Reading Holinshed's *Chronicles*

☙ READING
HOLINSHED'S
Chronicles

Annabel Patterson

The University of Chicago Press
Chicago & London

Annabel Patterson is professor of English at Yale University.

The University of Chicago Press, Chicago 60637
The University of Chicago Press, Ltd., London
© 1994 by The University of Chicago
All rights reserved. Published 1994
Printed in the United States of America
03 02 01 00 99 98 97 96 95 94   5 4 3 2 1

ISBN (cloth): 0-226-64911-3
ISBN (paper): 0-226-64912-1

Library of Congress Cataloging-in-Publication Data

Patterson, Annabel M.
    Reading Holinshed's Chronicles / Annabel Patterson.
        p.   cm.
    ISBN 0-226-64911-3 (cloth). — ISBN 0-226-64912-1 (pbk.)
    1. Holinshed, Raphael, d. 1580?   Chronicles of England, Scotlande, and
Irelande.   2. Historiography—England—History—16th century.   3. Great Britain—
History—To 1485—Historiography.   4. Great Britain—History—Tudors, 1485–1603—
Historiography.   I. Title.
DA130.P34   1994
                                        941—dc2093-47629
                                                    CIP

∞ The paper used in this publication meets the minimum requirements of the American
National Standard for Information Sciences—Permanence of Paper for Printed Library
Materials, ANSI Z39.48-1984.

Contents

❦ Preface

Let us (I say) as manie as will reape fruit by the reading of chronicles, imagine the matters which were so manie yeeres past to be present, and applie the profit and commoditie of the same unto our selves: knowing (as one wisely said) *Post sacram paginam chronici vivum veritatis typum gerere*, that next unto the holie scripture, chronicles doo carie credit.

A disciple of Socrates, by name Aristippus, a man suerlie of a verie sharpe judgement and pleasant wit, when he was demanded what profit he tooke by the studie of wisedome, made this answer: Forsooth this profit, that with all sorts of men I can frankelie and boldlie speake. Which answer might well be of that mans making; *bicause he bare a mind indifferentlie free*, as well from hope as feare: for he served no man, nor yet flattered anie person, nor otherwise behaved himselfe than his hart gave him. Of the same mind it were to be wished that all storie-writers were: for then should Chronicles approch next in truth to the sacred and inviolable scripture, and their use not onelie growe more common, but of greater account.

This book has a simple goal, though its task is unwieldy. It attempts to undo the neglect and, I believe, misunderstanding that have buried the greatest of the Elizabethan chronicles alive—neglect and misunderstanding that have been shared by both historians of early modern Britain and literary scholars of the same period. I hope that both groups, who increasingly trade across the boundary between their disciplines, will be startled to discover what riches accrue to both sides from revisiting "Holinshed's" *Chronicles* from a late-twentieth-century perspective, a perspective shaped by, among other altered assumptions, the young interdiscipline of cultural history.

"Holinshed's" *Chronicles* was itself, or can now be seen as, a giant interdisciplinary project. It was offered to the late-Elizabethan reader, in two editions a decade apart, as the work of a group, a collaboration (the term

"syndicate" can be loosely used) between freelance antiquarians, lesser clergymen, members of Parliament with legal training, minor poets, publishers,
and booksellers. The name of Raphael Holinshed, editor and major compiler of the 1577 edition, continues to distinguish it from the other Tudor
chronicles; but in my first two introductory chapters, "Intentions" and
"Authors," I explain the collaborative principle of the work, especially the
second edition produced after Holinshed's death.

The project was offered to the public as the culmination and accumulation of centuries of historiographical practice, while at the same time
making a bold new claim for significance. Both the statements quoted
above, which were added to the *Chronicles* for the second edition of 1587 by
Abraham Fleming, claim for the work a kind of authority undreamed of by
the great classical historians. "Next unto the holie scripture, chronicles doo
carie credit," wrote Fleming at the end of the pre-Norman history of
England; and at the beginning of the "Continuation" of the English history
past the point where Holinshed, now deceased, had let the story lapse,
Fleming repeated the claim: "Chronicles approach next in truth to the sacred and inviolable scripture."[1] Not only do both versions of this claim depend, obviously, on a Christianized culture; but they also derive from a
specialized program articulated by John Bale earlier in the sixteenth century to meet the needs of post-Reformation culture.

In the preface to his brief account of the life, trial, and execution of Sir
John Oldcastle, one of the first victims of anti-Wycliffite repression, Bale
had written in 1544:

> I wold wyshe some learned Englyshe man (As there are now most excellent
> fresh wyttes) to set forth the inglish chronicles in their right shappe, as
> certein other landes hath done afore them *al affections set a part*. I can not think
> a more necessarye thing to be laboured to the honour of God, bewty of the
> realme, erudicion of the people and commodite of other landes, next the sa-
> cred scripturs of the bible, than that worke wold be.[2]

Bale's own work as a historian would scarcely seem to merit the standard of
objectivity ("al affections set a part") he here proposed. A Carmelite monk
converted (in 1533) to a Protestant zealot, his scholarly reputation has
been flawed by the immoderation of his anti-Catholic propaganda.
Nevertheless, the very existence of such an appeal at this time (toward the
end of the reign of Henry VIII) is a sign of historical change; and it constituted vital protein in the genetic structure of the *Chronicles*, of the principles
of Raphael Holinshed and his colleagues as I will describe them in the following chapters. That Bale saw the reconstruction of English historiography as a project parallel to the dissemination of the Scriptures in English

helps me to introduce a central argument of this study. Both vernacular Bibles and national histories were essential to the Protestant educational mission that began with Wycliffe and continued as an underground movement through the fifteenth century and into the sixteenth: a mission in which wider literacy and the accessibility of books in the vernacular became a natural extension of the imperative to make the Bible legible by the laity, and in which, as it often turned out, spiritual and political consciousness-raising were to go hand in hand. The seeds of "Holinshed's" *Chronicles* were, then, sown as early as the late fourteenth and fifteenth centuries; and the fearsome systemic gymnastics set in motion in church and state by Henry VIII for alarmingly cynical reasons (but not without overt connections made to the so-called "proto-reformation" by more genuine reformers than himself) merely raised the stakes of enlightenment by clarifying its perils as well as its rewards.

Bale's appeal to an objectivity he was himself far from exemplifying was, I argue, all the more persuasive later in the sixteenth century, when thinking persons had had longer to meditate on the intricacy of the connections between religion and politics in the reigns of four successive Tudor monarchs. It is for this reason that Abraham Fleming restates his agenda as a compact that the historian must keep if he is to earn, with Aristippus, his reputation as a secular evangelist. The compact is to "frankelie and boldlie speake" to persons of all kinds (and status) and to bear "a mind indifferentlie free, as well from hope as feare." That word "indifferently," which has almost disappeared from our own vocabulary by its fatal attraction to apathy, recurs in the *Chronicles,* especially in those sections compiled by Raphael Holinshed himself, frequently enough to suspect its importance. While its simple meaning is impartiality or fairness, it comes to stand for a set of values which extend far beyond historiographical objectivity, into the territories of politics, law, economics, religion, citizenship, of relations between the classes, and even perhaps between the sexes. In other words, given the sociopolitical structure of early modern England, Holinshed's "indifference" placed him considerably further to left of center than it would today.[3]

At an early stage of his history of England, Holinshed attached this keyword to a doctrine that we now, thanks to John Pocock, can recognize as a branch of "ancient constitutionalism,"[4] but one that carries particularly generous foliage. Holinshed described the legislative reforms of Edward the Confessor, a model monarch in that he wished "to foresee as well for the welth of his subjects, as for himselfe, being naturallie inclined to wish well to all men" (1:747). Reform was necessary because by the accumulation of "manifold" lawes under different ruling nations "occasion was min-

istred to manie, which measured all things by respect of their owne private
gaine and profit, to pervert justice, and to use wrongfull dealing in stead of
right, clouding the same under some branch of the lawe naughtily misconstrued":

> Whereupon to avoid that mischiefe, he picked out a summe of that huge and
> unmesurable masse and heape of lawes, such as were thought most *indifferent*
> and necessarie, & therewith ordeined a few, & those most wholesome, to be
> from thenceforth used; . . . [in which all] might live in due forme and right-
> full order of a civill life. These lawes were afterwards called the common
> lawes, and also saint Edward his lawes, so much esteemed of the Englishmen,
> that after the conquest, when the Normans oftentimes went about to abro-
> gate the same, there chanced no small mutinies and rebellions for retaining
> of those lawes. (1:247)

This appeal to an ancient standard of justice as fairness, which entails si-
multaneously theories of acceptable monarchy, of the Norman Yoke as an
unacceptable model, of "civil" life as one in which the powerful were re-
strained from respecting only "their owne private gaine and profit," and of
the English common law as the "most indifferent" jurisprudential code
available, underpins the entire construction of the *Chronicles* as the story of
three nations from their origins up to what was then the present moment.
It is surely no coincidence that Abraham Fleming's definition of the historian who will bring the chronicles up to the level of truthfulness of the
Scriptures is one who bears "a mind indifferentlie free," or that Francis
Thynne signed off at the end of his extension of the Scottish chronicles
with the following apologetic:

> I desire thee reader to take it in good part, remembring *Ultra posse non est esse,*
> sith according to our old proverbe, A Man cannot pipe without his upper lip.
> . . . I commit myself and my labors to thy favorable judgement, . . . *measuring*
> *my meaning with the square of indifferencie."* (5:756)

But by using the phrase "justice as fairness" I intend a conflation of that
early modern moment and our own, a conflation provoked by continuing
debates on the status and usefulness of "liberalism" at the end of the twentieth century. This topic has been sadly disfigured by the definition of liberalism in the academy so as virtually to identify it with "possessive individualism." This property-centered and entrepreneurial definition of
liberalism tends to have a short historical memory, beginning with Locke
and Hobbes, who are assumed to share in its genesis.[5] But for someone primarily concerned with early modern England, not only do Hobbes and
Locke represent incompatible positions about how the individual relates to

the state, the one favoring a military dictatorship, the other a parliamentary republic, but the emphasis on economic self-determination seems only a late (and American) variant on other traditionally liberal (and American) themes: freedom of conscience, freedom of speech, the educability of all, the concept of the person in whom can inhere "natural" rights, equality before the law, some voice for all—if only symbolic—in the system of government. Perhaps liberalism was a faith whose outlines were clearer when the conditions for its instantiation were out of the question (which was certainly the case in early modern England) than when they could, much later and across the Atlantic, be approximated.

The phrase "justice as fairness," however, is intended to invoke John Rawls, whose *Political Liberalism* clarifies and extends the premises of his earlier *Theory of Justice.*[6] Rawls is a liberal with a sense of history, and to sanction his convictions he looks back to early modern Europe, identifying as developments that for ever after made unanimity impossible the Reformation, with its consequences in the religious wars of the sixteenth and seventeenth centuries, and the development of the modern state, "at first ruled by monarchs with enormous if not absolute powers,"[7] which forced the aristocracy or the rising middle classes to argue and occasionally fight for more reasonable arangements. The Reformation, for Rawls, had the greatest consequences for political philosophy, for it introduced a problem unknown to the ancient world:

> How is it possible that there may exist over time a stable and just society of free and equal citizens profoundly divided by reasonable religious, philosophical, and moral doctrines. . . . What are the fair terms of social cooperation between citizens characterized as free and equal [classical republicanism] yet divided by profound doctrinal conflict. . . . Of course Christianity already made possible the conquest of people, not simply for their land or wealth . . . but to save their souls. The Reformation turned this possibility inward upon itself. (xxv–xxvi)

Thus, Rawls argued (and I fully agree), "the historical origin of political liberalism . . . is the Reformation and its aftermath, with the long controversies over religious toleration in the sixteenth and seventeenth centuries. Something like the modern understanding of liberty of conscience and freedom of thought began then" (xxiv).

Rawls was here expressing, if rather tentatively, the insight that people learn to reason toward ideas like liberty of conscience or representative government by negative experience of enforced religious conformity or political oppression, and that such experience stays in the cultural memory, often at an unexamined level, as a prophylactic against a return to pre-democratic systems or impulses. The notion that "something like" political liberalism was in fact worked out in the second half of the sixteenth century in England, and that it found expression in the largest definition of the nation produced at that time, Holinshed's *Chronicles*, is the organizing theme of this book.

I am in general skeptical of the view that we cannot apply modern terminology to such evidence of *mentalités* as we can salvage from the early modern past. The notion of anachronism in *language* seems to me a shibboleth that permits modernity to shore up its own reputation for advanced thinking against earlier primitivisms. In the case of the *Chronicles*, as a result of three-quarters of a century of dramatic and destructive experiences in church and state, Holinshed seems to have developed a theory of justice as fairness that corresponds with some exactness to Rawlsian liberalism: as the pragmatic realization that irremediable diversity of opinion in all the most important matters had become a fact of early modern life, requiring a new working hypothesis of what constituted the civil society, a continued alertness to the value of checks and balances, and perhaps even some renegotiation of priorities.

For Holinshed himself (and in this he was considerably ahead of his colleagues) "indifference" even included religious toleration—up to a point. One of the last statements that he wrote for the 1577 edition is a meditation on the threat to Christianity posed by the Turks.

> It were therefore to be wished of all those that tender the suertie of the christian commonwealth, that princes would permit their subjects to live in libertie of conscience, concerning matters of faith: and that subjects againe would be readie in dutifull wise, to obeie their princes in matters of civill government, so that compounding their controversies among themselves, with tollerable conditions, they might emploie their forces against the common enemy.

But, Holinshed adds, in terms directly pertinent to his own writerly endeavors, "for matters in variance about religion, *rather to decide the same with the word, than with the sword*, an instrument full unfit for that purpose" (4:264; italics added).

One other important aspect of the *Chronicles* is the fact that they came from and were directed toward the already large and largely literate middle class. They were conceived and executed by an alliance of bourgeois entrepreneurs, bookmen, and bookish persons, reform-minded clergymen of middling status, and, in the case of John Hooker, a member of the House of Commons who was also a laywer and antiquarian. Like John Stow's *Chronicle*, which explicitly addresses a London citizen audience, the

Chronicles, especially when they deal with the sixteenth century, are an expression of citizen consciousness, though one that could imagine the entire nation as within the civil society. To this extent my project echoes Arthur Ferguson's account of the "articulate citizen" in the still earlier modern period of Edward's reign;[8] but it also carries the flavor of political independence and even protorepublicanism discerned by Patrick Collinson. In response to revisionist historiography, Collinson argued, first, that John Pocock "underestimated . . . the quasi-republican modes of political reflection and action" that were available as early as the sixteenth century, and *within* "existing modes of consciousness and established constitutional parameters"; second, that because Elizabethans lived proleptically with the anticipation of their queen's death without clear succession, "citizens were concealed within subjects," a phrase that implies an ideological conflict between the two terms; and third, that the more articulate and well-connected citizens, like Robert Beale, Dudley Digges, and Sir Thomas Smith, "pointed to a much wider body of citizenry, roughly equivalent to what Louis B. Wright, making a virtue of flagrant anachronism, called `middle-class culture.'"[9]

To place the work of Holinshed and his colleagues in such a context is a radical departure from the conventional view of the *Chronicles* constructed over the last three-quarters of a century. This traditional view not only involves misunderstandings of the chroniclers' historiographical objectives, but is often accompanied by a curious form of devaluation emanating from literary studies. As formulated by C. L. Kingsford, who was actually kinder to Holinshed and his colleagues than later evaluators have been, the *Chronicles* have basked in a reputation not their own:

> It is perhaps due to the service which he rendered to Shakespeare than to any merit of his own that Holinshed has long overshadowed Hall and Stow as an historian of the fifteenth century. . . . though his *Chronicles* were a meritorious compilation, which in default of printed originals were long of much historical value, their greatest interest now consists in their literary associations. . . . We may feel a just pride in realizing that so much of the rude material from which Shakespeare was to construct his chief historical plays was fashioned originally in our native English speech.[10]

In the main part of the book this invidious distinction between "rude material" and shaping genius should be seriously undermined by the new strategy of using the *Chronicles* as an archive for cultural history, by showing how rich is the material from which we might reconstruct the *conditions* of playwrighting (as only one among other social and intellectual practices) in late-Elizabethan England. And if Shakespeare's name appears only en passant or in the footnotes, that is itself a heuristic readjustment in the name of evaluative fairness.

Aiming at the largest picture possible, this book is divided into three sections. The first, containing four short introductory chapters, deals with the intentions of Holinshed and his successors, their careers insofar as they are known, the formal protocols of the project, and, as itself a protocol of great significance, its revision and expansion for the second edition. No systematic study has as yet been undertaken of these revisions performed on the *uncensored* text, in which Fleming and Thynne, with the evident cooperation of Stow and Hooker, not only continued the story where Holinshed's edition of 1577 left off, but returned to supplement his text, in ways that are themselves revealing of authorial intentions and historiographical principles. I study some of these revisions in the chapter called "Revision," primarily in order to show the value of such comparisons, and other examples of important alterations appear in later chapters.[11] Obviously, a complete account of the revisions would have to be performed on a scale much greater than its value. Here, as in the demonstration of what the *Chronicles* have to offer the cultural historian of early modern England, I rely on a principle the chroniclers themselves seem to have used. Since you cannot deal with everything, you offer *enough* of the texture of past history (in this instance, textual history) to make your point.

It is in the four central chapters, however, that this book takes its most enterprising and hence vulnerable stand. Chosen to represent fundamental aspects or conditions of social life, now as then, "Economics," "Government," "Religion," and "Law" make the case that the chroniclers saw it as their mission to instruct their readers how to understand a world of which these are the inescapable conditions. Despite the abstraction of their titles, each of these chapters is as stubbornly humanistic as my introductory emphasis on authors and their intentions. In "Economics" the focus is predominantly on the question of perception—on how the *Chronicles* register the human and amateur perception of economic change. In "Government," the chapter that most nearly approximates institutional history, I develop the theory of the ancient constitution as Raphael Holinshed understood it, as a story of the conflicts between all-too-human kings and their subjects. In both "Religion" and "Law" a single exemplary figure, Sir John Oldcastle and Sir Nicholas Throckmorton, come to stand respectively for the problems the chroniclers perceived in the overlap between church and state, between the law and political contingency. These chapters also contain certain local challenges to received opinion. I qualify some modern accounts (by Keith Wrightson and Steve Rappaport) of the sixteenth-century economy, and the effects of inflation; the revisionist view of the Elizabethan parliaments developed by G. R. Elton and his followers; and the now-standard assessment of the relationship between Henry V (as hero) and Sir John Oldcastle (as traitor), which is here set in vibration again with the counternarrative originating with Bale. But my favorite chapter, and the one that is perhaps the book's greatest claim to originality, describes the previously neglected: the trial for treason of Sir Nicholas Throckmorton in the first year of Mary's reign, and his magnificent self-defence which resulted in acquittal. This long (and digressive) section of the *Chronicles* is central to the project in more than one way. It looks as though Throckmorton came to stand for Holinshed as an alter ego, a man for whom the word "indifference" was at the center of his canny, informed, and courageous individualism.

The last section of the book, however, returns to types of history I experimented with earlier, in *Censorship and Interpretation* and *Shakespeare and the Popular Voice*. Two chapters, "Populism" and "Women" explore the surprising commitment of the *Chronicles* to the underprivileged, the demotic, the untitled (though not necessarily unnamed); and the final chapter is devoted to the still-unsolved mystery of the calling-in of the 1587 edition. By tracking the thematics of censorship in the text of the *Chronicles*, as a problem the chroniclers constantly anticipated, I offer a different perspective on that later "castration" and what might have motivated it. In all these areas, of course, my work is at least as much indebted to those predecessors as it diverges from them in emphasis and diagnosis, and especially in relation to the censorship of the *Chronicles*, where all readers should begin with Anne Castanien's precise and exhaustive analysis of the differences between the expurgated and unexpurgated versions.[12]

❧ Acknowledgments

It seemed at times as if this book, like Marvell's vegetable love, would "grow vaster than empires, and more slow." Fortunately, I was privileged to receive a triple benefit: a Mellon Foundation Fellowship, with tenure at the National Humanities Center, and the necessary leave and additional support from Duke University that allowed me to spend an entire year working on almost nothing else. My gratitude goes first, then, to all those who made that year possible, especially to Phillip Griffiths, then provost of my university; but I want also to mention the library staff at the National Humanities Center, whose patience and resourcefulness would translate a word or two on a scribbled request slip into a multivolume edition or an already-xeroxed article. To other potential Center applicants, let me suggest that this "fetching" service is perhaps the greatest (and most legitimate) luxury our profession affords.

My next largest debt of gratitude goes to the people who read all or parts of this manuscript and helped me to make it better: first, Fritz Levy, who not only has played the role of straw man with good humor, but was even so generous as to read the entire manuscript and send me his doubts and caveats; second, David Underdown, who read the manuscript for the Press, made many invaluable comments, and eventually directed me to William Whiteway, who features in the conclusion that Underdown asked for; and third, the historians whose interest in this project has given me confidence that other historians may find it useful—Lawrence Stone, Patrick Collinson, Linda Levy Peck, Cynthia Herrup, David Wootton, and Janelle Greenberg.

I am also indebted to a long list of friends, colleagues, critics, and students, who have weighed in with a reference, a fact, a translation, encouragement, or a practical helping hand: David Bevington, Peter Burian, Ellen Caldwell, Terence Cave, Cynthia Clegg, Ann Coiro, Richard Dickson, James Epstein, Wyman Herendeen, Richard Helgerson, Micaela Janan, David Kastan, Andy Kelly, John Knott, Scott Lucas, Janelle Mueller, Francis Newton, David Norbrook, Lena Cowen Orlin, Mark Phillips, David Harris Sacks, Thomas Scanlan, Gabrielle Spiegel, Jane Strekalovsky, Richard Strier, and Daniel Woolf. The most invaluable helping hands belonged to Patsy Batemen, who patiently xeroxed and mailed huge stacks of paper more than once and in many directions. I would like to think that this list is neither a boast nor a false modesty topos, but a reenactment of the very principle of collaboration and civic-mindedness that made "Holinshed's" *Chronicles* the broad-minded project described in this book.

Lastly, I take another opportunity to publish to the world (what a strange convention this is!) the name of my most important, most necessary collaborator, Lee Patterson, who constantly reminds me, and not only by exhortation, that there is more to life than work.

Part One

ONE   *≥₰ Intentions*

More then ten Hollensheads, or Halls, or Stowes,
Of triviall household trash he knowes.
> John Donne, *Satire 4*, ca. 1597

Vast, vulgar Tomes . . . recover'd from out of innumerable Ruins.
> Edmund Bolton, *Hypercritica*, ca. 1610

Voluminous Holingshead . . . full of confusion and commixture of unworthy relations.
> Peter Heylyn, *Microcosmus*, 1639

The project was large enough to absorb impure motives. So at least I have come to believe of the gargantuan work we continue to refer to as Holinshed's *Chronicles*, despite the fact that Raphael Holinshed was only one of nearly a dozen persons who contributed to the project over two decades and in two quite different editions, the first appearing in 1577, the second, expanded version of 1587 largely produced after Holinshed's death. In his grumpy old age, John Stow, one of the contributors of material for both editions, expressed his resentment at the way Holinshed's name had come to dominate it.[1] Rivalry and self-promotion were among the impure motives. What precisely pure motives would have been for a syndicate of middle-class entrepreneurs and antiquarians in the last quarter of the sixteenth century is a question of considerable subtlety. In this chapter I discuss the agenda of the project as Holinshed established it; and my own agenda is revisionary, in the sense that I believe the *Chronicles* to have been misunderstood, insufficiently studied, and undervalued.

    The reputation of "Holinshed's" *Chronicles* as it stands today can be quickly summarized. First, for its aphoristic clarity, stands the statement that "we care about *Holinshed's Chronicles* because Shakespeare read them." The author of this dictum was Stephen Booth, distinguished Shakespearean critic and editor, in the course of introducing a special presentation volume, for the California Book Club, of some leaves of the 1587 edition of the *Chronicles*. This occasion led to a discussion of the bibliographical problems created by the censorship to which the 1587 edition of the work was subjected.[2] But Booth was explicitly uninterested in the motives for that censorship, or in the *Chronicles* themselves, other than as ancillary to Shakespeare studies, the raw material on which genius drew. This premise, in existence long before Stephen Booth declared it in so naked a form in 1968, ensured that attention to the *Chronicles* was concentrated only on those sections Shakespeare used as sources; its products are those excerpts of the Lancastrian history found at the back of the Arden editions of Shakespeare, which for many students constituted "Holinshed" forever, and even a volume of such excerpts published as *Shakespeare's Holinshed*, which for many libraries represents their only "edition." Such overemphasis on the late-fourteenth- and early-fifteenth-century sections diverts us from precisely those materials that could broaden our cultural perspective on Elizabethan drama—the accounts of *sixteenth*-century events, persons, and practices.

Two other attitudes about the *Chronicles* are likely to be shared by literary scholars and historians. These, however, contradict each other on an issue fundamental to the philosophy of history—whether or not *grands récits*, grand narratives, are necessary, desirable, or possible. By one view, the *Chronicles* were an insignificant historiographical achievement because they *failed* to produce a grand narrative. Thus F. J. Levy's *Tudor Historical Thought*, published in 1967, disapproved of the *Chronicles* as baggy and undisciplined, erratic in their coverage, overzealous in their inclusion of the full texts of primary documents, and lacking the analytical and structural skills of the Continental historians. As Levy put it of the Tudor chronicles in general:

> There was [then] no conception of history writing as selective: a historian did not remake the past in his own image or in any other but instead reported the events of the past in the order in which they occurred. The criterion by which a historian was judged was the quantity of information he managed to cram between the covers of his book; if the matter of quality arose at all, it was relevant to accuracy. Once facts could be established as equal in authenticity, they were assumed to be equal in all other ways as well.[3]

This was especially true of Holinshed, who "demonstrated most fully the idea that history could be written by agglomeration." This made him "the ideal source for the playwrights; everything needful (and a great deal more) was included, but the `construction,' the ordering of events, was left to others."[4] Thus the historian's disapproval of the *Chronicles* renders them, in a mirror image of Stephen Booth's assessment, useful *only* for literary purposes. In a more recent unpublished paper Levy complained more explicitly about a level of interpretive indecision by Holinshed that "came close to abdicating responsibility altogether" and concluded, with disapproval, that "this was to leave the reader to be his own historian."[5] Abraham Fleming, the chief editor of the second edition, "exacerbated the situation, for he insisted on the importance of understanding the whole picture while simultaneously blurring its outlines." "Thus," Levy concluded, "the book which goes by the name of Holinshed . . . may be seen as a palimpsest, with each layer written over the incomplete erasure of the one below." And he cited in support of this position both Peter Heylyn's and Edmund Bolton's later assessments: Heylyn's "voluminous Holingshead . . . full of confusion, and commixture of unworthy relations," and Bolton's more generalized critique of the Tudor chronicles: "Vast, vulgar Tomes . . . [which] seem to resemble some huge disproportionable Temple . . . in which store of rich Marble, and many most goodly Statues, Columns, Arks, and antique Peices, recover'd from out of innumerable Ruins, are here and there in greater Number then commendable order erected."

What Levy did not emphasize was the class bias that inhered, none too subtly, in Bolton's negative judgment. Following a lament that they had been initiated by commercial printers, rather than by royal commission, Bolton had cited with approval Sir Henry Savile's epistle dedicating his own translation of Tacitus to Elizabeth. "Our Historians (saith the Knight) being of the Dregs of the Common People, while they have endeavour'd to adorn the Majesty of so great a Work, have stain'd and defiled it with most fusty foolerys."[6] In Savile's Latin the insults are even worse: for "the Dregs of the common People," read *"ex faece plebis."*

But there has been another, incompatible, reason for derogating the *Chronicles* as a historiographical achievement. This is the assumption that the *Chronicles* did indeed develop a *grand récit* in favor of the status quo. Whether described as "moral" as distinct from "political" history, or Ciceronian as distinct from Machiavellian/Tacitean history, or, more commonly, providentialism, the practice of the Tudor chroniclers has been assumed to be blindly (or hypocritically) clear on the separation of right from wrong. And yet, at the same time as their bondage to an absolute concept of value is asserted, it is claimed that they served a secular authority, that they worked, in the language of a providentialist theory of history, to legitimate a particular dynasty. These ideas emanated from E. M. W. Tillyard, whose views of the Tudor chronicles were formulated backwards, as it were, in relation to Shakespeare's history plays.[7] They were also (since the first edition appeared in 1944) produced in the context of the Second World War, when a providentialist view of national destiny was particularly acceptable; but they have been repeated in this decade, though from the perspective of disapproval, by a historian of historical thought in seventeenth-century England.[8]

The charge that Holinshed and his colleagues were engaged in legitimation of the house of Tudor simply will not stand. This is not to deny that there is a fair amount of editorial comment in the *Chronicles;* and that in some places, especially when Abraham Fleming was acting as editor-commentator, there is a heavy-handed emphasis on morality and political obedience. It is not necessary to conclude from this, however, that the project was commissioned or encouraged by the ruling monarch, as was true for Polydore Vergil and Edward Hall. Even if we acknowledge that by the last quarter of the sixteenth century such a program would have become more complex—to legitimate the institutions and practices, both secular and ecclesiastical, of the Elizabethan *state*—the complexity of the task cannot alone account for the unevenness of tone, attitude, and opinion that the *Chronicles,* if read with different assumptions, now seem to register. Nor can it be demonstrated that those who produced it were in any sense servants of the Crown.

It is an odd fact of intellectual history that new paradigms can sometimes be created by inversion rituals: not by discarding the views of the previous generation, but by retaining the insights and reversing the conclusions. There are strong signs throughout the *Chronicles* that what has been seen (contradictorily) as incompetence was a deliberate policy, the consequence of holding a different set of historiographical principles. Rather than being the author of a horrendous muddle, as Levy assumed, or merely the agent of God and *his* agent, as Tillyard and his followers believed, Holinshed initiated a procedure whereby "the reader was left to be his own historian," not because the historian had abrogated his interpretive task, but because he wished to register how extraordinarily complicated, even dangerous, life had become in post-Reformation England, when every change of regime initiated a change in the official religion, and hence in the meaning and value of acts and allegiances. What at one moment was loyalty, obedience, and piety could at the next be redefined as treason or heresy. As the 1587 edition put it, in summing up the reign of Mary Tudor:

> The death of this said queene made a marvellous alteration in this realme, namelie in the case of religion, which like as by the death of king Edward the sixt it suffered a change from the establishment of his time: so by the death of this queene it returned into the former estate againe. So that we see the uncerteintie of the world, and what changes doo come in times by their revolutions, and that everie thing is subject to unconstancie, and nothing free from variablenesse.[9]

Consequently, Holinshed believed in a humbler, or at least less interventionist, scholarly mission than that demanded by modern historiography. The following, I suggest, were its alternative principles.

1. One of the functions of a national history was to discover, salvage, and preserve in print ephemeral, manuscript, or otherwise endangered records; that is to say, the *Chronicles* were conceived from the start as "documentary history," as much a part of the national archive as the enrolled statutes stored in the Tower of London.

2. Given the nature of post-Reformation experience, which set Protestants and Catholics against each other in changing patterns of domination and repression, a national history should not and could not be univocal, but must shoulder the responsibility of representing diversity of opinion. Wherever possible, moreover, diversity should be expressed as multivocality, with the *Chronicles* recording verbatim what they found in earlier historians or contemporary witnesses. A corollary of this principle was that although the individual chroniclers might hold and express strong opinions of their own, especially on religion, the effect of the work *as a whole* would be of incoherence, here used as a positive term.[10]

3. The third principle answers directly, and also reverses, the class bias of Edmund Bolton's attack on the "vast, vulgar Tomes" of the *Chronicles*. For not only were they produced by middle-class citizens self-consciously acting as such, but they registered, as part of the drive toward completeness and multivocality, a greater interest than we have supposed in the voices and views of the groups below them, the common people, the artisanal and laboring classes. We might call this the anthropological level of the *Chronicles*, and it is invaluable in providing otherwise scarce data about subliterate and semiliterate culture in early modern England.

4. The last principle, in combination and extension of the other three, it would not be anachronistic to call "the right to know." The *Chronicles* do, paradoxically, contain several *grand récits*, though they are not presented in the triumphalist or tragic mode that usually signals such conceptions. As part of his protoliberalism, Holinshed himself was extremely interested in what we now call rights theory, specifically in constitutional and legal rights; and included in this theory were the conjoined rights of writing and reading, which in the late sixteenth century were much restricted. And all of the chroniclers had, as they frequently testify, good reason to believe that what they were doing teetered constantly on the edge of the illegal—that the general constraints on public expression had particular relevance to English historiography. That they chose to test the limits of the allowable in this arena of Elizabethan policy by carrying the second edition up to the minute, relating current events almost as they happened, and that

the 1587 edition was consequently called in by the Privy Council and "castrated" before being released again to the booksellers are both proofs of the brinksmanship they managed. Its motives were to make available to the reading public *enough* of the complex texture of the national history that the middle-class reader could indeed become his own historian—that is to say, a thoughtful, critical, and wary individual.

I shall return to the remarkable facts about the censorship of the 1587 edition at the end of my story, when the mystery that has hitherto surrounded them will be more capable of dispersion.

Chapter 11 will demonstrate, however, that the theme of censorship was already built into the *Chronicles* in 1577, and that it had been intensified by the revisions and additions of Fleming in earlier sections of the text that were evidently unscrutinized by the Privy Council a decade later. In the rest of this chapter I will, instead, line up what we know about the members of the "syndicate," another set of facts which should not only lay to rest the suspicion that this was a work of hegemony, but also show that the chroniclers were indeed self-conscious about the leading and educative role of the historian in testing the limits of allowable expression.

The conception of a national history for Elizabethans originated with a printer, Reginald or Reyner Wolfe, originally from Strassburg, who had been patronized by both Thomas Cranmer and Thomas Cromwell, and been employed as royal printer by Edward VI, with a patent for publishing Latin, Greek, and Hebrew. He became a prominent member of the Stationers' Company, and when Elizabeth confirmed their charter in 1559 he was named as Master. By the mid-century he had imagined a great work, a universal history and cosmography, to be illustrated with maps and other images, and to that end acquired a considerable collection of documents in manuscript. Much of his own collection, in turn, was purchased by John Stow when Wolfe died in 1573. From the start, then, the intellectual making of the *Chronicles* was inseparable from their financing; and in the absence of public libraries or collections of records to which the scholar might have access, the purchasing power of ordinary citizens was an essential ingredient of the antiquarian process.

About Raphael Holinshed we know very little, except that he was university-educated, probably at Cambridge, and had taken clerical orders. He has been identified as the son of Ralph Holinshed, of Cophurst, in Cheshire, and may have served for a time as steward to Thomas Burdet, of Bromcote, Warwickshire.[11] Initially he was employed by Wolfe as an assistant in the project, but his role must gradually have grown.[12] When Wolfe died, the financing of the project was taken over by John Harrison, Wolfe's son-in-law, Lucas Harrison, who had leased his shop from Wolfe, and

George Bishop. As Holinshed put it in his dedication to Burghley, those whom Wolfe "had left in trust . . . willed me to continue mine endevour." Though Wolfe knew William Harrison, the latter's involvement with the *Chronicles* seems to have begun after Wolfe's death. His *Description of England* was written in haste in 1576; and Richard Stanyhurst, who wrote the matching *Description of Ireland,* was also brought into the project late in the day by "some of those who were to bestow the charges of the impression," as Holinshed explained in his dedication of the Irish history to Sir Henry Sidney. Stanyhurst also completed the history of Ireland on the basis laid down by Edmund Campion. The first edition covered the history of England up to 1572, of Ireland to 1547, and Scotland to 1571. When Holinshed himself died in 1580, plans already having been made to produce a new edition, the publishers' team expanded to include Ralph Newberie, Henry Denham, and Thomas Woodcock, as also did the scholarly team, to include John Hooker, alias Vowell, Abraham Fleming, Francis Boteville, otherwise known as Thynne, and John Stow.

There is disagreement as to who was responsible for most of the second edition, the Dictionary of National Biography stating that Hooker was the editor in chief, a position subsequently adopted by Vernon Snow in his preface to the modern reprint of Sir Henry Ellis's early-nineteenth-century edition, although he acknowledged that there was no evidence of Hooker's official appointment.[13] He argued that Hooker's dedication of the Irish history to Sir Walter Ralegh has the marks of introducing the whole volume. Stephen Booth followed Sarah Dodson and William Miller in supporting the claim of Abraham Fleming, who certainly signed the preface to the "Continuation" and wrote a conclusion to it.[14] Elizabeth Story Donno believed that, as the title page of the "Continuation" asserted, the major figure was John Stow, who had provided Holinshed with material for the first edition, whose own major *Chronicle* (as distinct from the Reader's Digest versions) had been published in 1580 and whose qualifications as a historian were greatly superior to those of Fleming.[15] Stow himself spoke in his *Annals* (1605) of "*my* continuation of Maister Reine Woolfe's Chronicle."[16] However, the typographical practice of attribution in the *Chronicles,* whereby authorship of a particular section was indicated in the margin, seems to support the claims of Fleming as the actual compiler; not only because there are so many insertions marked by his initials, but also because specific materials attributed to Hooker and Stow in the margin are represented as if by a third party. Thus Fleming typically gives a page reference to Stow's *Chronicles* of 1580, along with his own initials, a technique that fails to distinguish Stow from, say, Edward Hall; and a similar but more elaborate technique is used for the insertion into the story of Edward VI's reign of

Hooker's account of the 1549 uprisings in Devon: "we adde a new report (new I meane, in respect of the publication, having not heretofore beene printed) though old enough, and sufficiently warranted by the reporter, who upon his owne notice hath delivered no lesse in writing" (3:926). The use of the editorial "we" here, while it may retain some aspect of collaboration, clearly identifies Fleming as the first person editorial, and Hooker as the "reporter" who has "delivered" his manuscript for appropriate disposition.

If we think back to the disapproval of Sir Henry Savile, repeated by Edmund Bolton, it is clear that only Stow could conceivably have deserved the charge of being of "the Dregs of the common People." Stanyhurst was the son of James Stanyhurst, recorder of the city of Dublin and speaker of the Irish House of Commons from 1557 to 1568. Richard himself graduated from University College, Oxford, studied law at two of the Inns of Court, and became the schoolmaster of the children of the earl of Kildare.[17] Hooker had been educated at Oxford and may also have taken a degree in law. He sat as a member of the Irish parliament of 1568–69, and subsequently sat for Exeter in the English parliament of 1572. Francis Thynne was the son of the famous editor of Chaucer, and a friend of Sir Thomas Egerton. He became an active member of the Society of Antiquaries formed around William Camden and managed, apparently thanks to Burghley, to become the Lancaster herald. Abraham Fleming was university-educated and became chaplain to the countess of Nottingham. William Harrison graduated from Oxford and became chaplain to William Brooke, lord Cobham. Only John Stow, who liked to be known as "Citizen," began life below the middle class, as apprentice to a tailor. But he was clearly a formidable autodidact, and like Thynne became a member of the Society of Antiquaries. His 1565 *Summarie of Englyshe Chronicles . . . Perused and allowed accordynge to the Quenes majesties Injunctions* was dedicated to Leicester, even as it was clearly addressed to a broad citizen audience.[18] On 8 March 1603, James I published an unusual document: Letters Patent commending Stow for his labors in the field of historiography, and authorizing him to "collect, amongst our loving Subjects, theyr voluntary contribution and kind gratuities, . . . having already, in our owne person, of our speciall grace, begun the largesse, for the example of others."[19] Evidently, we will need to look elsewhere than at the social status of these members of the syndicate to account for the social stigma later attached to the *Chronicles*.

Second, the several dedications of parts of the work to different members of the Elizabethan government may itself be a signal of disunity in high places. Holinshed dedicated the first edition of the *Chronicles* to William Cecil, lord Burghley, but in language that argues against an actual commission, or even patronage from the start.[20] William Harrison dedicated his *Description of England* to William Brooke, lord Cobham, who certainly was his patron; but Cobham was the inveterate enemy of Robert Dudley, earl of Leicester, to whom Holinshed dedicated the "History of Scotland." Leicester and Burghley themselves became leaders of opposing factions in Elizabeth's court and council, though modern historians disagree as to when their policies sharply diverged. Richard Stanyhurst dedicated his part of the "History of Ireland" to Sir Henry Sidney, Elizabeth's Lord Deputy in Ireland; but by the time the second edition of the *Chronicles* appeared Sidney had been recalled in some disfavor; which may help to explain why the eulogistic biography of him that had been included in the *Chronicles* was radically truncated during the 1587 censorship. When in 1586, in part as a move against Leicester, Burghley took Whitgift, Cobham, and Lord Buckhurst into the Privy Council, they apparently urged Thynne to compose his "discourse of the archbishops of Canturburie and the lord Cobhams, with the lord wardens of the five ports" (4:660), encouragement which must have felt particularly bitter to him when they were subsequently deleted.

This leads to a third point, that the publication of *both* editions of the *Chronicles* suggests, if not scofflawry, at least a degree of circumvention of the regulations. The first edition was not registered with the Stationers' Company until after it was fully printed (the register entry is for 1 July 1578, whereas all copies bear the 1577 date). In his late complaint about unfair competition, John Stow complained that his own *magnum opus* was "prevented, by Printing and reprinting (without warrant, or well liking) of Raigne Wolfes collection." Though this interested remark should not bear much weight, it should perhaps bear a little. There is at least one indication that the authorities in 1577 did not anticipate the appearance of this *kind* of chronicle. On 5 December 1577, two letters were written by the Privy Council in response to rumors they had heard. The first was to John Aylmer, bishop of London, telling him that a history of Ireland by "one Stanhurste" had recently been published, in which certain events were falsely recorded contrary to the ancient records of that realm. The bishop was ordered to summon the printer, for whose name a space was left in the record, and to discover how many of the histories had been printed, how many were sold in Ireland, and how many remained unsold. He was further to order the printer to refrain from printing or selling any more copies. The second letter was to Gerald Fitzgerald, eleventh earl of Kildare, ordering him to send them "his servant" Stanyhurst, who would then learn their pleasure.[21] On January 1578 the Acts of the Privy Council record that "forasmuche as the compyler thereof hathe shewed the cause how he was induced to those errors, and offerethe to reforme them, his Lordship is willed, after significacion made unto him from the Lord Threasurer that those faultes are reformed, he shall suffer them to passed and to be soulde, notwithstanding the former restrainte." The question still under debate is whether the cancellation in most surviving copies of leaves 2E6 through F7 was the result of this reformation. Anne Castanien accounted for the cancellands by way of the confusion that would have occurred when Stanyhurst took over this section of the work from Holinshed, and argued that the toning-down of some unsavory gossip does not indicate official censorship. She conceded, however, that perhaps "interest in some other problem connected with Irish administration led the Council to halt publication and sale of this history in Ireland until the motives behind it could be investigated." And she observed that at this very moment Kildare was in London to present an Anglo-Irish protest (over the imposition and collection of cess) to the Privy Council (pp. 122–23). Liam Miller and Eileen Power, who edited the Irish history for the Dolmen Press in Dublin, continued to believe that at least one of the cancellands was motivated by censorship, "designed to eliminate unfavourable references to Archbishop Alen."[22] In either event, the threatening tone implied by this correspondence is incompatible with the notion of an official national history appearing with the blessing of the authorities.[23] As for the second edition, publication had been planned since 1584, when it was twice entered in the *Stationers' Register*, on 6 October and 30 December. It is evident, though, that the revision kept being expanded to give it up-to-the-minute topicality; and it was precisely the most recent materials that should have been reviewed before a license was granted.[24]

Some of the chroniclers' own manifestos support these inferences. Since I have already mentioned Stanyhurst, let us start with his own 1577 dedication to Sir Henry Sidney, which, interestingly, did *not* appear in those few copies of the Irish chronicle that got into circulation without revision.

"How cumbersome . . . and *dangerous* a taske it is," Stanyhurst began:

> to ingrosse and divulge the dooings of others, especiallie when the parties registered or their issue are living: . . . if the historian be long, he is accompted a trifler: if he be short, he is taken for a summister: if he commend, he is twighted for a flatterer: if he reproove, he is holden for a carper: if he be pleasant, he is noted for a jester. (6:273)

Such standards, always expressed negatively, and impossible to reconcile, have in Stanyhurst's view created two types of historian, those who "taking the waie to be thornie . . . would in no case be medlers, choosing rather to sit by their owne fire obscurelie at home," and others who, "being resolute fellowes . . . rush through the pikes." Between these two extremes Stanyhurst claims to have chosen the middle path of proper caution. But, he adds:

> as for the passing over in silence of diverse events (albeit the law or rather the libertie of an historie requireth that all should be related, and nothing whusted) yet I must confesse, that as I was not able, upon so little leasure, to know all that was said or doone; so I was not willing for sundrie respects, to write everie trim tram that I knew to be said or doone.

This passage is particularly telling in its self-correction: the law "or rather the libertie" of historiography requires that everything be told, and nothing concealed; since the self-correction recognizes a conflict between law and individual liberty that the writing of history invariably brought to consciousness. Although it is possible to imagine that the insertion of this defensive manifesto into the revised copies of the Irish chronicle was merely the result of Stanyhurst's taking over the task and wishing to signify his presence, it is more tempting to see it as his response, half apologetic, half defiant, to his meeting with the Privy Council.

And Stanyhurst inserted into this otherwise ceremonial statement an anecdote which is typical of the project as a whole, in its comic, irreverent tone, its story (the first of several that I shall highlight) of master-servant relations: for in exemplifying the problems of selectivity, he wrote:

> And if anie be overthwartlie waiwarded, as he will sooner long for that I have omitted, than he will be contented with that I have chronicled; I cannot devise in my judgement a better waie to satisfie his appetite, than with one Dolie, a peintor of Oxford, his answer: who being appointed to tricke out the ten commandements omitted one, and pourtraied but nine. Which fault espied by his maister that hired him, Dolie answered, that in verie deed he painted but nine: howbeit, when he understood that his master had well observed and kept the nine commandements that alreadie were drawne, he gave his word at better leisure throughlie to finish the tenth. (6:274)

This cheeky "answer" was not, evidently, aimed at Sir Henry Sidney, whose grasp of the chronicler's predicament is not in question, and who figures throughout the *Chronicles* as one of its exemplary figures. Because even with proper caution Stanyhurst anticipates that "misconstruction" of it may be "perilous," he commits his work to Sidney's patronage, hoping "to be sheelded against the sinister glosing of malicious interpretors" (6:274).

My second exhibit is a quotation at second hand: that is to say, a state-

ment about the historian's predicament that occurs in Giraldus Cambrensis'
Expugnatio Hibernica, as translated by John Hooker for the 1587 edition. The
Expugnatio, which Giraldus wrote as chaplain to Henry II, presented to
Henry in 1188, and twice re-presented to king John, once when he was still
only duke of Poiters, and again upon his accession in 1199, was in certain
obvious ways the work of a king's servant. It is all the more interesting,
therefore, to hear Giraldus on the royal historian's dilemma. Like
Stanyhurst, but at the opposite end of the rhetorical and social scale,
Giraldus had taken up the metaphor of history as painting, and promised to
deliver a "lively portraiture" of the first conqueror of Ireland:

> For he being so noble an ornament to this time and our historie; we might
> not well . . . omit and passe him over in silence. Wherein we are to crave par-
> don that we may plainelie declare and tell the truth: for in all histories the
> perfect and full truth is to be alwaies opened, and without it the same wan-
> teth both authoritie and credit: for art must follow nature. And the painter
> therfore, whose profession and art is to make his protraiture [*sic*] as livelie as
> may be, if he swarve from the same, then both he and his worke lack and
> want their commendation.

If Giraldus had stopped there, this would be merely an orthodox preamble
to a eulogy; but he continues with the problem of truthful representation
until he too, arrives at the dangerous:

> And therefore, as things spoken in commendation either of a mans good dis-
> position, or of his worthie dooings, doo delight and like well the hearer: even
> so let him not be offended, if things not to be well liked be also recited and
> written. And yet the philosophers are of the opinion, that we ought to rev-
> erence so the higher powers in all maner of offices and dueties, as that we
> should not provoke nor moove them with anie sharpe speeches or disordered
> languages. . . . Wherfore *it is a dangerous thing* to speake evill against him,
> though the occasion be never so just, as who can foorthwith avenge the
> same. And *it is a matter more dangerous,* and he adventureth himself verie far,
> which will contend in manie words against him, who in one or few words can
> wreake the same. It were surelie a verie happie thing, and that which I con-
> fess passeth my reach, if a man intreating of princes causes might tell the
> truth in everie thing, and yet not offend them in anie thing. (6:175–76)

The brief biography that follows reproaches the now-dead Henry as lacking in religious devotion, a great promise-breaker, and as hostile to his
grown children as if he were a father-in-law! (6:176–77). It is impossible to
tell what John Hooker was thinking as he translated these twelfth-century
meditations on balanced and complete reporting; but that he *did* include

them was, in its own way, a small contribution to the indifferency of the *Chronicles.*

But to complete this exercise, we should hear from Raphael Holinshed himself, in his "Preface to the Reader." To this audience, the work was clearly not presented as a state history, but rather as a project of civic consciousness. Holinshed began with the word we have been following: *"It is dangerous* (gentle reader) to range in so large a field as I have here undertaken, while so manie sundrie men in divers things may be able to *controll* me."[25] The purpose of the project is described in conventional didactic terms: "the incouragement of . . . woorthie countriemen, by elders advancements; and the daunting of the vicious, by soure penall examples, to which end (as I take it) chronicles and histories ought cheefelie to be written." But the method selected (and here Holinshed would have acknowledged Levy's description of himself) is implicitly at odds with didacticism, which requires from the historian the certainty that leads, if not to a grand narrative, at least to a tidy one:

> I have collected [the history] out of manie and sundrie authors, in whom what contrarietie, negligence, and rashnesse sometime is found in their reports; I leave to the discretion of those that have perused their works: for my part, I have in things doubtful rather chosen to shew the *diversitie* of their writings, than by over-ruling them, and using a peremptorie censure, to frame them to agree to my liking: *leaving it neverthelesse to each mans judgement, to controll* them as he seeth cause. (Vol. 2, "Preface to the Reader"; italics added)

If, as I have suggested, we take this statement seriously as a defence of a hands-off historiography designed to encourage independent judgement in the reader, Holinshed's *Chronicles* can be reconceived, not as the successor to Hall's *Union,* but rather as a counterstatement: the evidence of diversity that historical inquiry discovers must not, at whatever cost to the historian, give way to the principles of unity and order.

I would now, therefore, want to develop in a stronger direction one of my earlier theories of the effects of censorship on early modern writers. Holinshed and his colleagues, as a group and over a decade, had evolved a larger notion than that of the safe corridor policed by self-censorship.[26] That notion was philosophical in the sense that it went beyond specific criticisms to the idea of an open society in which dissent must be spoken, in the different voices recorded throughout the *Chronicles,* and not least as it was represented by the individual differences of opinion and belief among the chroniclers themselves.

And crucial to the project as I am redefining it was the construction and education of a new kind of *readership* (already implied in the addresses to the reader cited above), a readership that would itself be composed of literate individuals spanning a fairly wide cross section of socioeconomic groups, but predominantly, like the members of the "syndicate" themselves, middle-class citizens. The question of who read the *Chronicles* was obviously determined in part by its price. The 1577 edition, both volumes, bound, sold for 26 shillings to Robert Devereux, earl of Essex, which suggests a high-quality binding. It is important to realize that one could purchase such books much more cheaply unbound.[27] The great book collector, Andrew Perne (ca. 1519–89), who was Master of Peterhouse College, Cambridge, and bequeathed his enormous collection of 2,900 books to the University Library, owned two copies of Holinshed's *Chronicles*, one (obviously finely bound) valued at 33s. 4d., the other (obviously unbound), valued at 16s., the same price as his copy of Foxe's *Acts and Monuments*. More important for my argument, Ambrose Barker, who graduated B.D. from Cambridge in 1582, had a far smaller collection (170 volumes), primarily theological in emphasis, and he owned a budget-priced copy of Holinshed valued in 1583 at only *four shillings*, which was one of only two historical works he acquired.[28] Perne was clearly not constrained by price, and Barker was a moderately prosperous clergyman. But we know that Edmund Spenser and Gabriel Harvey read the first edition of the *Chronicles*, and that Spenser apparently took a copy to Ireland, which shows that it was not financially out of reach for someone who made his living as a personal secretary.[29] At the end of this book I will identify other readers of the *Chronicles* in the late sixteenth and seventeenth centuries, readers whose social status falls somewhere between that of Perne and Spenser, and whose motives for investigating the *Chronicles* are partly revealed in their comments.

My use of the term "middle class" here and elsewhere is sustained in the face of J. H. Hexter's important critique of that concept as used by previous historians, especially in the form of a theory of a "rise" of the middle class in Tudor England.[30] It is necessary to focus on this problem in social history, in order to suggest that the *Chronicles* may themselves make a hitherto unrecognized contribution to that debate. The objective of Hexter's revisionist argument was to dispose of the "myth" of an unprecedentedly strong and successful middle class in early modern England, a group who encroached on the aristocracy and were particularly favored by the Tudor monarchy. In its place, he constructed an image of a rather meek group, still utterly committed to the medieval vision of an hierarchically ordered society, whose group solidarity was constantly undermined by the flight of successful mercantile capital to land in search of prestige, and by the failure of class loyalty in those servants of the Crown—Wolsey, Cromwell, Cecil, Gresham—whose personal rise to power often resulted in their conceiving regulations to prevent others from doing the same. Hexter cites William Cecil's plan to reserve public office for the aristocracy and bar middle-class families from the kind of education that would fit them for public service, which also incorporated an earlier plan of Thomas Cromwell's for keeping the middle class out of the land market.[31] And he generally suspected those who developed the "myth of the middle class" as reading backwards, with a shadowy Marxist agenda, from the late eighteenth and nineteenth centuries. The Tudor middle class, he concluded, "is no threat to aristocracy or monarchy because it has no ideology of class war or even of class rivalry. It does not seize on More's *Utopia* and the propaganda of the `commonwealth' group of social critics, as the man of 1789 seizes on the writings of Rousseau and the *philosophes*."[32]

Hexter's point was well taken so long as it remained with the terms and documents of economics, the facts about who bought land, and who engaged in industrial enterprises. Such material, however, cannot be made to prove or disprove the question of morale, and whether the Tudor middle class did or did not develop an ideology that distinguished them from other social, economic, or status groups. Holinshed's *Chronicles can* offer information on this point, by giving us access to the mind-sets of a group of Elizabethan citizens who had given some thought to this question.

The *Chronicles* are well supplied with stories of confrontations between court and city. In 1392 there was a conflict over the Londoners' refusal to lend Richard II a thousand pounds. "Some there be that write, how the king piked the first quarell against the maior and shiriffes, for a riot committed by the unrulie citizens, against the servants of the bishop of Salisburie," one of whom had stolen a loaf of bread from a baker's man and then "brake the bakers mans head, when he was earnest to have recovered the lofe" (2:818). As a consequence, "the liberties of the citie were seized into the kings hands, and the authoritie of the maior utterlie ceassed." Eventually the Londoners did penance to the king, first at Sheen and then at Westminster, offering him many costly presents, and received in return their liberties back again. "The Londoners believed, that by these gifts they had beene quite rid of all danger; but yet they were compelled to give the king after this, ten thousand pounds, which was collected of the commons in the citie, not without great offense and grudging in their minds" (2:320). In Henry VIII's reign there occurred the riot known as Ill May Day, to be described in chapter 9, which Holinshed again presents as a court/city confrontation. Although it was broadly motivated by trade protectionism, the 1517 episode was sparked by a very similar episode of violence toward a victualler.

In 1552, in connection with the trial of the Lord Protector, Edward, duke of Somerset, who is one of the heroes of the *Chronicles*, there occurs a remarkable episode in the history of the Edwardian Reformation. Somerset had appealed to the City to support him and had the king's signature attached to his request. The lords who had signed the proclamation against Somerset (who included Lord Rich, the Chancellor, St. John, Northampton, Warwick, Arundel, Shrewsbury) came to the Guildhall where the mayor was in council and requested the Londoners' support for themselves. Here was a cruel dilemma: "At the last," wrote Holinshed, "stepped up a wise and good citizen, named (as maister Fox saith) George Stadlow, and said thus":

> In this case it is good for us to thinke of things past to avoid the danger of things to come. *I remember (saith he) in a storie written in Fabians chronicle,* of the warre between the king and his barons, which was in the time of king Henrie the third, and the same time the barons as (our lords doo now) commanded aid of the maior and citie of London, and that in a rightfull cause for the commonweale, which was for the execution of diverse good lawes, whereunto the king before had given his consent, and after would not suffer them to take place, and the citie did aid the lords.

The barons defeated Henry, and among the conditions of the resulting peace treaty was a pardon not only for themselves but for the London citizens, ratified by act of Parliament. "But what followed?" asked Stadlow dramatically:

> Was it forgotten? No surelie, nor yet forgiven during the kings life. The liberties of the citie were taken awaie, strangers appointed to be our heads and governours, the citizens given awaie bodie and goods, and from one persecution to another were most miserablie afflicted: *such it is to enter into the wrath of a prince, as Salomon saith; The wrath and indignation of a prince is death.* Wherefore forsomuch as this aid is required of the kings majestie, whose voice we ought to hearken unto *(for he is our high shepheard)* rather than unto the lords: and yet I would not wish the lords to be clearlie shaken off, but that they with us and we with them may joine in sute, and make our most humble petition to the kings majestie, that it would please his highnesse, to heare such complaint against the governement of the lord protector as may be justlie alledged and prooved. And I doubt not but this matter will be so pacified that neither shall the king nor the lords have cause to seeke for further aid, *neither we to offend anie of them both.* (3:1018; italics added)

This phase of the story has a temporarily happy ending; after a short imprisonment in the Tower, on 6 February 1550, Somerset was released, "and that night he supped at sir John Yorks one of the shiriffes of London, also the proclamation before set foorth against him was revoked and called in" (3:1020).

Now, it would be certainly possible to align this anecdote with Hexter's view of the urban middle class as low in morale and no threat to anyone. On the other hand, it can also be read as a paradigm of the values in whose service, I claim, the *Chronicles* were compiled; first, a commitment to settling disputes by words rather than swords, and to the importance of constitutional government; second, a commitment of several of the chroniclers to the mixed ideals of the Edwardian Reformation, which they grasped as partly a theological and liturgical move toward a purer Protestantism, partly, under the influence of Somerset and the "commonwealthmen" who surrounded the young king, a tentative movement toward social reforms.[33] Third, and more important for my purpose here, is the fact that the story thematizes the historiographical memory, and the value of the English chronicles in developing civic prudence:[34] "it is good for us to thinke of things past to avoid the danger of things to come." Remembering "a storie written in Fabians chronicle" leads the Londoners out of their dilemma, and, it is implied, also leads to Somerset's release. That John Foxe remembered that story again before Holinshed came to it does not render Holinshed weakly agglomerative in procedure and belated in analysis (and certainly not abandoned to the endless recursiveness of deconstruction) but rather alert to the responsibilities of the historian as transmitter rather than "controller" of the past.

And finally, it is impossible not to read this anecdote without remembering also the constraints under which the chroniclers operated. There are two conflicting fables of monarchy in Stadlow's story. One is an image of humane protectiveness ("for he is our high shepheard"); the other is the image of leonine ferocity ("such it is to enter into the wrath of a prince, as Salomon saith; The wrath and indignation of a prince is death.") In one of his long catalogs of officeholders that was deleted from the 1587 edition, Francis Thynne had cited this same biblical caveat in connection with Archbishop Grindal's confrontation with Elizabeth over the "prophesyings," or public seminars on biblical interpretation, which the queen wanted suppressed and the archbishop wanted retained. Not surprisingly, although even then the disciplinary action was seen as excessive, the confrontation led to Grindal's sequestration from office. In Stadlow's story, the biblical proverb leads to conciliation; but to recall this exemplary tale of civic mnemonics is another, infinitely more subtle form of protest, which contravenes the apparent meekness of its message.

To sum up my own contribution to the "myth of the middle class" as it seems to have been articulated in the *Chronicles*, I shall engage in another "anachronism." There is some virtue in comparing the *Chronicles* to Jürgen Habermas's ideal of communicative reason, which he conceived of as operating in a special territory halfway between the mind and the world. This territory Habermas designated *bürgerliche Öffentlichkeit* (civic openness); though finding the term capable of mistranslation in overly spatial terms, he subsequently redefined it so as to avoid the charge of reification. In his final version, *Öffentlichkeit* is explained as including the media of public communication, along with voluntary organizations or institutions "which are neither bred nor kept by a political system for purposes of creating legitimation."[35] Rather they are sites where the "common consciousness" society has of itself "can be concentrated and more clearly articulated around specific themes and ordered contributions" (p. 359). Sites of *Öffentlichkeit* work, Habermas claims, in two directions; the one internal, a kind of gathering and strengthening process for the opinions of their members, a process which he elsewhere calls, more strikingly, "radical democratic will formation"; the other external, by way of bringing influence to bear on the seemingly immune, self-regulating and self-sufficient systems of power and money, or government and the economy.

Although Habermas writes evidently of the modern or postmodern world, there is nothing to prevent our applying this concept to the early modern environment of the *Chronicles*. Indeed, one of his own complaints is that contemporary social thought and political philosophy have lost all sense of historical perspective, by forgetting their origins in early modern Europe. For in the endless laments about alienation and other diseases of modernity, "the high price earlier exacted from the mass of the population (in the dimensions of bodily labor, material conditions, possibilities of individual choice, security of law and punishment, political participation, and schooling) is barely even noticed" (pp. 337–38). As Rawls insists on the shaping force of sixteenth- and seventeenth-century British history on the deep structure of American political thought, with its intuitive commitment to freedom of speech, Habermas posits an unconscious conspiracy among the European avant-garde to curtail that mnemonic activity.

Raphael Holinshed and his colleagues came to similar conclusions by way of meditation on the effects of the Reformation in England, effects which had the most widespread consequences for everyday life and social consciousness. It may well have been this civic aspect of the *Chronicles*, which happened to be conceived and executed by an alliance of middle-class entrepreneurs, bookmen and bookish persons, reform-minded clergymen and, in the case of Hooker, parliamentarians, that disturbed Sir Henry Savile and others like him.[36] And if there were no physical or institutional spaces that were, by their very nature, democratic and egalitarian in late-

Elizabethan England, where in the 1570s educational seminars on scriptural exegesis were banned just because they were public and well attended, one may imagine that civic-minded people (though they might have disagreed on many other matters) could have agreed to construct a *textual* space—the huge space of the *Chronicles*—in which the public's right to information could to some extent be satisfied. On that penultimate phrase, "to some extent," everything of course turns; and the extensive though extraordinarily obtuse censorship of the 1587 edition either proves my point or renders it invalid.

When England was all Popish under Henry the seventh, how esie is conversion wrought to half Papist halfe-Protestant under Henry the eighth? From halfe-Protestantisme halfe Popery under Henry the eight, to absolute Protestantisme under Edward, the sixth; from absolute Protestation under Edward the sixt to absolute popery under Quegne Mary, and from absolute Popery under Queen Mary, (just like the Weathercocke, with the breath of every Prince) to absolute Protestantisme under Queene Elizabeth.

In the somewhat parodic formulation of Roger Williams,[1] the coming of the Reformation to England produced, for at least the half century prior to the production of the *Chronicles*, a nationwide confusion of beliefs and allegiances. Where, then, was the "nation" to be found? This question is implicit in the event that marks the beginning of the reign that first demonstrated the "weathercock" nature of religion—that of Mary Tudor, whose determination to return the country to the papal fold motivated the rebellion of Sir Thomas Wyatt the younger. Holinshed had described how a band of the London militia sent out against Wyatt had instead revolted in his favor, crying out as they did so "We are all Englishmen, we are all Englishmen" (4:13). Subsequently he had described their execution, in terms that make it quite clear that he deplored it:

> a great multitude of their said poore caitifs were brought foorth, being so manie in number, that all the prisons in London sufficed not to receive them: so that for lacke of place they were faine to bestow them in diverse churches of the said citie. And shortlie after were set up in London for a terrour to the common sort (bicause the white cotes being sent out of the citie, as before ye have heard, revolted from the queens part to the aid of Wiat) twentie pair of gallowes, on the which were hanged in severall places to the number of fiftie persons, which gallowes remained standing there a great part of

the summer following to the great griefe of good citizens, and for example to the commotioners. (4:21)[2]

The *Chronicles*, I argue, were dedicated to the task of showing what it might mean to be "all Englishmen" in full consciousness of the fundamental differences of opinion that drove Englishmen apart. And the group of contributors and financial backers that I have referred to as a "syndicate" were themselves representative of the problem, in that, though they were socially homogenous, all of the "middling sort," their beliefs and values extended quite far in both directions on the scale that had Roman Catholicism as one of its poles and radical Protestantism as the other.

Having in the last chapter made certain claims for the chroniclers' respectability, I must also acknowledge that some of the syndicate had, as we say, trouble with the law. One of the five booksellers who subsidized the project, Thomas Woodcock, had been imprisoned in 1578 for selling Cartwright's *Admonition to Parliament*.[3] Stanyhurst's summons by the Privy Council in 1577 has already been mentioned. Shortly before 28 August 1580, his house was searched for unspecified papers. On 26 November 1580, Stanyhurst was examined by Robert Beale, secretary to the Privy Council, about a purported plot for conveying Gerald Fitzgerald, lord Offaley, into Spain at the instigation of a Catholic priest, and briefly imprisoned.[4] His later history confirmed these suspicions. Stanyhurst had become a private pupil of Campion, whom he had met at Oxford, with whom he returned to Ireland, and whose influence undoubtedly affected his religion. It was probably just after the November examination that Stanyhurst left England for the Continent, converted explicitly to Catholicism, and conspired with Catholic exiles in Flanders against Elizabeth's government.

When William Harrison wrote his account of English law, he included a calendar of the law terms, Hilary, Easter, Trinity, and Michaelmas, with acknowledgment to John Stow, "whose studie is the onelie store house of antiquities in my time, and he worthie therefore to be had in reputation and honour" (1:303). Stow's capacity for acquiring ancient manuscripts was indeed legendary, but it did not always lead to such positive evaluations. In 1568 he was examined by the Privy Council on the charge of possessing Roman Catholic propaganda against Elizabeth; and in February 1569 a search of his house revealed "old fantastical books" with papist tendencies, and "a great Parcel of old M.S. Chronicles, both in Parchment and Paper."[5] It is much to the point that the list of "unlawful" books that was given to Archbishop Grindal included four chronicles. From his own independent historiographical projects, as well as from the character of some of the manuscripts he collected (though he must have kept them more carefully

thereafter) it can be inferred that Stow was particularly interested in political protest and resistance.[6] In the preface to his *Abridgement* (1570), and as
an aspect of their rivalry as producers of condensed chronicles for wider audiences, Richard Grafton had complained that Stow's *Summarie* had contributed "to the defacing of Princes doinges," and that in his historiography
"the gates are rather opened for crooked subjectes to enter into the fielde
of Rebellion, then the hedges or gaps of the same stopped."[7] Stow took the
charge seriously, and its sting must have lasted at least two years. In one of
his manuscripts Stow wrote (but apparently never published) a heated
counterattack on Grafton for plagiarism, followed by a defence of his own
political loyalty during "the laste rebellyon," presumably the Northern
Rebellion of 1572.[8]

In 1575–76 Francis Thynne spent over two years in prison for debt,
and he appealed to Burghley for assistance. This seems more like bad luck,
the results of a family feud, than disreputable;[9] but Thynne also happened
to be the contributor most directly embarrassed by the censorship of the
1587 edition of the *Chronicles*, during which four of the massive catalogs he
had compiled, those listing the archbishops of Canterbury, the earls of
Leicester, the house of Cobham, and the Lord Wardens of the Cinque
Ports, were all deleted.[10] There is general agreement that at least his catalog of archbishops, though largely translated from Archbishop Matthew
Parker's lives of seventy bishops in *De Antiquitate Britannicae Ecclesiae*, fell prey
to the Council's sensitivity to religious dispute.[11] Had Thynne's catalog of
archbishops survived it would have put into circulation an epitaph for
Archbishop Grindal: he who had ordered the search of Stow's study, but
had himself fallen victim to Elizabeth's determination to suppress the so-
called "prophesyings," open seminars on scriptural exegesis. Of this scandal, Thynne had written the following oblique protest:

> For as the wheele, when it is at the highest, must turne; and as the fairest
> cedar is most subject to the power of the winds: so this man began somewhat
> to decline, and the beames of his honorable place were somewhat eclipsed,
> by the clouds of hir maiesties displeasure conceived against him. For he was
> called before authoritie, where standing upon the defense of his cause, and
> growing in mislike with hir maiestie therefore; he was committed to restreint
> in his owne house. In which estate he continued untill his death, without re-
> lease thereof. So greevous a thing it is to fall into the princes disgrace: which
> Salomon saith is death, *Sed vir sapiens placabit eam.* (4:772)

"But the wise man will please *her*"; if he can. The same biblical aphorism
(Proverbs 1:7) that Holinshed had cited in his emblematic story of citizen
prudence in 1549 reappears here in an Elizabethan tragedy of ecclesiastical

courage or impudence, take your choice. The Latin pronoun *eam* points by its gender to the Queen, and thereby declares the need for wisdom's constant updating.

Indeed, when Thynne took over the revision of the Scottish history, and added his own continuation from 1571 to 1586, he provided a pompous and cautious preface to the reader which echoes the note of danger in Holinshed's and Stanyhurst's prefaces of 1577:

> Now, if thou which art the reader, thinke that I (unacquainted with matters of state, especiallie in an other countrie . . .) am far unable to breake the dangerous ice of such matters, and so more unmeet to enter into the bosome of princes (whose harts as Salomon saith are unsearchable) should for my unadvisednesse seeme worthie the punishment of Prometheus, that stale the fier from Jupiter, and caried it abrode into the world, bicause the affaires of princes are not to be made common, to be submitted to the censure of their subjects . . . thou must yet remember that men have escaped punishment in dealing with higher matters than with things of chronicles, or of such like which onelie touch the life of the bodie. And therefore in punishing thereof upon Prometheus, Jupiter went beyond himselfe. For if the greater, that is for matters touching the soule, went not onelie free from punishment, but received eternall reward, [as Enoch, Elias and Paul], how much more should Prometheus have bene spared, that but onelie medled with the bodie? . . . much lesse ought I to be punished with Prometheus in medling with the discourse of matters upon the earth, and such as concerne the actions of mortall creatures, as battels, mutations of kingdoms, death of princes, and such other earthlie accidents. Into which yet I would not have so rashlie descended, or taken so hard a province in hand, had not (as before I said) the commandement of such as I durst not gainsaie, interponed it selfe as a shield to receive and beat backe the sharpe darts of envious toongs. (5:657)

There are no other suspicious characters among the (then) living authors of the *Chronicles*; but what of the dead ones?

What, in particular, of Edmund Campion, the original "author" of much of the history of Ireland, on whose work Holinshed and Stanyhurst merely expanded? Campion, one of the most brilliant scholars and fellows of St. John's College, Oxford, had at first tried to accommodate his Roman Catholic principles, developed during Mary Tudor's reign, to life in Elizabethan England and Ireland. There was a plan, jointly developed by James Stanyhurst and Sir Henry Sidney, to renovate the University of Dublin with Campion as its director, but after the scheme collapsed (6:251) he apparently lost hope of inclusion within the Elizabethan colonial system, and became first a religious outlaw, then a Jesuit, and finally, after reentering England as a missionary, was captured, tortured, and executed in 1581 on a charge of treason. Thus one of the "authors" of the 1577 edition appears in the 1587 edition as an actor in his own trial and execution,[12] even though Abraham Fleming was then doing everything in *his* authorial power to destroy Campion's reputation.

At the other end of the religious spectrum from Stanyhurst and Campion stand William Harrison, whose use of the *Chronicles* to argue for a more reformed version of Protestantism in England will be described in chapter 4, and Abraham Fleming, whose moralizing commentary in the 1587 edition has been largely responsible for the misunderstanding of its overall agenda.[13] But while both Harrison and Fleming could be described as strenuous Protestants, their convictions led them in different directions politically. Fleming's constant emphasis on political obedience is possibly consistent with his rather drab career as a minor literateur, moralist, and journalist, who published translations of Virgil and Musaeus, pamphlets on English dogs, blazing stars, and "A Paradoxe, proving by reason and example that baldnesse is much better than bushie haire."[14] After he dedicated his *Bucoliks . . . and Georgiks* of Virgil to Whitgift in 1589 his clerical career advanced, he delivered several sermons at Paul's Cross, and was preferred by Whitgift to a London rectory. Nevertheless, even Fleming contributed, as we shall see, to some aspects of "indifference" as Holinshed had defined it.

Unlike Fleming, Harrison was evidently unhappy both with the original Elizabethan church settlement and with Whitgift's later campaign to sharpen and police its borders. He was emphatically in favor of clerical marriage (he married Marion Isebrande by 1570),[15] a position obnoxious to Elizabeth; but he was acceptable to the ecclesiastical system administered by Grindal, being appointed an official of the archdeacon of Colchester's court, a position he held from 1569 to early 1576. Some of the most intriguing information we have about him was discovered by Georges Edelen, in the form of a brief Latin biography written on a blank page in Harrison's own copy of John Bale's *Scriptorum illustrium majoris Britannie . . . catalogus* (Basle, 1557–59), which Edelen found among the remains of Harrison's library at Derry:

> William Harrison was born in London. His parents, John and Anne, were honorable citizens of that city. In order that he be thoroughly instructed in the liberal arts, they sent him to [Christ Church college] Oxford, where he received his master's degree. While at the university he flung himself into the filth of papistry and became a shaven worshipper of Baal; . . . But God in His mercy recalled him from this insanity shortly before Mary's death, after he had heard, secretly but with good effect [*occulte sed feliciter*] Cranmer, Ridley,

Latimer, and other preachers of Christ. He would not, perhaps, have escaped
harm if that Jezebel had reigned longer, whom the Almighty Father wonder-
fully carried off, together with Pole, to the solace of the whole church. . . .
At present he is the rector of Radwinter, near Walden, in Essex, daily writing, as I understand, on an uncommon compendium of history in imitation of
Aelian, Gellius, Macrobius, Petrarch, and Politian. He was born in 1535 and
has now reached his thirtieth year—and will live much longer, God willing.[16]

Parry doubted that Harrison's claim to have heard Cranmer, Ridley,
and Latimer preaching "occulte" could actually have happened;[17] but this
Foxian reference to the Oxford Martyrs drives home the shape that this
minibiography was obviously intended to have—a shape responsive to the
weathercock national religion that could so mislead the young and endanger the converted. The threat of sudden death hanging over the anecdote,
and its openendness, "si deus voluerit," should both be remembered when
we come to Harrison's *Description of England* and the topics he decided to
tackle.

We also know that Harrison enjoyed the patronage of William
Brooke, seventh or tenth lord Cobham (depending on how one counts the
generations in an interrupted peerage), whose chaplain he became in 1558,
and who in February 1559 installed him at Radwinter, Essex. Brooke was a
leading Elizabethan magnate who, at least until after the 1587 *Chronicles*
were completed, can be counted as a staunch Protestant of reformist tendencies, which he had inherited from the Edwardian reformation. His father George, ninth lord Cobham, had been, according to Parry, "a protegé
of Thomas Cromwell and a die-hard supporter of Northumberland's policies, as a Privy Councillor signing the instrument which limited the succession to Lady Jane Grey."[18] George Brooke supported Northumberland
after Somerset's fall, and had been singled out by John Ponet for his fidelity to Northumberland's program.[19] William himself, as a young man, had
been a squire of the body to Edward VI and was knighted in 1549. Along
with his brothers, and presumably with his father's acquiescence, he had
participated in the rising of his cousin Wyatt against Queen Mary, which
had been motivated by her plans to marry Philip of Spain.[20]

Since William Brooke, lord Cobham, had been, after Burghley, at the
head of those to whom the *Chronicles* recommended themselves, the second
of the dedicatees whose protection the chroniclers sought in 1577, some
further definition of his role in Elizabeth's regime is in order. Peter Clark
has argued that, despite the friendship of Cecil and, through his second
wife, the favor of Elizabeth herself, despite securing the Lord Wardenship

of the Cinque Ports in 1559, and his huge landholdings in Kent, Cobham was never trusted with complete power in the county, perhaps because of his feud with Leicester.[21] But there was undoubtedly an important turning point in Cobham's fortunes in February 1586 when, in response to Leicester's mishandling of his campaign in the Netherlands and as part of his reprimand, Burghley brought Cobham, along with Whitgift and Lord Buckhurst, and instead of Leicester's own nominees, into the Privy Council, an event to which Francis Thynne refers in the preliminaries to his ill-fated catalogs, suggesting that Whitgift and Cobham thereupon "occasioned" him to write the three catalogs that related to these officers— the archbishops of Canterbury, the lords Cobham, and the lord wardens of the Cinque Ports (4:660).[22] Clark sees Cobham becoming more conservative in his religious policy at this stage (that is to say, going over to Whitgift) though he gives no evidence beyond Cobham's employment of the "crypto-catholic" Peter Hendley as his chaplain.[23] Harrison himself benefited from Burghley's coup by being promoted to a prebend in St. George's chapel, Windsor, in April 1586, and it has been suggested that this promotion, which greatly increased Harrison's income, moved his views on church and state toward religious and political orthodoxy. I doubt that Harrison sold his radical soul for the difference between £40 p.a. and £190.[24] The revisions he made to the second edition of the *Description,* at least some of which were made as late as 1586, not only fail to support such a hypothesis, but require us to construct a bolder and more interesting one: that Harrison felt required by Whitgift's reactionary policies to speak out more strongly in the second edition of the *Chronicles* than he had in the first. His dedication to Cobham, which was itself (and unusually for a dedication) revised in small ways in 1587, *still* ends by commending "the rest of your reformed familie."

The last member of the team that produced the 1587 edition was John Hooker, alias Vowell, whose role in the whole project is, as I have said, uncertain. Whether or not he was actively involved in restructuring the second edition, he certainly contributed large chunks of material, several of which had previously been or were subsequently published separately. Having translated Giraldus Cambrensis for the Irish section of the *Chronicles,* he then continued the Irish history from 1546, where Stanyhurst left off, to 1568. To the English section, for the reign of Edward VI, he contributed several blocks of material relating to his own region—an account of the popular uprising in 1549 caused by Edward's and Somerset's reform programs, along with a description and history of the city of Exeter. Hooker, as a young man twenty-four years old, had participated in the defence of Exeter against the rebels, and himself experienced the seige.[25] He was therefore able to offer an exceptionally colorful firsthand narrative of those events.

After the Western Rebellion, he entered the service of Miles Coverdale, the Marian exile who had returned to England in 1548 and become bishop of Exeter, probably in the role of secretary or translator.[26] As Vernon Snow points out, Hooker's commonplace book clearly reveals his commitment to the Edwardian reformation, since he recorded the sermons of Hugh Latimer as well as Coverdale's activities.[27] In 1551 he became, as local chamberlain, an official archivist for the Exeter corporation, and later served as tax collector, president of the court of orphans, and the admiralty court. In 1568 his legal skills gained him the appointment as solicitor to Sir Peter Carew, who wished to recover some estates in Ireland, and who employed Hooker to search the records for him. This led to his election for Athenry, Connaught, for the 1568 Irish parliament. The *Chronicles* contain a much condensed version of his biography of Carew,[28] along with a remarkable account of his own performance in the 1568 session.

In the service of an English colonialist, Hooker found himself on the opposite side from Stanyhurst, and the gregarious text of the *Chronicles* faithfully records their differences. Stanyhurst himself was, as the Privy Council noted in 1577, a "servant" of the eleventh earl of Kildare, Gerald Fitzgerald, and hence a member of a family that Hooker, without distinguishing between its two branches, saw as the root of all evil in Ireland: the Geraldines. In 1577 Kildare was in attendance before Elizabeth's Privy Council in England in relation to complaints made by the Anglo-Irish of the Pale about the cess—and Hooker records the careful responses of the four Irish lords whom Elizabeth consulted on this point in a way which obscures their probable sympathy for the grievance (6:392). In 1582, on suspicion of his treason, the earl's estates were placed under sequestration, and he and his son Henry were imprisoned in the Tower, but released on June 1583. Hooker, on the other hand, was employed by a military commander engaged in the suppression of Irish rebels.

We can learn a great deal about Hooker from the self-portrait he provided, barely concealed behind a third-person narrative, in describing the 1568 session of the Irish parliament. When the house met, with Sir James Stanyhurst as Speaker, a struggle began, for the Anglo-Irish of the Pale objected to the large number of nonresident Englishmen who were seated. They refused to get down to business, a bill for the granting of an impost on wines, although they would eventually carry by a small majority the repeal of Poynings Law (whereby it had been enacted under Henry VIII that no legislative action could be taken in the Irish parliament unless it had already received the assent of the English Crown). And, wrote Hooker, "in this matter they shewed themselves verie froward & so unquiet, that it was more like a bearebaiting of disordered persons, than a parlement of wise and grave men" (6:344).

> Wherewith a certeine English gentleman (the writer hereof) being a burgesse of the towne of Athenrie in Connagh, who had before kept silence, and still so meant to have doone; when he saw these foule misorders and overthwarting, being greeved, stood up, and praied libertie to speake to the bill.

It quickly (and unintentionally) emerges from Hooker's account that he was a pompous, long-winded, and authoritarian speaker; and he proceeded to threaten the Irish parliamentarians with a "preamble," a version of royal absolutism that Elizabeth herself might have been unwilling to articulate in her own parliament (6:344).

"And *when he had spent a long time in this matter,*" Hooker ingenuously continued, "he proceeded to the bill," claiming that the majority of the house approved "of the person and of the matter," but that (unsurprisingly) those he had "touched" with his rebuke were greatly offended. The result was a minidrama of confrontation between the "new English" and the Anglo-Irish, complete with threats, locked doors, "secret" government intervention, and a physical rescue of the "gentleman" from the consequences of his rhetoric:

> And thefore some one of them rose up and would have answered the partie, but the time and daie was so far spent above the ordinarie houre, being well neere two of the clocke in the afternoone, that the speker and the court rose up and departed. Howbeit such was the present murmurings and threatnings breathed out, that the said gentleman for his safetie was by some of the best of that assemblie conducted to the house of sir Peter Carew, where the said gentlemen then laie and resided. The lord deputie in the meane time, hearing that the lower house were so close, and continued togither *so long above the ordinarie time,* he doubted that it had beene concerning the questions before proponed, and therefore did secretlie send to the house to learne and know the cause of their long sitting. But by commandment of the speaker, order was given to the doore-keepers, that the doores should be close kept, & none to be suffered to come in or out, *so long as the gentleman was in deliverie of his speeches;* and after the court was ended, it was advertised to the said lord deputie, who thanked God that had raised up unknowen freends to him in that place. (6:345; italics added)

This self-serving narrative contrasts absolutely with the tactful presence of Raphael Holinshed, a well-named guardian angel, yet invisible as a *character* in his vast project.

Nevertheless, there is another side to this episode. The day after his long speech on the unlimited nature of the royal prerogative, Hooker was attacked in the house by Sir Christopher Barnewell and other lawyers of the English Pale, so vociferously that Stanyhurst was asked to discipline them. He requested advice as to the procedure of English parliaments in such matters. "Which was promised unto him and performed, and also promised that a booke of the orders of the parlements used in England should in time be set forth in print, which the said gentleman did, and presented & bestowed the same among them." What followed in the *Chronicles*, for all at home to read, was Hooker's own pamphlet, *The order and usage how to keepe a parlement in England in these daies* (6:344–45).

In fact his *Order and usage* was not written until after his second experience as an M.P., this time representing Exeter for the English parliament of 1571. During that parliament, Hooker claimed to have lost his voice, but not his reputation: "although by meanes of sicknes, the use of my speech not serving, I could not speak my minde in that place . . . yet in such credit of that assembly I was, that by a whole and a generall concent of the Parlement: I was eftsoones chosen to be A Comitte in sundry matters of charge and importaunce."[29] The committee was concerned with nothing more central than Bristol trade; but, more to our purpose, Hooker wrote a diary of the 1571 proceedings; he discovered a manuscript of the medieval *Modus tenendi parliamentum;* and he published it, along with his own *Order and usage*, in two separate editions. Consequently, he becomes a crucial figure in the parliamentarianism of the *Chronicles*, in which, as I argue in chapter 6, Holinshed led the way, and William Harrison and John Hooker, their principles fortified by later experience, became his not unworthy successors. The difference between Hooker's attitudes to Irish politics and those he apparently developed in relation to English parliamentarianism is only one more of the complications and nuances, derived from human diversity and inconsistency, which the following chapters will try to render intelligible.

THREE   ❧ *Protocols*

I n the previous chapter the concept of a collaborative agenda for the *Chronicles* was complicated (though not undermined) by considering the individual perspectives of the contributors, so far as they can be reconstructed. The question of motives, pure and impure, subdivides into impulses ranging from the most purposive to the most accidental, from the worldly to the ineffable, from patronage arrangements, through personal or family attachments, to conversion narratives. Now I turn from the *persons* engaged in the construction of the *Chronicles* to the *protocols* observed in its making, which reinstates the idea of shared understandings and common practices. By using the term "protocol" one implies a structure under control by its makers. Once beyond the premise that the chroniclers proceeded only by agglomeration, and that they produced a horrendous muddle, it is remarkable how many signs of effective if unorthodox construction gradually become visible. Toward the end of the English history there occurs an elaborate description of a technological miracle—the reconstruction of the port of Dover (as a symbol of national pride) out of the most unlikely materials (earth, chalk, sludge, faggots, and stakes) and in the most hazardous conditions, the workers up to their waist in the sea (4:857–68). This is not an incongruous metaphor for the construction of the *Chronicles* as a monument its compilers hoped would withstand the tides of time.

The most obvious structural protocol, and one which must have had at the time an ideological effect, was the production of parallel histories of England, Ireland, and Scotland, implying that the three countries should be considered as historically separate yet interdependent, a union of not quite equal partners. Each was provided with its own geographical "Description," although Harrison's *Description of England* was much the longest.[1] Yet the problem of Scottish and Irish nationalism is placed squarely before the reader, in ways that are compatible with the principle of diversity and multivocality. The claims of England to sovereignty over Ireland are frequently asserted in the text, yet, as we have seen, Stanyhurst and Hooker themselves took strikingly different positions on what constituted rebellion to English authority. In the Scottish history, the theme of independence from England is nowhere better expressed than in John Major's account of William Wallace, who in 1298 invaded England in defence of his own country against Edward I, to whom John de Balliol had sworn fealty; and Holinshed repeats after Major the stirring speech that Wallace delivered to Robert Bruce:

> If they have given their faith to the king of England, they are not bound to keepe it: in a wicked promise no oth is to be performed. . . . Wherefore imbrace you this thraldome (which is so much esteemed of you) to whom filthie servitude with ease seemeth more pleasant, than honest libertie with danger: for I had rather choose willing death with freedome (in which I meane to spend my bloud) than to doo as you have doone, because the love of my countrie shall not depart from my hart, before the life of my bodie depart from his office. (5:334)

Later in the history the old struggles are relived in the enigmatic figure of Mary, Queen of Scots, whom the continuators of the English history must render "malicious and murtherous" (4:897), but whom the Scottish history knew to have been caught in the geopolitical web of Europe's intermarried yet feuding royal families. Thus Thynne imports from John Leslie's *De Origine, Moribus, et Rebus Gestis Scotorum* (1578) an account of the negotiations between Marie de Guise and the Scottish parliament in 1558 on the occasion of her son's marriage to the princess Mary:

> let it be opened unto the Scots, what great benefit maie redound unto them by this signe of a thankefull mind. For it maie so happen, that if the king Dolphin shall feele himselfe increased with this title of honor by the Scots, as a note of their good favour to him [i.e., that he should be king during the life of the queen], that he maie raise up his father the king of France, that he will not by anie meanes permit the queene of Scots his wife to be excluded from the kingdome of England, after the death of queene Marie, who was not like to live long being sore troubled with the dropsie. (5:558)

In the margin (since his own position diverged from Leslie's), Thynne could not prevent himself protesting: "Well fished to catch a frog. Not so likelie as that lies drop out of your pen."

The effect, then, of the three parallel chronicles is of *competing* stories of the "British" isles; and the reader is encouraged to move back and forth between them by explicit cross-references. Toward the end of the project, however, these interdependent stories begin to converge. In the "Continuation" of the English history, for the year 1586, we find the following:

> In the chronicles of Ireland, upon occasion of service in the highest office there, mention was made here and there of sir Henrie Sidneie his saiengs and dooings, where promise did passe (by means of discoursing his death) that the reader was to looke for a full declaration of his life and death in the chronicles of England, as course of time should give direction. (4:869)

The promise was then fulfilled, by way of the verbatim inclusion of Edmund Molyneux's "Note" on Sir Henry's career. It seems to have been too well fulfilled, since the "Note" constituted a posthumous defence of Sir Henry's services as Lord Deputy in Ireland, which had earned him only the queen's ingratitude and a recall in moderate disgrace. "His ample authoritie," Molyneux had written," . . . procured him (and not his owne deserts) manie envious, heavie, and potent enemies. Howbeit, his inocencie was ever his buckler and shield of defense against them" (4:877).

This part of the "Continuation" was, not surprisingly, truncated during the 1587 censorship; as was another contentious form of cross-reference to the Scottish history, probably attributable to Abraham Fleming. In preparation for his presentation of the Babington Plot, Fleming inserted the following remarkable synopsis of Scottish history into his story of 1586:

> And here (by the waie) having entered into a remembrance concerning Scotland, it is noteworthie, a little to glanse at the present state of the same, whereof let the wise consider, how soever the lesse advised passe it over. The king himselfe we omit as touching his port be it as it is, nevertheless by name to be thought upon: Utpote nomen minimae felicitatis, maximi vero unfortunii perhibeter. For if a man tosse over the Scottish historie, and cast an eie upon the succession of their kings; . . . he shall see Fatale quoddam malum nomini annatum. (4:896)

After this none-too-hidden disparagement of James VI, in all probability the heir to the English throne, Fleming then proceeded to run through the disasters that had overcome all the James's of that nation, before returning to the subject he had pretended to omit:

The sixt and last of that name, of rare qualitie, and now in roialtie (the sonne of Marie Dowager malicious and murtherous, of whome in discourse here-after, as occurrences of consequence shall direct our pen) what dangers he passed, &c: by search into the Scotish annals maie appeere: what remaineth behind we leave to the Lord Gods counsell and working. Touching the coun-trie it selfe, it is divided into factions; a plague to kingdoms, and a verie en-trance to ruine and desolation. As for the tumults and seditions (which have often happened) they have had their beginning from a pretended care of re-ligion, which diverse times hath beene altered, not in profession but in dis-cipline; and which at this present (bishops remooved) is in the power of su-perintendents; neither can the same, by meanes of old hatred remaining in seed, be at quiet. (4:897)

Whatever principles of evenhandedness had motivated Raphael Holinshed in setting up his tripartite structure were here, under the stress-es of the 1580s and the unsettled nature of the succession, pushed into the background. This passage must have been what the Privy Council referred to in January 1587 as "such mention of matter touching the King of Scottes as may give him cause of offence."[2] It did not survive the subsequent "cas-trations."

The Use of Sources

It goes without saying that a central issue in the production of multivocali-ty is the one foregrounded by Holinshed in his preface to the reader, where-by he gave notice that he had "rather chosen to shew the diversitie" of opin-ion among his predecessors than "by over-ruling them . . . to frame them to agree to [his] liking." Accordingly, the typographical strategy of the *Chron-icles* was to indicate the source of a particular passage in the margin, although it is not often clear when an older authority is no longer speaking, and the convention is not scrupulously observed. It would, of course, be possible to argue, as I have done elsewhere, that this strategy provided some degree of self-protection for the redactor.[3] But whereas such a concern would have been paramount for, say, a dramatist using an ancient story to convey a top-ical message, and while the chroniclers seem to have no illusions about the danger of their task, the effect of the constant dialogue between historians old and current, of the marginal roll call of names, must have gone beyond such prudential considerations. It is important to realize that this was not the strategy of the English chroniclers of the earlier sixteenth century. Al-though the printer who reissued Fabian's *Chronicles* in 1559 added a few sources in the margin "to the ende you maie knowe the diversities of theim," and although this goal might conceivably be seen as embryonic of Holinshed's,[4] the scholarly apparatus was slight indeed compared to that of the *Chronicles* in 1577, which was still further enhanced in 1587. Both Hall and Grafton indicate in a marginal note that the whole of their account of Edward V and Richard III derives from Sir Thomas More, but this is a notable exception to their usual policy.[5] Grafton, in particular, calmly appropriated much of Hall's work, which he had, after all, been instrumental in both publishing and continuing; and without comparing them, you would never know that his account of Somerset's execution derives from John Foxe's *Acts and Monuments.*[6] Yet Holinshed, and after him Abraham Fleming, constantly recycle the names of Fabian, Hall, and Grafton, a procedure which makes it possible readily to determine what were their own principles of selection and supplementation.

In the Irish chronicle there is occasionally an ideological argument carried on between John Hooker, the translator of Giraldus, and his original. The *Expugnatio* was a text of which Hooker, as a Protestant, could only partially approve. Occasionally he inserted anti-Catholic footnotes (6:211). Once he engages Giraldus in the margin: "Aha Giraldus! could you see that curssed fault and abuse?" (6:227). The value of the medieval history to Hooker was, obviously, the support it provided for Elizabethan colonial policy; yet even so he found himself willy-nilly articulating a defence of the Fitzgeralds, or Geraldines, which was alien to his own opinions.[7] In the Scottish history, Francis Thynne, whom we saw above arguing in the margin with John Leslie, or perhaps with Marie de Guise, created an implicit dialogue between the accounts of John Major, whose Latin *History of Greater Britain, both England and Scotland,* had been published in Paris and dedicated to James V, and his ungrateful student George Buchanan, who had mocked Major in an insolent epigram:

> Cum scateat nugis solo cognomine Major,
> Nec sit in immenso pagina sana libro,
> Non mirum titulis quod se veracibus ornat:
> Nec semper mendax fingere Creta solet.
> Although he abounds in trifles, "Major" in name only,
> and there is not one sound page in his huge book,
> It's no marvel that he adorns himself with true titles:
> Even lying Crete isn't always accustomed to make things up.

If Major was a faithful Roman Catholic, Buchanan was a strenuous Protestant. If Major was, as the *Dictionary of National Biography* asserts, a liberal in politics, Buchanan, on the basis of his *De Jure Regni apud Scotos,* was already recognized as a notable European spokesman for the doctrine of limited and elective monarchy, of a mutually contractual relationship between king and people, and the occasional legitimacy of tyrannicide. The *De Jure* had been published in 1579, and suppressed by an act of Parliament in 1584. Buchanan's unremitting hostility to Mary, Queen of Scots and her party in the *Historia Scotorum*, which was first published in 1582, is remarked on by Thynne in an aside ("for by that name and epitheton [the rebellious faction] dooth Buchanan alwaies terme those that tooke the queenes part") (5:643); and in his catalog of writers at the end of the Scottish history, Thynne calls Buchanan "greatlie learned, but manie times maliciouslie affected" (5:754). Yet he remains the chief authority for the history of Scotland as Thynne revised it.

As for Foxe's *Acts and Monuments*, not only did Holinshed and his successors frequently turn to that huge work as a source of materials, especially for the reigns of Edward VI and Mary Tudor, but they also imitated the historiographical *practices* of Foxe: on the one hand, the grand-scale salvage and preservation in print of early documents, which made the work the monument that it is; on the other, the use and privileging, wherever possible, of eyewitness accounts. But in two respects, Holinshed diverged completely from Foxe. The first, as I shall show in chapter 7, was in eschewing Foxe's Protestant polemic for a more "indifferent" stance on religion; the second, not unconnected, is a self-conscious division of labor. The *Acts and Monuments* concerned itself with church history, the *Chronicles* with political history. Yet each was aware of the impossibility of completely severing these topics in practice, and from time to time commented upon it. Thus Foxe in his 1570 defence of Oldcastle against Harpsfield complained that he had never expected, in embarking on an ecclesiastical history, to be pressed "with such narrow points of the law" by his adversary that he had to reply in kind, demonstrating a formidable grasp of legal history;[8] and Francis Thynne, in his catalog of archbishops, disclaimed any intention of encroaching on the territory that Foxe had sufficiently covered: "it is beside my purpose to treat of the substance of religion, sith *I am onelie politicall, and not ecclesiasticall;* a naked writer of histories, and not a learned divine" (4:743; italics). That this intention was sometimes forgotten, not without disingenuity, may be inferred from the fact that Thynne had used his catalog of the archbishops of Canterbury to retell much of the story of the early Reformation, as also from that catalog's subsequent excision.

Eyewitness Testimony

In his preface to the reader, Raphael Holinshed put particular stress on the desirability of eyewitness accounts, asking his contemporaries to be aware "that no one can be eie-witnesse to all that is written within our time; much less to those things which happened in former times," but nevertheless assuring them that he has spared no pains either in searching out ancient authors, or inquiring of "moderne eye-witnesses for the true setting downe of that . . . here delivered" (2:np). It is partly this trust in eyewitness testimony that, interrupting the otherwise neutral march of facts, gives the *Chronicles* their unique and often eccentric flavor. The effect is of many different representatives of the "I" addressing the reader directly, sometimes intersecting a first-person comment by an editor-compiler, sometimes even competing with another "I" who has been present at the same event.

One striking example of this practice occurs in that section of the *Chronicles* that deals with the reign of Edward VI. The chroniclers chose to tell the story of Edward's reign as coming to a tragic climax with the consequences of the rebellions that took place in 1549, some of them clearly encouraged by Somerset's proclamation against enclosures. The tragedy, then, was Somerset's trial and execution in 1552. This section was reworked in interesting ways for the 1587 edition, so that we are given *two* different eyewitness reports of the execution. Both focus, one more sceptically than the other, on a "hurly-burly" that occurs in the crowd around the scaffold. The effect of this double reportage is not, as the *Chronicles'* bad press hitherto might lead one to suppose, of a gratuitous duplication, but rather of a bringing to consciousness, making visible, the facts of multivocality and diversity of opinion. Holinshed himself had been responsible for the inclusion of the first voice, which turns out to be that of John Stow, but instead of a marginal attribution (to what must at this stage have been only a manuscript account)[9] Holinshed played up the voice-on-voice montage: "Wherefore I thinke it good to write what I saw (saith John Stow)" he wrote vicariously:

> The people of a certeine hamlet which were warned to be there by seaven of the clocke to give their attendance on the lieutenant, now came thorough the posterne, and perceiving the duke to be alreadie on the Scaffold, the foremost began to run, crieng to their fellowes to follow fast after. Which suddennes of these men, being weaponed with bils and halberds, & this running caused the people which first saw them, to thinke some power had come downe to have rescued the duke from execution, and therefore cried Awaie, awaie; Thereupon the people ran, some one waie some an other, manie fell into the tower ditch, and they which tarried, thought some pardon had beene brought. Some said it thundered, some that the ground mooved, but there was no such matter. (3:1034)

In Stow's account, the entire commotion was caused by tardiness, the local constabulary arriving late for the job of superintending the crowds around the scaffold, and the crowd's misconception that their hasty, last-minute arrival constituted an insurrectionary "power." The tone is darkly comedic; and although Stow's presence at the scene in one sense makes him an ordinary member of the crowd, his rejection of the superstitious interpretations of the "great noise" creates some intellectual distance.

For the second edition, Abraham Fleming chose to supplement Stow's response, or to contrast it, with that of John Foxe. This incident, Fleming added, "is *in other words* recorded by John Fox . . . which because they be *effectuall* I thinke good to interlace" (italics added). What he means by "effectuall," the reader is left to deduce, but the new material clearly adds a religious, prophetic aura that Stow had as conspicuously declined:

> When the duke had ended his speech (saith he) suddenlie there was a terrible noise heard: whereupon there came a great feare on all men. This noise was as it had beene the noise of a great storme or tempest, which to some seemed to be heard from above: But to some againe it seemed as though it had beene a great multitude of horssemen running togither, or comming upon them; . . . some being affraid with the horrour and noise, fell downe groveling into the ground with their pollaxes & halberds, and most part of them cried out: Jesus save us, Jesus save us. . . . And I myselfe [and here the marginal note says, "Namelie John Fox the writer of this report"] which was there present among the rest, being also affraid in this hurlie burlie, stood still altogither amazed, looking when anie man would knocke me on the head. (3:1034)

Unlike Stow's, the "effectuall" strategy of Foxe's account and of its quotation is to merge the historian completely with the crowd, and to subject him (or at least his youthful past self as a gawking bystander) to the same limited and apocalyptic point of view. Whereas Stow records the crowd as crying in unison, "Awaie, awaie," what Foxe remembers is a corporate "Jesus save us, Jesus save us." But in accordance with Foxe's own development as a grand-scale historian of English Protestantism, he also sees the local "hurlie burlie" as speaking to the political nation at a crucial turning point. Seeing Sir Anthony Browne riding up to the scaffold, the people "conjectured that which was not true, but notwithstanding which they all wished for, that the king by that messenger had sent his uncle pardon":

> And therfore with great rejoising and casting up their caps, they cried out; Pardon, Pardon is come: God save the king. Thus this good duke, though he was destitute of all mans helpe, yet he saw before his departure, in how great love and favour he was with all men. (3:1035)

Here is a moment of popular consensus and celebration, of national enthusiasm ("God save the king"), but one, it turns out, that is illusory. There is to be no last-minute reprieve. On the contrary, Somerset's popularity with the common people merely underscores the gratuitousness of his removal from the political scene. The *Chronicles* look through Foxe's eyes at a past which shows no rationale for such horrific events, whose very frequency indicates that governments are run by faction rather than principle, and toward a future made only more threatening by the removal of the one figure who seemed concerned with something other than his own advancement:

> And trulie I doo not thinke, that in so great slaughter of dukes as hath beene in England within this few yeares, there was so manie weeping eies at one time: and not without cause. For all men did see in the decaie of this duke, the publike ruine of all England, except such as indeed perceived nothing. (3:1035)

Multivocality and Verbatim Reporting

The effect produced by the intertwined voices in this episode, Holinshed's, Stow's, Foxe's, and that of the crowd at large (the popular voice), is both subtle and troubling. Here the protocol of eyewitness reporting dovetails exactly with that of multivocality, the determination to register diversity of opinion. An essential protocol for producing multivocality, evidently, was verbatim reporting, whereby the chroniclers choose, if not wherever possible, at least by conventional standards unnecessarily, to retain the actual words of their sources, rather than filter them through a third-person narration. When more than one witness, living or dead, is engaged, the effect may be troubling insofar as it forces the reader to recognize how easy, indeed inevitable, it is for different persons to perceive the same events differently. But a different justification for verbatim reporting was offered by Francis Thynne, whose catalogs of officeholders gave less opportunity for deploying it. Toward the end of Thynne's roll call of the archbishops of Canterbury, which would culminate with Edmund Grindal and his successor Whitgift (and would be removed by the 1587 censorship), Thynne remarks:

> Which matter being set downe in manie of our chronicles, as in Caxton, Henrie Knighton, Eulogium, Scala chronicon, Campden, and others, I will deliver the words of the said Authors, least I might seeme (in being ambitious in names) to bring emptie casks without anie wine. The words of which au-

thors, although they be long and to some maie seeme needlesse to be so often remembred, *yet I have not refused to give everie author leave to tell his owne tale, for that I would not seeme to wrong them in misreporting thereof; and for that I desire to make common by manie copies (as occasion may serve) the writings of former ages remaining in private hands.* (4:773; italics added)

The concept of verbatim reporting also, therefore, dovetails in this historiography with the ideal of a documentary history that preserves and transmits from private to public hands the records of the past, whose integrity resides precisely in being left alone, untampered with.[10] "Verbatim" is a word that Thynne uses more than once.[11] It appears again in the editorial comment following "the note of Edmund Molyneux" which provides the biography of Sir Philip Sidney that was promised in the Irish section of the *Chronicles;* and here it is perhaps John Stow speaking, incidentally delivering important information about the way the project was printed:

This note you find here before set downe, touching sir Philip Sidneie, being a member of the discourse made of his father, was brought and delivered to the impression before there was either speech, or could be no imagination of his fatall end, which soone after happened: who for that he was reckoned . . . so complete a man to everie perfection, as the memorie of him ought not to be forgotten, I have entred the note *verbatim*, without adding or altering as it came first to my hands. (4:880)[12]

As with Thynne's catalog of archbishops, this decision was frustrated by the official censorship which overtook the second edition, and the tributes to the Sidneys, father and son, eventually appeared in a far less generous form. It appears that "altering" testimony is associated more with the authorities than with the chroniclers themselves, who theoretically wash their hands of it.

But one should not conclude that the verbatim protocol was innately oppositional. On the contrary, the words of the authorities, as represented by official pamphlets or speeches, are recorded with the same fidelity. This is especially true of Queen Elizabeth herself, whose speeches and proclamations form the last words of the 1587 edition; and her voice is equally heard earlier in the reign, as, for example, in this telling insertion made by Abraham Fleming with respect to her progress through Cambridge in 1564. Before she left she made "a notable oration in Latine . . . to the students great comfort." And, added Fleming:

A copie whereof I have set downe, as I received it in writing at the hands of one that then was present, and noted the same as hir majestie uttered it. Whose words unto me in a letter, wherewith the same oration was sent, I doo here set downe Bona fide. This hir majesties extemporall oration (saith he) lieng among my papers these twentie yeares and more, I thought good now to send to you, that if anie occasion be fitlie offered in the discourse of hir highnesse reigne, you maie (if you please) insert it. In truth, I my selfe never elsewhere read it, which hath made me even religiouslie to preserve it. Master Abraham Hartwell in his Regina literata, dwelling upon this onelie argument of hir comming and doings at Cambridge, glanceth in a distich or or twaine at the effect hereof. but this is the thing it selfe, as I my selfe (most unworthie) being both an eare and also an eie witnesse, can testifie. (4:225)

We can see here another example of one "I" superimposed on, or inserted into, the testimony of another, as Fleming incorporates the letter he has received from Thomas Newton. But what makes this passage particularly interesting theoretically is the cognitive play between "the thing it selfe" and "I my selfe" as copartners in this fully reified, fully individualist mininarrative, this collaboration between archivists of the cultural memory.

The Anecdote

Modern and postmodern culture has become suspicious of "the thing it selfe" and "I my selfe," the realist and subjective views of the world in which the chroniclers evidently believed, and assumed would make their work believable by others. Much has been written in our own time, not all of it intelligent, to make these concepts evaporate. Fortunately, history and historiography have proved resiliant against, if not impervious to, the deconstructive turn; and the *Chronicles*, by virtue of their own protocols of representation, by their refusal to produce a seamless narrative, are still more resistant. Realism and individualism as frames whereby to approach experience converge, I believe, in the anecdote. By "anecdote," I refer to a brief, independent narrative about human behavior, short enough to be emblematic, independent enough of its surroundings to be portable, and with one or more colorful individuals at its center. Sometimes these individuals are nameless, but their independence of spirit, their refusal to be absorbed into the unifying texture of a grand narrative, is evident nonetheless. The better anecdotes, therefore, contain snatches of conversation, whose verisimilitude is a key to their memorability, the cause of their having remained in the cultural memory; and they tend to function as signs that something in the "system" is under stress, something in the "official" account is up for question.

We see today the beginnings of a theoretical debate about the status of the anecdote in cultural history. Among the criticisms that have been leveled against the New Historicism or "cultural poetics" of Stephen Greenblatt and others is a distrust of the anecdotes with which many of their arguments begin. If one were to go beyond merely the suspicion that this strategy gives an unfair rhetorical advantage, such distrust implies that the anecdote is insufficiently representative of large cultural phenomena or that it privileges the individual rather than the group; a complaint that might be equally generated by Marxist criticism or a social history that demands statistics.[13] Holinshed, Stow, Stanyhurst, Hooker, and Fleming, however, deploy the anecdote in a way that suggests a cultural poetics of their own, one that rebuts these criticisms in advance.

Anecdotes will often be featured in the following chapters, especially in my account of popular, demotic culture as the *Chronicles* represent it, and of the life of women in early modern Britain. Perhaps there is a connection. The chroniclers appear to think that women's culture, unless they happen to be queens, is demotic, possibly therefore a challenge to authority. Anecdotes are *added* in the 1587 edition to the story of earlier reigns, carefully culled from the pages of Hall's *Union*, Foxe's *Acts and Monuments*, John Stow's *Chronicle*, and other sources. There is more at stake here than the provision of thick description or local color, although the chroniclers evidently felt that these were indispensable to their task. After one becomes familiar with the *Chronicles* the anecdotes begin to speak to each other across the vast expanses of military campaigns, state entertainments, and lists of officeholders, and the stories they tell come to acquire symbolic import.

In the *Chronicles*, predictably, there are tales of violent crimes, with the characters all named, including the overgrown anecdote of the murder of Arden of Feversham, which later became a play (3:1024–31); the story, derived from Matthew Paris, of a Jew who refused to pay the tax demanded by King John, and was condemned to have one tooth pulled out of his head every day, until, with one tooth left, he submitted (2:301); and the story, complete with references to Icarus, of an Italian abbot who in 1507 claimed he could fly, but who, to save face, "referred the default of his flieng wholie to his wings, because they were not made of eagles fethers and such like, but onelie of pullens fethers, not meet or accustomed to cut the aire with flight (and which by a certaine inward vertue (working according to the nature of those foules) did draw the fethers downe toward the doonghill (wherupon those birds live) as the adamant draweth iron" (5:467–68).

But none of these meets the criteria I am here suggesting for the paradigmatic anecdote—one that, at least from the perspective of this study, encapsulates the original historiography that Holinshed and his colleagues were developing, original even though, or because, they drew for its spirit on stories passed down from one teller to another. Here are three examples

of anecdotes that fulfil this condition. They stand respectively as signs of
the economic, social-domestic, and politico-religious conditions of life of
early modern England. All three, moreover, interrogate at different levels
of seriousness the master-servant relationship so engagingly broached by
Stanyhurst in his dedication to Sir Henry Sidney by way of *his* anecdote
about the painter Dolie.

The first is a story attributed to William of Malmesbury about William
Rufus, first son of William the Conqueror, but it could easily have occurred
in the 1540s: "I find," wrote Holinshed, "that in apparell he loved to be gaie
and gorgeous, & could not abide to have anie thing (for his wearing) esteemed at a small valure":

> Whereupon it came to passe on a morning, when he should pull on a new
> paire of hose, he asked the groome of his chamber that brought them to him
> what they cost? Three shillings saith he; "Why thou hooreson (said the king)
> doth a paire of hose of three shillings price become a king to weare? Go thy
> waies, and fetch me a paire that shall cost a marke of silver." The groome
> went, and brought him another paire, for the which he paid scarselie so
> much as for the first. But when the king asked what they stood him in, he told
> him they cost a marke: and then was he well satisfied, and said; "Yea marie,
> these are more fit for a king to wear," and so drew them upon his legs. (2:46)

It is impossible to read this anecdote without recognizing its irreverent intentions, its willingness to display the upstaging of a vain and silly monarch
by a shrewd and witty servant. Its underlying structure is that of the
Aesopian fable, the king of the beasts outwitted by the fox; but the fable
has been updated in terms of the *Chronicles'* interest in prices, and the spread
of conspicuous consumption.

My second example also has the structure of a fable, though blended
uncomfortably (as the fable often was in Elizabethan literature) with sardonic anti-pastoral. It appears as a detail within an extensive account provided by Holinshed of the floods that overtook the northeast coast in
October 1570, and its source would appear to be very local knowledge:[14]

> Also between Humerston and Grimsbie were lost eleven hundred sheepe of
> one master Spensers, whose sheepherd about middaie, comming to his wife,
> asked his dinner: and she being more bold than manerlie, said, he should
> have none of hir. Then he chanced to looke toward the marishes where the
> sheepe were, and saw the water breake in so fiercelie, that the sheepe would
> be lost, if they were not brought from thense, said, that he was not a good
> sheepherd that would not venture his life for his sheepe, and so went streight
> to drive them from thense, but he and his sheepe, were both drowned, and

after the water being gone, he was found dead, standing upright in a ditch. (4:256)

Why are we told this story, when the statistics of the devastation to sheep farming that Holinshed provided at length would seem adequate for agricultural history, the business in hand? Perhaps to people the drowned landscape, to offer something other than an economic accounting of the nature of loss. Why else are we given the gratuitous and memorable detail that the dead shepherd was found as a marker of catastrophe, a grotesque signpost "standing upright in a ditch"? But such old-fashioned humanism does not exhaust the anecdote's own economy of suggestiveness. Should the shepherd have given his life for "master Spenser's" sheep? Should his wife have taunted him to do so? Where does Holinshed stand on this conflict of duties, and on the "more bold than manerlie" woman who refused her husband his dinner, perhaps until he had seen to his charge, perhaps out of ordinary domestic rebellion? Given the familiar metaphor of the monarch as shepherd of his people (which has already appeared in chapter 1 in my citation of Holinshed's citation of Foxe's anecdote about George Stadlow, and will recur at significant moments hereafter), how far do the subtexts extend? That something is *wrong* with the shepherd's thinking is unexpectedly signaled in the margin, where Holinshed had added elliptically "Scripture abused," a sign to the reader not only to pay attention, but to wonder in what the abuse consists.

An anecdote like this is particularly open to interpretation in the light of D. R. Woolf's understanding of the vexed status of oral history in this period. Woolf cites William Lambarde's anxieties over the issue of '"feedback,' which occurs when writing influences, distorts or even creates outright an oral tradition"; and he also notes that, like the ballads suspected by the Elizabethan government as vagrant, uncensorable, and potentially subversive, oral tradition was "masterless history."[15] It answered to no one.

The last anecdote in my series is longer and still more complex in tone and function. It also involves an unfortunate marriage, but one inset in a larger tragedy of church and state. It occurs in Francis Thynne's deleted catalog of archbishops, which was originally inserted into the *Chronicles* under the year 1586, although the anecdote itself belongs to 1540. It has laughter within it, but it is not told facetiously. We can be confident of the historicality of its protagonists, being Henry VIII and Archbishop Cranmer; and Thynne was able to translate it verbatim from an unexceptionable source, the Latin history of the English archbishops by Matthew Parker,[16] himself a holder of that office.

Here Henry, to escape the "pontificals," as Thynne calls the antireform bishops, who are planning Cranmer's demise, "for recreations cause tooke barge to row up and downe the Thames," where he is joined at Lambeth by Cranmer. There was "long and secret talke" between them, the "watermen stil hovering with the bote on the river," and Henry pretended to ask Cranmer's advice about how to deal with a dangerous archheretic. This is the game of cat and mouse:

> Whereunto Cranmer (although he was in great feare) answered with a good countenance that the same counsell pleased him well, being verie glad to hear thereof, because by the punishment of that archheretike the rest of the flocke of heretikes would be bridled. But with this speech he did yet with a certein fatherlie reverence toward the king, modestlie admonish the king, that he shuld not judge them to be heretickes, who with the word of God strived against mens traditions. Whereunto the king said; It is rightlie spoken by you, for you are declared to us by manie to be that archhereticke of all our king-dome, who in Kent and in all your province doo so withstand us, that the beleefe of the six articles established in parlement be not received of the com-mon people; wherefore openlie declare unto us what you thinke, and what you have doone of and in the same. Cranmer replied, that he was still of the same mind which he openlie professed himselfe to be at the making of that law. . . . Then the king somewhat leaving this grave talke, merrilie asked of him, whether his inner and privie bed were free from those articles. To which Cranmer (although he knew it dangerous by that law for priests to have wives, and that he certeinlie understood that the king knew that he was maried) an-swered, that he contracted that marriage before he was archbishop . . . but now because he would not offend so rigorous a law, he had not touched his wife since the making thereof, because he had presentlie sent hir unto hir freends in Germanie. By which plaine answer he wan such favor with the king, that the king incoraged him to be of good comfort. (4:737)

Hovering on the river, king and prelate play out the game of acceptable speech, in the frame of the weathercock religion of the day. Cranmer's "good comfort" did not last. As Thynne ironically summed up the end of his story as a whole, in Mary's reign "he was consumed to ashes": "a death not read before to have happened to anie archbishop, who as he was the first that publikelie impugned by established lawes the popes authoritie in England, so was he the first metropolitane that was burned for the same" (4:744). The elegant structure of this sentence mocks the reversals of ec-clesiastical fortune in post-Reformation England, perhaps all the more ef-fectively for Thynne's withholding of overt expressions of sympathy and regret.

These anecdotes explain that the texture of history, if we could look more closely at every corner of it, would become visible as a web of complex human motivation. In short, they make nonsense of the poststructuralist claim that we cannot recuperate the alien cultures of the past except in our own distorting mirror. There are no aliens here. But in addition the anecdotes included in the *Chronicles* seem to belong there, to have a nonarbitrary relationship to the project seldom achieved by modern cultural historians who deploy some version of this strategy. They possess all the attributes of good fiction (shapeliness, thrift, vitality, the capacity to speak to social issues of importance, particularly those not yet fully or widely understood), while being, unmistakably, uninvented. And they finesse the problem of *representativeness* by virtue of their *representational* solidity, their sense of being a statistic come alive.

Literature as History

A focus on the aesthetics and hermeneutics of the anecdote should not be confused with postmodernist attempts not merely to renegotiate the theoretical frontier between history and literature, but to make it an open invitation to illegal immigration. In fact, although my own approach to the *Chronicles* depends on reading with a "literary" eye—one trained to consider nuance, ambiguity, subtexts, tone—I am committed to the opposite principle from that espoused by postmodernists: not that history (since all of its traces are textual) is only another form of literature, but that "literature," a category of texts that have acquired special privileges over time, is (among other things) an important source of historical knowledge.

In a slightly different sense, this view was also held by those who contributed to the *Chronicles*. Holinshed himself was interested in writers as contributors to the national culture. Although the catalogs of writers added at the end of each reign, in imitation of Bale's *Catalogus*, made no distinction between, say, poets and monastic chroniclers or pamphleteers, Holinshed took extensive note of the achievements of Chaucer and Gower in establishing the vernacular as a literary language (3:58). Literary figures would only enter his narrative proper, however, when they became embroiled in politics. As we will see in chapter 11, Holinshed's curiosity was sparked by the poet Collingbourne, executed for treason by Richard III for circulating the notorious couplet in which Richard and his advisors are billed as the protagonists in an Aesopian fable. In his history of Scotland, for the year 1521, Holinshed recorded that factional strife between the dukes of Albany and Angus resulted in a proclamation by the former requiring the latter with all his "complices," to appear before Parliament for trial:

Maister Gawin Dowglasse bishop of Dunkeld, hearing of this proclamation, fled into England, and remained in London at the Savoie, where he departed this life, and is buried in the church there. He was a cunning clearke, and a verie good poet: he translatd the twelve bookes of the *Aeneidos of Virgill* in Scotish meeter,and compiled also *The palace of honor,* with diverse other treatises in the Scotish language, which are yet extant. (5:492)

But Holinshed was also interested in royal entertainments as signs of the times, and capable of recording them with a certain ironic relish. Thus for the year 1564, he reported, on August 5:

the queenes maiestie in hir progresse came to the universitie of Cambridge, and was of all the students (being invested according to their degrees taken in the schooles) honorablie and joifullie received in the Kings college where she did lie during hir continuance in Cambridge. The daies of hir abode were passed in scholasticall exercises of philosophie, physicke, and divinitie: *the nights in comedies and tragedies, set foorth partlie by the whole universitie, and partly by the students of the Kings college.* (4:225; italics added)

Abraham Fleming felt compelled, ten years later, to add his own idea of the purpose and effect of these entertainments: "to recreat and delight hir maiestie, who both heard them attentivelie, and beheld them cheerfullie." Two years (but only a few pages) later, the rivalry between the two universities receives, as it were, aesthetic expression. On 31 August 1566,

The one and thirtieth of August, the queenes maiestie in hir progresse came to the universitie of Oxford, and was of all the students, which had looked for hir comming thither two years, so honorablie and joifullie received, as either their loialnesse towards the queenes majestie, or the expectation of their freends did require. Concerning orders in disputations and other academicall exercises, they agreed much with those which the universitie of Cambridge had used two yeares before. Comedies also and tragedies were plaied in Christs church, where the queenes highnesse lodged. Among the which the comedie intituled Palemon and Arcit, made by maister Edwards of the queenes chappell, had such tragicall successe, as was lamentable. For at the time by the fall of a wall and a paire of staires, and great presse of the multitude three men were slaine. (4:230)

Another of the chroniclers with literary affiliations was Richard Stanyhurst, whose amazing translation of the *Aeneid* into fourteeners was declared by C. S. Lewis to be "barely English," a verdict we need not share.[17] It is not, therefore, surprising to discover that Stanyhurst, as part of his defence of the Geraldines, incorporated into the text of the *Chronicles* the complete text of a sonnet by the earl of Surrey, whose "Geraldine" was Lady Elizabeth, daughter of Gerald Fitzgerald, the ninth earl of Kildare, and father of Stanyhurst's employer. The sonnet has the effect of dignifying her lineage ("From Tuscane came my ladies worthy race"), emphasizing her upbringing at the English court ("From tender yeares in Britaine she dooth rest / With kings child"), and referring to Surrey's imprisonment in Windsor Castle in 1537 ("Windsor, alas, dooth chase me from hir sight") (6:46). The muted protest of this sonnet against Henry VIII is compatible with the tone of Stanyhurst's history of Ireland, in which, according to Colm Lennon, the reign is to be seen "as an account of the passing of the most favorable political conditions for the expression of his society's aspirations."[18]

Because I suggested above that Holinshed's anecdote about William Rufus's stockings had the shape of an Aesopian fable (and also because fables were, in this period, one of the most urgent signs of a politicized literary consciousness), it is worth noting that Stanyhurst gratuitously appended to his discussion of barnacles a famous fable of political arbitrariness in interpretation. Stanyhurst reminded his readers that Parliament was entirely capable of changing the rules, and passing legislation that "it were high treason to eat flesh on fridaie, and fish on sundaie." "Trulie I thinke," he continued whimsically, "that he that eateth barnacles both these daies, should not be within the compasse of the estatute: yet I would not wish my friend to hazard it, least the barnacle should be found in law fish or flesh, yea and perhaps fish and flesh":

> As when the lion king of beasts made proclamation, that all horned beasts should avoid his court, one beast having but a bunch of flesh in his forehead departed with the rest, least it had beene found in law that his bunch were an horne. (6:20)

This casual allusion might pass without notice, unless as one of those "fusty fooleries" for which the chroniclers were berated. However, it changes its appearance when we recognize that Stanyhurst must have been reading More's account of Richard III, where he would have encountered this fable in Bishop Morton's warning to Buckingham, and which also appears in the *Chronicles*:

> In good faith my lord, I love not to talke much of princes, as a thing not all out of perill, though the word be without fault: forsomuch as it shall not be taken as the partie ment it, but as it pleaseth the prince to construe it. And ever I thinke on Aesops tale, that when the lion had proclaimed that (on paine of death) there should no horned beast abide in that wood: one that had in his forehed a bunce [*sic*] of flesh, fled awaie a great pace. The fox that saw him

run so fast, asked him whither he made all that hast? And he answered, In faith I neither wote, nor recke, so I were once hence, bicause of this proclamation made of horned beasts. What foole (quoth the fox) thou maiest abide well inough: the lion ment not by thee, for it is no horne that is in thine head. No marie (quoth he) that wote I well inough. But what and he call it an horne, where am I then? The duke laughed merilie at the tale, and said; My Lord, I warrant you, neither the lion nor the bore shall pike anie matter at enie thing heere spoken: for it shall never come neere their eare. (2:405)

But undoubtedly the chronicler most responsible for incorporating literary or cultural events into the historical record (and perhaps illuminating the latter by the former) was Abraham Fleming. It has been previously been assumed that for Fleming literary allusions were merely an aspect of an undistinguished belle-lettrism. Typically, when supplementing earlier sections of the history for the 1587 edition, Fleming would add a brief editorial comment of his own, nailed down with a Latin quotation from "the poet," usually Virgil or Horace, or, more interestingly, Juvenal, but sometimes from Christopher Ockland's polemical Latin verse history of Elizabeth's reign, *Anglorum Praelia*, published in 1580, a habit which C. L. Kingsford declared "does not impress the reader with a high sense of [his] literary discrimination."[19]

In fact, however, Fleming seems to have made a considerable effort to ensure that high or "official" culture would be part of the signifying structure of any recent reign. Thus for Henrician culture, Fleming returned to Hall's *Union* (p. 719) for the "goodly disguising" performed at Christmas 1527 at Gray's Inn, during the period of Cardinal Wolsey's ascendancy. The play was "compiled," Hall had written:

for the most part by maister John Roo, sergeant at the law manie yeares past, and long before the cardinall had any authoritie. The effect of the play was, that lord governance was ruled by dissipation and negligence, by whose misgovernance and evill order ladie publike weale was put from governance: which caused rumor populi, inward grudge and disdaine of wanton sovereignetie, to rise with a great multitude, to expell negligence and dissipation, and to restore publike welth againe to hir estate, which was so doone.

This plaie was so set foorth with rich and costlie apparell, with strange devises of maskes & morrishes, that it was highlie praised of all men, saving of the cardinall, which imagined that the play had been devised of him, and in a great furie sent for the said maister Roo, and tooke from his coife, and sent him to the Fleet; and after he sent for the yoong gentlemen, that plaied in the plaie, and them highlie rebuked and threatned, and sent one of them called Thomas Moile of Kent to the Fleet, but by means of friends maister

Roo and he were delivered at last. This plaie sore displeased the cardinall, and yet it was never meant to him, as you have heard. Wherfore manie wise-men grudged to see him take it so hartilie, and ever the cardinall said that the king was highlie displeased with it, and spake nothing of himselfe. [But what will you have of a guiltie conscience but to suspect all things to be said of him (as if all the world knew his wickednesse) according to the old verse: "Conscius ipse sibi de se putat omnia dici."] (3:714)

The signs of Fleming's adapting hand appear in that moral supplement. But to assume that his interest in the scandal over Roo's old play was restricted to Cardinal Wolsey's guilty conscience would be to miss an important point: the courtly entertainments Fleming inserted in the narrative were never *merely* literary, but always carried a political edge. In this case the morality play of state conveyed a barely veiled threat of popular insurrection ("wanton sovereignetie" leads to "rumor populi," which in turn causes the rising of "a great multitude") which might have offended more than Wolsey, and was certainly general enough to be still current in the late 1580s.

Then, for the brief reign of Edward VI (and in the context of Protector Somerset's fall, which we have already seen to be a focus of complex historiographical maneuvers in the *Chronicles*) Fleming reproduced verbatim the following story in Richard Grafton's *Chronicle:*

The duke being condemned (as is aforesaid) the people spake diverslie, and murmured against the duke of Northumberland, . . . and also (as the common fame went) the kings majestie took it not in good part. Wherefore as well to remoove fond talke out of mens mouths, as also to recreat and refresh the troubled spirits of the yoong king; who (as saith Grafton) seemed to take the trouble of his uncle somewhat heavilie: it was devised, [margin. Policie] that the feats of Christs nativitie, commonly called Christmasse then at hand, should be solemnlie kept at Greenwich with open houshold, and franke resort to court (which is called keeping of the hall) what time of old ordinarie course there is alwaies one appointed to make sport in the court, called commonlie lord of misrule.

Therefore George Ferrers, appointed for that year as "maister of the kings pastimes," put on an usually fine assortment of "rare inventions," "diverse interludes", and "matters of pastime," as fully to satisfy the "common sort," the "councell," and "best of all . . . the yoong king himselfe" (3:1032).[20] It would be hard to find a better instantiation of the charge that high culture can function as an ideological screen for repressive state procedures, though here the story is humanized in a way that neo-Marxist theory would find beneath it. Not only are there unmistakable agents of the strategy of diversion (Northumberland and his faction), but there is also an unhappy symmetry between the two supposedly quite different audiences at whom the diversion is aimed: the "common sort" and the young king, whose childish pleasure in the "pastimes" overcomes his concern for his uncle. Moreover, a *writer* (Ferrers) is fingered as complicit, consciously or not, in the scheme, for which, we are told, he was well rewarded; and lest any of his readers be seduced along with the others, Fleming inserted that accusatory marginal pointer: "Policy"!

For the reign of Mary Tudor, Fleming greatly diverted himself, as we shall see in chapter 9, by his sardonic accounts of the pageants devised for Philip II's arrival in London. Perhaps even more interestingly, he took this occasion to write his own Aesopian fable against the marriage, against the parliamentary complaisance in it:

> Howbeit, it was to be wished, even to the disappointing of that mariage (if God in counsell had so provided) that the whole bodie of the parlement had beene semblablie affected, as it is said, that all the nations of the world were, when the sunne would needs be maried. Against which purpose of the sun the people of all regions assembling, humblie besought Jupiter to cast in a blocke and impediment against that wedding. But Jupiter demanding of them why they would not have the sun maried; one stepping up made answer for the rest, and said: Thou knowest well enough Jupiter that there is but one sun, and yet he burneth us all: who, if he be maried and have children, as the number of suns must needs increase; so must their heat and ferventnesse be multiplied, whereupon a generall destruction of all things in their kind will insue. Hereupon that match was overthrowne. (4:27)

In this case the "one stepping up [who] made answer for the rest" is surely the chronicler himself, who assumes (like Buckingham) the privilege of the fabulist to engage in oblique political commentary,[21] but at a safe enough distance chronologically from the events he deplored that the convention was not put to the test.

When he came to the reign of Elizabeth herself, however, Fleming did not drop his concern with courtly entertainments. After Thynne's catalog of the chancellors of the realm, Fleming inserted, out of its chronological place by a full year, an account of Elizabeth's reception into Suffolk and Norfolk in 1578. He took the entire account from a pamphlet by T.[homas] C.[hurchyard], eyewitness of these festivities,[22] unwilling, he tells us, to "let it perish in three halfepenie pamphlets, and so die in oblivion" (4:375). Here there is no overt scandal, nor obvious "policy" drawn to the attention of reader; but especially in the sequence Fleming seems to have constructed, it is impossible to take the pageant's reproduction (as distinct from its first production) as entirely complimentary to the monarch. The first-person, on-the-spot reportage, the human element, with its tendency to demystification, jars with the idealizing texts of the Latin orations and English poems. Even "Mercury's" speech, which contains its own description of these pageants, is surprisingly candid about the organization that at every level underwrites such a show:

> With that a swarme of people everie waie
> Like little ants about the fields gan run,
> Some to provide for pompe and triumph well,
> Some for good fare, yea houshold cates and meate,
> And some they ran to seeke where poets dwell,
> To pen foorth shews and paint out trifles well. (6:387)

Without the worker ants, neither the literal consumption of provisions ("cates") by the royal party, nor the metaphorical consumption of literary sweetmeats ("trifles") would have been possible.

Nor is there any mistaking the mixture of humor and chagrin by which the reporter (Churchyard) himself acknowledged the gap between the ideal and the real. The pageants are plagued by material circumstances. The queen does not come when she is expected: "there having althings in readinesse, they hoovered on the water three long houres, by which meanes the night came on, and so they were faine to withdraw themselves and go homeward, trusting for a better time and occasion" (4:394); speeches are not delivered because they are cut off by rain (4:379); shows are not what they should be because of economic constraints ("by meane of some crossing causes in the citie"); and at one point we are told directly what the real costs are to a community of having to put on such entertainments:

But now note what befell after this great businesse and preparation. For as the queenes highnesse was appointed to come unto hir coch, and the lords and courtiers were readie to mount on horsseback, there fell such a showre of raine (and in the necke thereof came such a terrible thunder) that everie one of us were driven to seeke for covert and most comfort, insomuch that some of us in bote stood under a bridge and were all so dashed and washed, that it was a greater pastime to see us looke like drowned rats, than to have beheld the uttermost of the shewes rehearsed. Thus you see, a shew in the open field is alwaies subject to the sudden change of weather, and a number of more inconveniences. But what what should be said of what the citie lost by this cause; velvets, silkes, tinsels, and some cloth of gold being cut out for these purposes, that could not serve to anie great effect after? (4:401)

In fact, the question of what should be said is deliberately rephrased as what *could* be said by prudent recorders, who fall back on common wisdom or tactful silence:

> Well, there was no more to saie, but an old adage, that Man dooth purpose, but God dooth dispose, to whose disposition and pleasure the guide of greater maters is committed. So this thursdaie tooke his leave from the actors, and left them looking one upon another, and he that thought he had received most injurie, kept greatest silence, and lapping up (among a bundle of other misfortunes) this evill chance, everie person quietlie passed to his lodging. (4:401)

Three years later, on 15 and 16 May 1581, there occurred the cultural event we now know as the *Four Foster Children of Desire*, famous in literary studies as involving Fulke Greville and Sir Philip Sidney. This royal entertainment took the form of a tournament, which was advertised by a challenge issued a month earlier by a herald representing the figure of Desire. The text of this entertainment, written by Sidney, had already been published by Henry Goldwell, in a pamphlet entitled *A Briefe Declaration of the Shews, Devices, Speeches, and Inventions, Done & Performed before the Queene's Majestie, & the French Ambassadors* (London, 1581).[23] There has never been any doubt that the pageant was intended as a commentary on the queen's current negotiations for a marriage with the duc d' Alençon, whose commissioners arrived in London in May, to be followed by the French prince himself a few months later, though what precisely its message could have been remains, after much discussion by historians and literary critics, uncertain.[24] The first modern commentators assumed that the pageant expressed the hostility to the French marriage of the English court, or at least the Walsingham-Leicester faction, of which Sidney was naturally a member; but according to a more recent tendency to understand the Elizabethan shows as less obvious forms of persuasion, the *Four Foster Children* has been read as a meditation on the strategies of self-presentation and self-preservation required for a male courtier-politician in the service of a female monarch.[25] At any rate, the compilers of the 1587 *Chronicles* felt that the pageant was important enough to the cultural history of Elizabeth's reign, and perhaps to its political history also, that the entire text should be included.[26] Perhaps it was intended as a substitute for truly unrepresentable matters, Sidney's overt protest against the marriage in a private letter to the queen, which resulted in his voluntary or involuntary rustication on his sister's estate at Wilton, where the *Arcadia* was written. And in a later section of the *Chronicles*, for the year 1586, Fleming was to include the "note of Edmund Molyneux" praising Sidney as the young courtier on whom all eyes were fixed in expectation, not least for his composition of that highly political prose romance. Molyneux's praise would, had it survived the castration of the 1587 edition, have become an unusually interesting elegy, though written, as Fleming reminds the reader in what must have been a very late postscript, and *brought to the press* "when there could be no imagination of his fatall end" that same year, 1586; and it would have been interesting precisely in pretending that everything Sidney had done had been pleasing to the queen, when in fact he had frequently incurred her displeasure.[27]

The chroniclers, then, were convinced that what we call "literature" was integral to the cultural history they were compiling, an indispensable part of the record, both of the individual career and of the *bildungsroman* of the nation as a whole. They also had at their disposal a number of literary techniques and genres, which enliven and intensify the text they were constructing out of extremely diverse materials; but they did not make the mistake of some modern theoreticians in confusing literary *methods* with an endless, indiscriminate textuality. Reading the *Chronicles* with a literary intelligence may alert us to the mobile boundaries between "facts" and fictionality, or between documents and stories, but it does not require us to deny their existence; not, at least, if we also try to read as cultural historians.

FOUR   🌿 *Revision*

P erhaps the most underinvestigated aspect of the *Chronicles* is the fact
of their revision. The 1587 editors not only continued the histories of
the three nations from the point where Holinshed and Stanyhurst
had stopped, but returned to rework and supplement the earlier accounts of
the history of England and Scotland. One of the many overt signs of this
activity occurs at the end of the account of King Alfred, where there appears a Latin epitaph "(verse for verse, and in a maner word for word) translated by Abraham Fleming into English, whose no litle labor hath beene
diligentlie imploied in supplieng sundrie insufficiences found in this huge
volume" (1:676). But while previous commentators on Fleming's role in the
project have briefly noted this process of supplementation, there has been
no analysis of *why* the first edition was thought insufficient to the 1587 syndicate, or of whether there are any patterns of significance in the extensive
additions, deletions, and passages of detailed and subtle rewriting.

One of the most obvious changes between 1577 and 1587 was the removal of the illustrations. While the primary reasons for this change were
probably practical—space-saving and ease of printing—the *effect* of the removal of this form of emphasis deserves consideration. Or rather, the effect
of the presence of the illustrations in 1577 needs to be considered, although here we must really be guessing how the sixteenth-century reader
would have seen them. Although in a few rare instances individual wood-

cuts appear to have been created for special moments, such as the speech of the British queen Voadicea to her troops before their fatal engagement with the Romans, or Macbeth's meeting with the Weird sisters, the vast majority were formulaic designs endlessly repeated. As Liam Miller and Eileen Power explain, the woodcuts were assembled from many sources and "followed the Elizabethan principle of book illustration: to represent the general rather than the particular."[1] The general, however, has a decidedly violent and even sinister character, especially when the principle of repetition itself enforces the message that history is an endless series of battle, sieges, and pillagings, executions formal and informal, scenes of advice and submission to monarchs, courtly banquets, acts of recoinage, and the occasional murder and rape. Without these visual reminders that *plus ça change, plus c'est la même chose*, the reader of 1587 was presumably free to create his own theory of historical change or continuity.

For the Scottish history in 1587, the supplementary text was clearly signaled as the responsibility of Francis Thynne, who usually marked his insertions in the margin with his own signature (Fr. Thin.); in particular, Thynne apparently decided that Holinshed's choice of one primary authority, John Major, was too restricting, and he went back through the entire history adding material from Leslie and Buchanan. In the English history, the supplementation seems to have been the responsibility of Abraham Fleming, who also usually marks his insertions with his initials, but whose reasons for augmenting Holinshed's text are less easy to summarize than Thynne's. In the account of the reign of Henry VIII, for example, he imported massive blocks of material about international politics and military campaigns from Guicciardini, but he also filled out episodes that might be thought revelatory of trouble on the domestic front, usually by recourse to Edward Hall's *Union of the two noble & illustre famelies*. For the reign of Mary, whom Fleming decided to render an object of comic disesteem, he went constantly to Foxe's *Acts and Monuments*, a strategy that Holinshed had also used but more sparingly. And in earlier reigns, at least two discernible patterns emerge: an interest in economic history, which motivated him to search the fifteenth-century chronicles for details about dearths and prices, and, less surprisingly, an interest in the prehistory of the Reformation, which caused him to insert six of the twenty-three articles of Wycliffe's creed (2:705), Knighton's account of the bill for disendowment in the 1391 parliament (2:813), and the text of Richard II's commission against the Lollards "Englished by A.F." (2:826–28).

There is also the interesting possibility that, where additions or changes were made that do *not* carry Fleming's initials, or where subtle rewriting occurs of passages that were clearly tendentious, they were the second thoughts of Holinshed himself before his death. As we shall see in subsequent chapters, *someone* toned down for or prior to the second edition some of the most interesting passages on ancient constitutionalism, and on Sir John Oldcastle's rebellion, suggesting that self-censorship was a conscious consideration before the second edition was issued. Unlike most previous commentators on Fleming's contributions, I am not convinced that all such cautions proceeded from him. Rather, Fleming seems to have understood and developed in his own way at least some of the historiographical principles Holinshed established. Although his tendency was to blur the distinction between the ecclesiastical and secular history that was one of the project's protocols, the effect of his additions in the aggregate was to increase the multivocality of the work, and to sharpen its emphasis on religious and social dissent.

Revision is, therefore, another protocol of the *Chronicles*, perhaps the most important of all, whose study demands readerly patience. I trust that here and in the following chapters that patience will be rewarded; for it is often in the material added or altered that we can most clearly recognize or confirm the signs of intentionality, at least in the reviser. The difficulty of the task resides, of course, in the need to compare the 1577 and 1587 editions, for which neither the 1807–8 edition by Sir Henry Ellis nor its modern reprint is a reliable guide. Although the Ellis edition, which was based on 1587, gives warning of additions by paragraph markers or square brackets, it does not *always* do so, nor do such markers always indicate new material. And neither the 1587 edition nor the 1807–8 edition give any indication of material deleted or rewritten in complicated ways. Yet in order to retain a system of citation that best serves the needs of today's readers, I shall continue to refer to the Ellis edition as a good *enough* source of the text of the 1587 edition.

In order to establish the importance of the revisions in reconstructing the chroniclers' agenda, I shall begin with a comparatively simple exhibit, one where we can be reasonably sure who was responsible for the revisions, and therefore focus the question of intention with some precision. This is William Harrison's *Description of England*, which also happens to be a particularly interesting case of how the difference between 1577 and 1587 is more important than it has seemed to earlier editors, critics, and historians.

There are three such accounts, each of which tells a different (and in my view, somewhat misleading) story of Harrison. The first is Frederick J. Furnivall's 1877 edition of the *Description*. This was not a complete edition, but contained only Harrison's second and third books. Revealingly entitled *Harrison's Description of England in Shakspere's Youth*, it was published for the New Shakespeare Society, of which Furnivall was founder and director.[2]

Like Holinshed's *Chronicles* as a whole, then, this opening section was early annexed to the field of Shakespeare studies in their antiquarian or anthropological form. Furnivall was, above all, interested in local color, what he calls the "interesting home-life part" (viii); he included a map of "Shakspere's routes to London" and a long appendix by William Rendle on "The Bankside, Southwark, and the Globe Playhouse" (Part II, i–xxix); and fact and fiction are in his imagination inseparable. His notes on the excluded first book of the *Description* include the following gloss on chapter 11, "Punishments appointed for Malefactors":

> that the punishment for "robbing by the high waie" (like Sir John Falstaff's), "cutting of purses," "stealing of deere by night" (like Shakespere's, if he ever stole deer from Sir Thomas Lucy, who had no park in his time), was death. (xxi)

At the bottom of this page of Furnivall's edition appeared a note which reveals the intensity of his personal identification with his idol: "Did Shakspere ever turn out and chevy a Stratford thief, I wonder? He must have been able to hit and hold hard."

But one does not need such detailed symptoms to decipher *Furnivall's* intentions. His foreword says it all, including his reasons for omitting all but a few brief excerpts from Book I. "The *[Description]* is full of interest," it declares, "not only to every Shakspere student, but to every reader of English history, every man who has the least care for his forefathers' lives." Furnivall commends Harrison's "racy phrases" and the expansiveness of his social vision. "From its Parliament and Universities to its beggars and its rogues; from its castles to its huts, its horses to its hens; from how the state was managd, to how Mrs. Wm Harrison (and no doubt Mrs William Shakspere) brewd her beer; all is there." And "nothing could have kept it from being often reprinted and a thousand times more widely known than it is, except the long and dull historical and topographical Book I." Accordingly, Furnivall calmly omits it (iii–iv, ix).[3] In fact, however, Furnivall's emphasis on amusement and what he calls "capital bits" (xxvii) is slightly disingenuous. His decision to omit the first book and to begin, therefore, with the important chapter "Of the ancient and present estate of the church of England" has the same effect as his emphasis in the Foreword on "how the state was managd," through Parliament and the law courts: to foreground the politics of the work, which would indeed, even in the 1587 arrangement of the *Description*, have been relatively obscure to a desultory reader. It is also important to realize that Furnivall collated the first (1577) version of the *Description* with the second of 1587, or rather conflated them, with square brackets indicating material added in revision; and although this is scarcely a perfect system for registering changes when material is rewritten in complex ways, the edition nevertheless gives the modern reader a simple visual representation of a text that in crucial chapters was heavily supplemented. Furnivall, however, offered no comment on or analysis of these changes, and his typographical signals may well have appeared to later readers as eccentric as his treatment of Harrison's marginal notes, which he supplemented with marginalia of his own, in a quirky idiom that is half archaic, half nineteenth-century enthusiasm.

The second Harrison story was told by Georges Edelen, who, no doubt on the strength of his discovery of Harrison's mini-biography in Derry, in 1968 reedited the *Description* for the Folger Shakespeare Library.[4] Or rather, he reedited almost the same sections as had Furnivall, in modernized spelling, *without the collation of 1577 and 1587,* beginning also with Book II, though adding at the end a few more selections from Book I, in accordance with what he perceived as "Harrison's own range of interests" (viii). He omitted also what he saw as "four lengthy and readily detachable historical digressions" from the parts that Furnivall had included.[5] His aim throughout was apparently to update Furnivall (whose selection was now referred to as *the Description*) and beyond that to include only what was "relevant to the series on social and intellectual history" in which the edition was to appear (viii). The Edelen edition is an advance on Furnivall's only in the sense that it is apparently neutral in tone and less idiosyncratic. But because the collation of the two editions was dropped, nobody reading what had now become ingrained in editorial tradition as the first chapter, "Of the Ancient and Present Estate of the Church of England," would have any idea of how radically this chapter had been revised by Harrison before it arrived at its seemingly transparent state.

Also, the Harrison that emerges from Edelen's account, though not quite as quaint as Furnivall's, was both blander and less dignified. Represented as a man of unusual diligence, who "brought new standards of thoroughness and detail" to what was still residually a monastic chronicle, Edelen's Harrison was also represented as a victim of scholarly indulgences, oddly described in not-quite-dead metaphors of sexual transgression and humiliation. He "is *betrayed* into lengthy digressions." Humanism presented "a *constant temptation.*" Harrison "*cannot resist*" incorporating from Budé a discussion of the sizes of ancient vessels. "Like Shakespeare, he is *seduced* into the unhappy attempt to cast King John as a protoreformer." For him, historical evidence to support his antipapal biases is "a *golden apple.*" "Fortunately, most of these *lapses* are limited to the two chapters on the church which open *The Description of England.*" "Harrison *succumbed,* but we value him none the less for that" (xxii–xxiii). Attempting to "*straddle*" the mutually exclusive demands of panoramic range and exhaustive detail, he "sometimes was *thrown into ungainly postures.*" This picture of Harrison as a pantomime Eve, having eaten of the tree of unnecessary knowledge, and requiring our forgiveness, is, however, conflated with the more or less admirable picture of Harrison the patriot, enthusiastically supporting the Elizabethan church settlement (xxix), and drawing with "honesty and skill" "a deliberate survey of a nation on the threshold of a golden age" (xxxv). In fact, Edelen's description of Harrison's religious opinions, though based on the 1587 text exclusively, would have applied much better to that of 1577, before Harrison had become as indignant, or as cynical, or careless of consequences, as the second edition suggests.

The third story of Harrison and his *Description* is different again. It too was generated by the discovery of new Harrison material, in this case of a second manuscript of Harrison's great unpublished "Chronology." In 1851, one manuscript had been discovered at Derry,[6] and Furnivall had printed a very few excerpts from it before it disappeared, recently to reappear in the British Library.[7] Another version of the "Chronology" was subsequently recognized in Trinity College Dublin MS 165, and became the subject of a 1987 monograph by G. J. R. Parry.[8] The Harrison visible through the lense of the prophetic "Chronology" is neither the racy anthropologist of Furnivall nor the ungainly patriot of Edelen. Parry describes his Harrison as a Protestant visionary with an apocalyptic sense of history, whose *Description* conveys the tension between his godly ideals, which he believed the whole course of salvation history required him to follow, and the institutional reality of Elizabethan England.[9]

Yet if read as a separate work more inflected by the protocols of the *Chronicles* as a whole than the grand scheme of salvific history, the *Description* gives a more mundane impression. Harrison's interest in symbolic chronology is here represented only in a small section of Book I that in 1587 was appended to chapter 9, "Of the ancient religion used in Albion," which actually reveals a rather sceptical attitude to the numerology of Jean Bodin's *Methodus ad Facilem Historiarum Cognitionem* (1:49–51). And although Harrison included important discussions of the Elizabethan church, the overall effect of the *Description* is of a broadly imagined, geographical, social, and institutional account of a country, whose function is to lay down the base for the history to follow.

The first version of the *Description* seems to have been written, as Harrison himself says, in a great hurry, presumably in the second half of 1576. Its tone was comparatively bland and optimistic, compared to that of the revised version, which became in places highly polemical and even satirical. The new syndicate committed to a second edition of the *Chronicles* was formed shortly after Raphael Holinshed's death in April 1582, and Harrison did most of his revising thereafter. Although there is one addition internally dated "this 1579 year of grace" in the chapter "Of Baths and Hot Wells,"[10] Harrison was working away on his revisions through 1586. In "Of Gardens and Orchards" he spoke of a rose that "was to be seene in Antwarpe 1585" (1:353), implying that 1585 was past.

The process of revision was truly extraordinary. Harrison's second thoughts range from the insertion of words or phrases for the purposes of precision and clarification to the addition of new tirades on the subjects of bad landholding practices (the exploitation of tenants and enclosures), the abuse of the admissions process in the universities, usury, grain distribution in the country markets, and (a very important topic indeed for Harrison) the way the English clergy were taxed from all directions. Among the most significant additions for our purpose was an entirely new chapter on Parliament, to be discussed in chapter 6. Certainly not everything that Harrison added carried a polemical flavor; but the examples that follow should give some sense of what was involved.

One might suppose that, if the purpose and effect of the revision was to tidy up a too-hasty first version, chapter 18 in Book I, on "the aire, soile, and commodities of this Iland," would have been *pruned* of a short digression on the laws of the realm which had crept into it by way of a disregarded statute about growing flax. Not so. Instead, Harrison took the opportunity to rewrite this passage with remarkable care, a process the reader cannot deduce from Furnivall's edition, which prints this chapter in an appendix. In 1577 this section read as follows:

> The like I may say of flaxe, which by lawe ought to be sowen in every country towne in Englande, more or lesse, but I see no successe of that good & wholsome estatute,[11] sith it is rather contempteously [sic] rejected then otherwise dutifully kept. *Some say* that our great numbers of lawes, whereby it is impossible for any man to avoyde theyr transgression, is one great cause of our negligence in this behalfe. *Other affirme* that the often alteration of our ordinaunces do breed this general contempt of al good lawes, which after Aristotle doth seme to carye some reason withall.[12] But *very many let not to saye,* that facility in dispensation with them, and manifest breche of the same in the Superiours, are the greatest causes why the inferiours regarde no good order, beyng alwayes ready to offende without any such facultie one way, as they are to presume upon the example of the higher powers another. But as in these thinges I have no skyl, so *some wishe* that fewer licenses for the private commoditie, but of a fewe, were graunted: *this they say,* not that they denie the execution of the prerogative royall, but would wyth all theyr hearts that

it might be made a grievous offence, for anie man by feeed [*sic*] fryndeship or otherwise, to procure oughtes of the Prince (who is not acquainted wyth the botome of the estate of common things) that may be prejudiciall to the weale publike of his country. (38v)

In 1577, therefore, Harrison had found himself straying from agricultural scofflaws to the large and dangerous subject of the general contempt of the laws, to the dispensing power, to corruption in high places, and ultimately to monopolies and the royal prerogative.

   Notice that, precisely because these topics are dangerous, Harrison resorted to the rhetorical strategy of the sociopolitical critic who is not quite ready to assume these views as his own. "Some say," "other affirme," "but very many let not to saye," "some wish," "this they say." This, as I have argued elsewhere,[13] was the conventional rhetorical strategy of radical critics of church and state throughout the later sixteenth century. Its effectiveness had been marked by Sir Thomas More himself in his *Apology*, directed in 1533 against a church reform pamphlet anonymously published by Christopher St. German, not least by the obsessiveness with which More kept returning to what, in his opponent, was only an occasional ploy. For example, wrote More in exasperation:

And as touchynge that he sayth not the thynges as of hym selfe, but bryngeth them in wyth a fygure of *Some say:* to that poynt some other say, that for that curtesy no man hath any cause to can hym any thanke. For under hys fayre fygure of *some say* he maye ... devyse to brynge in all the myschyefe that any man can saye. And yet over thys wythout hys masker of *Some say* he saith open faced some of the wurste hym selfe.[14]

   In the 1587 edition Harrison restructured the latter phase of his argument phrase by phrase, sometimes merely rearranging, sometimes introducing substantial changes, indicated here by italicization:

Some saie that our great number of lawes doo breed a negligence and contempt of all good order; bicause we have so manie, that no subject can live without the transgression of some of them, and that the often alteration of our ordinances dooth much harme in this respect, which (after Aristotle) doth seeme to carie some reason withall, *for (as Cornelius Gallus hath:)*

Eventus varios res nova semper habet. (Eleg. 2)[15]

   But verie manie let not to affirme, that *the greedie corruption of the promoters on the one side,* facilitie in dispensing with good lawes, and *first* breach of the same in the *lawmakers &* superiors, *& private respects of their establishment* on the other, are the greatest causes whie the inferiours regard no good order, being alwaies

> so redie to offend without anie facultie one waie, as they are otherwise to presume, upon the examples *of their betters when anie bold is to be taken*. But as in these things I have no skill, so *I wish* that fewer licences for the privat commoditie but of a few were granted (not that *I thereby* denie the *maintenance* of the prerogative roiall), *but rather would with all my hart that it might be yet more honorablie increased*) & that everie one which by feed friendship (or otherwise) dooth attempt to procure oughts from the prince, *that may profit but few and prove hurtfull to manie, might be at open assizes and sessions denounced enimie to his countrie and commonwealth of the land.* (1:187)

Harrison's alterations move in two diametrically opposite directions. On the one hand he has found reason to be cautious about the royal prerogative, whose "extension" has disappeared from the text, to be replaced by "maintenance" and a wish for its "honorable" increase, a nice ambiguity; on the other, just when he reaches the most dangerous topic of the royal prerogative he drops the pretence of reporting only the sayings of others, and it is now in his own voice that these "wishes" (both loyal and critical) are expressed. Prudence has recognized the tactlessness of suggesting that the prince "is not acquainted wyth the botome of the estate of common things," a phrase which leaves no residue in 1587; courage has increased the vehemence of his antimonopolist sentiments, and the legal sanctions that might be possible in his "commonwealth" utopia.

This example may suffice to show that Harrison's *Description* must be misrepresented by any edition that fails to provide the reader with the text(s) of its first book. Furnivall's and Edelen's theories of what was important and interesting have had the same deleterious effect on the *Description* as the far-better-known castrations performed on the "Continuation." I now turn to those parts of the *Description* that they did include, but whose revisions have so far only been considered (by Parry) as an aspect of Harrison's "Protestant Vision," the big picture and long story of salvific history.

In 1577 the second book of the *Description* contained a fifth chapter, "Of the number of Bishopricks in Englande and Wales, and of the present state of the church there" (pp. 75–78). It was preceded by three chapters on rivers, and one on the division of the country into shires and counties. In 1587 the rivers had been moved back to Book I, and the subject of ecclesiastical history and polity took pride of place, the original chapter being subdivided into two, entitled respectively "Of the ancient and present state of the church of England" and "Of the number of bishoprikes and their severall circuits." Subdivision was required by Harrison's considerable expansion of his accounts of ecclesiastical history and contemporary practices, and the inclusion of some fairly heavy-handed criticism, not to say satire, against the higher clergy. The question at issue must be, therefore, the direction of his polemic. Was it only and safely against the medieval church and the papacy? Or do his revisions imply a more contemporary target? More specifically, how would his 1587 text have been read in the context of a church that had been, since Whitgift's ascension to the archbishopric in 1583, experiencing a campaign to enforce uniformity at almost any cost?

Unlike Edelen, who saw Harrison as enthusiastically supporting the Elizabethan church settlement, and inveighing only against the papacy, Parry perceived that Harrison was far from sanguine about the present state of the church, that he regarded it as at best half-reformed, and that his comments on the system waver between moral indignation and a self-protective prudence. These views, for which Parry uses the strong terms "radical" and "revolutionary," he aligned with the various agendas of those who petitioned the Convocation of 1563,[16] including Alexander Nowell, Harrison's former headmaster at Westminster School and later his fellow scholar; with Archbishop Edmund Grindal and the "Grindalian" vision of the church; with the Puritan George Withers, who was a close friend; with Thomas Cartwright, author of the *Second Admonition to Parliament* in 1572; and behind them with the "commonwealth" preachers of Edward's reign, including John Ponet.

Certainly the new version is astonishingly critical of the princes of the church. Whereas the 1577 version began simply "There are two provinces in England, of which the first and greatest is subject to the see of Caunterbury, the seconde to that of Yorke," in 1587 Harrison added the statement that the see of Canterbury now comprehends "a parte of Lhoegres, whole Cambria, & also Ireland, which in time past were severall, & brought into one by the archbishop of the said see & assistance of the pope; *who in respect of meed, did yeeld unto the ambitious desires of sundrie archbishopes of Canturburie,* as I have elsewhere declared" (1:221; italics added). In 1577 he had already complained that the archbishops of Canterbury and York had often "in tyme past" presumed to equal the king in authority, as witness their own "actes, epistles, and aunsweres." In 1587 he took the trouble to update this phrase in a way that cast doubt on its reference only to the past ("that this is true, it may easilie appeere by their owne acts, yet kept in record; beside their epistles & answers written *or in print,*" 1:222; italics added), and added a direct challenge:

> Our adversaries will peradventure denie this absolutelie, as they doo manie other things apparant, though not without shamelesse impudencie, or at the leastwise defend it as just and not swarving from common equitie; bicause they imagine everie archbishop to be the kings equall in his owne province. (1:222)

The phrase "our adversaries" has a topical ring which is not, perhaps, sufficiently removed by Harrison's claim that the examples he will adduce (massively expanded in 1587) are all from "the time of poperie."[17]

As for the state of the church produced by this ecclesiastical hierarchy, the 1587 text is outspokenly shocked by it. For example, after a passage praising the bishops for their diligence in preaching, Harrison added an *occupatio* attacking the whole structure of clerical ambition and promotion, including a gibe at the royal abuse of "legal" precedent for personal gain:

> Of their manifold translations from one see to another I will saie nothing, which is not now doone for the benefit of the flocke, as the preferment of the partie favoured, and advantage unto the prince, a matter in time past much doubted of, to wit, whether a bishop or pastor might be translated from one see to another; and left undecided, till prescription by roiall authoritie made it good. For among princes a thing once doone, is well doone, and to be doone oftentimes, though no warrant be to be found therefore. (1:227–28)

But the most unmistakably daring move was still to come. In the first edition Harrison had given a very positive and detailed description of the so-called prophesyings, which had subsequently been suppressed by order of the queen. In his catalog of the archbishops of Canterbury, and by way of his biography of Edmund Grindal, Francis Thynne cautiously alluded to this episode. Harrison's response to the queen's intervention was not nearly so cautious; but hidden away in his revisions it apparently went unnoticed. He inserted a few new minor caveats intended to reassure his readers of the general decency of the meetings, the proper qualifications of those who led them, and the silence of the laietie *unless* some irrepressible maverick be present ("except some vaine and busie head will now and then intrude themselves with offense"); but he also engaged in open defence of the prophesyings against their enemies in high places, adding remarks which could not possibly have been construed as anything other than a criticism of the queen's actions against Grindal:

> But alas! as sathan the author of all mischeefe hath in sundrie manners heretofore hindered the erection and maintenance of manie good things: so in this he hath stirred up adversaries of late unto this most profitable exercise, who not regarding the commoditie that riseth thereby so well to the hearers as spekers; but either stumbling (I cannot tell how) at words and termes, or at the least wise not liking to here of the reprehension of vice, or peradventure taking a misliking at the slender demeanours of such negligent ministers, as now and then in their courses doo occupie the roomes, have either by their owne practise, their sinister information, or suggestions made upon surmises unto other procured the suppression of these conferences, condemn-

ing them as hurtfull, pernicious, and dailie breeders of no small hurt & inconvenience. But hereof let God be judge, unto whome the cause belongeth. (1:228–29)[18]

The reappearance of that word "adversaries" (with its intimations of the Psalms) suggests an embattled group of reformers whose enemies are determined to think the worst of their educational outreach, and who are using rumor and exaggeration as a justification for its suppression.[19] It is surely to the point that in the 1584 parliament, which met in November about a year after Whitgift was appointed to the archbishopric, a broad coalition of reformers, including at least two Privy Councillors, Sir Walter Mildmay and Sir Henry Knollys, attempted unsuccessfully to roll back the program of enforced conformity and ceremonical uniformity that Whitgift had already unveiled. And, along with specific proposals for improving the methods by which clergymen were appointed to livings, the reform group proposed that the prophesyings should be restored.[20]

Another major topic of this chapter is the more self-serving one of the financial state of the lower clergy—a topic on which Harrison expanded greatly for the 1587 edition, again by speaking in the personal rather than the impersonal voice, so that "they" becomes "we" in the new complaints. For example, in turning to the topic of how the clergy are taxed both by the church and the state, Harrison protests:

> We are also charged with armor & munitions from thirtie pounds upwards, a thing more needfull than diverse other charges imposed upon us are convenient by which & other burdens our case groweth to be more heavie by a great deale (notwithstanding our immunitie from temporall services) than that of the laitie, and for ought that I see not likelie to be diminished, as if the church were now become the asse whereon everie market man is to ride and cast his wallet. (1:231)

From the maintenance of the lesser clergy, Harrison proceeded to the subject of the liturgy and church services, about which, in 1577, he had written a little Protestant manifesto, commending the fact that "there is nothing read in our churches but the canonicall scriptures,"[21] that there was a strong emphasis on preaching," that services were all conducted in the vulgar tongue, "that each one present may heare and understand the same," without singing except of the Psalms, and those so plainly sung that "each one present may understand what they sing." He also remarked approvingly that "all images, shrines, tabernacles, roodlofts, and monuments of idolatrie are remooved, taken downe, and defaced," with stained glass windows gradually being replaced as economics permitted. In 1587 he further congratulated the English church for reducing the ninety-five church festivals of the Old Religion to twenty-seven, "and with them the superfluous numbers of idle waks, guilds, fraternities, church-ales, helpe-ales, and soule-ales, also called dirge-ales, with the heathnish rioting at bride-ales, are well diminished and laid aside," a catalog that would have still more clearly identified him as a reformer; and he stated his conviction that all church festivals should be reduced to Christmas, Easter, and Whitsun, and that those of the Virgin Mary should be "utterlie remooved from the calendars, as neither necessarie nor commendable *in a reformed church*" (1:233).

This brings us back to the question of Harrison's preferment to the prebendary of Windsor in April 1586. Did this promotion tie his tongue and bring him over to the policy of Whitgift, or did he maintain his reformist zeal to the end? In my view, the material that Harrison added to the *Description* on the subject of religious practice not only confirms Parry's view[22] that Harrison *remained* a committed reformer, but also suggests that he became a more daring one. In the decade between the first and second editions of the *Chronicles* (and this will be confirmed by his contributions, to be discussed in subsequent chapters, on the subjects of Parliament and economics) Harrison developed a darker view of the state of England in its entirety, of which his distrust of the Whitgiftian church was only the most deeply felt instance. In fact, Harrison appears to have exhibited that rare quality, the capacity to be *more* critical of an institution after receiving its rewards than from a posture of disappointment. In 1587 the crucial chapter "Of the ancient and present estate of the church of England" ends with material directly pertinent to Harrison's own situation in 1586. Nostalgic for the now-abandoned system of training the clergy in the old cathedral churches, Harrison concluded with some sour remarks on the status and qualifications of prebends. "But what is that in all the world," he laments, "which avarice and neligence will not corrupt and impaire?" The general contempt of the ministry results in less hope of their "competent mainte-nance by preaching the word," and consequently, in a vicious circle, fewer intelligent and well-trained ministers. With a fair system of financial sup-port would come proper rotation. Then "prebends should be prebends indeed, there to live till they were preferred to some ecclesiastical function, and then other men chosen to succeed them in their roomes, whereas now prebends are but superfluous additaments unto former excesses, & perpetu-all commodities unto the owners" (1:235).[23]

It is not entirely surprising, then, to discover nesting in the center of this chapter a remark that both draws attention to Harrison's outspoken-ness, and indicates that he still, as Windsor prebend, felt himself to be op-erating under constraints:

More I could saie, and more I would saie of these and other things, were it not that in mine owne judgement I have said inough alreadie for the advertisement of such as be wise. (1:234)

The differences between the two versions, a decade apart, of Harrison's *Description of England* do more than support the commonsense idea that authors can change their minds. They also speak to a central question of cultural history: to what extent were early modern persons aware of and capable of articulating *changes* in their environment? There is currently a trend among historians of this period toward drawing a much darker picture of the last three decades of Elizabeth's reign than has been conventional: a picture marked by economic problems and social malaise; by fears of what would happen when the queen died without a direct successor; by renewed confrontation on religion sparked by, on the one hand, fear of Roman Catholic conspiracy following the pope's 1570 excommunication of Elizabeth, and on the other by the ascension and rigor of Whitgift and his hard-line bishops such as Richard Bancroft. Inevitably the religious confrontation brought with it turmoil in Elizabeth's parliaments, as the more radical Puritan members struggled to get their reform agenda onto the floor. Although this book, which has no reason to look beyond 1587, will not encounter the really dark days of the late 1590s, whose climactic event was the Essex rebellion, it computes with John Guy's theory of the "two reigns of Elizabeth," the first, from the accession to the early 1570s an extended period of conciliation and restored fiscal stability, and the second, beginning around 1585, conceivable even at the time as a period of national decline.[24] Christopher Haigh has argued that in the last decade of the reign there was a marked disparity between such perceptions of malaise and the tone, sanguine or uplifting, of Elizabethan propaganda and image-making.[25]

These more sceptical interpretations of the second half of the reign may well bear a more than coincidental relation to the plan formulated in the early 1580s for a new edition of the *Chronicles*, which appears to have been modified, perhaps from 1584 onwards, in the direction of more and more revision to its earlier sections. The "Continuation" itself is structured in a way that becomes intelligible in the light of Guy's and Haigh's theories; that is to say, it is structured as a tragedy of church and state, beneath a canopy of idealizing speeches and iconography. There is a disproportionate emphasis on ceremonial occasions: thirty-one pages detailing the queen's visit to Norfolk in 1578 (which is actually inserted "somewhat out of place" for the year 1579 [4:375]): eleven pages devoted to the pageant of the Four Foster Children of Desire in 1581, in which Arundel, Windsor,

Sir Philip Sidney, and Fulke Greville participated; twenty-six pages to the departure of the French duc d'Alençon, the queen's last suitor, from England to Antwerp and the festivities laid on for him there; and thirteen pages to the reception in the Netherlands of Leicester in December 1585 (an account subsequently truncated in the 1587 censorship).

But there is an equally disproportionate emphasis on state violence: among the highlights are seemingly overextended treatments of the trials and executions of Edmund Campion, William Parry, and Francis Throckmorton, the whole volume tending to a dying fall in the long and bloodthirsty account of the Babington Plot and its fatal consequences for the conspirators, as well as for Mary, Queen of Scots. The "Continuation" opens with a story supplied by John Stow: "The tenth day of November, in the citie of Worcester, a cruell and unnaturall brother (as an other Cain) murdered his owne naturall and loving brother" (4:343); and it ends with Abraham Fleming's prayer for the interception of traitors, "to whom the Lord in vengeance give the judgement of Judas, as they have been partakers of his sinne; let them be intangled and taken in the traps of their trecheries ... that they be no more a familie" (4:953). Any thoughtful reader must have been able to perceive the ironic contrast between festive material and brutal punishments, not to mention the total *omission* of matters of national concern, such as the national opposition to Elizabeth's proposed marriage to Alençon, or the anti-Whitgift campaign in the parliaments of 1584 and 1586. To the extent that earlier historians and literary critics have been misled by Elizabethan propaganda into believing, like Georges Edelen, that the late decades of the sixteenth century were a golden age, reading the *Chronicles* as a strenuous act of revision may itself contribute to a revisionary view of the 1570s and 1580s.

Part Two

FIVE ‏ﷺ‎ *Economics*

This onelie I know, that everie function and generall vocation striveth
with other, which of them should have all the water of commoditie run
into hir owne cesterne.

William Harrison, *Description of England* (1:275)

To be short, the poore citizens of London were this yeare plagued with
a threefold plague, pestilence, scarcitie of monie, and dearth of vittels,
the miserie whereof were too long to write: no doubt the poore remember it, the rich by flight into the countries made shift for themselves.

Raphael Holinshed, for the year 1564

In 1978 Joyce Appleby entered a subtle critique of the thinking represented by Peter Laslett's formula, "the world we have lost" (a mythic,
preindustrial era where economic disruption would have been accepted
"as man's lot under God's dispensation"). As Appleby observed, evidence
for such a world is hard to find: "Each cut of the historian's axe backward in
to the layers of the past," she wrote, "proves that the roots of modern society are very deep, and the ordered world against which to project the dis-
ruptive forces of modernity retreats";[1] yet she began her evolutionary account of economic self-consciousness with the seventeenth century,
implying that prior to the 1620s no one was able to analyze economic factors in isolation from political policy or moral persuasions.

I propose in this chapter to appropriate Appleby's corrective to my
reading of Holinshed's *Chronicles,* but to push the boundary between the archaic and the early modern still farther backward, at least to the late 1570s;
nor will I share her assumption that economic thought comes to maturity
only by abstracting the economy from its social context. But as a cultural
historian my purpose is elegantly served by Appleby's definition of *her* task
as a historian of economic consciousness:

Novelty acts like a wedge between the social and private world, for it is
thrust in between what has been learned and what must be coped with spon-

taneously by the single person. . . . It forces the imagination to rearrange remembered experience. . . . For historians, the question is to discover what
form reflections took.[2]

The wedge that novelty thrusts between traditional expectations and present conditions, the gap between memory and imagination in diurnal coping mechanisms, are particularly appropriate metaphors with which to
reapproach the greatest of the Tudor chronicles, which institutionalize
memory and make it a tool of civil society. Wedge and gap, though of
course themselves no more than mental constructs, seem to belong with
Appleby's other metaphor for the modern historian's task, the axe that implies clearing a path through the forest of the past, but without (in today's
ecology of the mind) clear-cutting.

In clearing my own path through the forest of the *Chronicles*, I have
tried to discover what form the reflections of the chroniclers took on the
world they inhabited, as well as the world farther back in time they determined should not be lost to reflection. I assume that perceptions of economic conditions are at least as pertinent to historical inquiry as are the statistics derived by modern historians from consulting, say, the account
books of the London guilds; which is not to abandon the claim that in certain cases the information recorded in the *Chronicles* may corroborate or re-
fute (or be corroborated or refuted by) that derived from very different
archives.

Any student of the economy in sixteenth-century England will, at the
beginning of her inquiry, encounter certain classic propositions. Economic
historians are virtually unanimous that the last half of the sixteenth century was a period of dramatic inflation ("the price revolution"). They are far
from unanimous as to its causes. The competing explanations may invoke
major, long-term socioeconomic changes that can now be perceived as the
heralds of modernity: population growth, the commercialization of agriculture, a huge increase in the demand for consumer goods, especially in
the clothing and metal-working trades, international traffic in those goods,
and expansion of markets. Other explanations are local, political and specific to England: events that either drained the country's fiscal resources—
Henry VIII's wars and the taxes raised to support them—or, conversely,
put new wealth into circulation—the dissolution of the monasteries and
the redistribution of their endowments. One seemingly irreducible category of explanation relates short-term price fluctuations in the food supply to
the quality of harvests; but there is a disturbing circularity in an argument
that deduces the quality of harvests not from direct evidence of yields but
by inference from an analysis of grain prices.[3] One central monetary expla-

nation, capable of expression as a mathematic equation, is the "quantity theory of money," or the doctrine that inflation is primarily caused by the amount of coin in circulation; in modern terms, too much money chasing too few goods. For some years the favorite version of the quantity theory, and one that rendered English problems only a version of a pan-European inflation, was that the money market was flooded by imported Spanish silver. In addition, the local monetary policies of the Tudors—Henry VIII's debasement of the currency and Elizabeth's attempts to restore it—became and remain a focus of attention; but it has proved difficult to support the theory by hard evidence of how much coin was actually in circulation.[4]

The two greatest periods of inflation were ten years at the end of Henry VIII's reign and the beginning of Edward's (1542–51) and a briefer period toward the end of Elizabeth's reign (1593–97), when prices skyrocketed by nearly 50 percent.[5] While the first crisis was almost certainly triggered by Henry VIII's debasement of the currency, and was thus compatible with monetary theory, the second was almost certainly generated by a series of disastrous harvests, an old-fashioned explanation which unites the two meanings of the Tudor word "dearth," high prices, and harvest failure. Yet these were only the peaks in a slower process that requires a more complex accounting.

It should be noted here, however, that historians disagree about the impact of inflation on actual standards of living. Steve Rappaport's study of London provided a relatively conservative analysis, perhaps intended to discount the darker picture drawn by some earlier economic historians.[6] By using retail rather than wholesale prices, Rappaport claimed that the real wages of skilled and semiskilled workers declined by only 29 percent throughout the century, as compared to a previous estimate of 57 percent; and he argued that, except for the two sharp periods of inflation noted above, the decline was so gradual that most people could accommodate themselves to it.[7] Even in the period of rapid inflation at mid-century, Rappaport argued, there is a striking *"absence* of complaints about rising prices and impoverishment."[8] His general conclusions (which are limited by their almost exclusively urban focus) therefore stand at the other end of the scale (whose points are optimism and pessimism) from that of Lawrence Stone, who declared that the fall of real wages, and hence of living standards for the laboring classes, during the century "was undoubtedly of a magnitude for which there is no parallel in English history since the thirteenth century." On the other hand, Stone remarked throughout the whole of the sixteenth century and much of the seventeenth, "a striking rise in the material comforts of all classes from yeomen upwards, groups who benefitted from rising agricultural prices, increased commercial activity, and increased demand for professional services," a spread in the wealth/poverty differential that Stone found reprehensible.[9] Between these two positions stands Paul Slack's cautious conclusion: "According to the available indices, the real value of wages fell by about a quarter in the course of Elizabeth's reign. However, there are serious problems in measuring how far (and how many) people were dependent on money wages, and hence in determining what the drop meant in actuality."[10]

I referred above to the view that early modern citizens were incapable of economic *thought*, as distinct from uninformed grumbling. In 1971 Peter Ramsey introduced a collection of essays on the "price revolution" in the sixteenth century with the statement that "those who lived through it lacked the statistical techniques and grasp of economic theory that would have enabled them to interpret their painful experience, and to establish chains of cause and effect."[11] He cited the Elizabethan pamphlet, *Discourse of the Common Weal*, as symptomatic of Tudor attempts to grapple with the causes of inflation empirically, without an analytical model or an economic vocabulary.[12] Eighteenth- and early-nineteenth-century political economists regarded as one of their greatest achievements the explosion of the theory that higher rents (for agricultural land) lead to increased food prices. Because all farmers within the same agricultural system receive more or less the same return for their investment and labor (and would presumably cease to farm if it ceased to be profitable), later political economists would look with condescension on such thinking as appeared in William Forrest's *Pleasant Poesye of Princelie Practise* (1548) that raising rents from twenty to fifty pounds, combined with unreasonable fines, will produce "great Dearthe" (high prices).[13] But Forrest's nostalgic yearning for the concept of fair rents and fair prices, to be reestablished by "owre hedde pearis," is embedded within a larger calculus: "But heere liethe a mateire muche Difficulte, . . . / Pryvate Commoditye withe Commone wealthe to scorse [balance]." This is a bargain we in the supposedly advanced societies have yet to drive successfully. It would be possible to argue that early modern thinkers were indeed capable of positing economic cause and effect (although the explanations they proposed for inflation have subsequently been debunked), and of intuiting a complex set of relations between inflation, standards of living, shifts in the wealth/poverty differential, currency regulation, wage control, and less tangible factors such as economic trust. Despite the inadequacies of a largely moral vocabulary for discussing the distribution of wealth, they grappled with the difference between healthy competition and destructive exploitation.

There was also available the concept of a *political* economy in the prudential sense, of the direct relationship between the perception of economic injustice and political instability. The anonymous author of the Edwardian "Policies to reduce this realme of England unto a prosperus wealthe and estate," a set of manuscript proposals dated 1549 and dedicated to Somerset, took the position that the Edwardian reforms of the church should facilitate secular reforms of the commonwealth. He was probably a member of the group of "commonwealthmen" whose advice was, ironically, discredited by the uprisings of 1549.[14] The author of these proposals drew some of his conclusions from his reading of English chronicles, as he argues for economic reform on the grounds that it will prevent popular unrest:

> For as much as it is right evident *by cronicles* that the skantenes and derthe of victuall and other necessaries . . . hathe ofte tymes cawsede as well in this realme as also in meney other places greate discorde ande tumultes to ryse betwein the comonaltye and the majestrates.[15]

In fact he had been reading the 1548 edition of Edward Hall's chronicle,[16] where several pages had been devoted to a chain of causes: Wolsey's excessive and unparliamentary "subsidy" leading to widespread layoffs and ultimately to industrial revolt in the clothing industry.[17]

Inflation and the Standard of Living

Any inquiry into economic thought in the *Chronicles* should begin where the Elizabethan reader began, with William Harrison's *Description of England.* Oddly, with the exception of Book II, chapter 15, "Of the coines of England," a rather muddled history of coinage, and chapter 10, "Of provision made for the poore," largely a tirade against the "thriftless" poor or vagabonds, there are no signposts directing the reader to consider economic issues. The *Description,* however, does in fact contain a great deal of information on inflation, international trade, the new consumerism, wages and working conditions, and especially on the standard of living. In "Of degrees of people in the commonwealth of England," Harrison digressed into an attack on merchants, "whose number is so increased in these our daies, that their onelie maintenance is the cause of the exceeding prices of forreine wares." He hearkened back to an earlier period of free trade, when "everie nation was permitted to bring in hir owne commodities," and when imports were "farre better cheape and more plentifullie to be had. . . . Whereas in times past when the strange bottoms [vessels] were suffered to come in, we had sugar for foure pence the pound, that now at the writing of this treatise is well worth halfe a crowne, raisons or corints for a penie that now are holden at six pence," etc. "Whereby we may see," he added, that the consequence of changes in the regulations is "verie seldome . . . such as is pretended in the beginning" (1:274–75). The "suspicious voiages" of the English merchants that were supposed to increase the quantity of rare foodstuffs have only increased their price exorbitantly.

More important, the *Description* demonstrates how, and in what terms, Harrison himself and his neighbors experienced economic change. This information is inserted into the chapters on cities and towns, on social status and degree, "Of the Maner of Building and Furniture of our houses," and on markets (in both the literal and the economic-theoretical sense). Not only is it inserted (or perhaps insinuated) where we would not expect to find it; but in the differences between the 1577 and the 1587 editions of the *Chronicles*, in Harrison's careful revisions and expansions of this economic commentary, we can see what another decade has done to sharpen, and darken, his own perceptions and those of his contemporaries.

In his invaluable introduction to early modern society, Keith Wrightson took this same decade—more precisely, the year 1580—as his starting point. Wrightson found William Harrison useful as a witness to the contemporary perception of social change, "however blurred might be [the] perception" of its nature and causes," and noted that he had discussed inflation "with the greybeards of his home parish in Radwinter," who regarded three things as "marvellouslie altred" within their lifetimes: the number of chimneys, the improvement in bedding, and the "exchange of vessell" (that is, tableware) from wood to pewter and even silver. But, continued Wrightson, these advances had their costs:

> His informants also picked out three "very grievous" developments: "the in-hansing of rents"; the "dailie oppression of copyholders" forced by their landlords to pay increased entry fines or to forfeit their holdings; the spread of usury and charging of interest upon loans.[18]

Yet although he used Furnivall's edition of the *Description*, which had roughly indicated Harrison's revisions, Wrightson did not observe that what he was citing was the text of 1587; and that precisely in the differences between it and the text of 1577 lay still other observations, perhaps rather less "blurred," of economic change. Most important, Wrightson overlooked the fact that the three changes for the worse offsetting the three signs of rising standards of living were *not* included in the 1577 version, but were added by Harrison in the less optimistic, more critical perspective that generally marks his revisions.

Because this passage of recorded "oral" history is of considerable import to cultural history, bearing as it does on the ways in which people untrained in economic analysis can nevertheless create working models of change, we cannot rely on Wrightson's summary. On the contrary, the care with which Harrison first constructed this passage and then reconstructed it, both in the small details and in the large picture, must be demonstrated, as before, by full quotation of the final version, and partial comparison with the earlier one. In what follows, the italicized phrases were added for the 1587 edition; and the words in square brackets were then replaced by what precedes them:

The furniture of our houses also exceedeth, and is growne in maner even to passing delicacie: and herein I doo not speake of the nobilitie and gentrie onelie, but likewise of the lowest sort in most places of our south countrie, that have anie thing at all to take to. Certes in noble mens houses it is not rare to see abundance of Arras, rich hangings of tapistrie, silver vessell, and so much other plate, as may furnish sundrie cupbords, to the summe often-times of a thousand or two thousand pounds at the least: whereby the value of this and the rest of their stuffe dooth grow to be almost inestimable. Likewise in the houses of knights, gentlemen, merchantmen, and some other wealthie citizens, it is not geson to behold generallie their great provision of tapistrie, Turkie worke, pewter, brasse, fine linen, and thereto costlie cupbords of plate, worth five or six hundred or a thousand pounds, to be deemed by estimation. But as herein all these sorts doo far exceed their elders and predecessors, *and in neatnesse and curiositie, the merchant all other;* so in time past, the costlie furniture staied there, whereas now it is descended yet lower, even unto the inferiour artificers and manie [1577: most] farmers, who *by vertue of their old and not of their new leases* have *for the most part* learned also to garnish their cupbords with plate, their *joined* beds with tapistrie and silke hangings, and their tables with *carpets &* fine naperie, whereby the wealth of our countrie *(God be praised therefore, and give us grace to imploie it well)* dooth infinitelie appeare. Neither doo I speake this in reproch of anie man, God is my judge, but to shew that I do rejoise rather, to see how God hath blessed us with his good gifts; and *whilest I* behold how that in a time wherein all things are growen to most excessive prices, & *what commoditie so ever is to be had, is dailie plucked from the communaltie by such as looke into everie trade,* we doo yet find the means to obtein & atchive such furniture as heretofore hath beene unpossible. There are old men yet dwelling in the village where I remaine, which have noted three things to be marvellouslie altered in England within their sound remembrance; *& other three things too too much increased.* One is, the multitude of chimnies latelie erected, wheras in their yoong daies there were not above two or three, if so manie in most uplandish townes of the realme (the religious houses, & manour places of their lords alwaies excepted, and peradventure some great personages) but ech one made his fire against a reredosse in the hall, where he dined and dressed his meat.

The second is the great *(although not generall)* amendment of lodging, for (said they) our fathers (yea and we our selves also) have lien full oft upon straw pallets, *on rough mats* covered onelie with a sheet under coverlets made of dagswain or hopharlots (I use their owne termes) and a good round log under their heads in steed of a bolster *or pillow.* If it were so that our fathers or the good man of the house, had within seven years after his mariage purchased a matteres or flockebed, and thereunto a sacke of chaffe to rest his head upon, he thought himself to be as well lodged as the lord of the towne, that peradventure laie seldome in a bed of downe or whole fethers; so well were they contented, and with such base kind of furniture: which also is not verie much amended as yet in some parts of Bedfordshire, and elsewhere further off from our southerne parts. Pillowes (said they) were thought meet onelie for women in childbed. As for servants, if they had anie sheet above them it was well, for seldome had they anie under their bodies, to keepe them from the pricking straws that ran oft through the canvas of the pallet, and rased their hardened hides.

The third thing they tell of, is the exchange [of vessell, as of] treene platters into pewter, and wooden spoones into silver or tin. For soe common were all sorts of treene stuff in old time, that a man should hardlie find foure peeces of pewter (of which one was peradventure a salt) in a good farmers house, and yet for all this frugalitie (if it may so be justly called) they were scarce able to live and paie their rents at their daies without selling of a cow, or an horse, or more, although they paid but foure pounds at the uttermost by the yeare. Such also was their povertie, that if some one od farmer or husbandman had beene at the alehouse, a thing greatlie used in those daies, amongst six or seven of his neighbours, and there in a braverie to shew what store he had, did cast downe his pursse, and therein a noble or six shillings in silver unto them (for few such men then cared for gold bicause it was not so readie paiment, and they were oft inforced to give a penie for the exchange of an angell) it was verie likelie that all the rest could not laie downe so much against it: whereas in my time, although peradventure foure pounds of old rent be improved to fortie, fiftie, *or an hundred* pounds, yet will the farmer *as another palme or date tree* thinke his gaines verie small toward the end [1577: middest] of his terme, if he have not six or seven yeares rent lieng by him, therewith to purchase a new lease, beside a faire garnish of pewter on his cupbord, *with so much more in od vessell going about the house,* three or foure featherbeds, so manie coverlids and carpets of tapistrie, a silver salt, a bowle for wine (if not an whole neast) and a dozzen of spoones to furnish up the sute. This also he taketh to be his owne cleere, for what stocke of monie soever he gathereth & laieth up in all his yeares, it is often seene, that the landlord will take such order with him for the same, when he renueth his lease, which is commonlie eight or six [ten] yeares before the old be expired (sith it is now growen almost to a custome, that if he come not to his lord so long before, another shall step in for a reversion, and so defeat him out right) that it shall never trouble him more than the haire of his beard, when the barber hath washed and shaven it from his chin. (1:317–18)

Up to this point in his discussion, and in his 1577 text, Harrison had offered the following information. First, and most obvious, that despite its being "a time wherein all things are growen to most excessive prices," the standard of living in England has improved dramatically since the first decades of the century. The measure of that standard is twofold: material comforts (the raising of chimneys, to provide smoke-free dwellings, and the softening of bedding), and the widespread display of the *signs* of wealth, in "tapistrie, Turkey worke, pewter, brasse, fine linen," and especially the "costly cupbords of plate" that may have had marginally more use value over wooden platters, but were also capable at need of instant conversion back into money.[19] Second, he declares that this development is good, separating himself from those mid-century writers who deplored rampant consumerism as a cause of inflation: he writes not "in reproch of anie man . . . but to . . . rejoise rather, to see how God hath blessed us." Third, he reassures his reader that the standard of living has not only risen in the upper strata of his society, but has extended down the social scale to "inferiour artificers and most farmers"; and fourth, he provides a *mechanism* for documenting this trickle-down effect: appealing to living memory, the "sound remembrance" of the old men of his Radwinter parish. A Marxist critic might see this material, especially the farmer's capacity to acquire portable property as a form of savings ("his owne cleere"), as empirical evidence for the principle of primitive accumulation, yet extended lower down the class structure than the theory itself might be able to accommodate,[20] although Harrison also makes the point that this form of saving is required for survival. For when the time comes for the tenant farmer to renew his lease, or rather well before it, his landlord will deprive him of any *money* he has accumulated as deftly as the barber can shave him. The suggestion that the two processes are equally painless is certainly Harrison's irony.

These perceptions, from a man who already in 1577 was highly sympathetic to the laboring classes, can certainly be used to set in perspective, and mediate between, the optimistic and pessimistic reconstructions by modern historians. It seems clear that Harrison's account of 1577 was consistent with Rappaport's calculation of an upturn in real wages in the 1570s.[21] And there are two reasons to regard Harrison, though a lone observer, as a credible witness to national economic trends. The first resides in the verisimilitude, the representational facsimile of "truth," that emanates from detail. The discrimination between types of bedding, the use of dialect words ("dagswain or hopharlots") to which Harrison himself draws our attention ("I use their owne termes"), these have the texture, and sometimes the rhythms, of genuine oral history, of an anthropological fidelity of observation. It is nice to know that pillows were reserved for women in childbed.

The other reason to credit Harrison's accuracy as a witness, however, resides in his revisions. Between 1577 and 1587 he went over his account of contemporary standards of living with a fine-tooth comb, in certain places merely increasing its specificity, in others clearly qualifying his previous optimism. While he did not withdraw his disclaimer that the passage was not intended as a moralistic reproach of wealth, he made a number of changes that in fact carry such reproach, at least to the point of showing where the trickle-down process stopped. "Most" farmers becomes "manie." The "amendment of lodging" is still great, but now "not generall."

As for agricultural rents, Harrison shows that he understands the force of competition in driving them upwards ("another shall step in for a reversion"), but he also shows his sensitivity to an increase in competitive pressure. Although landlords now look for a new lease six or eight years, not ten, before the old is expired, the accumulation of the farmer's capital has been possible on the basis of their old, not their new leases. The rents have increased from four pounds not only to forty or fifty, but even to a hundred pounds.

Still more significantly, when he reworked this passage for the 1587 edition Harrison added the "other three things too too much increased." For this, if we are to believe him, he went back to his Radwinter elders and consulted them again. The result is the following list of grievances:

> And as they commend these, so (beside the decaie of housekeeping whereby the poore have been relieved) they speake also of three things that are growen to be verie grievous unto them, to wit, the inhansing of rents, latelie mentioned; the dailie oppression of copiholders, whose lords seeke to bring their poore tenants almost into plaine servitude and miserie, dailie devising new meanes, and seeking up all the old [meanes] how to cut them shorter and shorter, doubling, trebling, and now & then seven times increasing their fines, driving them also for everie trifle to loose and forfeit their tenures (by whom the greatest part of the realme dooth stand and is mainteined) to the end they may fleece them yet more, which is a lamentable hering. The third thing they talke of is usurie, a trade brought in by the Jewes, now perfectlie practised almost by everie christian, and so commonlie that he is accompted but for a foole that dooth lend his monie for nothing.

At this point Harrison launched into a tirade against excessive interest rates. While it is important to realize that Harrison's discussion of usury took place in the aftermath of the Elizabethan Act against Usury of 1571, which reconfirmed the ancient taboo against loans with a contract for interest that had been undermined by Henry VIII's statute of 1545,[22] the topic is digressive, both for him and for us; and his real concern in this passage is with the sharp practices that distort the supposedly inevitable effects of competition:

> Forget not also such landlords as use to value their leases at a secret estimation given of the wealth and credit of the taker, whereby they seeme (as it were) to eat them up and deale with bondmen, so that if the leassee be thought to be worth an hundred pounds, he shall paie no lesse for his new terme, or else another to enter with hard and doubtfull covenants. I am sorie to report it, much more greeved to understand the practise; but most sorowfull of all to understand that men of great port and countenance are so farre from suffering their farmers to have anie gaine at all, that they themselves become grasiers, butchers, tanners, sheepmasters, woodmen, and "denique quid non," thereby to inrich themselves, and bring all the wealth of the countrie into their owne hands, leaving the communaltie weake, or as an idoll with broken or feeble armes, which may in a time of peace have a plausible shew, but when necessitie shall inforce, have an heavy and bitter sequele. (1:318)

It seems clear that, from the perspective of the later 1580s, Harrison perceived that the distance had widened between the rich and the poor, thereby aligning himself closer to the pessimists than the optimists among modern socioeconomic historians. Despite its intuitive basis, his story of the social consequences of high "fines" (the lump sum payable at the beginning of a lease, supposedly to permit a lower rent thereafter), rack-renting, and engrossing matches the conclusions of the economic historian C. G. A. Clay. Harrison, of course, lacks the recognition of historical hindsight, that agricultural change led to more efficient farming; but Clay's judicious summary discounted the sharp practices described above as exceptional. Thus Clay's statement that agricultural rents for tenant farmers "could only be increased on the expiry of their leases," which gave them, as well as stability, "all the advantage of the long term rise in product prices,"[23] is somewhat undercut by Harrison's account of the pressure applied by landlords to renegotiate a lease considerably before expiration; while the concept of "reasonable" rent increases that continued in some part of the country to govern copyholders of inheritance could equally be undermined by the practice of raising the rent exactly to the level where the tenant could still pay it, but have nothing left over.[24] Indeed, by the

time that Harrison had completed his revisions he had come to sound remarkably like an Edwardian reformer; or perhaps like Lawrence Stone.[25]

In two other chapters, though again apparently en passant, Harrison
expanded his analysis of how the wealth of rural England seemed more unjustly redistributed than before. Into "Of Cities and Townes in England" (in
1587 Book II, chapter 13) he had originally inserted a tirade against engrossing, the creation of large estates by agglomeration, and the concen-
tration of land in fewer and fewer hands. This tirade had ended with the
following confident statement: "a great number complayne of thincrease of
povertie, but few men doo see the verye roote from whence it dooth pro-
ceede" (82v). In 1587 this sentence was rendered more complex by
Harrison's disagreement with the theory that population growth is the
cause of the country's economic ills: "Certes a great number compleine of
the increase of povertie, laieng the cause upon God, as though he were in
fault for sending such increase of people, or want of wars that should con-
sume them, affirming that the land was never so full, &c: but few men doo
see the verie root from whence it dooth proceed" (1:324). In addition, he
enhanced his already extensive protest against engrossing by providing information on the involuntary vegetarianism of the rural poor:

> by incroching and joining of house to house, and laieng land to land, . . . the
> inhabitants of manie places of our countrie are devoured and eaten up, *and
> their houses either altogither pulled downe or suffered to decaie by litle and litle, although
> sometimes a poore man peradventure dooth dwell in one of them, who not being able to repare
> it, suffereth it to fall downe, & thereto thinketh himselfe verie friendlie dealt withall, if he may
> have an acre of ground assigned unto him whereon to keepe a cow, or wherein to set cabbages,
> radishes, parsneps, carrets, melons, pompons, or such like stuffe, by which he and his powre
> household liveth as by their principall food, sith they can doo no better.* . . . a poore estate
> God wot! (1:325; italicized section added in 1587)

And he shrewdly quoted from Leland's *Itinerary* ("latelie come to my hands")
to the effect that the result of this depopulation of the countryside was to
concentrate the tax burden also in fewer and fewer households. *"It is not yet
altogither out of knowledge,* that where the king had seven pounds thirteene
shillings at a taske gathered of fiftie wealthie householders of a parish in
England: now a gentlemen having three parts of the towne in his owne
hands, foure housholds doo beare all the aforesaid paiment" (1:325; italics
added). Here living memory serves as a tool, not only for registering economic change, but for making a pragmatic point about the rebarbative effect on the tax structure of a flow of wealth upwards in society.

In "Of Faires and Markets," Harrison offered a graphic account of how
country markets operated (of considerable interest to a cultural historian),

while implicitly developing an argument that markets do not operate by invisible laws, but can be affected by human chicanery and inadequate government supervision. At the heart of his critique are two problems: too many middlemen, and the greed of those who have the resources to corner the market in grain. In addition, he was concerned that existing regulations were often unenforced. In 1577 Harrison had already complained that the magistrates were not so careful to regulate the markets as they should be; by 1587 he had also noted the political implications of a decentralized system. "Neither are the magistrates for the most part *(as men loth to displease their neighbours for their one yeares dignitie)* so carefull in their offices, as of right and dutie they should be" (1:339; italics added).

Harrison's eyewitness testimony is here several times offered as the criterion of veracity ("I will saie yet a little more, and somewhat by mine owne experience," 1:340; "but sith I see it not, I will not so trust mine eares as to write it for a truth," 1:341). A comparison between the 1577 text and that of 1587 implies that he went back to his local markets for a closer inspection of the abuses of the regulations against hoarding. Consider this analysis of how grain prices were manipulated (the italicized sections having been added for the second edition):

At Michaelmasse time poore men must make monie of their graine, that they may paie their rents. So long then as the poore man hath to sell, rich men will bring out none, but rather buie up that which the poore bring, under pretense of seed corne, *or alteration of graine, although they bring none of their owne,* bicause one wheat often sowen without change of seed, will soone decaie and be converted into darnell. For this cause therefore they must needs buie in the markets, though they be twentie miles off and where they be not knowne, promising there if they happen to be espied (which God wot is verie seldome) to send so much to their next market, to be performed I wot not when.

If this shift serve not (neither dooth the fox alwaies use one tracke for feare of a snare) they will compound with some one of the towne where the market is holden, who for a pot of hufcap or merie go downe, will not let to buie it for them, and that in his owne name. Or else they wage one poore man or other, to become a bodger, and thereto get him a licence upon some forged surmise, which being doone, they will feed him with monie, to buie for them till he hath filled their lofts. . . . But who dare find fault with them, when they have once a license? . . . If anie man come to buie a bushell or two for his expenses unto the market crosse, answer is made; Forsooth here was one even now that bad me monie for it, and I hope he will have it. And to saie the truth, these bodgers are faire chapmen, for there are no more words with them, but Let me see it, what shall I give you, knit it up, I will have it, go carie it to such a chamber, *and if you bring in twentie seme [sic] more in the weeke daie to such an Inne or sollar [sic] where I laie my corne, I will have it and give you pence or more in everie bushell for six weekes day of paiment than an other will. Thus the bodgers beare awaie all, so that the poore artificer and labourer cannot make his provision in the markets.* (1:340)

The principle of verbatim reporting that governs the *Chronicles* at large results here in a record of small-scale racketeering patter.

No one who read this chapter in 1587 could have believed that Harrison in the *Description* was engaged only in the art of describing. This is not a neutral description. It hovers somewhere between a memorandum of economic advice to the local magistrates and a caveat emptor to the Elizabethan consumer, with obvious traces of moral indignation. The question of his qualifications to discuss these matters certainly occurs to Harrison, and is settled by a compromise between consumer entitlement and the more abstract demands of theory, between an egalitarian (*because subjective*) interest in fair pricing, and some superiority of perspective: "But what do I talke of these things," he concluded, "or desire the suppression of bodgers being a minister? Certes I may speake of them right well, as feeling the harme in that I am a buier, neverthelesse I speake generallie in ech of them" (1:343). This last statement, seemingly so innocent, is actually a complex move of historiographical and anthropological self-consciousness. Harrison claims that speaking personally to economic change, in the sense of providing eyewitness and earwitness testimony, is not only compatible with speaking "generally" but an essential condition of critique's legitimacy.

It seems reasonable to assume that Elizabethan readers who worked their way through the *Chronicles* from beginning to end might have Harrison's protests ringing in their ears when they came upon information as to what, over the *longue durée* in England, had happened to prices. City chronicles, including Stow's own, typically included such information, but it looks as though considerable effort was made to include it in the *Chronicles*, and that the process of revision increased the emphasis on economics. Thus, for the reign of Henry III, Holinshed extracted from Matthew Paris an account of "an exceeding great dearth" caused in 1258 by bad harvests, during which "a quarter of wheat was sold at London for foure and twentie shillings, whereas within two or three yeares before, a quarter was sold at two shillings" (2:444). The dearth was partly alleviated by the arrival of fifty great ships carrying grain from "Almaine" (Germany), and Henry published a proclamation against engrossing,

and not without cause: for the wealthie citizens were evill spoken of in that
season, bicause in time of scarsitie they would either staie such ships as
fraught with vittels were comming towards the citie, and send them some
other way foorth; or else buy the whole, that they might sell it by retaile at
their plesure to the needie. By means of this great dearth and scarsitie, the
common people were constreined to live upon hearbs & roots, and a great
number of the poore people died through famine. (2:444)

In 1587 Abraham Fleming took this occasion to define famine as "the most
miserable calamitie that can betide mortall men," and added an appropriate
poetic gloss from Ovid's *Metamorphoses*, 8: fable 11 ("Quaesitam famem lapi-
doso vidit in antro").

For 1391 Holinshed reported on both the extent and the easing of a
dearth, in a magnificent sentence packed with social conscience.

The price of corne that had continued at an high rate, almost for the space
of two yeares, began to fall immediatelie after harvest was got in, to the great
reliefe of the poore, which before through immoderate eating of nuts and ap-
ples, fell into the disease called the flix, thereof manie died, and suerlie (as
was thought) the death and dearth had beene greater, if the commendable
diligence of the lord maior of London had not beene, in relieving the commons by such provision as he made for corne to be brought to London, from
the parties of beyond the seas. (2:815)

Not content with his predecessor's coverage of this event, Fleming later incorporated "a large discourse" from Henry Knighton's chronicle, for the
sake, I infer, of its multicausal explanation:

In this yeare [1390] (saith he) was a great dearth in all parts of England, and
this dearth or scarsitie of corne began under the sickle, and lasted till the
feast of saint Peter ad vincula, to wit, till the time of new corne.... But yet
there was such plentie and abundance of manie yeares before, that it was
thought and spoken of manie housekeppers and husbandmen, that if the seed
were . . . sowen in the ground, which was hoorded up and stored in barnes,
lofts, and garners, there would be inough to find and susteine all the people
by the space of five yeares following. But the cause of this penurie, was
thought to be the want of monie in a great manie. For monie in these daies
was verie scant, and the principall cause hereof was, for that the wooll of the
land lay a sleepe and hoong heavie in some mens hands by the space of two
yeares; and in others three years, without a chapman. For it was enacted in a
certeine parlement, that the merchants of England should not passe out of
the land with wooll and other merchandize, but should bring the same unto
twelve places within the realme appointed for the same purpose, that the

merchants strangers might have recourse thither with their commodities and so by exchange should transport our merchandize for theirs. By meanes whereof the merchants of England did forbeare to buy wooll and other wares until the next parlement insuing, wherein it was granted them to traffike whither they would with their commodities. In these daies wooll was dogcheape: for one stone of good wool of the chosen and piked sort, was sold for three shillings, and in Leicester and Kent at some times for two shillings or two and twentie pence. This scarsitie of victuals was of greatest force in Leicester shire, & in the middle parts of the realme. And although it was a great want, yet was not the price of corne out of reason. For a quarter of wheat, when it was at the highest, was sold at Leiceister for 16 shillings 8 pence at one time, and at other times for a marke or fourteene shillings: at London and other places of the land a quarter of wheat was sold for ten shillings, or for litle more or lesse. (2:816)

For the early Tudor period, the *Chronicles* register short-term price fluctuations in detail that might seem obsessive. Their concern seems to be to record anything unusual, to include where possible the response of citizens of different status to these fluctuations, and the theories that were circulated at the time about causes. For example, in March 1543:

Wood was sold verie deare in the winter season of this yeere, and likewise vittels both flesh and fish grew to an high price towards the spring, *by reason (as was thought) of the untemperate wet summer last past, causing great death among cattell.* A quarter of mutton was sold for two shillings, or seven grotes, a lambe at three shillings, or three and foure pence, which afore that time was esteemed scarse woorth sixteene pence. (3:831; italics added)

The first observation, incidentally, seems to contradict Rappaport's statement that the price of wood rose 44 percent less than grain during the Tudor period, and that it "did not increase *at all* in price *until the late 1540s*."[26] The response of the city magistrates to these prices was also noted—a kind of self-denying ordinance whose motives probably combined concern for the municipal budget and a sense of moral leadership in hard times:

Against Easter at a court of aldermen kept in the Guildhall the twentith of March 1542, it was enacted by the lord maior and his brethren, that the maior and shiriffs should be served at their tables but with one course at dinner and supper in their houses; the maior to have but seven dishes at the most at one messe for his owne table, and the shiriffs and everie other alderman but six dishes, upon paine to forfeit for everie dish fortie shillings at everie time when they offended in this ordinance. (3:831)[27]

The harvests of 1555 and 1556 were destroyed by disastrous rains, so that 1556 was the highest point for prices of the early Tudor period. This the *Chronicles* confirm. Abraham Fleming transferred from Stow's *Chronicle* (1580, p. 1105) the following report for 1557, indicating that the dearth has been marvellously relieved:

> This yeare before harvest, wheat was sold for foure marks [53s. 6d.] the quarter, malt at foure and fortie shillings the quarter, beans and rie at fortie shillings the quarter, and pease at six and fortie shillings and eight pence: but after harvest wheat was sold for five shillings the quarter, malt at six shillings eight pence, rie at three shillings foure pence. So that the penie wheat loafe, that weied in London the last yeere but eleven ounces Troie, weied now six and fiftie ounces Troie. In the countrie, wheat was sold for foure shillings the quarter, malt at foure shillings eight pence; and in some places a bushell of rise for a pound of candles which was foure pence. (4:86)

For 1574, however, which should have been a good year in relation to harvest quality, Fleming supplied the following information:

> This yeare about Lammas, wheat was sold at London for three shillings the bushell: but shortlie after it was raised to four shillings, five shillings, six shillings: and before Christmas to a noble [6s.8d], and seven shillings, which so continued long after: beefe was sold for twentie pence, and two and twentie pence the stone, and all other flesh and white meats at an excessive price, all kind of salt fish verie deare, as five herrings two pence, &c: yet great plentie of fresh fish, and oft times the same verie cheape: pease at foure shillings the bushell, otemeale at foure shillings eight pence: baie salt at three shillings the bushell, &c. All this dearth notwithstanding (thanks be given to God) there was no want of anie thing to them that wanted not monie. (4:324)[28]

At seven shillings a bushell, that is, fifty-five shillings a quarter, wheat had surpassed its price (53s. a quarter) following the two rained-out harvests of 1555 and 1556. We may detect some social irony in the last sentence. In the margin the point is made more sharply, that the two meanings of dearth have no structural relation: "Dearth [high prices] without scarsitie, and afterwards plentie to them that had monie." What then was causing the rise in prices? Fleming added a postscript a few paragraphs later: "This yeare at London after harvest, the price of wheate began by little and little to fall, from seven shillings to three shillings the bushell, at which price it staied . . . all the yeare after: but baie salt was raised from three shillings to foure shillings, five shillings, and six shillings the bushell, *the like whereof had never beene seene or heard within this realme"* (4:326; cf. Stow, pp. 1179–80; italics added). This seems to imply some unusual degree of concern and discussion.[29]

Currency Manipulation and Its Consequences

In general, however, the chroniclers handle price fluctuations as a matter of course, with only a slight inflection of ethical or prudential reproach. Rather different is their treatment of what some have called "the great debasement" of the currency, by reducing its bullion content or specie.[30] This should not be confused with "decrying" or "calling down," namely, devaluation by proclamation of the exchange value of specific coins, in belated recognition that their bullion value (and hence purchasing power) had decreased. Debasement in the first, technical, sense was, as previously mentioned, an expedient used by Henry VIII to increase the *volume* of coinage at the Mint, thereby increasing the yield of seignorage or the king's commission on minting. For the year 1544, Abraham Fleming inserted into the accounts of Henry's wars in Scotland and France a statement taken from Stow's *Chronicle* (p. 1029):

> In the moneth of Maie proclamation was made for the inhancing of gold to eight & fortie shillings, & silver foure shillings the ounce. Also the K. caused to be coined base monie, which was since that time called downe, the fift yeare of Edward the sixt, and called in the second of queene Elizabeth. (3:838)

The addition to the second edition of the *Chronicles* is made without other comment; yet the placing of this brief statement, with its own built-in historical perspective revealing that Henry's fiscal policy was rejected by his successors, permits the judgment that economic historians have subsequently made.[31]

The chroniclers also knew, however, that Henry VIII was not the first to practice debasement. Edward III was advised by William de Edington, bishop of Winchester, and lord treasurer, to try the same expedient in the early 1350s, resulting in the coinage of the first silver groats and half groates of four pence and two pence, respectively. "Bicause these new peeces wanted of the weight of the old sterling coine," Holinshed observed: "the prices as well of vittels as of other wares, did dailie rise, and servants and workemen waxing more craftie than before time they had beene, demanded great wages" (2:652). In consequence, by the Statute of Laborers of 1352, wage ceilings were legislated in Parliament, prohibiting servants and laborers "to receive above the rate which they were accustomed to take before the yeare of the great mortalitie." It appears that even in the mid–fourteenth century monetary explanations for inflation were conceivable, along with a grasp of the price-wage cycle:

> Servants and laborers were in deed growen to be more subtill than before time they had beene; but by reason of the prices of things were inhanced, it is like they demanded greater wages than they had doone before time: and one cause of the dearth [inflation] was imputed to the new coine of monie, being of lesse weight in the value thereof, than before it had beene, so that *the bishop of Winchester being lord tresuror, who had counselled the king to ordeine those grotes and half grotes, was evill spoken of amongst the people.* (2:652; italics added)

One of the most intransigent problems facing the monarch of a trading nation was a direct consequence of a bimetallic system of coinage; more precisely, that the ratio between the two metals was subject to fluctuations in terms of supply and demand. If, for example, gold was undervalued in England in relation to silver by comparison to the ratio in Flanders, it would provide an incentive to export gold, producing an excess of silver at home.[32]

So for the year 1526 Holinshed reported a crisis in the currency exchange between England and Flanders. In this he followed Hall's *Union* (p. 718), whose account, being somewhat fuller, is more intelligible, and the source of the interpolated phrases in italics:

> In this season the angell noble was just the sixt part of an ounce Troie, so that six angels were just an ounce, which was fourtie shillings sterling; [i.e., one angel= 6s. 8d.] & the angell was worth two ounces of silver: so that six angels were worth twelve ounces, which was but fourtie shillings in silver. [*But in Flaunders, Braband, and Zeland, the Angel was worth 7s. 4d. so that merchants daily caried over much money, to the great hinderance of the merchandise of this realme, for most men caried gold, & and when it was there, it was losse in every noble viiid. to bryng it hether again: & when thenglishmen spake to the rulers there, to leave thenhauncying of the kynges coyne, thei laughed them to skorne.*] . . . So that, to meet with this inconvenience, in September proclamation was made through all England, that the angell should go for seven shillings foure pence, the roiall for eleven shillings, & the crowne for foure shillings foure pence. [*And to bryng out of Flaunders the great nomber of Englishe golde whiche was there*] on the fift of November following, by proclamation againe, the angell was inhanced to seven shillings six pence, and so everie ounce of gold should be five and fourtie shillings, and an ounce of silver at three shillings and nine pence in value. (3:713)

In 1551, Edward, seeing the inflationary effect of his father's debasement, moved to correct it by an extensive revaluation. As Holinshed reported:

> At this time also the king with the advise of his privie councell, and having also great conference with merchants and others, perceiving that . . . such coins and copper monies, as had beene coined in the time of the king his father . . . [were] not worth halfe the value that they were currant at, to the great dishonor of the kings majestie & the realme, and to the deceit & no little hinderance of all the kings maiesties good subjects, did now purpose not onelie the abasing of the said copper monies, but also meant wholie to reduce them into bullion, to the intent to deliver fine and good monies for them. And therefore in the moneth of Julie by his graces proclamation, he abased the peece of twelve pence, commonlie called a teston unto nine pence, and the peece of foure pence unto three pence. And in August next following, the peece of nine pence was abased to six pence, and the peece of three pence unto two pence, and the pennie to an halfe-pennie. (3:1031)

Although he does not so indicate, his source here was probably the money-conscious John Stow, whose *Abridgement* (1570) had given disproportionate space to these Edwardian proclamations and their consequences, offering in addition a moral-social analysis that Holinshed omits. Stow had reported that the May proclamation had "caused great dearth of al thinges, for the people covetyng to reyse the losse of theyr mony, upon suche kynde of wares or victual as they occupied, did dayly enhaunce the pryce, most myserablye oppressing the poore" (pp. 215–16). The Edwardian Council, in their concern to allow people to prepare for the crying down of the coinage, had not grasped the inflationary effect of a delay between proclamation of the new values and their formal adoption. In consequence, Stow reported, the time for the proclamation to take effect was shortened, by another proclamation, from the end of August to July 9th; and a second decrial had to follow the first.[33]

The continued presence of a stock of debased coinage in the system, however, caused enormous problems. One of Mary's first acts after her accession in the summer of 1553 was to mint new "fine" coins and determine their currency value; the next year she tried again; while from 1560 to 1562 Elizabeth wrestled with the same problem, issuing no fewer than nine proclamations.[34] An inevitable effect of her 1560–61 interventions was to generate popular distrust of the currency, just as her father's interventions in 1551 had also resulted in "a flight from money and abiding suspicion of government intentions."[35] In a climate of distrust of the coinage of the realm, rumors could render fiscal policy nugatory.[36] As her brother had discovered in 1551, in the expectation that coins were about to be "decried,"

that is, their face value lowered, merchants would raise prices, and the inflationary spiral would continue. A spate of rumors in 1562 that the newly
minted coin was about to be called down set off such a crisis that Elizabeth
was almost persuaded to make them self-fulfilling prophecies.[37] Indeed, so
paranoid was the Crown on this topic that Elizabeth issued a second
proclamation (13 March 1562), defining currency prognoses as "seditious
rumors," and requiring that offendors could be imprisoned for three
months without bail, and after conviction pilloried.[38]

Another inhibition, or unanticipated side effect, of the struggle to *reverse* debasement was the disappearance of small change, a serious hardship
for the poor whose transactions were mainly at that level. John Stow, in his
Abridgement (1570), had noted that in the Edwardian calling down of 1551
"no word [was] spoken of the small money, as pence & half grotes, by reason wherof, there was no small mony to be gotten to geve the poore people" (fol. 215–16). Elizabeth's Council apparently did not learn from previous experience. Her proclamation dated 15 November 1561, "Announcing
New Small Coins," states "that ther is risen great annoyance amongst the
poorer sort of her subjects for lack of small moneys of fine silver."[39]

For the year 1560, Holinshed reported neutrally on the beginning of
Elizabeth's great recoinage:

> The queenes maiestie by the advise of hir most honorable councill, meaning
> to abolish all corrupt, base, and copper monies then currant in this realme of
> England, coined in the times and reignes of king Henrie the eight, and king
> Edward the sixt, to the great hinderance and decaie of the commonwealth of
> this realme, and therewith to restore unto all hir subjects fine and pure ster-
> ling monies, both of gold and silver, to the great honor and benefit of the
> whole realme: published a proclamation on Michaelmasse even before
> noone, that the teston coined for twelve pence, and in the reigne of king
> Edward embased by proclamation to six pence, should now foorthwith (that
> of the best sort marked with the portculeis) be current for foure pence
> halfepenie: the second marked with the greihound for two pence farthing:
> the third and worst sort not marked as afore, not to be currant at all, nor re-
> ceived for anie value. The grote to be currant for two pence, the former
> peece of two pence for a penie, &c.
>
> It was not long after this, but that hir grace restoring to hir subiects fine
> sterling monie, called all the said base and corrupt coines into hir majesties
> mint, allowing to them therefore after the rate before mentioned, so much of
> the said fine monies as they brought in of the said base monies. (4:201–2; cf.
> Stow, p. 1115)

The source of this information is marked in the margin as John Stow. A few paragraphs later, however, Holinshed also reported on the queen's reaction to the disappearance of small change that is so eloquently documented in her proclamation of 15 November 1561, "wherein," as Holinshed reported, "she restored to the realme diverse small peeces of silver monie, as the peece of sixpence, foure pence, three pence, two pence, and a pennie, three halfe pence, and three farthings." Whereas a modern economy would have quickly invented a substitute for change (compare the use of postage stamps and candy in Italy in the early 1980s), such resourcefulness would have been highly dangerous in Elizabethan England. For the year 1569, the *Chronicles* recorded, a man was hanged at Tyburn for casting testons of tin (4:234).

Much has been said about the naive nature of Tudor thought on the question of intrinsic value (bullion content), a principle carrying a strong symbolic or idealizing subtext that privileged "pure" gold and silver over "base" metals, and the tone of Elizabeth's proclamations charting her "victory and conquest of this hideous monster of the base moneys"[40] supports the charge of archaism. Certainly to use as one's instrument of control in such a crusade the inherently conventional "fiat value,"[41] that is, the value imposed on coins by government decree, was to fight against the approaching tide of the market as the regulator of exchange rates with a weapon that itself revealed the illusory concept of intrinsic value; but in certain respects it seems that Elizabeth was more old-fashioned and idealistic in her thinking than some of her subjects. It is impossible to tell for certain whether Holinshed and his colleagues, from a position of hindsight, understood that attempts to keep the two metals in balance or to regulate the exchange value (as distinct from the face value) of particular coins were doomed to fail. Yet the fact that they continually return to such attempts tells its own story. The facts alone, arranged as a consecutive narrative in the way I have presented them here, reveal without further commentary the incoherence in government policy.

A valiant attempt was made by Abraham Fleming, in the second edition of the *Chronicles*, to bring out the idealizing subtext of the recoinage as Elizabeth herself evidently imagined it, reinstating the Edwardian connection with reform in religion:

> Thus did her majestie in all her actions directed to common utilitie shoot at *a certeine perfection, purenesse, and soundnesse,* as here in hir new stamps and coines of all sorts; so also in God's religion, setting the materiall churche of her dominion free from all popish trash. (4:203–4)

But if any of his readers remembered William Harrison's historical description "Of the coines of England," they would have to set beside this image of perfection a bewildering (and bewildered) impression of an economy flooded with coins old and new, native and foreign, of competing authenticity and changing value. And listing the coins he believed to be current, he entered a man-in-the street disclaimer: "if there be anie other, in good sooth I know them not, as once scarselie acquainted with any silver at all, much lesse then (God it wot) with any store of gold" (1:367).

Wages and Working Conditions

In this last section I return to the contested question of wages in a period of high inflation, the focus being not on standards of living but on the wages paid to the artisanal classes. As Phelps Brown and Hopkins put it in 1956, "the lowest point [of real wages for building craftsmen] we record in seven centuries was in 1597, the year of the *Midsummer Night's Dream*."[42] This statement economically suggests that in the 1590s the Elizabethan dream was primarily upheld by art and illusion.

In the late sixteenth century, one of the most obvious reasons that real wages did not keep up with inflation is that there were rigid state-decreed wage controls, whose records we can follow in a series of royal proclamations, which would presumably have kept the problem of wage levels firmly in public view. In general the *Chronicles* have little to say on the subject of wages. With the important exception of the protests generated by widespread layoffs in the clothing industry, themselves provoked by Wolsey's exactions, or the protectionist issues motivating Ill May Day (to be described in chapter 9) the prehistory of industry is not apparently a matter of concern. No mention was made for the year 1563 of the Statute of Artificers, or of the many other proclamations for establishing *maximum* wages which followed it. For the year 1580, the proclamation regulating London wages set the level for clothworkers at five pounds by the year with meat and drink, for common laborers five pence by the day with meat and drink, nine pence without. These levels were reinstated in July 1586, and they find no mention in the *Chronicles*.[43]

Yet there is one episode that does address the question both of wages and working conditions, and in so graphic a way as to make amends for earlier omissions. This is the account of the rebuilding of the port of Dover under the supervision of Sir Thomas Scot, an account provided by his kinsman Reginald Scot, whose working relationship with Abraham Fleming we shall have cause to consider in chapter 10. Reginald, himself an expert surveyor of Romney marshworks, becomes another of the many eyewitnesses whose testimony both enlivens and complicates the *Chronicles*.

Despite the fact that this project began, at the queen's instigation, in 1583, this account is chronologically deferred until 1586, when the story of the reign as the chroniclers conceive it is already drawing to a close. Dover had been allowed to fall into disrepair at the time of the loss of Calais, and its state was therefore a matter of national confidence and prestige. From Scot we learn everything we could possibly want to know about the technology of construction on sand against water: what "provision of stuffe should be made, to wit, of timber, thorne, faggots, needles, keies, beetels, piles, pasture, earth"; how between April and harvest, when they were not needed in the fields, hundreds of workmen, carts and oxen were summoned from the market towns by proclamation. Since Scot had a personal and family interest in promoting a positive account of this project, he proposed to "omit all contentions and factions concerning these proceedings, as also all injurious practices against those works" (4:857), a declaration which, by summoning up the specter of dissent, accomplishes rather the opposite.

We also learn that the Romney marshmen were the preferred workmen and what they were paid, in relation to the superior officers in the project:

> Sir James Hales, treasurer: for every £50 disbursed, 6s. 8d. Since the total costs of the two main walls of the harbor was £2,700, Hales's commission was at least £18.
>
> His clerk, £5 yearly.
>
> Master Digs, esquire, general surveyor: 20 marks yearly.
>
> 8 guiders ("standing at . . . places of most danger"), 8 pence a day.
>
> 8 untingers (to undo the tackle of every cart before unloading), 8 pence a day.
>
> 8 shelvers (to pull down the carts where they should unload, "the strongest and nimblest men"), 10 pence a day.
>
> 8 tingers (to lift up the unloaded carts as soon as they were empty, and make fast their tackle), 8 pence a day.
>
> General laborers (to shovel and spread the contents of the carts) 6 pence and 8 pence a day.
>
> Beetlemen, (to beat the sludge to the sides of the walls, level the earth and compact it), 8 pence a day.
>
> Armorers (to arm the walls with faggots and stakes after they were constructed), 12 pence or 16 pence a day.

In other words, the rates were eight to sixteen pence per day for a ten-hour day, from six in the morning to six at night, with a two-hour midday break (4:862).

By comparison with the wage schedule for urban workers for 1584, these wages are low, unless we posit that food and drink was provided by the Crown, and especially given the danger and difficulty of the work. It also emerges that the workers had to report at 5 A.M., "and such as were absent had no allowance that daie: if they came late, their wages was tot-ted at the expenditors good discretion" (4:863). Sir Thomas Scot and his officers "did (not seldome times) bestow rewards bountifullie upon the poore workmen, who upon sundrie occasions were driven to worke longer than the rest, and with more difficultie; for some at some times wrought in danger of life, and offtimes in the waters up to the wast or shoulders" (4:861–62). But the suggestion that the wage schedule was sometimes sup-plemented conflicts with Scot's other statement, that the writing of this industrial history is (in some mysterious territory where psychology merges with public relations) reparation for inadequate material compen-sation:

> In the declaration hereof also, the parties which have deserved commenda-tion or consideration maie perhaps in some sort have a kind of recompense: for other reward was not looked after, or sought for by the best executioners hereof, sith the better sort imploied their travell with great charges, the meaner sort their readie furtherance to their power, the poorer people their labor at a small rate to the preferring and performance of this worke; and all with such forwardnesse and willingnes of mind, as the like hath not beene knowne or seene in this age. (4:858)

The reconstruction of Dover, then, was presented by Scot as an instance of high-minded collaboration between classes, of benevolent industrial relations, in the service of a project enhancing the nation's pres-tige.

Yet, as if by attraction to the anthropological spirit of the *Chronicles* as a whole, tensions and contradictions in his narrative reveal the presence of a more realistic attitude on the part of the workers to their work. There is one astonishing passage, in which Scot records how they responded to the issue of the strict timekeeping that the overseers insisted upon:

> For they never ceased working the whole daie, saving that at eleven of the clocke before noone, as also at six of the clocke in the evening, there was a flag usuallie held up by the sargent of the towne, in the top of a tower, ex-cept the tide or extraordinarie busines forced the officers to prevent the houre, or to make some small delaie and staie thereof. And presentlie upon the signe given, there was a generall shout made by all the workers: and wheresoever anie court [cart] was at that instant either emptie or loden, there was it left, till one of the clocke after noone or six of the clocke in the morn-ing, when they returned to their businesse. But by the space of halfe an houre before the flag of libertie was hanged out, all the court drivers entered into a

song, wherof although the dittie was barbarous, and the note rusticall, the matter of no moment, and all but a jest, yet is it not unworthie of some briefe note of remembrance. (4:865–66)

It is, then, not so remarkable that the chroniclers decided to end their story of Elizabeth's reign, and indeed the *Chronicles* as a whole, with her January 1587 proclamation for the relief of the poor in time of dearth, including a summary of the specific orders sent out to local officers. These orders included provisions against many of the abuses listed by William Harrison in his *Description*. For example, "None to buie such kind of corne as they shall bring to sell, but by warrant upon reasonable cause. . . . Inquirie to be made against ingrosers: . . . No badger to buie corne but in open market, and with a sufficient license in writing" (4:945). The *Chronicles* were thus, as it were, framed by a concern for greater economic "indifference," justice as fairness, in the sense of concern for those most likely to suffer from economic fluctuation, which at the end of the story they could claim as also the concern of the state: "Able poore people to be set to worke: Stocks of monie for provision of works for poore people: Clothiers to continue their workefolks" (4:945).

To call this a frame makes the economic strain in the *Chronicles* sound neater than it was, as my system of quotation may make it sound more pervasive than, in the great bulk of the work, it actually could be. Nevertheless, to look back over those quotations does suggest that the chroniclers believed that educated citizens needed to be alert to price and currency fluctuation, to understand them as best they could, and to watch out for sharp practice. They catch the *perceptions* both of their contemporaries and of much earlier periods, perceptions which include very little passive acceptance ("man's lot under God's dispensation") and a good deal of empirical questioning. In addition, the subdued ethical strain, most evident in William Harrison but also audible in Fleming, Stow, and Holinshed himself, is compatible with the tendency of the project to harken back to the brief period of social reform inaugurated under Edward VI. Paul Slack has argued that the strain of social engineering evident in Elizabeth's reign was predominantly attributable to Protestant or Puritan religious enthusiasm,[44] and the evidence for that seems clear. Yet perhaps such thinking was also a product of the secular social contract that the *Chronicles* as a whole presented as a model to the nation.

SIX   🕯 *Government*

The purpose of this chapter is simple: to recount what the *Chronicles* offered as a history of Parliament, and to show how they inflected that history with political theory. Raphael Holinshed evidently regarded Parliament as *the* institution on which a secular history should focus, because of its potential contribution to the rights or protections of subjects, not against each other, but against the arbitrary exercise of sovereign power. He produced, therefore, a history of Parliament which could be called both evolutionary, in that it reached a peak in the reign of Richard II, and devolutionary, in that that level of parliamentary responsibility was not sustained.

Holinshed's views on this topic may well have been developed or strengthened during the decade prior to the first edition of the *Chronicles*, when the most recent history of the Elizabethan parliaments illustrated how easily subjects' rights, as represented by parliamentary liberties, might be encroached upon. His successors in the 1587 edition, perhaps even more anxious about the prognosis for constitutional government to be calculated from recent events, supplemented his earlier history of Parliament to bring out its thematics more clearly. They also added material that, for all its descriptive or antiquarian format, was probably recognizable as the vehicle of a clear and ideologically potent theory, a theory of Parliament's role as the emblem (if not the guarantor) of limited monarchy, government by consent of the governed, and the freedom of speech necessary to arrive at that consent.

With respect to current views of the Tudor chroniclers, who are still regarded as uninterested in or underequipped to engage the history of institutions, this proposal is revisionary. It has been customary to draw an epistemological line between the chroniclers and the members of the Society of Antiquaries founded in 1586 by William Camden, despite the fact that both John Stow and Francis Thynne were members of the Society, and that John Hooker, as we shall see, had interesting connections with it. But that the Society of Antiquaries was founded in 1586 may have no more compelling relation to the appearance of Camden's *Britannia* in that year than to the fact that the second edition of the *Chronicles* was in press, and about to become a historiographical scandal. In at least one instance, the case of the Ricardian *Modus tenendi parliamentum*, the interests of the chroniclers converged directly with those of the Society of Antiquaries.[1] Whether the Society as a whole was, as some have claimed, a disinterested group of scholars intensely loyal to the Crown, or, as others have inferred, they had given some reason for Elizabeth's 1602 refusal of their request for formal incorporation, and for James's demand in 1608 that their meetings cease entirely,[2] at this one point of their convergence the Society and the chroniclers both provided ammunition for Parliament's search into its own origins, as a ground for at least the defensive claims of the moment.

But with respect to the Elizabethan parliaments, my argument is counterrevisionary, in that it challenges an extremely influential position set in place by Sir Geoffrey Elton. In 1979 Elton delivered what seemed at the time a fatal blow to the earlier paradigm constructed by J. E. Neale and Wallace Notestein,[3] in Elton's own summary, "that the real significance of the institution's history lay in its political function . . . its ability and willingness to provide a counterbalance to monarchic rule," and secondly "that the sixteenth century witnessed a maturing of the house of commons . . . from a rather primitive state into a sophisticated political instrument."[4] Elton implied that Neale's selection of materials for analysis was itself structured by unspoken assumptions, and he doubted whether "the affairs of Peter Wentworth and Arthur Hall" corresponded to "what people in parliament saw at the time," or to "the main interests of contemporaries" (p. 258). By shifting the inquiry from debates to the parliamentary journals, where daily business was recorded in all its mundaneness, by concentrating on the queen's view of her parliament's purpose and strategies for its management, and by citing Sir Thomas Smith as an authority on parliament's functions, Elton arrived at the following dicta:

Parliament was not called for political reasons. Nor was it thought of as a
political assembly: it was a court, and the best contemporary opinion of its
functions brings in politics only very obliquely. The long list of its compe-
tences put together by Sir Thomas Smith (choosing his order of priorities
carefully. . .) speaks of making and repealing laws, of altering rights and possessions, legitimating bastards, establishing forms of religion, altering
weights and measures, settling the succession of the Crown, defining rights
where the law had not settled them, granting taxes, issuing pardons, restoring in blood and condemning by attainder. We should never forget that
Smith knew very well what he was talking about, or that when he spoke of
"the parliament" he did not mean the House of Commons alone. And he had
nothing to say about providing a stage upon which those apprehensive of
the rule of their monarch may express their opinions or push their solutions,
whatever Peter Wentworth—about as unrepresentative a burgess of the
House as the reign produced—may later have asserted. (p. 258)

Elton therefore concluded that Neale and Notestein had achieved their
grand simplicities by reading backwards from the history of the Long
Parliament, and that they were unsupported by any evidence of new powers achieved by the Elizabethan parliaments. "Nor," he added, "need this
suprise us, for on the whole the House had little occasion in this reign to
seek such power" (p. 270).[5] The influence of this new doctrine on the role
and status of the Elizabethan parliaments was so broad that the next generation either followed Elton's lead with enthusiastic denigrations of Neale,[6]
or entered only cautious disclaimers.[7]

  While some of Elton's critique was indeed therapeutic, it was probably
an overstatement that will itself be modified, as the energy generated by
the controversy finds new material to work on.[8] In particular, "Holinshed's"
Chronicles is a source of information about Elizabethan conceptions of
Parliament that has been almost completely overlooked by revisionist history; but it is one that surely belongs in any reconstruction of what
Elizabethan political thinkers, professionals or amateurs, "saw at the time,"
to use Elton's own phrase. If it is the business of cultural history to decipher
"the main interests of contemporaries," the major chronicle of the reign
would surely be a place to look. But before turning to this underinvestigated archive, I need to enter some theoretical caveats about Elton's thesis
that the last decades of the sixteenth century could not have flexed parliamentary muscles for the contests of the seventeenth because no procedural advances were made. One might logically question whether citing the
queen's intentions as to what a parliament should accomplish, or her well-

documented determination to control debate and her success in silencing the more intransigent members, constitute evidence against a growing *conception* of the political importance of Parliament, whether or not that conception produced any concrete alterations in practice. On the contrary, one might well suppose that the more rigorously debate was curtailed, the stronger the belief might have grown in those silenced that the institution was unable to fulfill its rightful function. The question that Elton himself asked, as to why Fulk Onslow, clerk of the Commons, took notes of speeches that he never transcribed into the official journal (p. 266), could itself point to the inadequacy of that record as an authentic account of what was heard at the time to be important, not to mention the fact that in 1628 "the Commons sensibly insisted on restoring . . . earlier practice by removing all record of debate" (p. 266), where "sensibly" connotes self-protection.

In addition, Elton relied for his formal definition of Parliament as a court on the great modern legal scholar, F. W. Maitland, whose theory of the exclusively judicial origin of parliaments has often been challenged.[9] And he had privileged, as "the best contemporary opinion" of Parliament's function, Sir Thomas Smith's *De Republica Anglorum*, published in 1583. If we are looking for contemporary opinion, the *Chronicles* belong in this story as well, not least because of their *response* to Smith's account.

It is well known that in 1587 William Harrison inserted into his *Description of England* a new chapter "Of the High Court of Parliament and Authority of the Same," taken in large part from Smith. Harrison gave due credit for this material to Smith, in terms that are either testy, joking, or generous, depending on one's ear:

> As Sir Thomas Smith dooth deliver and set them downe, whose onelie direction I use, and *almost word for word* in this chapter, requiting him with the like borowage as he hath used toward me in his discourse of the sundrie degrees of estates in the common-wealth of England, which (as I hope) shall be no discredit to his travell. (1:292; italics added)

This reference to "like borowage" refers to an earlier phase of the relation between the two texts, in which, it appears, Smith had access to a manuscript version of Harrison's chapter 5, "Of degrees of People in the Commonwealth of England," and transferred its contents, though without acknowledgment, into the *De Republica*, Book I, chapters 17–24. This relationship between the two texts has been fully explicated by Mary Dewar;[10] but her focus on the problem of plagiarism may have distracted her attention from the differences that emerge from the exchange.[11]

In fact, Harrison's procedure was a fairly strenuous rewriting of Smith's prose, so that while the substance (except in one crucial instance) remains the same, it is actually quite difficult to align any two passages exactly. This would be a trivial correction, were it not that the two texts diverge significantly on the question here in dispute, the precise role of Parliament in the nation.

Even Smith's own views on the matter have been disputed, because his opening sentence, "The most high and absolute power of the realme of Englande, is in the Parliament," contained a phrase, *absolute power*, which was likely to activate the constitutional reflexes. Dewar took the view that Smith's use of this term was not tendentious, and that it, too, had been misunderstood by reading backwards from the more radical constitutionalist perspective of the seventeenth century.[12] But when we compare what Smith wrote with what Harrison rewrote and represented as "borowage," the charge of tendentiousness seems unavoidable. "The Parliament," Smith had written:

> abrogateth olde lawes, maketh newe, giveth orders for thinges past, and for thinges hereafter to be followed, changeth rightes, and possessions of private men, legitimateth bastards, establisheth formes of religion, altereth weights and measures, giveth formes of succession to the crowne, defineth of doubt-full rightes, whereof is no lawe alreadie made, appointeth subsidies, tailes, taxes, and impositions, giveth most free pardons and absolutions, restoreth in bloud and name as the highest court, condemneth or absolveth them whom the Prince will put to that triall: And to be short, all that ever the people of Rome might do either in *Centuriatis comitiis* or *tributis*, the same may be doone by the parliament of Englande, which representeth and hath the power of the whole realme both the head and the bodie.[13]

Now if Smith was indeed, as Elton asserted, "choosing his order of priorities carefully," what should we think of the fact that when William Harrison imported this material into his *Description*, he transferred it from the second paragraph where Smith had placed it (after a more general description of how the three estates functioned as a legislative body) to a frontal position (immediately after the phrase, "absolute power," that later generations would find so provocative) and substantially changed its content? "This house," wrote Harrison:

> hath the most high and absolute power of the realme, *for thereby kings and mightie princes have from time to time beene deposed from their thrones, lawes either enacted or abrogated, offendors of all sorts punished, and corrupted religion either disannulled or reformed,* which commonly is divided into two houses or parts. (1:291; italics added)

And only then followed the rest of Smith's opening paragraph, with its delineation of the three estates. By juxtaposing the phrase "absolute power" with a new and threatening first function, deposing kings, and by condensing Smith's long list of functions to only four, none of which could be seen as administrative busywork, Harrison completely altered his readers' apprehension of what "absolute power" might consist in. The structural rearrangement of the material has itself the effect of prioritization, rendering Parliament's actions more important than those who perform them, more grandly and simply constitutional.

And in place of Smith's Erastian assertion that Parliament *"establisheth formes* of religion," Harrison's version offers the Puritan or Grindalian hope that *"corrupted* religion [will be] either *disannulled or reformed."* Although Smith's locution might not, in Dewar's phrase, "have offended even Elizabeth's sharp sense of the Crown's authority,"[14] it is hard to see how, had the queen noticed Harrison's adjustment, she could have failed to see it as a challenge. For from 1572 onwards, she had adamantly refused to allow church reform to be a matter of parliamentary debate.

Harrison's new chapter on Parliament therefore established certain expectations for the readers of the 1587 edition of the *Chronicles,* which later chapters on the medieval parliaments would strikingly confirm; or, if we reverse the chronology to emphasize the authorial *construction* of the work, Harrison responded to the theme already established a decade earlier by Holinshed during those chapters, which would build to one climactic instance of monarchical deposition, that of Richard II, and so wrote a "description" of the English parliament and its functions that acted, as it were, as a tiny but sinister table of contents.

Holinshed's "Ancient Constitutionalism"

It may appear to be cheating to begin with an incident from medieval history that is, by any standard, preparliamentary. Yet since my claim is that Raphael Holinshed wrote a discontinuous story of "ancient constitutionalism" we should not overlook a very early episode, the abortive rebellion against the Romans in A.D. 62, led by a figure, Boadicea, or Voadicea, whom Holinshed represents as a spokeswoman of national self-consciousness and political freedoms. In his otherwise economical account of ancient Britain, Holinshed paused to permit Voadicea to deliver a long speech on the subject of "ancient liberty," a speech that he had troubled to unearth in Dion Cassius, despite the fact that it duplicates a briefer one translated directly from Tacitus, his primary source at this point. Voadicea had exhorted her followers to suicidal resistance rather than accommodation to a colonial power; and Holinshed's subtle updating of Dion's locutions are not difficult to spot:

> Againe, in that a number of you have rashlie preferred an externall sovereigntie before the customes and lawes of your owne countrie, you doo at this time (I doubt not), perfectlie understand how much free povertie is to be preferred before great riches, whereunto servitude is annexed; and much wealth in respect of captivitie under forren magistrats, whereupon slaverie attendeth. . . . We therefore that inhabit this Iland, . . . are now contemned and troden under foot, of them who studie nothinge else but how to become lords & have rule of other men. Wherefore my welbeloved citizens, friendes, and kinsfolkes (for I thinke we are all of kin, since we were borne and dwell in this Ile, and have one name common to us all) let us now, even now (I saie, because we have not doone it heretofore, and *whilest the remembrance or our ancient libertie remaineth*) sticke togither, and performe that thing which dooth perteine to valiant and hardie courages, to the end we maie injoie, not onelie the name of libertie, but also freedome it selfe, and thereby leave our force and valiant acts for an example to our posteritie. (1:497; italics added)[15]

This speech is structurally connected to what follows by the theory of the four great conquests: Roman, Saxon, Danish, and Norman. Voadicea's speech, and the failure of her resistance, ushers in a period that Holinshed renders, efficiently but bleakly, as a dark age of political incoherence.

Not completely dark, however. For, as I indicated in the preface to this book, Holinshed's ancient constitutionalism began, as also would that of Coke and Lambarde, with the apocryphal laws of Edward the Confessor. To repeat the crucial point: for the year 1053, Holinshed described the legal reforms of this third Edward before the Conquest, as an extraction out of "that huge and unmesurable masse and heape of lawes" that had accumulated during previous reigns "such as were thought most indifferent and necessarie," which laws "were afterwards called the common lawes, . . . so much esteemed of the Englishmen, that after the Conquest, when the Normans oftentimes went about to abrogate the same, there chanced no small mutinies and rebellions for retaining of those lawes" (1:747).

Holinshed was here translating closely from Polydore Vergil's *Anglica Historia*, the source from which much of his ancient constitutionalism is drawn. It is worth noting, however, that his phrase "such as were thought most *indifferent* and necessarie" translates Vergil's less ideologically potent "optima quaecque & necessaria"; while he has *added* without any mandate from the Latin the gloss on "wrongful dealing," as "clouding the same under some braunche of lawe, naughtily misconstrued."[16] This shows that Holinshed's legal reflexes were excited by this emphasis in Vergil, which he gives a characteristic push in the direction of legal hermeneutics; and, even more germane to the history of Parliament for which he was here (without saying so) laying the foundations, Holinshed returned to this theme when he came to the Conquest itself.

According to John Pocock, "the story that among the Conqueror's first acts had been to codify and confirm the Confessor's law had found its way into most of the chroniclers."[17] For Holinshed, however, the Conqueror's legal revisionism had the opposite effect:

> Whereupon abrogating in maner all the ancient lawes used in times past, and instituted by the former kings for the good order and quietness of the people, he made new, *nothing so equall* (cf. *parum justas*) or easie to be kept; which neverthelesse those that came after (not without their great harme) were constreined to observe: as though it had beene an high offense against GOD to abolish those evill lawes, which king William (a prince nothing friendly to the English nation) had first ordeined, and to bring in other and more tollerable. Here by the waie I give you to note a great absurditie; namelie, that those lawes which touched all, and ought to be knowne of all, were notwithstanding written in the Norman toong, which the Englishmen understood not; so that even at the beginning you should have great numbers, partly by the iniquitie of the lawes, and partlie by ignorance in misconstruing the same, to be wrongfully condemned: some to death, and some in the forfeiture of their goods; others were so intangled in sutes and causes, that by no means they knew how to get out, but continuallie were tossed from post to piller; in such wise that in their minds they cursed the time that ever these unequall lawes were made. . . . Howbeit this is most true, that the Norman kings themselves would confesse, that the lawes devised and made by the Conqueror were *not very equall*; insomuch that William Rufus and Henrie the sonnes of the Conqueror would at all times, when they sought to purchase the peoples favor, promise to abolish the lawes ordeined by their father, establish *other more equall* (cf. *meliores*) and restore those which were used in S. Edwards daies. (2:13; italics added)

From the threefold repetition of the term "equal" (as that which denotes a just and acceptable code of law, and that Holinshed himself has imposed on Vergil's less choric vocabulary), we can tell that equality has joined indifferency as a constitutional ideal. And the *Chronicles* thus made available in the vernacular not merely the concept of the Norman Yoke but also Vergil's sophisticated insight into the way religion may be used to bolster the claims of law and the state ("as though it had beene an high offense against GOD to abolish those evill lawes").[18]

However, even this account is inadequate to the complexity of how

the *Chronicles* fought to transmit the story of the ancient constitution without giving overt provocation; for I have here quoted the 1587 version. In
1557 Holinshed had given his readers a characteristic sign of his own presence as translator, when instead of "Here by the waie I give you to note a
great absurditie," he had written "Neither can I in this place omitte to give
a note of that which may seeme to such as do *indifferently* consider of things
a greate absurditie." And at the end of the passage, after he had described
how the descendants of the Conqueror had, whenever they wished to curry
popular favor, promised to restore the laws of the Confessor, Holinshed
had originally written:

> But their meaning was so far to the contrary, that their deeds declared their
> dissimulation, so that many of those Norman lawes remayne in force even
> unto these dayes. The cause as some thinke, is for that they make more to the
> Princes behoofe, than to the commoditie of the people. (2:304)

With these ideological guideposts, it is not hard to follow the story of
the ancient constitution's *fortuna* throughout the Middle Ages. After
William's death, Henry I, permitted to succeed instead of his eldest brother Robert, attempted to ingratiate himself with his subjects: "somewhat to
releeve the common-wealth, he promised to restore the lawes of good king
Edward [the Confessor], and to abolish or amend those which by his father
and brother were alreadie ordeind *to the hurt & prejudice of the old ancient liberties
of the realme of England*" (2:48; italics added). This phrase, which supplants the
neutral *"ad incommodum Anglorum"* of Polydore Vergil,[19] leads by a now visible logic to what might otherwise seem a digression on the beginnings of
parliamentary government, an event that Vergil had located, ca. 1116, in
the reign of Henry I.

Again, as with Voadicea's speech, attention to Holinshed's translation
reveals additions (marked here by square brackets) and locutions that updated the material for the benefit of an Elizabethan reader (marked here by
italicization):

> Here is to be noted, that before this time, the kings of England used but sel-
> dome to call togither the states of the realme after *any certaine maner* or gener-
> all kind of processe, to have their *consents* in matters to be decreed. [But as the
> lords of the privie councell in our time doo sit onlie when necessitie re-
> quireth,] so did they whensoever it pleased the king to have any conference
> with them. So that from this Henrie it may be thought the first use of the par-
> lement to have proceeded, which sith that time hath remained in force, . . .
> and in such decrees (established by the authoritie of the prince, the lords
> spirituall and temporall, and the commons of this realme thus assembled in

parliament) consisteth the whole force of our English lawes. [Which decrees are called statutes, meaning by that name, that the same should stand firme and stable, and not be repealed without the *consent* of an other parlement, and that upon good and great consideration.] (2:65–66)[20]

Holinshed had discovered in Polydore Vergil a theory of the origins of Parliament that suited his agenda perfectly: not only because those origins predated Magna Carta; but also because Vergil's account, with a few salient adjustments, provided the basis for an ancient system in which "consent," rather than counsel, was what the king needed from his parliament, and in which regular rather than eccentric sessions were part of the understanding. Subjection to the arbitrary meeting, called at the monarch's pleasure, has been deftly redefined by Holinshed as the fate of the Tudor privy council!

More important still, Holinshed had discovered in Vergil an explanation for the bicameral structure of the early modern parliament that suited his own convictions—convictions that he did not hesitate to support by judicious mistranslation:

> The maner of their consulting heere in England in their said assemblies of parlement is on this wise. Whereas they have to intreat of matters touching the commoditie both of the prince and of the people, *that everie man may have free libertie to utter what he thinketh* (cf. "ut aequa unicuisque loquendi potestas fiat") they are appointed to sit in severall chambers, the king, the bishops, and lords of the realme sit in one chamber to conferre togither by themselves; *and the commoners called knights for the shires, citizens of cities, and burgesses of good towns in another* (cf. "at procuratores civium populique alterum proximum"). These choose some wise, eloquent, and learned man to be their prolocutor (as they terme him), who propoundeth those things unto them that are to be talked of, and asketh everie mans opinion, concerning the conclusion thereof. In like sort, when any thing is agreed upon, and decreed by them in this place [(which they call the lower house in respect of their estate)] he declareth it againe to the lords that sit in the other chamber called the higher house, demanding likewise their judgement touching the same. For nothing is ratified there, except it be agreed upon by the *consent* of the more part of both those houses. (italics added)

It has been said, indeed by J. E. Neale himself, that the formal privilege of freedom of speech for members of Parliament first appeared in the reign of Henry VIII. "We can be reasonably certain that no medieval Speaker asked for such a privilege, and, so far as we know, Sir Thomas More was the first to do so, in 1523."[21] But this older concept of a *structure* designed to free debate in the lower house from the surveillance of the more powerful figures in the Lords was a feature of parliamentary theory that Sir Edward Coke would think worthy of special comment, perhaps having been alerted to it by John Hooker, who in turn may have learned it from Holinshed.

In the 1587 edition of the *Chronicles*, this entire passage was drawn to the reader's attention by being printed in ostentatiously larger type, and together with Harrison's new chapter on Parliament, might be said to constitute the first two stages of a theoretical framework that would be completed—not where one might expect to find it, in the "Continuation" to the history of England—but in Hooker's *Order and usage of the keeping of a Parlement in England*, tucked away in the history of Ireland.

But to return to the medieval history of Parliament, Holinshed's next opportunity for ancient constitutionalism was provided by the reign of King John, who in 1215 returned from his continental wars to deal with dissention at home:

> For the people being set on by diverse of the superiours of both sorts, finding themselves greeved that the king kept not promise *in restoring the ancient lawes of S. Edward*, determined from thencefoorth to use force, since by request [they] might not prevaile. . . . the Nobles supposing that longer delaie therein was not to be suffered, assembled themselves togither at the abbeie of Burie . . . where they uttered their complaint of the kings tyrannicall maners. . . . There was brought foorth and read *an ancient charter made sometime by Henrie the first . . . conteining the grant of certeine liberties according to the lawes of king Edward the confessor*, profitable to the church and barons of the realme, which they purposed to have universallie executed over all the land. And therefore being thus assembled in the queers of the church of S. Edmund, they received a solemne oth upon the alter there, that if the king would not grant to the same liberties, with others which he of his owne acord had promised to confirme to them, they would from thencefoorth make warre upon him, till they had obtained their purpose, and inforced him to grant, not onelie to all these their petitions, but also yeeld to the confirmation of them under his seale, for ever to remaine most stedfast and inviolable. (2:317–18; italics added)

Despite a first furious response, "Why do they not aske to have the kingdome also?" John measured his strength against that of the barons, estimated at 2,000 knights and a huge army of commoners, and agreed to the signing of the two great charters, Magna Carta and the Charta de Foresta.

The story of the charters has also experienced the fluctuations of historiographical fashion, and Magna Carta itself has been subject to interpretive distortion at different ends of the ideological scale.[22] It looks as though Holinshed's position were somewhere to the left of center, and that

he wished Magna Carta to be thought of as a declaration of political liberty explicitly connected to others that had preceded or would follow it.[23]
Not incidentally, he recorded both the 1225 reconfirmation of the two
great charters ("these good lawes and laudable ordinances," 2:357) and the
repeat performance of 1237, when, in return for the grant of a subsidy the
request for which "was not verie well taken," Henry III "granted and confirmed the liberties and customes conteined in the two charters, the one
called Magna charta, and the other Charta de foresta" (2:380). Moreover,
Holinshed inserted the epilogue added at that time to Magna Carta which
bound Henry's successors "in perpetuum" to observe all the aforesaid liberties and free customs (2:381).[24]

In the reign of Henry III onwards the focus of the *Chronicles* begins to
shift, to problems of subsidy and taxation. During this reign there occurred
what is now recognized as the first parliamentary debate,[25] when in January
1242, at a meeting of the great council, Henry asked for financial support
for his campaign to seek his rights in France. According to Butt, the barons,
"having remarked pointedly on the King's other resources, on the poverty
of the kingdom and on Henry's failure (since they had given him the thirtieth) to observe the charter (instead, they said, he had oppressed them
more than usual) `told the king flatly that for the present they would not
give him an aid.'"[26] Holinshed provided a rather more detailed account of
how the Parliament "stifflie denied" the request for funds, citing the various
taxes levied on such things as ploughland, and expressing their conviction
that the thirtieth they had granted him "remained unspent, bicause it could
not be understood about what necessarie affaires for the common-wealth it
should be laid foorth and imploied." Since it had been levied on condition
that it should not be expended without the advice of four great peers of the
realm, their lack of comprehension was understandable (2:396).

Denial of subsidy, whether absolute or negotiable, would become an
explicit theme of the history of the medieval parliament as Holinshed
chose to relate it, especially in the reigns of Edward III and Richard II; but
before reaching that stage in his own narrative, he noted the emergence of
the practice of parliamentary impeachment, and what that could lead to. In
1321 Edward II's third parliament, popularly known as the "parliament of
white bands," because of the special livery adopted by the baronial retinues
who were gathered in London as a show of force, demanded the exile of the
Spensers, father and son, from Edward's council. "The king, being brought
into streict, durst not but grant unto all that which they requested, establishing the same by statute" (2:561–62). Again, this concession is only the
preliminary to civil war, in which the queen led a rebellious army against
her husband. In 1327, with Edward a prisoner, a new parliament opened,

"in which it was concluded and fullie agreed by all the states (for none durst speake to the contrarie) that for diverse articles which were put up against the king, he was not worthie longer to reigne, *and therefore should be deposed, and withall they willed to have his son Edward duke of Aquitaine to reigne in his place*" (italics added). The parliamentary action was followed by a sermon in Westminster by the archbishop of Canterbury, "taking his theame, Vox populi, vox Dei" (2:584). From the impeachment of members of the royal council to deposing the king himself, parliamentary history was evolving as (according to Harrison's 1587 *Description*) it was entitled to do. Edward's deposition was a crucial step in the self-definition of Parliament because, although it had been accomplished by force, both houses had been involved in legitimizing the change. Although it was undoubtedly true, as G. L. Harriss argued, that this action of the magnates and the Commons was "corrective, the intention being to restore royal government, not to abrogate it," it was also true, as Butt observed, that "a new precedent had been set."[27]

If one were to rely on Holinshed alone, one would assume that parliamentary sessions in the reign of Edward III were exclusively focused on taxation; and here his readers could clearly see a development. From the early years of heavy taxes on wool, wheat, and money, we arrive at the so-called Good Parliament of 1376, in the fiftieth and last year of the reign, where, Holinshed reported:

> was demanded a subsidie of the commons for the defense of the kings dominions against his enemies. Whereunto answer was made *by the common house*, that they might no longer beare such charges, considering the manifold burthens by them susteined in time past. And further they said, it was well knowne the king was rich inough to withstand his enimies, if his monie and treasure were well imploied: but the land had beene of long time evill guided by evill officers, so that the same could not be stored with chaffer, marchandize, or other riches. (2:703; italics added)

Through the mouth of their speaker, the Commons identified the chief culprits—the duke of Lancaster, lord Latimer, the Lord Chamberlain, Sir Richard Sturrie, and Alice Perers, the king's mistress—and *"required* that those persons might be remooved from the king" (2:703; italics added). These demands were acceded to; and "shortlie after, the commons granted to the king his whole request, so that he had of everie person, man and woman, being above the age of fourteene yeares, foure pence, poore people that lived of almesse onelie excepted" (2:703). This series applies the practice of negotiation established by Magna Carta to a broader fiscal sphere, where access to the country's tax revenues can be traded in return for the resolution of grievances; and it also, unmistakably, identifies the Commons as the source of initial resistance, whose language, as Holinshed reports it, was far from deferential.

The Deposition of Richard II

But it was in the reign of Richard II, as I have said, that Holinshed's parliamentarianism finds its fullest ancient confirmation, a theme made available to him by the frequency of the Ricardian parliaments and the increasingly conflictual tone of their proceedings. In 1380 Lords and Commons requested the replacement of the king's councillors by the single figure of Thomas Beauchamp, earl of Warwick, because "it was perceived that they had sought to inrich themselves, & had doone little to the advancement of the kings honor, or state of the common-wealth, but rather emptied the kings cofers" (2:726). In the Lenten season of 1384 there was, in Holinshed's phrase, "hard hold," that is, reluctance amounting to resistance, in response to a request for funds supporting the bishop of Norwich on a crusade against Pope Clement, to which he had been enjoined by Pope Urban. "Diverse there were," wrote Holinshed:

> that thought it not good that such summes of monie shuld be levied of the kings subjects, and the same togither with an armie of men to be committed unto the guiding of a prelat unskilfull in warlike affaires. Other there were that would needs have him to go, that the enimies of the church (as they took them) might be subdued. And *although the more part of the lords of the upper house, and likewise the knights and burgesses of the lower house were earnestlie bent against this journie:* yet at length those that were of the contrarie mind, prevailed; & so it was decreed. (2:756; italics added)

In translating from his source Holinshed increased the emphasis on majoritarianism ("the more part"), although here mysteriously the minority is victorious, and the indications of approval and disapproval are reversed.[28]

By 1386, the tensions apparent in earlier parliaments were coming to a head. Lords and Commons united in an attack on Robert Vere, earl of Oxford, just created duke of Ireland, and on Michael de la Pole, recently created earl of Suffolk and Lord Chancellor. Again there emerged the politics of the deal. Parliament responded to the king's request with the severe rebuke that "he needed not any tallage of his subjects, sith he might furnish himselfe with such a summe at the hands of the said earle, that was justlie indebted unto him therein." At the persuasion of some of the "great lords," a subsidy was granted, under the condition that the lords who had argued for it should account for it. "But before this paiment might be granted, there was much adoo, & *hard hold.*" For "the whole bodie of the parlement made answer thereto, that without the king were present (for he was then at Eltham) they could make therein no answer at all: and herewith they tooke occasion at length to say further, that except the said earle of Suffolke were remooved from the office of chancellorship, they would meddle no further with any act in this parlement, were it never of so small importance" (2:774). Although he was here translating fairly closely from Henry Knighton's Latin,[29] it appears that Holinshed relished, and accentuated through the rhythms of his prose ("were it never of so small importance") the parliamentarians' intransigence.

This intransigence set the stage for the famous occasion where, first, Richard refused to attend the parliament and instead demanded that forty leading members of the Commons should attend him at Eltham; second, and not surprisingly, rumors developed that this was a plot, and that the king intended "to intrap and destroie them that followed not his purpose"; third, that at a meeting of both houses together, it was agreed *"with one consent"* that Thomas, duke of Gloucester, and Thomas Arundel, bishop of Ely, should meet with Richard in the name of the whole Parliament. At this meeting, the Lords Appellant insisted the king meet with his parliament if he wished them to continue in his service. "They further declared, that one old statute and laudable custome was approved, which no man could denie, that the king once in the yeare might lawfullie summon his high court of parlement;" and that "by an old ordinance it was enacted" that if the king absented himself from the parliament unduly, "they then may lawfullie returne home to their houses" (2:775).[30] Their warning was evidently received. By the "whole consent of the parlement," Suffolk was dismissed from the chancellorship, and convicted of a long list of crimes. Parliament appointed thirteen lords "to have oversight under the king of the whole government of the realme," and thereby to deprive him of any autonomy.[31]

My point in rehearsing these early struggles at such length is to build up a picture of how Raphael Holinshed liked to focus on parliamentary resistance, on the conditions exacted for the granting of subsidies, on the word "consent," and on the antiquity of the principles that, already at the end of the fourteenth century, were invoked when a showdown threatened between king and parliament. I shall pass over the long struggle between Richard and the Lords Appellant and move to its climax in 1397, initiated by the murder of Gloucester, and the arrests of Arundel and Warwick, along with John, lord Cobham and Sir John Cheyney. The trials that were processed through the so-called Great Parliament resulted in the execution of Arundel and the exile of Warwick, Cobham, and Cheyney. After the Christmas adjournment, all of the legislation of the Merciless Parliament was repealed, and Richard obtained a number of devices for avoiding parliamentary process, such as a general pardon for persons unnamed. "Manie other things were doone in the parlement, to the displeasure of no small number of people; namelie, for that diverse rightfull heires were disherited" (2:844). These unconstitutional acts heralded the onset of what would later be called Richard's tyranny; as Holinshed put it, "he forgot himselfe, and began to rule by will more than by reason, threatning death to each one that obeied not his inordinate desires" (2:844).

The climactic parliament of the reign would once again reverse the direction of history; but in between there occurred the story that Shakespeare's play has made almost too familiar: the duel betwen Mowbray and Bolingbroke, their exile, Richard's Irish campaign, Lancaster's death and Richard's seizure of his estate, which proved to be merely the prelude to a rash of forced loans, exactions, blank charters, and arbitrary imprisonments. A group of discontented magnates, "perceiving dailie how the realme drew to utter ruine, not like to be recovered to the former state of wealth, whilest king Richard lived and reigned (as they tooke it)" (2:852) invited Bolingbroke, now duke of Lancaster, to return. After a brief period of civil war, with huge defections to Bolingbroke, a parliament was "called by the duke of Lancaster, using the name of king Richard in the writs" (2:859) to begin on 13 September 1399. Thirty-three articles were drawn up charging Richard with unconstitutional behavior: for instance, that he interfered with elections; that "he said, that the lawes of the realme were in his head" and "he most tyrannouslie and unprincelie said, that the lives and goods of all his subjects were in his hands, and at his disposition"; that "contrarie to the great Charter of England," he incited young men to challenge old men under martial law, with the result that the elderly submitted to his extortions (2:860–61). And while Edward Hall had also included this list of charges as a preface to the reign of Henry IV (which is where Hall prudently decided to begin his chronicle), one has only to compare Hall's treatment of the deposition with Holinshed's to see how strongly the latter insisted on *Parliament*'s role in these events, where for Hall it was largely a matter of personalities.[32]

The question of whether one can properly speak of Parliament's role in the deposition has been debated by modern historians.[33] Yet Raphael Holinshed, with whose version of history we are here concerned, did everything he could to imply that "Parliament," kingless or not, was in fact the scene, the spirit, and the instrument of the deposition. Where Hall, after listing the articles, focused on Bolingbroke's role in persuading Richard that it would be in his best interests to resign, and describes a staged resignation at the Tower of London, with a highly emotional and metaphorical speech by Richard complaining that he has not been permitted time to grow up and mend his ways,[34] Holinshed rejects such pathos. Instead he offers the full text (which he found in Fabian) of the "instrument" drawn up by the parliamentary commissioners who received the resignation, or, more likely, made Richard read aloud the speech they themselves had prepared (2:861–63). On 30 September the resignation was, according to Holinshed, formally confirmed in both Houses; and "it was then declared, that notwithstanding the foresaid renouncing, so *by the lords and commons admitted and confirmed*, it were necessarie in avoiding of all suspicions and surmises of evill disposed persons, to have in writing and registred the manifold crimes and defaults before doone by king Richard, and after *to remaine of record amongst other of the kings records for ever*" (2:864; italics added). Holinshed reported with some perplexity (and apparently mistakenly) that the articles were mysteriously never read in parliamentary session.[35] It seems reasonable to assume that the care he bestowed on these formalities and his reproduction of the official documents was intended to correct the omission.[36]

How, then, are we to account for the fact, observed by H. A. Kelly, that in giving his final evaluation of the reign Holinshed reverts to a personal tone of sympathy for Richard and moral disapproval of Bolingbroke?[37] Having included a catalog of still other abuses of kingly power and resources derived from Hardyng via Fabian, Holinshed entered the following quite uncharacteristic demurral:

> Thus have ye heard what writers doo report touching the state of the time and doings of this king. But if I may boldlie saie what I thinke: he was a prince the most unthankfullie used of his subjects of any one of whom ye shall lightlie read. For although (through the frailtie of youth) he demeaned himselfe more dissolutelie than seemed convenient for his roial estate, & made choise of such counsellors as were not favoured of the people, whereby he was the less favoured himselfe: yet in no kings daies were the commons in greater wealth, if they could have perceived their happie state: neither in any other time were the nobles and gentlemen more cherished, nor churchmen lesse wronged. But such was their ingratitude towards their bountifull and loving sovereigne, that those whom he had cheiflie advanced, were readiest to controll him; for that they might not rule all things at their will, and remoove from him such as they misliked, . . . and that rather by strong hande, than by gentle and courteous meanes, which stirred such malice betwixt him and them till at length it could not be asswaged without perill of destruction to them both. (2:369)

And this is followed by a strong critique of Bolingbroke's lack of moderation, loyalty to his sovereign, and the natural affection due to kin, "that thought it not inough to drive king Richard to resigne his crowne and regall dignitie over unto him, except he also should take from him his guiltlesse life."

Taken out of context, this passage appears to fit the older paradigm by which the Tudor chroniclers were seen to be promoting a providential view of history, especially since Holinshed states that Bolingbroke "and his lineall race were scourged afterwards, as a due punishment unto rebellious subjects." And it is perhaps too convenient for my thesis simply to suggest that these concluding statements were inserted for prudential reasons, to protect the *Chronicles* from the fate that befell Sir John Hayward's *History of Henry IIII* two decades later. But taken as Holinshed's last thoughts on the history of medieval parliamentarianism, the personal sympathy for Richard, which focuses chiefly on his assassination and the previous interference by his overweening magnates, reads more like an expression of Holinshed's own "indifferency" than a contribution to providentialist grand narrative. The facts of the reign continue to speak for themselves. Holinshed made possible, therefore, their deployment in the debates of the next century, and Richard's reappearance as a precedent for the parliamentary trial of Charles I. In 1648, in *The Tenure of Kings and Magistrates*, written to encourage the Long Parliament to bring their monarch to justice, John Milton invoked "our Ancestors who were not ignorant what rights either Nature or ancient Constitution had endowed them," and who therefore "thought it no way illegal to depose and put to death thir tyrannous Kings. Insomuch that the Parlament drew up a charge against Richard the second, and the Commons requested to have judgement decree'd against him, that the realme might not be endangerd."[38] And we know that Milton *twice* took note in his commonplace book of the thirty-three articles, citing the 1587 edition of Holinshed as his source.[39]

Holinshed, then, had identified the reign of Richard II as a point of definition of ancient constitutionalism. It is striking to observe how much less attention he pays to constitutional issues during the fifteenth century. Although there were a few sessions over which he paused, his story of Parliament's evolution seems to have gone into remission. Of the ten short parliaments held during Henry's militaristic reign, Holinshed mentions only five. Likewise, important sessions of 1429 and 1433 during the reign of Henry VI, when the Commons addressed the problem of lawlessness, were preempted in Holinshed's narrative by almost unbroken accounts of the French campaigns and the doings of La Pucelle. He does not mention the issue of privilege that arose in 1454, when the Speaker of the Commons, Thomas Thorpe, was sent to the Fleet by suit of the duke of

York, and the Commons petitioned unsuccessfully to have him released.[40]
Nor did he articulate what has since become a commonplace of modern
historians, that Edward's reign was "one of the least constructive and in-
spiring phases in the history of the English parliament," an early premoni-
tion of "personal government" by the monarch and parliamentary docility
achieved through "management."[41] We might reasonably conclude that
Holinshed's cavalier treatment of the fifteenth-century parliaments was a
sign that he, like modern historians, had registered a contraction in
Parliament's role and a debasement of its principles during the dynastic
wars and the rapid exchange of factions.

Henry VIII and His Parliaments

According to Butt, the English parliament did not recover from the managed or fractured docility of the fifteenth century until the long parliament
of Henry VIII, which over the seven years of its continuance provided an
occasion for a renewed sense of corporate identity and importance.
Holinshed, however, took a different view of the Reformation Parliament,
and in his story the recovery began considerably earlier, in 1523, when parliamentary resistance was generated by Cardinal Wolsey's demand for "a
great subsidie" to support the king's wars, of four shillings in the pound, or
one-fifth of every man's income. The 1523 session was also that first occasion, mentioned above, when the Speaker of the House, Sir Thomas More,
explicitly petitioned the king for freedom of debate, and the petition was
granted. But although this important moment entered the chronicle tradition through Hall, and was of obvious importance to Abraham Fleming as
he supplemented Holinshed's account for the second edition, Holinshed
himself passed over it in favor of developing the role of the Commons in
resisting the subsidy.[42] He also used a locution we have heard before in his
accounts of fourteenth-century resistance to taxation: *"Hard hold* there was
about this demand";[43] and he asserted the leadership of the Commons in
relation to the Lords: "The cardinall to moove them thereto, bare them in
hand that the lords had agreed to foure shillings of the pound, which was
untrue: for they had granted nothing, but *staid till they might understand what the
commons would doo*" (3:685; italics added). Eventually (to considerably over-
simplify) the grant was of two shillings in the pound, or one-tenth.[44]
Among other material retrieved from Hall for the 1587 edition of the
Chronicles was the ironic response of the burgesses' constituents to the threat
of the one-fifth: "Sirs, we heare say you will grant foure shillings of the
pound, we advise you to doo so that you may go home: with manie evill
words and threatnings" (3:686).

This reminder of the accountability of the members to their constituents leads directly to the next phase of this story, when, in 1525,
Wolsey turned to extraparliamentary means for raising money, and ordered
the notorious exactions of one-sixth that led to armed risings in Norfolk
and Suffolk. Here Holinshed radically truncated Hall's account of the arguments made by Wolsey to the London magistrates and of the anti-tax
demonstrations as a whole; but he wrote an important sentence of his own
providing the latter with a rationale: "And in excuse of their deniall it was
alledged, that wrong was offered, and the *ancient customes & lawes* of the
realme broken, which would not anie man to be charged with such pai-
ment, *except it were granted by the estates of the realme in parlement assembled*" (3:709;
italics added).[45]

We now arrive at the "long" or "Reformation" Parliament which first
convened in 1529. The two strands to my argument may by this time require restatement. Raphael Holinshed himself assessed the value of parliamentary sessions in terms of their capacity to embody, maintain, and develop principles that revisionist historiography has claimed were
inconceivable prior to the middle of the seventeenth century: that
Parliament, especially the lower house, was responsible for holding the
monarch to long-established contractual terms for constitutional government, and was also responsible to the nation at large for the monarch's tax-
generated revenues. According to these principles, Holinshed himself was
uninterested in the first session of the Reformation Parliament. His account
in the 1577 edition runs to little under a column, and consists of a dry report of complaints in the Commons of the oppressions by the church of the
laiety—the costs of probate and mortuary expenses, and the abuses of non-
residency and pluralism.

But in the decade between the first and second editions of the *Chronicles*
the antiquaries who expanded and revised his project had their own parliamentary reflexes alerted by what occurred in the Elizabethan parliaments
of 1576, 1581, and 1584–85; and, depending on their interests, they supplemented Holinshed's work with material calculated not only to support
his agenda but also to achieve some objectives of their own. In the case of
Abraham Fleming, who seems to have been responsible for augmenting the
sections on the Henrician parliaments, it is clear that his own Protestant
fervor and hence hostility to Wolsey left him unsatisfied by Holinshed's
largely secular and fiscal approach to this session. He therefore greatly expanded it, again by recourse to Hall's *Union*, from which he retrieved
More's extraordinary speech about Wolsey's disgrace that was intended to
conciliate the Commons and make them receptive to doing the king's business. In this speech, More developed the metaphor of Henry as a good

shepherd who has driven a bad sheep from his flock—developed it at such length that it became, in effect, an Aesopian political fable:

> And as you see that amongst a great sort of shepe some be rotten & faultie, which the good sheepheard sendeth from the good sheepe: so the great wedder which is of late fallen (as you all know) so craftilie, so scabbedlie, yea and so untrulie jugled with the king, that all men must needes ghesse and thinke, that he thought in himselfe that he had no wit to perceive his craftie dooing. (3:743–44; cf. Hall, p. 764)

The point of the fable was to assure the Commons that the king had always been undeceived by this wolf in sheep's clothing, and that the praemunire against Wolsey constituted sufficient punishment. However, the sacrifice of Wolsey released a torrent of anticlerical feeling, articulated in the "six great causes" that would ultimately motivate clerical disendowment (3:744–45); and this response was explicitly rendered by Fleming (via Hall) in terms of a new theme—freedom of debate:

> *These things before this time might in no wise be touched,* nor yet talked of by anie man, except he would be made an heretike, or leese all that he had. For the bishops were chancellors, and had all the rule about the king, so that no man durst once presume to attempt anie thing contrarie to their profit or commoditie. But now, when God had illuminated the eies of the king, and that the subtile dooings were once espied; then men began charitablie to desire a reformation: *and so at this parlement men began to shew their grudges.* (3:745; cf. Hall, p. 768; italics added)

By the same token, when in 1532 "divers froward persons" of the lower house insisted that Henry should extend to the laity the general pardon he had granted to any of the clergy endangered by the praemunire (1577, p. 1556), Fleming added (from Hall) that phase of the struggle between king and Commons when "some light persons" circulated rumors of a breach in the privilege of liberty and confidentiality of debate, alledging that "Thomas Crumwell . . . had disclosed the secrets of the Commons" (3:766) whereupon Henry decided on conciliation, sending a pardon to the House by his attorney Christopher Hales.

From 1532 onwards, Parliament's involvement in the affairs of Henry's various marriages is tersely related in the *Chronicles*, without any evaluative comment. Holinshed does not show us his burgesses, from 1529 to 1536, forging a powerful parliamentary instrument; after 1532 we are not permitted to audit a single debate. On the contrary, the bleak record implies an increasingly pliable group, whose own anticlericalism has rendered them complicit in the creation of a new tyranny, greater than that which they had complained of under Wolsey or the canon courts. Indeed, in 1539 a new parliament, which began with a string of attainders and executions, proceeded to pass the notorious Six Articles, intended to obstruct the development of a genuinely theological and pastoral reformation: "Of some," wrote Holinshed, "it was named the bloodie statute, as it prooved indeed to manie. . . . For such was the rigor of that law, that if two witnesses, true or false, had accused anie, and advouched that they had spoken against the sacrament, there was no waie but death; for it booted him not to confesse that his faith was contrarie, or that he said not as the accusers reported, for the witnesses (for the most part) were beleeved (3:808; cf. Hall, p. 828).

The Elizabethan Parliaments

It is all the more unexpected, then, when for the year 1542 Holinshed, who had hitherto merely been condensing Hall's materials, suddenly decided to expand on an issue of parliamentary privilege—the privilege of immunity from legal process during a session. This was the case of George Ferrers, member of Parliament for Plymouth, who was arrested for debt, and the Commons were determined to have him released. Where Hall told this story in a single short paragraph (p. 843), Holinshed gave it as much space as the 1523 defiance of Wolsey, citing Henry's own speech confirming the privilege, and adding an explanation of its significance: "Bicause this case hath beene diverslie reported, and is commonlie alleged as a president for the privilege of the parlement; I have endevored my selfe to learne the truth thereof, and so set it forth with the whole circumstance at large according to their instructions, who ought best both to know and remember it" (3:826).

Why would Holinshed in 1577 have had cause to dwell on parliamentary privilege? And with whom, we may wonder, did he research the question? Who among his contemporaries "ought best both to know and remember" the Ferrers case? There is a pleasing symmetry in discovering that this brings us back to the question with which this chapter opened, the contested understanding of the Elizabethan parliaments, the contest between Neale and Elton and their followers. Both Neale and Elton cited the case of Ferrers as evidence for their own position, the former that the Commons were interested in the history of privilege as a route to the expansion of their own power, the latter that they could not possibly have been so. For Neale, Ferrers's case was the first precedent for the House's forcible intervention on behalf of an imprisoned member that was available either to sixteenth-century commentators or later historians, and Henry's speech supporting the action should have given him "misgivings about the precedent he was condoning."[46] For Elton, Ferrers's case, in its very exceptionality, proved his point that the Commons had nothing to go on:

> Privileges and liberties were supposed to be proved by precedents, but where could such precedents be found? Even by the end of the period, the Commons' record, such as it was, stretched back barely thirty years: before that they had only the medieval Roll in which the only point relevant to their claims was the Speaker's petition. Events in Parliament from Edward III's reign onwards were sometimes cited, with notable inaccuracy and general irrelevance. The uncertainty about Ferrers' case, remembered by some committees and forgotten by others, can be understood: it was not on record at all, being vouched for only in a short passage in Hall's *Chronicle* and possible memories of surviving participants in the event. Indeed, *it was Smalley's case of 1576 that moved Ralph [sic] Holinshed to investigate and to produce that detailed account on which ever since our knowledge of the case has rested.* (italics added)[47]

This remark of Elton's, however, seems oddly rebarbative against his case. Not only does it remind us of the importance of the *Chronicles* in filling the gaps in the more conventional archives of parliamentary history; not only does it register the importance of Holinshed's unique contribution at this point; but it draws an inference about Holinshed's motive for engaging in this research that flies in the face of Elton's larger position. For it implies that Holinshed was concerned with the story of parliamentary privilege as it evolved over time, and that his interest was sparked by an event—the release from gaol of Edward Smalley, Arthur Hall's servant—that took place in the year that the first edition of the *Chronicles* was being readied for the press. Holinshed's interest was therefore *topical*, in the sense that it was generated by, and possibly intended to support, the debates on privilege generated by that incident. In fact, Ferrers's case had been cited not only by William Fleetwood, standing fast "for the liberties of the House," on 20 February 1576, but was also mentioned twice in the Commons in 1572.[48]

To me, it shows how committed, by 1576, the Commons had become to the defence of their liberties that they would take the wretched case of Arthur Hall's unscrupulous servant as their own, and even send a committee to search the rolls for other precedents. And however we may subsequently weigh them in the overall picture of Parliament's day-to-day business, the chain of events that Neale related retains a certain explanatory force in accounting for that level of commitment. I rehearse them again here in order to show what might have motivated Holinshed to produce the *history* of Parliament that the preceding pages have outlined, and the *theory* of Parliament that his emphases, his vocabulary, and his omissions all point to. I hope, in addition, to show what Holinshed had in common not

only with Sir Edward Coke but also with another of the 1587 chroniclers—
with John Hooker, whose own theory of Parliament is inscribed in his *Order
and usage of the keeping of a Parlement in England,* as also in his parliamentary
diary.

On 9 November 1566, Paul Wentworth had asked the House
"whether her Highness's commandment, forbidding the Lower House to
speak or treat any more of the succession . . . be a breach of the liberty of
the free speech of the House, or not." Wentworth's challenge was to extend
the privilege claimed by Sir Thomas More, limited to discussion of legislation introduced by the government, to the right to *initiate* agenda items.
The queen must have taken note. At the closing ceremony of 2 January
1567, in which the Commons had been deliberately obstructive, she delivered a disciplinary speech threatening to restrict the privilege of debate:

> As to liberties, who is so simple that doubts whether a Prince that is head of
> all the body may not command the feet not to stray when they would slip?
> God forbid that your liberty should make my bondage, or that your lawful
> liberties should anyways have been infringed.[49]

At the opening of the 1571 parliament, she sent a message through Sir
Nicholas Bacon, the Lord Keeper, that the petition for freedom of speech
was to be strictly interpreted as excluding any "matters of state *but such as
should be proponed to them.*"[50] Apparently this injunction was provoked by a
speech by Robert Bell against licenses granted to courtiers. As Peter
Wentworth reported later, "This speech was so disliked of some of the
Council that [Bell] was sent for and so hardly dealt with that he came into
the House with such an amazed countenance that it daunted all. . . . For
ten, twelve, or sixteen days there was not one of the House that durst deal
in any matter of importance."[51] Obviously, this episode also involved the
issue of confidentiality, invoked by Peter Wentworth himself in his speech
on 20 April 1571.[52] Neale called it a "novel claim" that the speeches of
members should not be reported to the queen; but we have already seen
this issue raised by the Commons in 1531, and seen it resolved by Henry
more or less in their favor.

When William Strickland produced a bill for the reformation of the
Book of Common Prayer, which incorporated every reform for which the
Puritans had been campaigning during the Vestiarian controversy, he was
called before the Privy Council during the Easter recess in 1571 and re-
strained from further attendance in the House. Accordingly, after the recess George Carlton rose to declare that Strickland's detention infringed
parliamentary privilege, and Christopher Yelverton claimed that the action
set a dangerous precedent for subsequent reigns. The Privy Council

thought better of it, and Strickland was released. But the struggle over privilege continued.

The principle of unfettered debate was finally carried to its highest degree of articulation by Peter Wentworth, in the famous or notorious speech
of 8 February 1576, in which, to open the new session in a fighting spirit,
he declared:

> It is a great and special part of our duty and office, Mr. Speaker, to maintain
> freedom of consultation and speech. . . . I desire you from the bottom of your
> hearts to hate all messengers, tale-carriers, or any other thing, whatsoever it
> be, that in any manner of way infringe the liberties of this honourable
> Council. . . . We are incorporated into this place to serve God and all
> England, and not to be time-servers and humour-feeders.[53]

Wentworth had gone too far, not least in declaring that "her Majestie hath
committed great faults" in rejecting legislation designed to protect both her
and the state. He was summoned before a parliamentary disciplinary committee freighted with Privy Councillors, and ultimately sent to the Tower;
but only for a month. Elizabeth decided that it would be a conciliatory gesture to release him, two days before the ending of the session. If we seek for
a motive, then, for Holinshed's special interest in the Ferrers case of 1543,
its ideological reappearance in 1576 in relation to Arthur Hall's servant was
only part of a ten-year process in which the Commons attempted, if not to
expand their privileges, at least to protect the ones they thought they had.
If there was one arena in which they sought expansion, it was on the matter in which the queen most resolutely sought to contain them, namely on
whether they were entitled to propose agenda items themselves, or merely
to 'speak "to such as should be proponed to them." And on this subject, as
we shall see, John Hooker, in continuing Holinshed's parliamentarianism
in his own manner, had a contribution to make.

The manner in which Holinshed decided himself to tell the story of
the Elizabethan parliaments may bear on this question of what could and
could not be said. He provided a generous summary of the debates about
the religious settlement in the first parliament of the reign. He also displayed the text of the petition from the Commons to be allowed to address
the queen with respect to her marriage, and the text of her complaisance as
it had been read to the House on 10 February and printed in Richard
Grafton's *Chronicle* (4:178–79). The 1559 parliament granted the new queen
a subsidy as large (discounting inflation) as that they had so stoutly resist-
ed when Cardinal Wolsey demanded it. But the parliamentary honeymoon
was not to last. There is no record at all of the 1566 session, when, as we
know from other sources, "Paul Wentworth's tactic of intertwining the

problems of the succession with the grant of the subsidy led to considerable difficulties for the government."[54] Holinshed's report on 1571, the
year of Bacon's initial warning, of Bell's speech, and Strickland's proposal to
reform the prayerbook, consists of a single sentence detailing the subsidy
granted. For the 1572 session, the year of the Puritan *Admonitions to
Parliament*, we learn only of the creation of certain barons, and legislation
against vagabonds. It is hard to believe that Holinshed's interest in parliamentary history, and his research into the precedents for legal immunity,
would have ended so abruptly—unless we assume that prudence dictated
such silence, a prudence justified, perhaps, by the hope that the medieval
history of Parliament as he had reconstructed it could carry its message forward.

Knowing as little as we do about Raphael Holinshed, we can make no
direct connection between him and the precedent seekers of the
Commons. There was, however, a connection between them and John
Hooker, in that Hooker was not only a member for Exeter of the 1571 parliament, but wrote a journal of its proceedings, in which is mentioned Sir
Nicholas Bacon's rebuke to the House for its unwarranted pressure on the
limits of privilege, along with Bell's speech on the queen's prerogative,
William Strickland's detention, and Wentworth's speech on the privilege
of confidentiality of debate.[55] Indeed, Hooker's note on Elizabeth's restric-
tion, via Bacon, of the privilege, is unusually full and colorful, indicating
that he saw the significance of everything that was said, and exactly what
was said:

> Her highness thinketh that it not meet that any sholde have further lybertie
> to speke or talke yn that howse of any matter *other then that which is there to be
> proponed* and that they sholde leave to talk *rhetoricè* and speak *logicè* to leave
> long tales . . . that going effectually to the matter they might dyspatche *that
> they were sent for* & that they might the souner returne home. . . . This doune
> the Quene arose wishing they wolde be more quiet than they were at the last
> tyme.[56]

Hooker sat with Fleetwood on a committee to polish the Bristol trade Bill,
his only committee assignment, and one of which he was exorbitantly
fond.[57] And Vernon Snow points out that in September 1572 Fleetwood,
along with Sir Peter Carew, Hooker's patron, Sir Thomas Wroth, and
Henry Knollys, were authorized to enter the Tower to look for records.[58]
Whatever the purpose of their search, Snow surmised that Hooker thereby
obtained a manuscript of the *Modus tenendi parliamentum*. This he edited and
prefixed to two separate issues of his own *Order and usage of the keeping of a
Parlement in England*, which appeared, apparently privately printed, between

May 1571 and November 1575, one dedicated to Sir William Fitzwilliam, the Lord Deputy of Ireland, the other to the mayor and civic leaders of Exeter.[59] In the preface to the Fitzwilliam edition, Hooker described the research he personally conducted after his term of service in the 1571 parliament: "I did then confer with the exemplars and presidents of tholde and aunceint Parlements used in tymes past within the said Realme of England," and having found two, one dating from Edward I and the other, he believed, from Edward the Confessor, he chose the latter, stating his reasons in the language of ancient constitutionalism: "as wel for antiquities sake, as also for a presedent to the good government in tholde yeeres" (p. 206).

The *Modus* insists on the importance of the Commons, or "communitates," so that, while any of the other elements may be absent without abrogating the Parliament, the absence of the Commons voids the proceedings. More strikingly, the *Modus* offers a model for direct criticism of the monarch: "If, for example, they argue that the King does not govern them as he should and mention particular matters in which he has not ruled correctly, then there would be no parliament at all."[60] And it contains a section devoted to the king's *required* presence, a matter on which Richard II's Commons had taken a strong stand by way of the Lords Appellants.[61]

The importance of the *Modus* for my story consists in the way in which Hooker's modernization of it, the *Order and usage*, became imbricated with the *Chronicles*, and how that work was perceived at the time. Was it, in fact, merely a handbook of parliamentary procedure? Or was it even then understood in something of the same way that the *Modus* itself was taken in the seventeenth century? Sir Edward Coke, Speaker of the Commons in 1593, makes an interesting confusion between the two, and on a point that the *Chronicles* had rendered ideological:

> At first we were all one House and sat together, by a precedent which I have of a Parliament holden before the Conquest by Edward the Son of Etheldred. For there were Parliaments before the conquest. This appeareth in a Book which a grave Member of this House delivered unto me, which is Intituled *Modus tenendi Parliamentum;* . . . And this Book declareth how we all sat together, but the Commons sitting in presence of the King and amongst the Nobles disliked it, and found fault that they had not free liberty to speak. And upon this reason that they might speak more freely, being out of the Royal sight of the King, and not amongst the great Lords so far their betters, the House was divided and came asunder.[62]

If Hooker was the "grave Member" in question, as Snow surmised, it is all the more interesting to note that Coke here conflated the *Modus*, which says nothing of the sort, with Hooker's statement in his *Order and usage* that the development of the separate Houses was for the protection of the freedom of speech of the less powerful members:

> th'olde usage and maner was that all the whole degrees of the parlement, sat togither in one house, and every man that had there to speak: did it openly before the king and his whole Parlement, but heerof did growe many inconveniences, and therfore to avoid the great confusions which are in such great assemblies: as also to cut of th'occasions of displeasures which eftsoones did happen, when a mean man speaking his conscience freely, either could not be heard, or fel into the displeasure of his betters [the division of the Houses occurred].[63]

Snow states that Hooker is "the first commentator to discuss the evolution of parliament from a unicameral body to a multicameral assembly" (p. 153). But Hooker's causal relation between bicameralism and freedom of debate in the Commons had been anticipated in Holinshed's description of its genesis: "that everie man may have free libertie to utter what he thinketh, they are appointed to sit in severall chambers" (2:66).

When Hooker's *Order and usage* was reprinted in the 1587 edition of the *Chronicles*, it could be read as a modern redaction of the *Modus*, and manuscript copies of that version, as well as of the separately printed pamphlets, show that individual readers went to the *Chronicles* to find a copy. In addition to his liberal explanation for bicameralism, Hooker had incorporated several aspects of the *Modus* that seem to speak to the Elizabethan context. That the presence of the Commons, alone of the estates, is essential for legislation, was carefully stated, in language derived from the *Modus* but brilliantly adapted:

> If the Commons be summoned, and wil not come, or comming wil not appeer, or *appeering wil not consent to doo anything, aledging some just and weightie and great cause.* The King (in these caces) cannot with his Lords devise, make, or establish any Law. (p. 182; italics added)

Moreover, Hooker *three times* insisted on the need to keep debates secret;[64] and after having given the conventional request for freedom of debate as the Speaker made it "that . . . every one of the house may have libertie of speech, and freely to utter, speake and declare his minde and oppinion to any Bil or question *to be proponed*" (p. 166; italics added), he returned several pages later to the topical question of who retained the initiative to propose the parliamentary agenda. It cannot be a coincidence that what he had so fully noted in his *Journal*, the queen's denial of this initiative to anyone but herself, is reclaimed in the *Order and usage* for the members of either House:

Also every person having voices in Parlement: hath free libertie of speach to speak his minde, oppinion and judgement to any matter proponed, *or of him self to propone any matter for the commoditie of the Prince and of the common welth.* (p. 184; italics added)[65]

So, in conclusion, if we read John Hooker's account of parliamentary procedure attentively, its implications extend considerably beyond the territory of procedure alone and merge in spirit with Raphael Holinshed's version of ancient constitutionalism. Each of them was capable, as was J. E. Neale four centuries later, of drawing back in embarrassment when libertarian tactics in the Commons crossed some kind of boundary. Holinshed had disliked the behavior of certain members in Henry VIII's 1531 parliament; Hooker's preface to his two treatises complained about the presence in the Commons he had observed of the "rash and yung councellors of Rohoboham" (p. 123);[66] and his self-serving account of his experience in the Irish parliament of 1568, which served as the pretext for inserting his *Order and usage* into the *Chronicles*, was almost entirely focused upon discipline. In addition, his lack of sympathy with Irish nationalism led him to deliver there a speech on the royal prerogative that, had it been given in the 1572 parliament, would certainly have alienated him from Fleetwood and other defenders of privilege. Yet the fact remains that the boundary Hooker wished to police between decency and repression in the Commons was in slow but constant movement, though not without many reversals, away from what is pleasantly referred to as personal monarchy, and in the direction of constitutional government. To that movement, Harrison's bold proposition about Parliament's role, Holinshed's demonstration of that role in the history of the medieval parliaments, and Hooker's disinterring of the *Modus* and development of an early modern handbook that incorporated its spirit made a not inconsiderable contribution.

SEVEN   ᴥ *Religion*

T he title of this chapter is slightly misleading, in that its real subject
is not religious doctrine or practice, but the convergence of church
and state in the enforcement of religious orthodoxy. This was a
topic in which the *Chronicles* were deeply invested, although individual
chroniclers differed as to whether this convergence was legitimate or desirable. We have already seen evidence of William Harrison's desire for further reforms of the English church, and his views on Erastianism expressed
in a bold defence against the queen's own policy of suppression of the
"prophecyings" that Archbishop Grindal had also defended, to his cost. At
the other end of the religious spectrum was her policy of rigorous dealing
with Roman Catholics, a topic that dominates the "Continuation" of the
English chronicles in 1587, where the trials of Edmund Campion and others accused of Jesuit conspiracy appear as *the* political events that define the
period from 1570 through 1584.

    We must, I think, conclude that Abraham Fleming was an ardent sup-
porter of the Elizabethan merger of church and state, and of the anti-
Catholic measures that resulted from Elizabeth's excommunication. But
however much he railed at Campion, Francis Throckmorton, or William
Parry, the effects of his overemphasis of these events brought clearly into
view the issue that Holinshed had himself introduced by imagining the
possibility of freedom of conscience. For 13 April 1579, Fleming reported

that "Matthew Hamont, by his trade a ploughwrite of Hetharset three miles from Norwich, was convented before the bishop of Norwich, for that he denied Christ our saviour":

> At the time of his appearance it was objected that he had published these heresies following. That the new testament and gospell of Christ are but meere foolishnesse, a storie of man, or rather a meere fable . . . that the Holie ghost is not God . . . that baptisme is not necessarie in the church of God, neither the use of the sacrament of the bodie and bloud of Christ. For the which heresies he was condemned in the consistorie, and sentence was pronounced against him . . . And bicause he spake words of blasphemie (not to be recited) against the queenes majestie and others of hir councell, he was by the recorder, master sergeant Windham, and the maior sir Robert Wood of Norwich condemned to lose both his eares, which were cut off on the thirteenth of Maie in the market place of Norwich, and afterwards, to wit on the twentith of Maie, he was burned in the castell dich of Norwich. (4:405–6)

This episode illustrates (unself-consciously?) the interinvolvement of political and religious repression in the second phase of Elizabeth's reign, a confusion that the government was concerned *not* to make visible to the public.

For 1583 Fleming recorded that "Elias Thakar tailor was hanged at saint Edmunds burie in Suffolke on the fourth of June, and John Coping Shoomaker on the sixt of the same moneth, for spreading and mainteining certeine bookes seditiouslie penned by one Robert Browne against the received booke of English common praier, established by the lawes of this realme their bookes (so manie as could be found) were burned before them" (4:505). And 10 January 1585, the *Chronicles* report that William Carter was convicted of treason and hung, drawn, and quartered for printing *The Treatise of Schism* at his secret London Press (4:511).

These events evidently created unfavorable publicity, in response to which was published in December 1583 an anonymous pamphlet now attributed to Burghley, *The Execution of Justice in England*, shortly after joined by *A Declaration of the Favorable Dealing of Her Majesty's Commissioners*, both in defence of the state against charges of torture, and having wrongfully applied the law of treason against those who were merely writers or publishers.[1] It is "pretended" (wrote Burghley) that "these late malefactors . . . offended but as scholers, or bookemen; or at the most but as persons that onelie in words and doctrine, and not with armour did favour and helpe the rebels and enimies." To which Burghley countercharged that "their persons have not made the warre, but their directions and counsels have set up the rebellions" (4:531). An Elizabethan reader could see the inclusion of this government pamphlet in the *Chronicles* as proof of the political and religious loyalty of the chroniclers; or he might, setting it beside Holinshed's plea for "libertie of conscience" and the settlement of religious disagreement "rather . . . with the word than with the sword" (4:264), conclude that the tolerationist position was, after all, rather easier to defend.

Those who had read Cardinal William Allen's response to Cecil's pamphlet, *A True, Sincere, and Modest Defense of English Catholics*, published in August 1584, would also have seen his defence of William Carter, "a poor innocent artisan, who was made away only for printing a Catholic book, *De schismate*, in which no word was found against the state, the quarrel only most unjustly being made upon a certain clause which by no likely honest construction could appertain to the Queen's person; viz., that the Catholic religion should once have the upper hand of heresy and Judith cut off the head of Holofernes, which they in their extreme jealousy and fear of all things would needs wrest against Her Majesty."[2] In other words, the issue of whether religion was being persecuted under the pretence that it was politically dangerous to the state was set squarely before the public, in a case where the innocence of the protagonist from anything approaching treason was self-evident. And one of the most ironic moments in this debate occurred in November 1590, when Elizabeth ordered a *second* castration of the 1587 *Chronicles*, on the grounds that they contained a tactless account of the trial and execution of Edmund Campion, and the chronicler's evaluation that he "died not for treason but for Religion." The irony resides in the fact that it was Abraham Fleming, champion anti-Romanist, who was responsible for this suggestion.[3]

The point of beginning near the end of the sorry story of state religion in the structure of the *Chronicles* is to sharpen the ironies that some, at least, of their readers would have been able to perceive in this turn of events. That is to say, the earlier history of England, as Holinshed retold it with his own differences of emphasis from the medieval (and usually monastic) chroniclers, had been occasionally dominated by the efforts of the monarchy, in collaboration with the upper clergy, to eradicate any challenges to orthodoxy, which was then, of course, the Roman Catholic religion. The main topic of this chapter, then, is a paradigmatic episode in that through-the-mirror world of medieval ecclesiastical polity, the story of Sir John Oldcastle, the Lollard knight, early in the reign of Henry V, and of his being burned alive, hanging in chains, for a crime so ambiguous in the historical record that it was told and retold, with different ideological emphases, throughout the sixteenth century.

In 1544 John Bale, whose efforts on behalf of the survival and transmission of English historical records are themselves legendary, attempted to rewrite one of the legends of the "proto-reformation" of the early fifteenth century. He published a revisionary account of Oldcastle's examination for heresy in 1413; of the armed rebellion that he may or may not have led in 1414; and of his eventual execution in December 1417.[4] It was in the preface to this work, as I noted in my own preface, that Bale introduced his appeal to "some learned Englyshe man . . . to set forth the inglish chronicles in their right shappe . . . *al affections set a part,*" and compared the project in importance to the vernacular transmission of the Bible (A5v).

In this program, the story of Sir John Oldcastle was to assume a privileged position, as one of those cultural icons in which are epitomized a society's conflicting and shifting values. Although the events in which Oldcastle was involved occupied Raphael Holinshed for only a few pages, the manner in which he deployed the "sources," the preceding accounts of Walsingham, Titus Livius, Edward Hall, and John Foxe, can also stand as an epitome—of the methods and purpose of the *Chronicles* as a whole. Precisely because the story is short, it provides a manageable experiment in discussing the relation of Holinshed to his sources, a topic that cannot elsewhere in this book be documented with the same completeness and precision. And insofar as Holinshed withheld judgement on the crucial issue (what did Oldcastle and his followers actually do, and why were they executed?), this episode stands in little for the principles of open-mindedness and freedom of information, as that bears particularly on historiography. This chapter, then, intertwines several themes: the historiography of Raphael Holinshed, as compared to those who preceded him; the connected topics of book distribution, translation, and literacy; and the development of the English reformation, from what has been defined as its "premature" anticipation at the end of the fourteenth and beginning of the fifteenth centuries, to the middle of the Elizabethan era.

The Oldcastle story constituted from the beginning an unstable component of Henry V's own legend, of his reputation as the most successful incarnation of English nationalism. That reputation involved internationally a commitment to an aggressive military foreign policy and domestically a strong alignment between church and state in the interests of national unity. Modern readers are more familiar with the military aspect of Henry V's character, defined for the record by the battle of Agincourt, and transmitted to popular culture by Shakespeare's play, and its transformations into film for audiences of the 1940s and 1990s, by Sir Laurence Olivier and Kenneth Branagh respectively. This was equally true for the popular culture of the fifteenth and sixteenth centuries. Immediately after Agincourt there were ballads written celebrating the English victory, which survive in many manuscripts.[5] And we know, from the existence of the *Famous Victories of Henry V,* as well as what appear to be references to two other plays on this subject, that Henry V was popularly celebrated by the Elizabethan stage as the military leader par excellence.[6]

One can fully understand the epic impulse in the fifteenth-century balladeers and perhaps (though this is more debatable) in the sixteenth-century playwrights; but it is clear that some modern historians have equally yearned for the model of ruthless efficiency that Henry seems to have represented. In a lecture originally delivered to the Workers' Educational Association in London in November 1954 and subsequently incorporated into his summary of the reign, K. B. McFarlane offered this evaluation: "Take [Henry] all round and he was, I think, the greatest man that ever ruled England."[7] The statement rings with the popular patriotism (or its promotion) necessary to survive the Second World War and its aftermath.

I am not here concerned, however, with British nationalism or with militarism as the focus of historiographical evaluation of the past and political evaluation in the present, except insofar as they have distracted our attention from the story of Sir John Oldcastle, which spoke to the other side of Henry's character, his strategic alliance with the Church and Archbishop Arundel, and hence his acceptance of the principle of religious persecution. It is worth noting that one of the first applications of the terrible statute *De heretico comburendo,* the anti-Lollard statute of 1401 introduced by his father at the urging of Archbishop Courtenay, which provided for the first time in England the penalty of burning heretics at the stake,[8] gave Henry, as heir apparent, an opportunity for a dramatic public demonstration of his own orthodoxy. As Holinshed records the episode, which took place in 1410:

> During this parlement one John Badbie a tailor, or (as some write) a smith, being convict of heresie, was brought into Smithfield, and there in a tun or pipe burnt to death, *in pitifull manner.* The kings eldest sonne the lord Henrie prince of Wales being present, offered him his pardon, first before the fire was kindled, if he would have recanted his opinions; and after when the fire was kindled, hearing him make a roring noise *verie pitifullie,* the prince caused the fire to be plucked backe, and exhorting him being with *pitifull paine* almost dead, to remember himselfe, and renounce his opinions, promising him not onelie life, but also three pence a daie so long as he lived to be paid out of the kings coffers: but he having recovered his spirits againe, refused the princes offer, choosing eftsoones to tast the fire, and so die, than to forsake his opinions: Whereupon the prince commanded, that he should be put into the tun againe, from thencefoorth not to have anie favour or pardon at all, and so it was doone, and the fire put to him againe, and he consumed to ashes. (3:48-49; italics added)

Although the source here is Walsingham, who saw the story as proof of Henry's magnanimity, Holinshed's triple emphasis on the "pitiful" aspect of this case produces an effect quite different from that which Walsingham intended.[9] At any rate, when after his coronation Henry received complaints from Arundel that Oldcastle had been supporting unorthodox preaching and was in possession of heretical books, after trying personal persuasion unsuccessfully Henry agreed to hand over his old friend and companion in arms to the ecclesiastical authorities, and may even have personally ordered his arrest. It was after his formal examination and condemnation that Acton and other supporters of Oldcastle were themselves arrested and executed, on the grounds that they had led an armed insurrection against church and state. The question that Bale and his successors in the Protestant tradition wished to bring to the attention of later readers was whether Oldcastle and his followers were guilty as charged; whether they were, to put it sharply, vicious traitors or unjustly martyred religious reformers.

One of the most thoughtful and pertinent assessments of Henry's confrontation with Lollardry is Margaret Aston's *Lollards and Reformers*, which includes an important chapter on the transmission of Lollard texts into the sixteenth century.[10] Aston also raises a central historiographical question about the Oldcastle movement, as to whether we can trust the sources: not only the early chroniclers, but also the official documents recording the indictments against Sir Roger Acton and his colleagues. The earliest chroniclers include Walsingham, who as a monk was an inveterate enemy of the Lollards; Titus Livius de Frulovisiis, whose *Vita Henrici Quinti* was written in the context of his patronage by Humphrey, duke of Gloucester, Henry's younger brother; and the anonymous cleric who wrote the *Gesta Henrici Quinti* as explicit propaganda for use at home and abroad—domestically to justify Henry's second campaign in France and the need for additional taxes to support it, in Europe to fortify Henry's negotiating position in the Council of Constance. In the next generation of historians the Oldcastle story passed to Polydore Vergil, to Fabian, and to the anonymous translator of Titus Livius, who produced what is known as *The First English Life of Henry V*, in order to apply its lessons to the times of Henry VIII.[11] For all of these writers Oldcastle is a demon whose appearance at the beginning of the reign has to be exorcised before the miracle of Agincourt can take place. Since Holinshed himself draws attention to his consultation, thanks to John Stow, of *The First English Life*,[12] it seems fair to cite its account (which we know to be erroneous on at least one crucial point) as representative of the standard position:

> In the first yeare of this most excellent Kings raigne, . . . fortuned a marvelous insurrection of heretiks; of which supersticious sect two knights were

principall chieftaines, of whome the one was Sr. John Oldcastell, Lord Cobham, who before the Kings coronacion was forsaken of the Kinge for the same opinions, and utterlie abject from his service and presence. And th'other knight was named Sr. Roger Acton. After these two knights as chieftaines followed a great multitude of people, also erringe from the waie of trueth, with theire armed power intendinge to oppresse the church, the spirituallitie, the Kinge and the realme. When the newes thereof was first brought to the Kinge at his Mannor of Eltham in the solemnitie of the Epiphanie, and that he was informed that they were assembled in a fielde near London . . . called Ficket fielde, immediatlie . . . the good Kinge hasted him to his mannor of Westminster, where in all hast possible he assembled his people, *with whome he sent his Brother, the Duke of Clarence, against those scelerate and misbeleevinge rebellions,* whome almost without resistance he vanquished, and tooke part of them, and put the remnant to flight. And those that were taken the Kinge caused to be put to execucion after theire deserts. Amongest whome the aforesaide Lord Cobham was taken and dampned by the Church, was put into the Tower, from whence he escaped by breakinge of the prison, and fledd into Wales. . . . *Thus the first victorie of that noble King after his Coronacion was against these cursed supersticious heretiques for Christ and the defence of the Church of God, in the defence and supportacion of our Catholique faith.*[13]

In this opening manifesto, the sections in italics were either additions to or expansions of Titus Livius by the Henrician writer, whose work has been dated quite precisely as having been compiled in the context of Henry VIII's treaty with France in 1513, which the historian chose to interpret as the "reconciliation of the same French King and his confederates unto our ghostly mother of the Church of Rome."[14] Apart from its agenda, this account perpetuates the mistake of transposing Oldcastle's condemnation by the ecclesiastical authorities and subsequent imprisonment and escape from *before* the confrontation in St. Giles' or Fickett's Field to its aftermath. Not trivially, possible cause is therefore made into legitimate consequence.

As Aston points out, we know a good deal about the Lollard program for reform from their own documents; but

when argument was translated into action and issued in rebellion, the evidence for Lollard deeds and intentions comes almost completely from the other, and hostile side. The story can hardly be a whole one when we have to watch it at moments of crisis from an entirely adverse viewpoint.

Aston adds a note to the effect that the *Coram Rege* Rolls and the Ancient Indictments are the main sources for the events of 1414, and that on other occasions, such as after the Peasants' Revolt of 1381, it has been shown that such indictments might lie. "When it comes to determining the aims and intentions of the Lollard rebels," she warns, "one is usually not in a position to verify the facts."[15] Aston does not, however, ultimately question whether a Lollard armed rebellion of any significant scale occurred in 1414, precisely that which Bale and consequently Foxe subjected to interrogation.

It is worth looking more closely at this historiographical dilemma. As Aston admits:

> None of the bills written "in his favour" which were advertised and circulated by Sir John Oldcastle and his accomplices seems to have survived, but the judicial proceedings taken after the revolt provide the names of persons who wrote and distributed them, (such as Thomas Ile of Braybrooke), as well as indications of the aims of the rebels, which, *presumably*, they contained. (italics added)

The objectives there attributed to the Lollards were "wholly to annul the royal estate as well as the estate and office of prelates and religious orders in England, and to kill the king, his brothers, . . . the prelates and other magnates of the kingdom, and to turn men of religion . . . to secular occupations: totally to despoil cathedrals and other churches and religious houses of their relics and other ecclesiastical goods, and to level them completely to the ground." Oldcastle himself was to be appointed regent. And, Aston concluded, *"as is well known,"* the adherents to these plans proposed to meet together, from various parts of England, "to the number of 20 thousand men," at St. Giles' Field, on 10 January 1414 (italics added).[16] Between "presumably," which retains a shadow of the suspicion raised earlier that even official indictments may lie, and the summative phrase, "as is well known," lies a gap of credibility which, given the nature of the sources (and Walsingham's figure of twenty thousand persons has long been recognized as at least an exaggeration), it is no longer possible to close.[17]

It is not my purpose here to attempt to erase "Oldcastle's rebellion" from the record, although, as will appear in what follows, there do seem to be grounds for doubt: not only about Walsingham's figures but also about Oldcastle's presence at Fickett's Field and hence about his direct responsibility for what happened there. More important still is the question that would subsequently be raised by Foxe, as to whether what happened there was really an armed rebellion, a more peaceful demonstration, or merely a clandestine religious meeting whose motives and scale had been gravely distorted. My point in rehearsing these doubts is, rather, to draw a distinction between the completely biased though revisionary history of Bale and Foxe, and the procedure of Raphael Holinshed, who might appear better to represent Bale's ideal of a historiography "al affections set a part" than did Bale himself. Indeed, Holinshed echoed this phrase when he assessed the causes of the Peasants' Revolt of 1381, for which Walsingham is again a primary source, warning his readers that "they that wrote in those daies, may happilie in that behalfe misse the trueth, in construing things according to their affections" (2:751). In attempting to produce a version of "Oldcastle's rebellion" that set affections aside, or, better still, rendered them visible, Holinshed passed on to his readers a set of doubts about what had actually happened in 1414 that are really quite striking, both in their debts to those who preceded him and in their independence.

It is, of course, true that Oldcastle and his followers inherited a situation already politicized in 1381, when the Peasants' Revolt brought the teachings of Wycliffe into disrepute as possibly having motivated the uprising. As Aston put it, "a heretical movement and a major upheaval among the lower orders of society had arrived, in point of time, together" (p. 1), and the coincidence formed in the minds of Richard's government an ugly appearance. Despite the fact that Wycliffe emphatically denounced the rising, and that there is no hard evidence to connect either his doctrines or Lollard preaching with the revolt, "somehow, through deliberate falsification, fixed prejudice, or plausible hypothesis, the conviction seems to have become established that Lollardy was associated with revolt. And opinions once lodged are themselves historical facts: and, as such, may influence events."[18]

But there is some evidence that the Lollards had more in mind than purging the medieval church of what they regarded as decadent or unnecessary beliefs and practices: the hierarchy of the priesthood, celibacy, transubstantiation, auricular confession, pilgrimages, and the worship of images. Not all of the twelve articles of the manifesto nailed to the door of Westminster Hall (the parliament house) and St. Paul's in 1395 targeted church doctrine. The *first* of these articles called for the disendowment of temporalities (the worldly possessions of the church), the tenth opposed itself to war and capital punishment ("He who lives by the sword shall die by the sword"), and the last inveighed against "unnecessary arts," including those of goldsmiths and weapon makers. Clearly, the issue of disendowment was the immediate motive for the church's strong campaign to suppress the Lollards and was capable of disquieting extension to the realm of secular property; but it is worth noting that Lollard pacifism could also have seemed particularly dangerous to a monarch like Henry V who intended to make wars of aggression his strongest claim to legitimacy.[19] The 1395 manifesto had ended with verses that press home an antiwar message:

Qui reges estis, populis quicunque praeestis,
Qualiter his gestis gladios prohibere potestis?[20]

There is also a final reference to a larger book of Lollard policy that had already been circulated.

In Bale's account of Oldcastle there is an odd reference to book distribution: "He admonished the kinges, as Richard the second, Henry the
fourth, and Henry the fyft, of the clergies manifolde abuses, and put into
the parlament house certain bokes concerning their just reformacion, both
in the yeare of our lord 1395 and in the yere 1410." The first of these
"books" (perhaps bills) Bale attributes to Oldcastle himself, and cites its
opening line: "Quando ecclesia Angliae" (A6v); the second he attributes to
John Purvey. This statement needs to be used with caution, since Oldcastle
was not a member of Parliament until 1404. The first evidence of
Oldcastle's writing on behalf of church reform, his letters to Wok of
Waldstein and King Wenceslaus of Bohemia, date from 1410 and ca. 1411.
But we should perhaps be equally sceptical of W. T. Waugh's notion of
Oldcastle as a man of few intellectual abilities and small learning, "slow to
grasp new ideas but tenacious of anything once assimilated."[21] The bias of
this early-twentieth-century biography, if not quite as visible as Bale's, is
evident in its arbitrary decisions as to which early chroniclers to believe on
which points; and it scarcely demonstrates Oldcastle's lack of intellectual
ability to note that Archbishop Arundel ordered at his trial that the "authorised doctrines on the chief matters at issue should be written out for
him, and translated into English, on account of Oldcastle's lack of learning
(*pro leviori intellectu eiusdem*),"[22] when Oldcastle had extensively demonstrated
his literacy in English—the reformers' language of ideological choice—his
forensic skills, and his command of the available media of publicity. Long
before printing began, specifically by 1388, the authorities recognized that
a lively traffic had developed in what they called *published* "books, booklets,
schedules and quires," and Lollard posting of bills and broadsheets is well
attested.[23]

By Bale, we are told that Oldcastle "toke paper & penne in hand, & so
wrote a Christen confession or rekening of his faith . . . and both signed
and sealed it with his owne hande. Wherein he also answereth to the iiii
chefest Articles that the Archebishop layed against him,"[24] and took it to
Henry, who refused to read it. In preparation for the ecclesiastical examination itself, Oldcastle "caused . . . the aforsayd confession of his faith to
be coppyed agayne and the answere also (whiche he had made to the iiii
articles propounded agaynst hym) to be wryten in maner of an indenture in
two sheets of paper. That whan he shuld come to his answere, he might

geve the one copy unto the Archbisshop, and reserve the other to himselfe" (C3v). This Oldcastle read before his examiners. When questioned further, Oldcastle refused to "declare his minde nor yet answere unto hys articles [other] than was Expresslye in hys Wryttinge there conteyned" (C6v). This testimony by Bale, who used both Arundel's "Magnus Processus" and the report of Thomas Netter of Walden, himself one of the examining clerics,[25] is particularly interesting in showing the strategies of self-defence that Oldcastle may very well have used, and suggests that literacy was already not only a tool of Lollardism, but also recognized as a political and juridical weapon.

According·to Bale's account of the second examination, which was taken down verbatim by two official notaries, Oldcastle conducted his defence with a tremendous aplomb and theatrical effect. He questioned the authority of his examiners, citing Scripture as the only true adjudicator of his case:

> Where do ye fynd in all Gods lawe, that ye should thus syt in judgement on any Christen man, or yet sentens anye other man unto death as ye do here daily? No ground have ye in all the scripturs so lordely to take it uppon ye, but in Annas and Cayphas, which sate thus uppon Chryst, and upon his Apostles after his ascensyon (D7v)

When they pressed him on the question of whether he would worship the cross, he "spreade his armes abroade" and said "This is a very crosse yea, and so moche better than your crosse of wood, in that it was created of God. Yet will not I seke to have it worshipped" (E4r). And after the bill of his condemnation had been read aloud, deprived of a jury of his peers, he took his case to the common people:

> And therwith he turned him unto the People, casting hys handes abroade, and saying with a very loude voice. Good Christen people, for Gods love be wel ware of these men. For they will else begyle you and lead you blinde-lynge into hell with them selves" (F1r).

Did Oldcastle actually say these things? These things exactly? This is not, of course, any longer possible to determine. Arundel's "Magnus Processus" in the *Fasciculi Zizaniorum* omits the first of these statements, as it clearly omits much else that was said on both sides; the second appears in a less colorful (and therefore less plausible) form as Oldcastle's statement that he would only worship the body of Christ on the cross and not the cross itself; and for the third the Latin text replicates Bale's version almost exactly, with the exception of that striking word "blindelynge."[26] We might here decide to choose the unconventional and unexpected reading over the flat, the orthodox, and the unmemorable, since the former would have been difficult to invent, the latter all too easy to substitute in a document whose principles, as well as whose function, were regularization and control.

But to quote from Oldcastle's examination is to leap ahead to the events of 1413. There is another issue we need to follow from 1395 onwards, of equal pertinence to Holinshed's *Chronicles*. While the disendowment issue was unquestionably the lever that turned the political machine against the Lollards, what complicated its turning was the role that the medieval parliaments seemed to have played, and the fact that economic anticlericalism was rampant in the knightly class in Richard's reign and thereafter, at least until what happened in 1414 poured very cold water on such feelings. By 1410 the issue had taken the form of a petition sent by the Commons to Henry IV and lords of the upper house outlining certain reappropriations of church properties. From Walsingham onwards, it was claimed that this was a sweeping proposal of confiscation indeed, a story accepted by some modern historians, denied by others.[27] Holinshed, following Hall, bought into it, explaining seductively how church revenues "lewdlie spent, consumed and wasted by the bishops, abbats, and priors," could be reappropriated to fund 150 earls, 1,500 knights, 6,200 esquires, and 100 hospitals for the poor. As Holinshed put it, the king "misliked of the motion, & thereupon commanded that from thenceefoorth they should not presume to studie about anie such matters" (3:48). Significantly, "an other thing the commons sued to have granted unto them, but could not obteine" in 1410 was some modification of *De heretico comburendo*. The parliamentarians were warned that any attempt to have the legislation withdrawn or amended would result only in its being "made more rigorous and sharpe for the punishment of such persons" (3:48). At the Leicester Parliament in April 1414, the petition respecting disendowment reappeared, with the addition: "and the king to have cleerelie to his coffers twentie thousand pounds"; a budget, as it were, with something for everyone! (3:65). Aston suggests that something similar had been mooted in the Coventry Parliament of 1404, was discussed and refuted in the parliamentary session of 1406, and might even have been in the air in 1395. Comparable proposals had gone before the parliament of 1371;[28] and, as Hall pointed out, and Holinshed followed him exactly, the 1414 petition was recognized as a reincarnation of that "exhibited in the parlement holden at Westminster in the eleventh yeare of king Henrie the fourth (which by reason the king was then troubled with civill discord, came to none effect" (3:65). In other words, from the middle of Richard II's reign through to 1414, when the clergy finally discovered what Holinshed called "a sharpe invention" (the

war with France) to put a stop to it, the medieval parliaments were the site
of a struggle between anticlericalism and secular acquisitiveness, on the
one hand, and on the other a reaction against the Lollards led by the bishops but fuelled, no doubt, by fears of the lower orders. Given the constant
reappearance of this issue in successive parliaments, it is worth considering
whether, if we wish to credit the occurrence of Oldcastle's rebellion, it
might not have been partly motivated by the perceived failure of earlier attempts to move through Parliament; yet by the same token, for the
Commons to *return* to the theme of disendowment in 1414, having just witnessed the execution of twenty-eight Lollard leaders, must signify very
considerable determination.

What neither Hall nor Holinshed chose to report was that the
Leicester Parliament *also* effectively eradicated Lollardry as an open political movement by enrolling the secular arm against it. As the church had
sponsored the earlier legislation and persuaded Parliament to give over into
ecclesiastical jurisdiction the rights of arrest and incarceration for those
suspected of heresy, so now the state was to create its own decentralized
machine, one that would make concealment virtually impossible. Heresy
hunting became part of the job description of the chancellor, treasurer, justices, and all local officers. Secular courts were authorized to receive heresy
indictments, and judges given full powers of inquiry into sermons, schools,
and "conventicles," a hostile term for nonconformist meetings that now entered the culture definitively. In 1416 this system was extended by
Archbishop Chichele to an ecclesiastical surveillance system, with biannu-
al inquiries into every deanery. As Aston put it, "the mesh of controls which
persistent heretics had to evade was now closer, and also double. . . . If
Lollardy emerged full grown from the head of rebellion the church had
thereby acquired most strong defensive armor."[29] In the late sixteenth century a very similar story could be told, as the antagonistic relation between
church and sect, between center and margins, was replayed, now with
Archbishop Whitgift in the seat at the center, and the Presbyterian and
Puritan reformers occupying the marginal and vulnerable position. Once
again, attempts to make their case in Parliament, in 1572 through the
Admonitions, and in 1584, when Cope's "Bill and Book" were presented,[30]
would provoke the same message from Elizabeth that Henry IV sent his
Commons in 1410, that "from thencefoorth they should not presume to
studie about anie such matters." Whitgift's notorious articles of 1583, the
visitations of parishes referred to in the preceding chapter, as well as his
1586 regulations of the press, effectively prevented such study by private
citizens. The two editions of Holinshed's *Chronicles,* in 1577 and 1587,
could scarcely have been innocent of the parallel.

"That Great Valhalla of the English Reformation":[31]
The Historiographical Countertradition

The coming of the Reformation to England necessitated a reversal of historical values, one from which Henry V himself was only partly exempted, but which required the transformation of Sir John Oldcastle and other Lollard figures from villains into heroes, from subversives to proto-Protestant martyrs. John Bale wrote from exile during Henry VIII's reign, and in explicit continuance of the work of Tyndale, who seems to have been responsible for the publication of a little *Boke of thorpe or Oldecastelle*, published in 1530, and condemned by Archbishop Warham and John Stokesley, bishop of London, in 1531.[32] Bale describes his own historiographical method in the *Brefe Chronycle* (itself proscribed in 1546)[33] as follows:

> I remember that xiiii yeares ago the true servaunt of God Willyam Tindale put into the press a certain brefe examination of the sayd lorde Cobham. The which examination was written in the tyme of the sayd lordes trouble by a certain frinde of his & so reserved in copyes unto this our age. But sens that tyme I have founde it in theyr owne writtings (which were than his uttre ennemyes) in a moche more ample fourme than there. Speciallye in the great processe which Thomas Arundell the Archbischop of Caunterbury made than against him written by hys owne notaryes and clerkes, tokened also with his owne signe & seale, and so directed unto Rychard Clyfford than Bisshop of London with a generall commaundement to have it than published by him and by the other Byshops the whole realme over.
>
> Furthermore I have seane it in a copy of the writting which the said Richard Clifforde sent unto Robert Mascall a Carmelyte fryer & Bishop of Herforde under his signe and seale & in a coppy of his also directed to the Archdeacons of Herforde & Shrewesbury. . . . Besides all this Thomas Walden, being in those daies the kinges confessoure, and present at hys examination, condemnacion & excreacion, regestred it amonge other Processes more in hys boke called Fasciculus zizaniorum wiclevii. . . . Only such reasons have I added therunto as the aforenamed Thomas Walden proponed to him in the tyme of the examinacion, as he mencioneth in his first and second bokes adversus Wiclevius as with the maner of hys Godlye departing out of his frayle lyfe, which I found in other writinges and chronicles. (A3v–4r)

As Aston observes, Bale, more than any other English reformer, deserves the credit of having grasped, as early as 1544, that "the exile of the Papacy from England meant the ending of a whole historical tradition" and the opportunity for a new one; and what he also perceived, and Aston, with matching brilliance, recognized, was that the new historiographical project "involved more than the piecemeal editing of heretical literature":

> It meant taking over enemy territory, and using enemy ammunition. Official records, works compiled by the authorities to condemn and eradicate heresy, were to be used as they had never been used before; for an anti-Catholic purpose.[34]

Thus somehow Bale acquired possession of the famous documentary history, the *Fasciculi Zizaniorum*, which contained, among other things, the text of Arundel's "Magnus Processus," and Oldcastle's "uttre enemies" were enrolled in his defence, long after they relinquished control over those materials.

It was also part of Bale's agenda to point out the inevitable presence of bias in preceding chroniclers, especially in Polydore Vergil, as a writer in direct communication with the pope, and as one, moreover, who manifestly got his dates wrong. John Foxe, as we know, inherited Bale's agenda, had access to many of his documents, and for the story of Sir John Oldcastle inserted the whole of Bale's *Brefe Chronycle* into the 1563 edition of the *Acts and Monuments* along with materials from the *Fasciculi Zizaniorum* and from Fabian. But in the story of sixteenth-century historiography, Foxe is preceded by Edward Hall. In Hall, whose chronicle was explicitly in the service of Henry VIII, the process of creating a new, Protestant archive was uncertain and transitional, as befitted a reign in which the break with Rome was manifestly motivated by the king's nonreligious and unedifying needs, and which was itself distinguished by its persecuting temper, beginning with the execution of Sir Thomas More for *refusing* to abandon his allegiance to Rome, and concluding in 1546 with the racking and burning of Anne Askew for convictions of the opposite temper. Hall's own signature appears on Askew's confession, indicating that he was willing to participate in Henry's reaction against those forces of change he had himself unleashed. There is some reason to believe, however, that Hall's own convictions were unsettled, and that their instability surfaced in his treatment of the Oldcastle episode.

Hall's account of the opening of Henry V's reign is heavily dependent on the fifteenth-century chroniclers, from whom he inherited his eulogistic, not to say hagiographical, tone with respect to the king himself; his emphasis on Henry's personal reformation ("he determined with hymself to put on the shape of a new man . . . turning insolencie and wildnes into gravitie and sobernes," p. 46); and his interest in the Council of Constance, at which Henry established himself as a significant force in international Christendom.

Hall's account of Oldcastle's rebellion, however, is not only more succinct than that of Walsingham, Titus Livius, and the anonymous author of the *Gesta,* but entirely free of their hostility.[35] Hall, by comparison, sounds noncommittal and nonevaluative. An innocent reader would be unable to detect where his own opinions reside:

> During this firste yere, sir John Old Castle, whiche by his wife was called lorde Cobham, a valiant capitain and an hardy gentleman, was accused to the Archbishop of Cauntorbury of certain poynctes of heresy. Whiche bishoppe knowying hym to be highly in the kynges favor, declared to his highnes the whole accusacion. The kyng first having compassion of the noble man, required the prelates that if he were a straied shepe, rather by gentlenes then by rigoure to reduce hym to his old flocke. After that he sendyng for hym, godly exhorted and lovyngly admonished hym to reconcile hymself to God and his lawes. The lorde Cobham not onely thanked the kyng of his most favourable clemencye, but also declared firste to hym by mouthe and afterwarde by writyng the foundacion of his faith, the ground of his belefe and the botome of his stomacke, affirmyng his grace to be his supreme hed and competent judge & none other persone, offeryng an hundred knightes and esquires to come to his purgation, or els to fight in open listes with his accusors.
>
> The kyng not onely knowing the lawes of the reame, but also persuaded by his counsaill, that hereticall accusacions ought to be tried by the spiritual prelates, sente hym to the tower of London there to abide the determinacion of the clergie according to the statutes in and for that cace provided. After which tyme the 23 daie of Septembre,a solempne session was appoincted in the Cathedrall churche of sainct Paule, and another the 25 da of the said moneth in the hal of the Friers preachers in London, in whiche places the said lord was examined, apposed and fully heard, & in conclusion by the archbishop denounced an hereticke and so remitted again to the toure of London: From which place, ether by help of frendes or corrupcion of kepers, he prively escaped and cam into Wales, where he remained by the space of thre yeres and more.[36]

Though Hall sounds noncomittal, what he does *not* say would have carried its own message. He states only that Oldcastle was accused of heresy by Arundel and that the charge was confirmed by his formal examination. There is no indication that Oldcastle might have stood accused out of his own mouth, as Bale had enthusiastically conceded; and for Oldcastle himself, as distinct from Acton and his colleagues, Hall gives no sign that his offences included treason or sedition. Indeed, the firm statement that he escaped to Wales and remained there for three years effectively avoids the charge that he was present at Fickett's Field in January 1414.

If we can believe John Foxe, Hall's account represented a dramatic conversion away from the hostile view of the fifteenth-century chroniclers. In the 1570 edition of the *Acts and Monuments*, Foxe responded to the Catholic counterattack on the new version of Oldcastle that he and Bale had put into circulation by claiming, among other things, that Hall had been influenced by Bale's work while his own was going through the press:

> The truth hereof is this, that as the said Edward Hall . . . was about the com-
> piling of his story, . . . others there were of the same sodality, who be yet
> alive, and were then in the house of Richard Grafton, he being both the
> printer of the said book, and also, as is thought, a great helper of the penning
> of the same. It so befell, that as Hall was entering into the story of sir John
> Oldcastle, and of sir Roger Acton and their fellows,the book of John Bale,
> touching the story of the lord Cobham, was at the same time newly come
> over: which book was privily conveyed by one of his servants into the study
> of Hall, so that in turning over his books it must needs come to his hands. At
> the sight whereof, when he saw the ground and reasons in that book con-
> tained, he turned to the authors in the aforesaid book alleged; whereupon,
> within two nights after, moved by what cause, I know not, but so it was, that
> he, taking his pen, rased and cancelled all that he had written before against
> sir John Oldcastle and his fellows, and which was now ready to go to print,
> containing near to the quantity of three pages. And . . . the very selfsame first
> copy of Hall, rased and crossed with his own pen, remaineth in my hands to
> be shown and seen, as need shall require.[37]

This is a great anecdote: replete with the aura of the surreptitious book trade, anthropologically rich in its intimation of the relation between masters and their more radical servants, and at least as strong in what Aston called circumstantial detail as the official documents charging Oldcastle and his followers with treason. If Foxe's story is true, the book by Bale "newly come over" must have been the 1544 Antwerp edition of his *Brief Chronicle*, which requires what Hall was then working on to be the posthumously published edition of 1548.[38]

At any rate, Foxe proceeded to specify what had been erased from the text prepared for the press: an account derived from Polydore Vergil of how the Lollards "here in England, after the death of John Huss . . . being pricked, as he saith, with a demoniacal sting, having for their captains sir John Oldcastle the lord Cobham, and sir Roger Acton, knight," rose in arms against the king:

> All which matter, notwithstanding, the said Hall with his pen, at the sight of
> John Bale's book, did utterly extinguish and abolish; adding in the place

thereof the words of Master Bale's book, touching the accusation and condemnation of the said lord Cobham before Thomas Arundel, archbishop of
Canterbury, taken out of the letter of the said archbishop, as is in his own
story to be seen.[39]

Obviously Foxe wished that a stroke of *his* pen could "utterly extin-
guish and abolish" the main core of the Oldcastle story as Lancastrian historiography had established it—that is, as "Oldcastle's Rebellion"—and
which indeed survived his own efforts and those of Bale. His use of Hall as
the model of a convert points clearly at the goal of other recantations in the
future.

But perhaps even more telling than the psychological drama here created is Foxe's analysis of the stance that Hall ultimately adopted, when he
came to the end of the first phase of the Oldcastle story, the executions of
Acton and (by his count) twenty-eight others for heresy and treason.
"Some saie," Hall had written in 1544:

> that the occasion of their death was the conveighance of the Lorde Cobham
> out of prisone. Other write that it was bothe for treason and heresy as the
> record declareth. Certaine affirme that it was for feined causes by the spiri-
> tualtie more of displeasure then truth: the judgement whereof I leave to men
> indifferent. For surely all conjectures be not true, nor all writyinges are not
> the Gospell, & therefore because I was nether a witnes of the facte, nor pre-
> sent at the deede I overpasse that matter and begin another. (p. 49)

At this extraordinary moment, Hall uncharacteristically raised the problem
of historical verifiability and the fact of diversity of opinion.[40] And not
only did he use the ventriloquist's formula "some say . . . other write" that,
as I showed in chapter 4, William Harrison adopted from the rhetorical tradition of political protest; but he anticipated the term that, I have suggested, was definitive of the values promoted by Holinshed and his colleagues:
"The judgement whereof I leave to men *indifferent.*"

The meaning of this term as Hall uses it did not go unnoticed by Foxe,
who, being of another disposition, did not approve:

> Moreover so doubtful he is and ambiguous, in declaration of this story, that
> no great certainty can be gathered of him. First, as touching the confession
> of them, he confesseth himself that he saw it not, and therefore leaveth it at
> large: and as concerning the causes of their death, he leaveth the matter in
> doubt, not daring . . . to define or pronounce any thing thereof, but only to
> recite the surmises and minds of divers men diversely, . . . And thus your au-
> thor Hall, having recited the variety of men's opinions, determineth himself
> no certain thing thereof; but, as one *indifferent,* neither bound to the conjec-

tures of all men, nor to the writings of all men, referreth the whole judgment of the matter free unto the reader.[41]

Nevertheless, Foxe himself a few pages later testifies, perhaps unconsciously, to the difficulties of assessment, not to mention other constraints upon the Tudor historians, that might indeed lead to their pulling their punches. Referring to the doubts that he himself had cast on the existence of any Lollard conspiracy to rebellion in the first edition of *Acts and Monuments* by showing how the different chroniclers got their dates wrong, he wrote:

> touching the matter of this conspiracy, I did not affirm or define any thing thereof in my former history so precisely that he [Harpsfield] could well take any vantage thereof against me, who, in writing of this conspiracy laid against sir Roger Acton, and sir John Oldcastle, do but disjunctively or doubtfully speak thereof, not concluding certainly this conspiracy either to be true, or not true, but only proving the same not to be true at that time, as Polydore Virgil, and Edward Hall, in their histories do affirm. . . . My words are plain, and are these: "Wherefore it is evident that there was either no conspiracy at all against the king, or else that it was at some other time, or done by some other captains," &. These be my words, with others besides; in which proposition disjunctive, if either part be true, *it is enough for me*.[42] (italics added)

Foxe rightly complained that there was little probative value in the preamble to the statute passed at the Leicester Parliament, which cited "great rumours, congregations and insurrections" as the context for the new anti-Lollard legislation, and on which Harpsfield had relied as official proof of the rebellion. Entering a long debate as to the status of preambles to statutes (which Sir Nicholas Throckmorton in 1554 had already entered on the other side of the argument) Foxe declared in favor of their merely rhetorical or ideological function: in this case, "to make mountains out of molehills, first of rumours [it] maketh congregations, and from congregations riseth up to insurrections; whereas in all these rumours, congregations and insurrections, yet never a blow was given, never a stroke was stricken, no blood spilled, no furniture nor instruments of war, no sign of battle, yea no express signification of any rebellious word, or malicious fact, described in records, or yet in any chronicle" (3:358). Much of Foxe's strategy is satiric. He points to the implausibility of twenty thousands Lollards having encamped in the thickets in the "hot month of January"! "And peradventure, if truth were well sought," Foxe suggested, "it would be found at length, that instead of armies and weapons, they were coming only with their books, and with Beverly their preacher, into those thickets"

(3:359). It was part of his program, inherited from Bale, to make this contest indeed a battle of books, instead of weapons; and given the pacificist emphasis of the Lollards' manifesto, he might indeed have had truth on his side.[43]

"Closely Hid for the Time from King Henries Reach"

While Foxe scored some points in his battle with Harpsfield, not only in recording the way the early chroniclers contradict each other, but in noting the absence of official documents proving an armed insurrection,[44] even he was unwilling to go beyond the point that his Catholic predecessors were *not* indifferent, and therefore not to be trusted.[45] But his account of what *might* have happened acquired a life of its own in the historiography of Raphael Holinshed, whose account of the Oldcastle story was more than usually finely tuned.

Holinshed was familiar with Bale's scholarship, as well as with the *Acts and Monuments.* Indeed, Bale appears in the third paragraph of the first book of the history proper, after Harrison's *Description,* as "John Bale our countrieman, who in his time greatlie travelled in the search of such antiquities," and at the beginning of the second chapter appears the first of many references to Bale's *Scriptorum illustrium majoris Britanniae . . . catalogus,* which might well be called the first history of English letters. The *Catalogus* was first published in 1548 under the auspices of the Edwardian Reformation, and it reappeared in a new Basel edition at the beginning of Elizabeth's reign. It was, we remember, in William Harrison's own copy of this important work that someone inscribed Harrison's own biography, thereby enrolling him among England's major authors; and from his account of Henry II onwards, Holinshed developed the habit of listing at the end of each reign its major writers as Bale had inventoried them.

This is not to say that Holinshed accepted all of Bale's values and priorities; their attitudes to King John, in particular, were radically divergent, Bale in his play of that name presenting him as a heroic prototype of the king who was willing to assault the church's temporalities, Holinshed as the tyrannical monarch whose irresponsible behavior resulted in the signing of the two great petitions, Magna Carta and the Charta de Foresta. Yet Holinshed was attracted to the mandate Bale had articulated in the preface to his *Brefe Chronycle* of Oldcastle, the call for "some learned Englyshe man . . . to set forth the inglish chronicles in their right shappe . . . al affections set a part."

In retelling the Oldcastle story, Holinshed makes no overt mention of Bale or Foxe. The sources he cites in the margin are Titus Livius,

Walsingham, and Hall. In fact, Titus Livius is a red herring. Holinshed's account could best be described as having used a close but much condensed paraphrase of Hall as the story's frame, that frame surrounding an epitome of Walsingham's version of the events of 1414,[46] which appears to grant that an armed rebellion did indeed take place. Nevertheless, there are crucial omissions from and additions to both of his major (and incompatible) sources that result, as it were, in an entente between them, in the creation of a text that is even more "indifferent" than that of Hall. In one crucial spot—the beginning—that effect is achieved by Holinshed's having silently inserted material that he found in Foxe. Holinshed chose to open the reign with a sinister portent. Hall had dated Henry's accession with a spiritual flourish but made the coronation an afterthought:

> Henry prince of Wales . . . toke upon him the high power & regiment of this realme of Englande the xx. daie of Marche in the yere after that Christ our savior had entered into the immaculate wombe of the holy virgin his naturall mother a thousande foure hundred and xii. and was crouned the ix. daie of Aprill then next ensuying. (p. 46)

Foxe avoided dating the accession precisely, but on the coronation he was darkly specific. It took place on "the ninth day of April, called then Passion Sunday, which was an exceeding stormy day, and so tempestuous, that many did wonder at the portent thereof" (3:319). As for Holinshed, he too avoids the "papistical" dating of the accession; and remarks that Henry was crowned "the ninth of Aprill being Passion Sundaie, which was a sore, ruggie, and tempestuous day, with wind, snow and sleet, that men greatlie marvelled thereat, making diverse interpretations what the same might signifie" (3:61).

   It is perhaps overreading to see this opening as itself a procedural portent—of the historiographical method to be employed in this section of the *Chronicles*, whereby "diverse interpretations" are indeed to be encouraged; but that Holinshed has Foxe before him as he writes, and that he somewhat overgoes his model, seems inarguable.

   It is also telling that Holinshed completely omits any reference to the Council of Constance, which for Hall had served as the opening proof of Henry's benign role in Christendom at large. Yet when Holinshed embarks on the Oldcastle episode, he follows Hall almost verbatim. He would already have known from Foxe's anecdote in the 1570 edition of *Acts and Monuments* that this account was a conversion narrative under the influence of Bale; but even so there are signs that when the transmission is not verbatim, the slightest of changes may carry significance. Thus where Hall had written of Oldcastle's escape from the Tower, "from whiche place, ether by help of frendes or corrupcion of kepers, he prively escaped and cam into Wales, where he remained by the space of thre yeres and more" (p. 48), Holinshed wrote, "from which place, either by helpe of freends, or favour of keepers, he privilie escaped and came into Wales, where he remained for a season" (3:63). The first alteration, from "corrupcion" to "favor," resonates ironically with Holinshed's emphasis, derived from Walsingham, on the failure of the rewards offered by Henry for Oldcastle's recapture, a failure that Holinshed glosses as a proof of Oldcastle's great national popularity; the second, "for a season" instead of the three years or more proposed by Hall, accords with Holinshed's expressed uncertainty (which he certainly did not derive from Walsingham) as to whether Oldcastle himself had ever appeared at the head of an armed body in Fickett's Field:

> The king . . . was advertised, that sir Roger Acton knight a man of great wit and possessions, John Browne esquier, John Beverlie priest, and a great number of other were assembled in armour against the king . . . suerlie (had it not been thus prevented and staied) there had issued foorth of London to have joined with them, to the number (as it was thought) of fiftie thousand persons. . . . Diverse also that came from sundrie parts of the realme . . . chanced to light among the kings men, who being taken and demanded whither they went with such speed, answered, they came to meet with their capteine the lord Cobham.
>
> But whether he came thither at all, or made shift for himselfe to get awaie, it dooth not appeare; for he could not be heard of that time (as Thomas Walsingham confesseth) although the king by proclamation promised a thousand marks to him that could bring him foorth, with great liberties to the cities or townes that would discover where he was. By this it maie appeare, how greatly he was beloved, that there could not one be found, that for so great a reward would bring him to light. (3:63)

To a careful reader, even though this seems to be an account of an armed rising, Holinshed nowhere states that one occurred. On the contrary, it was "advertised" to the king; it was "thought" that a great company would have joined Acton's group from the city had not Henry ordered the gates barred. Walsingham is made to "confess" that Henry's proclamation produced not a single traitor to Oldcastle; and in the margin of his chronicle Holinshed cast doubts on Walsingham's credibility by pointing to the exaggeration of his figures: "By this excessive number it may appeare, that Walsingham reporteth this matter according to the common fame, and not as one that searched out an exquisite truth" (3:63). In other words, as Foxe had said in his attack on the preamble to the anti-Lollard statute of 1414, "to make mountains out of molehills, first of rumours [he] maketh congregations, and from congregations riseth up to insurrections."

Finally, after an extremely curt account of the trials and executions of Acton and twenty-seven others, Holinshed turned to Hall's summary of the "diverse interpretations" of these punishments, as I have cited it above, and as Foxe had turned it to Hall's discredit. Holinshed, however, was of another mind than Foxe. For after the sentence in which Hall acknowledged the countertradition, whereby "Certain affirme, that it was for feined causes surmized by the spiritualtie, more upon displeasure than truth," Holinshed took off with conjectures of his own:

> and that they were assembled to heare their preacher (the foresaid Beverlie) in that place there, out of the waie from resort of people, sith that they might not come togither openlie about any such matter, without danger to be apprehended; as the manner is, and hath beene ever of the persecuted flocke, when they are prohibited publikelie the exercise of their religion. But howsoever the matter went with these men, apprehended they were, and diverse of them executed (as before ye have heard) whether for rebellion or heresie, or for both (as the forme of the indictment importeth) I need not to spend manie words, sith others have so largely treated thereof; and therefore I refer those that wish to be more fullie satisfied herein unto their reports. (3:63–64)

Like Hall, Holinshed invited his readers to participate in the historiographical exercise; unlike Hall, he urged them to read further in the matter in order to increase their skills in indifferency; and one of those to whom he surely referred them, one who had "so largely treated thereof" that no Elizabethan reader of the *Acts and Monuments* could be ignorant of the problems with the indictment, was John Foxe, whose suggestion that "instead of armies and weapons," Acton and his companions were "coming only with their books, and with Beverly their preacher, into those thickets," had apparently taken root and grown in Holinshed's imagination.

But this is not all; for I have cited above from the 1587 edition of the *Chronicles*, whereas in the first edition of 1577 Holinshed had continued his indifferency in a rather startling manner:

> I refer those that wish to be more fully satisfyed herein unto their discourses, having for mine owne part rather chosen to shewe what I finde recorded by Writers, than to use any censure, to the prejudice of other mens judgements, and therefore to leave this matter, and also the Lord Cobham, eyther in Wales, or else where, closely hid for the time from king Henries reach. (2:1168)

In this extraordinary gesture, the chronicler seems suddenly in league with the Lollard leader, "closely hid for the time" in nonevaluative statements and deference to other writers. Since this was not a part of the 1587 edition that came under revision as a result of official censorship, the *disappearance* of this passage must be seen as a form of self-censorship, either by Holinshed himself or by his successors; though for the knowing (habitual readers of the chronicles) what Holinshed had retained in his own brief chronicle of Oldcastle was more than enough to indicate which of the two countertraditions he adhered to.

The *Chronicles*, however, do not leave the story of Oldcastle an unfinished mystery. On the contrary, true to his theme of how "books" are central to this story, Holinshed went back to Walsingham's *Historia Anglicana* for the account of how Oldcastle had hidden for a while in "an husbandman's house" near St. Albans, that some of his servants had been captured there, and that he had narrowly escaped himself. His pursuers did, however, find an ideological treasure trove:

> books written in English, and some . . . trimlie gilt, limned, and beautified with images, the heads whereof had beene scraped off, and in the Letanie they had bolted foorth the name of our ladie, and of other saints, till they came to the verse Parce nobis Domine. Diverse writings were found there also, in derogation of such honor *as then was thought due our ladie.* The abbat of Saint Albons sent the booke so disfigured with scrapings & blottings out, with other such writings as there were found, unto the king; who sent the booke againe to the archbishop, to shew the same in his sermons at Paules crosse in London, to the end that the citizens and other people of the realme might understand the purposes of those that then were called Lollards, to bring them further in discredit with the people. (3:92; italics added)

Once again, Holinshed showed his presence, and his sense of historical change, by substituting what was *then* thought for Walsingham's emphasis on the multiple blasphemies against the Blessed Mary "which on account of horror he refrains from describing" ("quaedam scripta plena blasphemiae in Beatam Mariam, quae propter horrorem scribere supersedi").[47]

One kind of erasure, blotting out, produced another. Oldcastle was captured in the Marches of Wales, and brought to London "in a litter, wounded as he was," and returned to safekeeping in the Tower; and, Parliament being conveniently assembled "for the levieng of monie, to furnish the kings great charges" for the French wars, Oldcastle was brought before the duke of Bedford, acting as regent in Henry's absence, and the other estates in Parliament, and after his condemnation, "consumed with fire, the gallowes and all" in St. Giles' Field, the site of the supposed insurrection of 1414. While he followed Walsingham where it suited his theme,

Holinshed calmly ignored the suggestion that Oldcastle had been treacherously dealing with the Scots earlier in the year;[48] as for the execution itself, he avoided Walsingham's tale that at his execution Oldcastle had promised his own resurrection in three days, in order to secure toleration for his followers. For Walsingham, this was evidence of religious mania.[49] But perhaps, if indeed Oldcastle "really" made that promise, it was even at the time only a metaphor for the vitality of his own legend, for the iterability of the great tales from the distant past of resistance and nonconformity.

We have therefore followed Oldcastle from the hostile Catholic tradition of the fifteenth century through the Protestant countertradition of the sixteenth, and arrived at 1587. What followed Holinshed, as is well known to literary scholars, is a reprise of this historiographical duel on the stages of the public theater. This is not the place to rehearse the mystery of how Shakespeare's unhistorical "Sir John Oldcastle" of his *Henry IV*, Part I, became the still more unhistorical Sir John Falstaff.[50] But Holinshed was used as a source in the counterplay, *The First Part of Sir John Old-Castle*, collaborately produced by Michael Drayton, Richard Hathway, Anthony Munday, and Robert Wilson, for which payment was recorded in Philip Henslowe's diary for 16 October 1599. The *First Part* includes a series of accusations against Oldcastle, but insists that he was never involved in any rebellion or conspiracy against Henry, and that people only mention his name in that connection because of his reputation for probity in religion. A few more or less comic or disreputable figures, Acton, Beverly, and Murley, plan and carry out a pathetic uprising; but when confronted by Henry and Oldcastle on the question of the latter's involvement, Acton admits that his plan to meet with Oldcastle at St. Giles' Field was only because he "heard it was reported so":

> To cleere my conscience ere I dye my Lord,
> I must confesse we have no other ground
> But onely rumour to accuse this Lord,
> Which now I see was meerely fabulous.[51]

However, while Henry is convinced of Oldcastle's innocence with respect to the charge of treason, the bishop of Rochester's hatred of him initiates a new wave of accusations focused on heresy (the dramatists were revising the historical sequence to suit their own agenda), and Oldcastle is carried off to the Tower to await his examination by the ecclesiastical authorities. Here we can see most clearly how the proto-Reformation of the early fifteenth century worked in the cultural memory to authorize the not entirely submissive or state-approved Protestantism of the end of the sixteenth century.

The sign of Oldcastle's religious beliefs in this turn-of-the-century play is his ownership of books in English, and a scene of censorship is staged accordingly:

> Enter Sumner with bookes.
> Bishop: What bringst thou there? what, bookes of heresie?
> Sumner: Yea my Lord, here's not a Latine booke,
> Not so much as our Ladies Psalter:
> Here's the Bible, the Testament, the Psalmes in Meeter,
> The sickman's salve, the Treasure of Gladnesse,
> All English, not not so much but the Almanacke's
> English.

And the bishop replies, "All English, burne them, burne them quickly" (p. 121). It has been observed that this collection would be appropriate for a sixteenth-century Puritan's library.[52] And the separation of Oldcastle from Acton et al. has been seen as a concern to place his views and behavior "within acceptable contemporary political parameters," in contrast to the more extreme Puritan fundamentalists.[53] Perhaps so; but the play's sympathies seem to be decisively against the ecclesiastical authorities, with the bishop of Rochester standing in for Whitgift, and his complaint that the Lollards "give themselves the name of Protestants, / And meete in fields and solitary groves" (p. 72). And the stress on books in English belongs to the long struggle in which Wycliffe, Tyndale, and Bale were the progenitors of the *Chronicles*, at least in the arena of religious openness and self-education.[54]

EIGHT   ♊ *Law*

In the middle of Raphael Holinshed's treatment of the reign of Mary Tudor, there is recorded with remarkable fullness the trial for treason of Sir Nicholas Throckmorton. This is a unique section of the *Chronicles*. It is the only instance within the entire project of a trial where both prosecution and defence have full representation, though the ambiguity of that term "representation" will itself need further discussion. In the second edition of 1587, readers could compare, with some irony, Throckmorton's trial for complicity in a Protestant conspiracy with its ideological converse, the treason trial of Sir Nicholas's nephew, Francis Throckmorton, in 1584, for engaging in a Roman Catholic conspiracy. The source for this trial was a government pamphlet published in June of that year. Sir Francis's trial, which resulted in his execution, is told in consecutive narrative. An insistently editorial voice asserts the defendant's guilt, the rectitude of the proceedings, and the necessity of torture. We are told that the commissioners' questions are "for the more brevitie . . . omitted" (4:543). The trial of Sir Nicholas, however, is presented as what we now recognize as dramatic form, complete with speech prefixes and occasional stage directions. This convention allows him to represent himself with extraordinary freedom and cleverness.

Because of the fullness of representation, and more important, because Throckmorton's remarkable self-defence led to his acquittal, this trial as recorded in the *Chronicles* became a model for the reporting of subsequent trials in the sixteenth and seventeenth centuries, and in more than one case a model also of how to *prepare* a defence. It was also, in the longer perspective, awarded the status of a historical document, if partly by default of other records. Holinshed's account is the *only* surviving source of our detailed knowledge of the trial itself,[1] and was consequently reprinted in all the various collections of *State Trials*, with their broadly "whig" agenda, that began to be published in the early eighteenth century.[2] But there is something more at stake here than even these tests of significance. In Holinshed's eyes, Throckmorton's trial stood for his own theory of law in relation to the ancient constitution; and Throckmorton himself became the most articulate spokesman for what "indifference" meant in the territory of law.

In describing the Norman Conquest of England by William I, Holinshed, as we have seen, had focused on the new legal code, "nothing so equall or easie to be kept" (2:13) that the Conqueror established, and its disadvantages for the subject nation. And, Holinshed had continued:

> Here by the waie I give you to note a great absurditie; namelie, that those lawes which touched all, and ought to be knowne of all, were notwithstanding written in the Norman toong, which the Englishmen understood not; so that even at the beginning you should have great numbers, partly by the iniquitie of the lawes, and partlie by ignorance in misconstruing the same, to be wrongfully condemned.

He also indicated that it was rather inconvenient for ancient constitutionalism that William I originated the trial by jury; for while there are some "that will mainteine this maner of proceedinge in the administration of justice by the voice of a jurie to have beene in use before the conqueror's daies," they are unfortunately not "able to proove it by any ancient records."

But the importance of the jury trial in Holinshed's system of justice as fairness may be judged by what he had *added* to Polydore Vergil's account of the origins of this institution: added, that is, in the 1577 edition, where after his and Vergil's account of how the jurors reached their verdict, Holinshed observed: "And when they were once agreed, these 12 men, as it were the 12 Apostles (that in the number yet some respect of religion even wise appere) came in before the judges" (2:303).

And a little later he again diverged from his source, in a highly topical manner:

> Their judgement also or consent is called a verdict, that is to saye, a true saying: but I woulde to God that name myghte rightly and with good cause be ever applyed thereto, that men might have their causes justly adjudged,

rather than prejudiced by the verdicts of suche freeholders as are accustomed
to serve the Prince and the Countreys at assises and Sessions. (2:304)

Neither of these statements survived into the 1587 edition of the *Chronicles,*
a salient example of the self-censorship that took place as the second edition was being conceived.

Even without these particular signs of intention, those early indications of Holinshed's philosophy and history of law were likely to be remembered by Elizabethan readers of the *Chronicles* when, hundreds of pages
later, they came across what appeared to be a complete transcript of
Throckmorton's trial. Their attention would surely have been sharply focused by Holinshed's editorial appearance at this point:

> But now for as much as a copy of the order of Sir Nicholas Throckmorton's
> arreignment hathe come into my hands, and that the same may give light to
> the history of that dangerous rebellion I have thought it *not impertinent* to in-
> sert the same: not wishing that it should be offensive to anie, sith it is in every
> mans libertie to weie his words uttered in his owne defense, and likewise *the
> dooings of the quest* [jury] *in acquitting him,* as maie seeme good to their discre-
> tions, sith I have delivered the same as I have it, without prejudicing anie
> mans opinion, to thinke thereof otherwise than as the cause maie move him.
> (4:31; italics added)

His readers were therefore alerted to the highly unusual circumstances of
this trial, in which both the words of the defendant and the actions of the
jury are deserving of later analysis.

Both the charge of treason here and the defence against it were direct
consequences of Reformation history and the brief counter-Reformation
inaugurated by Mary Tudor. The "dangerous rebellion" that Holinshed
mentioned as the context (though not, I think, the real motive) for his "not
impertinent" introduction of the trial was the uprising led by Sir Thomas
Wyatt the younger against Mary Tudor, who had just assumed the throne
in defiance of the rival Protestant faction. Wyatt's uprising was explicitly
motivated by Mary's determination to return the realm to Roman
Catholicism and to marry Philip II of Spain, which many feared would
bring England under Spanish domination.[3] Throckmorton was one of a
group of eight members of the gentry who were charged with conspiring
with Wyatt and others in London to seize the Tower and levy war against
the queen. Of these, as David Loades has pointed out, two (Sir Peter Carew
and Sir William Pickering) had already escaped to France, and four
(William Winter, Sir Edward Warner, Sir Edward Rogers, and Sir Nicholas
Arnold) were never brought to trial. Only Throckmorton and Sir James

Croftes stood to the indictment. According to Loades, their examinations (which have not survived) may have been conducted primarily for the purpose of incriminating the princess Elizabeth and Edward Courtenay, earl of Devon, and once these men were in custody the Council's interest in most of them waned.[4]

Sir Nicholas, who was thirty-seven at the time of his trial, was the fourth son of Sir George Throckmorton of Coughton, in Warwickshire. His mother was aunt by marriage to Queen Catherine Parr, who in 1543 intervened to get Sir George released from prison, where he had been sent for refusing to take the oath of supremacy. Unlike his father, a zealous Roman Catholic, Nicholas became an ardent Protestant. According to John Strype, he and two of his brothers attended Anne Askew at her execution for heresy in 1546, where they were warned by the bystanders to "take heed to their lives, for they were marked men."

Nicholas's career began in court service, as page to the duke of Richmond, Henry's illegitimate son, who died in 1536. Like three of his brothers, he was several times elected to the House of Commons, and from 1545, for over twenty years, he repeatedly sat in Parliament for a series of different constituencies. During Edward VI's reign he made a second entry into court service. In 1547 he accompanied Protector Somerset's army to Scotland, and after the battle of Musselburgh he had brought news of the victory to the king, who knighted him and appointed him to the privy chamber.[5]

Although this period of favor, dependent as it was on Somerset and the young king, was inevitably short lived, Throckmorton seems to have played his political cards reasonably well, surviving Somerset's fall and the chaotic transition to the new reign. His signature appears on the letters patent of 7 June 1553, which limited the succession to Lady Jane Grey; but on the day of the king's death, he sent a messenger to Mary to inform her that, her brother being dead, she needed to act fast and defensively against Northumberland. In other words, Throckmorton (who sported a bright red beard) was one of Nature's foxes. Nevertheless, on 20 February 1554 he was sent to the Tower, on the testimony of one of Wyatt's lieutenants, Cuthbert Vaughan, that he and Throckmorton had discussed together the plans for the insurrection. He was tried in the Guildhall on April 17 by a commission of oyer and terminer, after fifty-eight days of close imprisonment.

Throckmorton conducted his own defence. This was usual procedure in the sixteenth century, since no defendants in criminal cases were permitted legal counsel, a rule that persisted for treason until altered by a statute of William III in 1696, and in all other capital cases until well into the eighteenth century.[6] As Sir Thomas Smith explained in his account of the English legal system, in a case where the "prince is endammaged," "he that speaks for the prisoner shall be rebuked, as speaking against the prince."[7] To this extent, the special commissioners were within the law (however reprehensible it now seems) in refusing to let John Fitzwilliams speak as a witness on behalf of Throckmorton, though merely to the untruth of some of the charges. But the practice was archaic in the sense that the accused was *required* to speak for himself, in the full expectation that he would incriminate himself; in other words, self-defence was expected to serve, in the residually magic political rituals of the day, as a form of confession.[8]

In the trial for treason, moreover, as in no other legal confrontation, the defendant is accused of the most complete alienation from his society conceivable: challenging the authority of its government. We now prefer to blur the political edge of a treason trial by defining the crime as "betrayal of one's country," an ideological ploy that barely conceals the conflicts of loyalties and principles that underlie such asymmetrical confrontations between state and individual. In early modern England, where the confrontation was posed as between monarch and subject, treason was, of course, a capital crime. The defendant therefore was impelled by what Hobbes would later define as the second "Fundamentall Law of Nature . . . By all means we can, to defend our selves."[9] In the real world of the treason trial, as distinct from an imaginary state of nature, self-defence meant not merely proving one's innocence of a specific charge, but refusing alienation, insisting on one's continued membership in the civil society, in which differences of opinion about politics are the inevitable consequence of rational participation.

Throckmorton was a poor subject for political magic, and psychologically immune to the alienation syndrome. He was unusually well informed, not only about legal procedure, but about the history of treason law, and he managed not only to infuriate the prosecution lawyers by his procedural sophistication, but also to persuade the jurors that the law was being unjustly manipulated. In short, Throckmorton was acquitted, to the large embarrassment of Mary Tudor's neophyte government. Throckmorton survived to become a significant, though unpopular, diplomatic figure under Elizabeth, negotiating on her behalf in Scotland and France throughout the 1560s, where he maintained his strongly Protestant stance. In his last year of life he was arrested on suspicion of sympathy with Norfolk during the Northern Rebellion, but was released to die in his bed in February 1571. Given the hazards of weathercock religion, Throckmorton had learned as well as any which way the wind was blowing.

The more closely one studies Throckmorton's defence, the more clearly it emerges as a brilliant articulation of values and insights to which the *Chronicles* as a whole were committed. What better instance of the right of every man to tell his own story than his self-defence before the law? What better illustration of the need for independent judgment in the citizen than "the dooings of the quest in acquitting him," as Holinshed put it?

Were not the readers of the *Chronicles* themselves being invited to take on the responsibility of jury duty, since "it is in every mans libertie" (a very loaded word) to "weigh" Throckmorton's words uttered in his own defence, and draw their own conclusions?

In this case, also, judgment of the defendant by the law was balanced by judgment *of* the law by the defendant. Throckmorton's words, as so remarkably saved for posterity, indicate that in the middle of the sixteenth century it was possible for a thinking person, especially, of course, when his own life was in jeopardy, to develop a critical perspective on "Law" as a set of socially and politically constructed rules, rules that particularly at this stage in history were subject to sudden and continuous change. William Harrison had himself slipped into his *Description of England* a sardonic account of common law, as "so variable, & subject to alteration and change, that oft in one age, diverse judgements doo passed upon one maner of case." And, he added, "these words; in such a yeare of the prince, this opinion was taken for sound law; doo answer nothing else, but that the judgement of our lawiers is now altered, so that they saie farre otherwise" (1:302).

It has already been established by Donald Kelley that the Reformation, with the rival loyalties it spawned, threw into relief the ambiguities of "law" as an absolute concept and made it possible for the Marian exile John Ponet in his *Short Treatise of Politike Power* (1556) to exclaim, "Wo be unto you . . . that maketh unrighteous lawes."[10] The anonymous *Certayne questions demaunded and asked by the noble realme of Englande*, published perhaps the previous year "at the requeste of Myles Hogherde," was more challenging still. Specifically addressed to the problem of the Spanish marriage and to the unstable content of the term "treason", the pamphlet included among its questions the following items:

> Item, whether the Kynge thursteth the bloud of his subjectes, when he seketh meanes to put his subjectes to death, after he is lawfully quyte by the lawes of his Realme, and punished those men, who have passed upon hys lyfe. . . ?
> Item, whether actes made by a parcial Parliament, chosen by craft and pollicy, for the compassing of the Princes wilfull purpose, oughte to be obeyed or not?
> Item, whether it be Treason to aske a question?
> Item, whether it be treason to saye God save the noble Realme of England from the captivitie, bondage, and conqueste of the vyle Spanyardes?

Evidently, the first of the questions I have selected from the original 48 is a veiled allusion to the Throckmorton trial and the fate of its jury, while the last three address the problem of Marian treason law and its application.[11]

The distinctive contribution of Throckmorton to this early modern relativism was this: he grasped the point that, if the laws governing treason, the most serious offence that the law recognized, could change arbitrarily to accommodate the policies of particular regimes, the relation between man-made law and justice was brought into even sharper focus than by the clash between one's duties to God and to the state, or between one judicial decision and another. By alluding to Throckmorton, *Certayne Questions* suggests that its own mixture of religious, political, and legal skepticism was partly inspired by that case, which thus becomes the origin of Marian resistance theory.

It is highly probable, also, that the poem that appears first in all surviving editions of *The Mirror for Magistrates* was recognized as an allusion to the Throckmorton trial. "The fall of Robert Tresilian chiefe Justice of Englande, and other his felowes, for misconstruying the lawes, and expounding them to serve the Princes affections," though literally set in the reign of Richard II, was all too easily applicable to the events of 1554. It is larded with Tresilian's "confessions" of the way he and his fellows had abused their trust, in language reminiscent of Throckmorton's protests:

> The lawes we interpreted and statutes of the lande,
> Not trulye by the texte, but nuly by a glose:
> And wurds that wer most plaine whan thei by us wer skande
> We turned by construction lyke a welchmans hose.
> Wherby many one both lyfe and lande dyd lose

Like Throckmorton, the *Mirror* tragedy, which is attributed to George Ferrers, warns judges that if on earth they abandon "the pathes of equitie" to "serve kings in al pointes" they will ultimately face a higher judge: "Remembre well your reckening at the daye extreme." And the poem calmly ends by appealing to the contemporary situation, in which equally corrupt judges have *not* yet met with Tresilian's punishment:

> If sum in latter dayes, had called unto mynde
> The fatall fall of us for wrestyng of the ryght,
> The statutes of this lande they should not have defynde
> So wylfully and wyttingly agaynst the sentence quyte:
> But though they skaped paine, the falte was nothing
> lyght[12]

If one reads these lines with Throckmorton's trial in mind, it was really not very surprising that, as William Baldwin advised his readers in the second edition of 1559, the first edition of 1554 was suppressed by Bishop Gardiner. "The wurke was begun," wrote Baldwin, "& part of it printed .iiii yeare agoe, but hyndred by the lord Chauncellour that then was." Later editions replaced this with "but staid by such as then were chiefe in office.[13]

Unofficial Reporting

The questions that Throckmorton himself formulated during his weeks in the Tower interrogated both the source of law and the agents of its application. Was Parliament or the common law the likeliest source of rules protective of the individual, as well as of the state? Were judges capable of "objectivity" (which in Throckmorton's vocabulary was, significantly, rendered as "indifference") when their own political self-interest was at stake? And what was the role, both in usual practice and ideally, of the jury? In posing these questions during the course of his trial, Throckmorton was not only an early modern critical legal theorist, but also a mighty convenient spokesman for Holinshed's own belief in justice as fairness, not to mention liberty of conscience, and the right to disagree peaceably. The question of whether Throckmorton was guilty of plans to disagree violently can never now be settled, and is not my concern here. But with relation to his "words," there are such telling echoes of Throckmorton's vocabulary in Holinshed's editorial commentary that the boundaries between them blur; or, to put it differently, the empty space in Holinshed's biography might be partially filled, if not with facts, with Throckmorton's foxy and historically conscious personality.

In introducing Holinshed's record of the trial, I used the term "transcript" provisionally but still seriously. We do not know who produced it, nor how Holinshed would have acquired it, but we can make an educated guess. John Bellamy, one of the few historians to treat this trial as a significant event in legal history,[14] assumed that the account was probably compiled by Throckmorton himself after Mary's death, though "based on notes taken at the time."[15] But it does not read like a protagonist's reconstruction after the event, which is more likely to have been told in the first person. Rather, the *vraisemblance* of the dialogue and its air of completeness demands one of three solutions: either very extensive notes made at the time, by another interested party or parties, since Throckmorton could scarcely have been scribbling while he spoke; subsequent *fabrication* by someone with a great ear for dialogue and a lively political imagination, a political playwright, as it were; or some combination of the two.[16] G. Kitson Clark, who challenged Sir Leslie Stephen's naïveté in the *Dictionary of National Biography* on the topic of the truth-content of the "transcript," admitted that "the trial certainly reads as if it were taken down verbatim," and, as one of the possible explanations for its existence, that "it may very well have been reconstructed from the memories of people who had actually been present in the Guildhall at the time of trial, possibly assisted by their notes, possibly assisted by the recollections of Sir Nicholas himself."[17] Clark's preference was for distrusting its documentary status, on the grounds that the much later writer Daniel Defoe could achieve "the language of real men" in a manifestly fictional form; yet Clark could not rule out of possibility what I offer here as the compromise view.

Official transcripts of trials did not come into play before the eighteenth century. But in the early fifteenth century ecclesiastical examinations were taken down in detail by official notaries, as in the case of Sir John Oldcastle's examination in 1413, recorded in Archbishop Arundel's *Magnus Processus*, where Thomas Netter served as one of the notaries.[18] Kitson Clark himself remarked that "if people speak slowly it is possible to take down what they say in long hand," using as an example the detailed records of clerical interrogations in sixteenth-century Catalonia.[19] It is reasonable to assume that someone who intended that his friends could take notes would indeed speak slowly. Books on how to write swiftly were published in England from 1588 onwards and may well refer to methods in use before then. But shorthand as such was not considered crucial to the Tudor government when in 1572 it placed Thomas Norton, the queen's printer, in a favored spot in the Guildhall so that he might write an official account of the trial of Thomas Howard, duke of Norfolk, which also happens to be recorded in dialogue or dramatic form.[20]

It is also important to grasp that the *motive* for note-taking derived from the existence of an opposition, whether religious, political, or both. Kitson Clark's notion that during the four years between Throckmorton's trial and Elizabeth's accession the climate "would not be propitious to any account of this trial being preserved, least of all published,"[21] is clearly as naive in its own way as Sir Leslie Stephen's uncritical acceptance of its documentary status. Well before Throckmorton's case, as Duncan Derrett has shown, unofficial manuscript accounts of the trial of Sir Thomas More (in 1534) were generated, from which several pamphlets were printed, all by continental presses. All of these can be traced to a single account which has now disappeared, compiled perhaps by an eyewitness, perhaps by someone who, in Derrett's words, "avidly took down what was brought to him from the scene of the trial."[22] Derrett reconstructs the profile of this witness as someone with antigovernmental sympathies, concerned with the trial "from a technical, even juridical standpoint," and with the means to convey "this highly-skilled précis" to Paris within a fortnight of the execution; someone, perhaps, with diplomatic immunity. More's trial would have been of particular pertinence to Throckmorton, since he was tried under that notorious Henrician Treason Act of 1534; while at the same time the religious content of the questions put to him placed him squarely, if ironically, in the line of those, from Oldcastle to Lady Jane Grey, who were interrogated by the ecclesiastical authorities, and to whose supporters it was of the utmost importance that their version of events should reach the public. Those who themselves held a strong (doctrinal) concept of truth, and believed that they were required to promulgate it at whatever cost to themselves, were unlikely to have consciously distorted the record.

But the account of More's trial was still, as Derrett acknowledged, a précis. The other side of the frame for Throckmorton's trial, speaking both chronologically and technologically, is supplied by the trial of John Lilburne in 1649. Here we have stronger information as to how it entered the archives. An apparently verbatim account of Lilburne's trial, even longer than Throckmorton's, was published in London almost instantly after *his* dramatic acquittal,[23] which had caused huge public demonstrations of joy. It was published by "Theodorus Verax," the pseudonym of Clement Walker, whose hostility to the Long Parliament was as great as Lilburne's.[24] Halfway through the pamphlet, Walker desired the reader "to take notice" that it is not quite a complete record:

> that in the Indictment itself there was *a great many other things than in this is ex-*
> *pressed . . . that were more neglected to be taken* [i.e. taken down] *than the pleadings;* be-
> cause it was not supposed, but the Indictment (being a record) a true copy of
> it might easily be had; considering that by law all records ought freely to be
> used by any freeman of England, and copies of them denied to none that de-
> sire to take them. But that privilege being in this cause already disputed and
> denied; in which regard, the Reader must at present accept of *the best imperfect*
> *notes that the publisher could pick up.*[25]

Walker's polemical point, that legal records ought "freely to be used by any freeman of England," indicates that he thought he was contributing to that freedom by assisting the public's right to know, a staunchly polemical purpose. But this also implies that Walker believed that the pleadings (Lilburne's self-defence) had the same documentary status as the indictment. More important still, we can be reasonably sure from this apology that his account of the trial was based on notes taken at the time, by someone other than Walker himself. Further, this transcript was, apparently, checked by Lilburne himself, as indicated in a "Certificate" at the end: "At the earnest desire of the Printer, I have read this following Discourse, and cannot say but that I do verily believe, the penman of it hath done it with a very *indifferent* hand betwixt the Court, and myself the Prisoner: And so far as in me lies, I am for my part willing the world should see it" (4:1421; italics added). The presence of the word "indifferent" in this certificate implies an ideal of historiographical accuracy, along with evenhandedness; and historians of the Leveller tracts have concluded that Walker worked "under Lilburne's direction, from documents provided by him and *a stenographic report* of the trial."[26]

I suggest that at least some of these conditions pertained also in the case of Throckmorton: that one or more persons deeply interested in this political trial took notes; that the notes were conflated; and that after the event the "transcript" was compared with those that Throckmorton had obviously taken to *prepare* for his defence.[27] It may then have been published as a pamphlet, which has now, unsurprisingly given its clear opposition to Mary's government, disappeared without trace. In the *Chronicles*, the title, THE ORDER OF ARREIGNEMENT OF SIR NICHOLAS THROCKMORTON, KNIGHT, IN THE GUILDHALL OF LONDON, THE SEVENTEENTH DAIE OF APRILL 1554, EXPRESSED IN A DIALOG FOR THE BETTER UNDERSTANDING OF EVERY MANS PART, was set in display type as if to replicate the appearance of a pamphlet. The inclusion of complete texts of pamphlets was, as we have seen, common practice in the *Chronicles*; and we have no reason to distrust Holinshed's veracity when he speaks of how he came by this material.[28]

It is also much to my point that Lilburne himself explicitly drew the connection between Throckmorton's trial and his own, which he had apparently studied with care as a model for his own defence. Early in his testimony, Lilburne referred to

> Throgmorton, in queen Mary's time, who was impeached of higher Treason than now I am; and that in the days of the commonly accounted bloodiest and cruellest prince that this many hundred of years hath reigned in England: . . . Throgmorton was in this place arraigned as a Traitor, and enjoyed as much, if not more [procedural] favour, than I have now enjoyed, although his then judges and prosecutor were bent to take away his life.[29]

And Walker's edition carried, at the place where Lilburne remembered Throckmorton, this telling marginal annotation: "Whose remarkable and excellent Defence you may at large read in Hollingshead's Chronicle, in the Life of Queen Mary, *which discourse is excellently well worth the speedily reprinting,*

especially seeing men are made traitors for words; which cruelty Queen Mary abhorred, as may clearly be read in that excellent statute of her's, made in the
first year of her reign" (p. 21; italics added). That men were indeed still being
made traitors for words in 1649 is demonstrated by Walker's own fate.
Thanks to the appearance of the second part of his *History of Independency*, and
also, surely, to his determination to enter Lilburne's trial in the public
record, on 13 November 1649 he himself was arraigned on a charge of treason, and placed in the Tower, where he died, never having come to trial, in
1651.

Tudor Treason Law

One cannot, however, understand the brilliance of the model to which
Walker so poignantly directs us without some basic understanding of those
arbitrary changes in the law to which I alluded earlier. John Bellamy
demonstrates that the Throckmorton case occurred at one of several crisis
points in the early Tudor period when law and politics merged so dramatically that their collusion became visible. Although during the late medieval period, scarcely an untroubled era politically, the Yorkist and
Lancastrian dynasties were able to manage fairly well, and reasonably fairly, with the basic treason statute devised by Edward III in 1352 (25 Edw. III
st. 5. c. 2), the coming of the Reformation to England and still more the
bizarre marital history of Henry VIII inaugurated a period of rapid and arbitrary legal innovation, whereby the definition of what might be classified
as treason expanded to meet the local and contingent needs of particular
monarchs. The result was a widespread confusion about what did and did
not count as treason; in Bellamy's words, a confusion "fortuitous for the
government, dangerous for the subject." And, he observed, the problems in
the law were exacerbated by the heightened political and religious tensions
of the era, which "tended to make men curb their tongues for fear of being
regarded as betrayers of their prince, church and realm." As compared to
the magnates of the fourteenth and early fifteenth century, who, according
to Bellamy, "had been great experts on illegal accusations and precedents in
general," and willing to oppose any monarchical incursions upon justice as
they understoood it, in the sixteenth century "all those with a good knowledge of the law seem to have been in thrall to the crown."[30]

This tendency to hold one's tongue was undoubtedly reinforced by the
fact that the Henrician Treason Act of November 1534 (26 Hen. VIII. c.
13) identified three brand-new treasons, including treasonable words that
were merely spoken. In G. R. Elton's summary, it was now treason either to

express (maliciously) in speech or writing a desire or intention to endanger or depose the monarch and his immediate family, or "to call the King, in express writing or words, slanderously and maliciously, a heretic, schismatic, tyrant, infidel, or a usurper of the crown." The saving word "maliciously" had been insisted upon and possibly inserted by the House of Commons. Yet, Elton pointed out, it was precisely spoken objections to Henry's policies, to the Boleyn marriage and the break with Rome—that is to say, ordinary political criticism or grumbling—that, being rather widely reported around the country in 1534, had motivated the new legislation in the first place. Political and religious dissent, which to modern eyes is scarcely *de facto* malicious, was now explicitly labeled treason; while the failure to report it was misprision of treason.[31]

Bellamy also pointed out that, whereas each of the Tudors expanded the scope of treason during the course of their reigns to deal with specific problems caused by themselves, expansion was not continuous. On the contrary, *contractions* tended to occur at the beginnings of reigns, "when a new monarch, probably in search of additional popularity, . . . removed the most disliked features of the treason law which his predecessor had operated."[32] One can reasonably infer that such expressions of leniency, even more than their opposite, and especially when they themselves imply or articulate a critique of more repressive policies, would create a climate of scepticism.

In 1547, at the opening of Edward VI's reign, a number of concepts were put into circulation that could not thereafter be withdrawn. The Edwardian treason statute (1 Edw. VI. c. 12) began by describing the laws of the king's father as "verie streighte, sore, extreme and terrible." The act claimed to be a return to that of 1352, but in fact it retained certain provisions of the treason act of 1534, as well as the succession act of 1543, with respect to challenging the royal supremacy over the church or the king's legitimacy. On the other hand, if these challenges were only *verbal*, and not written or translated into overt action, they were only to be treasonable on the third offence. When Mary Tudor came to the throne in 1553 amid the flurry of factional activity in support of Lady Jane Grey, her first opponents, including Northumberland, were tried under the treason acts of Edward III and Edward VI. However, a new treason act soon followed. Perhaps in order to mitigate public horror at the string of recent executions, Mary proceeded to outdo her brother in juridical leniency, at least in theory. The act opened with a preamble declaring the queen's commitment to abide by the treason law of Edward III alone. In particular, the preamble focused on the fact that under her predecessors men had been convicted of treason "many times, for woordes onelye without other facte or dede doone or perpetrated," a slap in the faces of her father and brother.

The Trial: The Mnemonics and Hermeneutics of Survival

I shall now discuss the "transcript" as though it had been arrived at by the compromise method described above and was therefore, like Walker's account of Lilburne's trial, closer to truth than fiction. In one sense it does not matter whether Throckmorton actually spoke all the words attributed to him, was possessed of the legal and mnemonic skills here evinced, or dominated the proceedings as completely as he here appears to have done. What matters for cultural history is the structure of thought articulated in his defence, the legal strategies employed to validate it, and that fact that the transcript reappeared in the *Chronicles*. But with regard to the issue of truth content or documentary status, the likelihood that he did conduct his defence in this brilliant manner is supported by the fact that he won his acquittal, a rare result in major political treason trials.

Sir Nicholas Throckmorton was a striking exception to Bellamy's description of a tongue-tied generation. When the transcript of his self-defense appeared in the *Chronicles*, its disproportionate length (as compared to the rather brief preceding accounts of the departures of Northumberland, Lady Jane Grey, and Wyatt) would have been remarkable in itself; but Holinshed's disclaimer that its insertion is "not impertinent" is a curious echo of Throckmorton's disingenuous early statement that the "few words" he intends "are not altogither impertinent to the matter" (4:32). Actually, both Throckmorton and his chronicler were being decidedly impertinent. Two minutes into the trial, and we suddenly realize we are not only latter-day jurors, but also the audience of a theatrical production, of whose surprise ending ("the dooings of the quest in acquitting him") we have already been informed, and whose tone is somewhere between a legal satire and a comedy of legal manners.

There is one moment during the trial when Throckmorton himself not only draws the analogy between the real-life drama of the courtroom and literary conceptions, but reminds us that this play of state could have turned out very differently. In the course of a dispute about jury packing (to be discussed below), he referred to an earlier trial he had personally witnessed in which packing not only took place, but was blatantly discussed by the judges, including Cholmley: "I trust," he said:

> You have not provided for me this daie, as in times past I knew an other gentleman occupieng this wofull place was provided for. It chanced one of the justices upon gelousie of the prisoners acquitall, for the goodnesse of his cause, said to an other of his companions a justice, when the jurie did appeare; I like not this jurie for our purpose, they seeme to be too pitifull and

too charitable to condemne the prisoner. No no, said the other judge (to wit Cholmeleie)[33] I warrant you, they be picked fellowes for the nonce, he shall drinke of the same cup his fellowes have doone. *I was then a looker on of the pageant as others be now here: but wo is me, I am a plaier in that wofull tragedie.* Well, for these and such other like the blacke oxe hath of late troden on some of their feet: but my trust is, I shall not be so used. (4:33; italics added)

The black ox did not come for Throckmorton. His refusal to be passive in his own courtroom drama had the effect of transforming a tragedy of state into a major embarrassment for the government.[34]

A large part of Throckmorton's strategy in the opening moments of the trial consisted in a struggle for control over procedure:

Sendall [clerk of the crown]: [lists the charges] Of all which treasons and everie of them in manner and forme &c: art thou guiltie or not guiltie?
Throckmorton: Maie it please you my lords and maisters, which be authorised by the queenes commission to be judges this daie, to give me leave to speake a few words, which dooth both concerne you and me, before I anser to the indictment. . . .
[Sir Thomas] Bromley [Lord chief justice]: No, the order is not so, you must first plead whether you be guiltie or no.
[. . .]
Throckmorton: But things spoken out of place, were as good not spoken.

Throckmorton's concept of "out of place" was the very opposite of that assumed by his judges, as based on established procedure.[35] But his determination to raise in the minds of the jury another conception of procedure—that which would give the accused the greatest opportunity to explain himself—had the secondary advantage of making his judges impatient, a fatal error that impugned their assumed objectivity, if indeed it were assumed:

Bromley: These be but delaies to spend time, therefore answer as the law willeth you.
Throckmorton: My lords I praie you make not too much hast with me, neither thinke not long for your dinner, for my case requireth leasure, and you have well dined when you have doone justice trulie. Christ said, Blessed are they that hunger and thirst for righteousnesse.
Bromley: I can forbeare my dinner as well as you, and care as little peradventure.
[Francis Talbot, fifth earl of] Shrewsbury: Come you hither to checke us Throckmorton? We will not be so used, no no, I for mine owne part have forborne my breakefast, dinner, and supper to serve the queene.

Throckmorton: Yea my good lord I know it right well, I meant not to touch your lordship, for your service and pains is evidentlie knowne to all men . . . so I will answer to the indictment, and doo plead not guiltie to the whole, and to everie part thereof.

When Sendall asked him the next question, "How wilt thou be tried?" the only proper answer was "By God and the Countrie." But Throckmorton continued his strategy of wilful misunderstanding:

Throckmorton: Shall I be tried as I would, or as I should?
Bromley: You shall be tried as the law will, and therefore you must saie by God and the countrie.
Throckmorton: Is that your law for me? It is not as I would, but sith you will have it so, I am pleased with it, and doo desire to be tried by faithfull just men, which more feare God than the world. (4:32)

In this opening sally, Throckmorton assumed the high moral ground, the highest religious sanction, with remarkable ease and adroitness. Continually thereafter he would imply that God was watching the proceedings, and virtually in his corner. He also deftly established the tone as debate between equals, forcing his opponents not only onto the defensive (by the invocation of the Beatitudes) but into the picayune. The anticipatory echo of Pope's sardonic line in *The Rape of the Lock,* "and wretches hang, that jurymen may dine," shows both that Throckmorton takes his place in a long tradition of antilegal satire, and how different is the social valence in this case, where jurymen will be the heroes. The choices those jurymen will face are already established, before any evidence has been heard, in the simple contrasts between "tried as I should, or as I would," between procedural formalism and fairness, and between those who answer to God and those who answer to some other master.

What followed the plea of not guilty in trial procedure was the swearing in of the jury. The transcript's slightly muddled account of this stage manages nevertheless to make it clear that, although it is unusual ("a rare case") for prosecution lawyers to challenge a juror, the attorney general, Edward Griffin, proposed to Sir Roger Cholmley that "certeine" jurors should be challenged, and was told that "no exceptions were to be taken to them, but onelie for their upright honesties," a locution full of complex irony. Nevertheless, Griffin persevered, and by "prompting" Dyer, one of the two sergeants-at-law, he managed to get rid of two jurors. With a different kind of irony, not of statement but of fact, their replacements were Whetston and Lucar, whom the text designates as "other honest men," and so indeed they proved. Throckmorton, however, who could not have anticipated the positive results of this change, did not let his opportunity pass to discredit Cholmley, by the allusion (mentioned above) to his interest in a well-packed jury. The transcript includes a dramatic "stage direction": "Whilest this talke was, Cholmeleie consulted with the atturnie, about the jurie, which the prisoner espied, and then said . . . Ah ah master Cholmeleie, will this foule packing never be left?"[36]

Along with his attacks on the restrictive formalism of accepted courtroom procedure, Throckmorton had clearly decided to take aim at the heart of jurisprudence, legal interpretation itself. Accordingly, in the guise of appealing to the commissioners for ethical conduct of his trial, he explained to the jury what to expect:

> I praie you remember I am not alienate from you, but that I am your christian brother; neither you so charged, but you ought to consider equitie; nor yet so privileged, but that you have a dutie of God appointed you how you shall doo your office; which if you exceed, will be greevouslie required at your hands. It is lawfull for you to use your gifts which I know God hath largelie given you, as your learning, art, and eloquence, so as thereby you doo not seduce the minds of the simple and unlearned jurie, to credit matters otherwise than they be. For master sergeant, I know how by persuasions, inforcements, presumptions, applieng, implieng, inferring, conjecturing, deducing of argument, wresting and exceeding the law, the circumstances, the depositions and confessions, that unlearned men may be inchanted to thinke and judge those that be things indifferent, or at the woorst but oversights to be great treasons; such power orators have, and such ignorance the unlearned have. Almightie God by the mouth of his prophet dooth conclude such advocates be curssed, speaking these words: Cursed be he that dooth his office craftilie, corruptlie, and maliciously. And consider also, that my bloud shall be required at your hands, and punished in you and yours, to the third and fourth generation. Notwithstanding, you and the justices excuse alwaies such erronious dooings, when they be after called in question, by the verdict of the twelve men: but I assure you, the purgation serveth you as it did Pilat, and you wash your hands of the bloudshed, as Pilat did of Christs. (4:33–34)

At the ethical level the point of this speech lay in its refusal of alienation ("I praie you remember I am not alienate from you, but that I am your christian brother"). But Throckmorton's jurors were thereby *also* instructed in the hermeneutics of suspicion ("applieng, implieng, inferring, conjecturing . . . wresting and exceeding the law"), and warned to be on their guard against such tactics.

Throckmorton proceeded to argue that the law was being wrested and exceeded in two crucial respects. In the first place, he had effectively been indicted under a statute no longer in force. The indictment claimed that Throckmorton and ten other gentlemen, in the company of certain traitors, "had compassed to deprive the queen of her crown" (which had been made treason in 1534 and again in 1547, but repealed in 1553), and that he had also "compassed" to levy war against her, which (as distinct, of course, from actually levying it) was not treason by any act. Bellamy inferred that those lawyers who drew up the indictment against Throckmorton "did so without having the recent amendments to the treason laws in mind," a quite remarkable supposition.[37] He also supposed that the Crown's lawyers worked from the indictments of Northumberland and his adherents, which had preceded the Marian statute of repeal. In fact, a charge of imagining the queen's death should have been treasonable under the statute of 1352 and sufficient to incriminate Throckmorton as merely one of a group of conspirators, regardless of whether he had subsequently supported the "imaginings" by overt act; but by drawing the indictment incorrectly the Crown's lawyers made, from their perspective, a fatal mistake, which permitted Sir Nicholas to claim illegal procedure.

The second aspect in which, Throckmorton warned the jury, the judges might be found "applieng, implieng, inferring, conjecturing, deducing of argument, wresting and exceeding the law" must be understood, paradoxically, in terms of the sixteenth-century expansion of the doctrine of equity, the territory in which "interpretation" makes its first appearance in a legal sense, to describe the judicial handling of *statutes*.

By the mid-sixteenth century, as acts of Parliament begin to acquire the force of modern legislation, and as Plowden's *Commentaries* and the mid-century *Discourse upon the Exposicion & Understanding of Statutes* witness, judges began to argue that even statutes needed to be restricted or extended by equity, and there appeared the secondary doctrine of interpretation according to the original intention of the lawmakers.[38]

We can tell from the *Discourse* that the doctrine of original intention was already perceived as problematic. In the first place, the concept of reading *ex mente legislatorum* must be subject to the knowledge that the makers of statute law (the members of previous parliaments) were not of a single mind: "so manie heades as there were, so many wittes; so manie statute makers, so many myndes; yet, notwithstanding, certen notes there are by which a man maie knowe what it was." Second, the task of the careful interpreter is "not onlie to knowe where a statute shall be taken by equitie, but also where it shall be taken straightelie accordinge to the naked & bare letter" (p. 151).

And the first condition where strict or literal application of statutes must apply is "when the law is penall, for in those it is true that Paston sai-

ethe, *Poenas interpretatione augere non debere:* for the lawe alwaies favoureth hym
that goeth to wracke, nor it will not pulle hym on his nose that is on his
knees" (p. 155). In the main part of his defence Throckmorton developed
an anti-interpretive position, in which he too appealed to the "naked & bare
letter" of the law as determined by parliamentary majority, and which he
trusted better than his judges not to pull him on his nose (or worse).

The charge against Throckmorton was not of merely being an acces-
sory in Wyatt's conspiracy but—it seems extraordinary now to look back at
the lawyers' hyperboles—"that he was a principall deviser, procurer, and
contriver" and that Wyatt "was but his minister." The evidence for this consisted entirely in the statements made by men involved in Wyatt's conspiracy, some of whom were already dead, but significantly none by Wyatt
himself, who had before his execution taken sole responsibility for the conception and organization of the uprising, nor by young Edward Wyatt,
whom Throckmorton had asked, unsuccessfully, should be brought into
court to testify or at least examined. Some of the testimony that was adduced, like Winter's statement that Throckmorton knew of Wyatt's plan to
seize the Tower of London and "misliked" it, was trivial, not to say (as indeed Throckmorton did say) exculpatory; some of it—notably the testimony of Cuthbert Vaughan, who was brought into court and sworn—
Throckmorton simply challenged as lies extracted from a condemned man
who thereby hoped for clemency.[39] All of the testimony consisted in reports of conversations, sometimes at second hand. Throckmorton did not
deny that such conversations had taken place—indeed, he had signed a
confession to that effect—but he did deny that conversations alone were
treasonable. Nor did he deny what his sympathies were; but his strategy
was to make those sympathies seem typical of a loyal Englishman rather
than treasonable and eccentric: "I confess," he said in court:

> I did mislike the queenes mariage with Spaine, and also the comming of the
> Spaniards hither, and then me thought I had reason to doo so: for I did learne
> the reasons of my misliking of you master Hare, master Southwell, and oth-
> ers in the parlement house, there I did see the whole consent of the realme
> against it; and I a hearer, but no speaker, did learne my misliking of those
> matters, confirmed by manie sundrie reasons amongst you; but as concerning
> anie sturre or uprore against the Spaniards, I never made anie, neither pro-
> cured anie to be made. (4:36)

Throckmorton hereby appealed to his fellow parliamentarians who had
now become his judges—Sir Nicholas Hare, master of the rolls, and Sir
Richard Southwell, privy councillor—to remember the debates in Mary's
first parliament during which they themselves had expressed concern at the

plans for the Spanish marriage. And his own description of his conversation with Vaughan becomes, in effect, a daring Protestant polemic:

> We talked of the incommodities of the marriage of the queene with the prince of Spaine, and how grievous the Spaniards would be to us here. Vaughan said, that it should be verie dangerous for anie man, that trulie professed the gospell to live here, such was the Spaniards crueltie. . . . Whereunto I answered it was the plague of God justlie come upon us; and now almightie God dealt with us as he did with the Israelites, taking from them for their unthankefulnesse their godlie kings, and did send tyrants to reigne over them. Even so he handled us Englishmen, which had a most godlie and vertuous prince to reigne over us, my late sovereigne lord and maister king Edward. (4:41)

Throckmorton was unintimidated by the ludicrous charge that he was the *éminence grise* of the entire uprising, with Wyatt acting merely as his catspaw. He assumed he was being treated as a pawn in a greater game. He asked that his own confession be read aloud in full, rather than selectively, so that his "words be not perverted and abused to the hurt of some others, and especiallie against the great personages . . . for I perceive the net was not cast onelie for little fishes, but for the great ones" (4:42), by which he probably alluded to attempts to incriminate the princess Elizabeth. But he also, addressing the jury directly, made mock of the nature of the testimony: "For what maner of resoning or proofe is this, Wiat would have taken the tower, Ergo Throckmorton is a traitor" (4:35). And he was master of the reductio ad absurdum: "Of all which treasons, to prove me guiltie, the queens learned councell hath given in evidence these points materiall . . . for the compassing or imagining the queenes death . . . that I should saie to the said sir Nicholas [Arnold] in Glocestershire, that maister John Fitzwilliams was angrie with William Thomas" (4:44)

From the perspective of legal history and theory, however, the most significant part of the trial was yet to come; for Throckmorton, in his determination to draw a distinction in the jury's mind between conversations and "overt acts" of treason, asked that the lawyers read aloud in the courtroom both the Marian statute repealing all previous treason laws except that of Edward III, and that ancient Edwardian statute itself. Unsurprisingly, this request was refused; "No sir, there shall be no bookes brought at your desire, we doo all know the law sufficientlie without booke," said Bromley (4:45); whereupon, despite his pose of legal ignorance, and with an extraordinary display of mnemonic power, Sir Nicholas proceeded to instruct the jury in the precise *wording* of the Marian statute, which restricted treason to its definition by the statute of 1352:

You seeme to give and offer me the law, but in verie deed I have onelie the
forme and image of the law; neverthelesse, sith I cannot be suffered to have
the statutes red openlie in the booke, I will by your patience gesse at them as
I maie, and I praie you to helpe me if I mistake, for it is long since I did see
them. The statute of repeale made the last parliament, hath these words: Be
it enacted by the queene, that from henceforth none act, deed, or offense,
being by act of parlement or statute made treason, petit treason, or misprision of treason, by words, writing, printing, ciphering, deeds, or otherwise
whatsoever, shall be taken, had, deemed, or adjudged treason, petit treason:
but onelie such as be declared or expressed to be treason, in or by an act of
parlement made in the five and twentieth yeare of Edward the third, . . . that
is to saie: Whosoever doth compasse or imagine the death of the king, or
levie warre against the king in his realme, or being adherent to the kings enimies within this realme, or elsewhere, and be thereof probablie attainted *by
open deed* by people of their condition; shall be adjudged a traitor. Now I praie
you of my jurie which have my life in triall, note well what things *at this daie*
be treasons, and how these treasons must be tried and decerned; that is to
say, by open deed, which the lawes dooth at some time terme (Overt act.)
(4:46; italics added)

At which point, we can still over all these years hear the querulous voice of
Sir Thomas Bromley raised in indignation:

Bromley: Why doo not you of the queenes learned councell answer him? Me
thinke, Throckmorton, you need not have the statutes, for you have them
meetlie perfectlie.

With the text of the current statutes thus inscribed in the minds of the
jurors, thanks to Throckmorton's canny direction of their attention ("note
well what things *at this daie* be treasons") the laywers became desperate, and
invoked cases from the common law which, they said, showed that merely
verbal complicity in or procurement of a crime was held fully as punishable
as action. It was this move that elicited Throckmorton's personal version of
legal literalism, which had two components: the first, that statute law is superior to common law, precisely by being written, and therefore capable of
literal interpretation; the second, that statute law, precisely by implying
the whole consent of the realm, is impersonal, whereas judges are subject
to interest and political pressure.

In pressing these principles, Throckmorton returned to the fact that
his present judges were once his colleagues—a powerful move which si-

multaneously denied his alienation from them and charged them with hypocrisy:

> I have remembered and learned of you maister Hare, and you maister Stanford in the parlement house, where you did sit to make lawes, to expound and explane the ambiguities and doubts of law sincerelie, and that *without affections.* There I saie I learned of you, and others my maisters of the law, this difference betwixt such [common law] cases as you remembred one even now, and the statute whereby I am to be tried. There is a maxime or principle in the law, which ought not to be violated, that *no penall statute maie, ought, or should be construed, expounded, extended, or wrested, otherwise than the simple words and nude letter of the same statute dooth warrant and signifie.*[40] And amongest diverse good and notable reasons by you there in the parlement house debated (maister sergeant Stanford) I noted this one, whie the said maxime ought to be inviolable. You said, *considering the private affections* manie times both of princes and ministers within this realme, for that they were men, and would and could erre, it should be no securitie, but verie dangerous to the subject, to refer the construction and extending of penall statutes to anie judges equitie (as you termed it) which might either by feare of the higher powers be seduced, or by ignorance and follie abused: and that is an answer by procurement. (4:48)

Throckmorton was not only citing written law but also instructing the courtroom in the principles of evenhanded justice. But his capacity to produce out of his memory the letter of the law was vital to his point, and one which he sprung as a late surprise, after having complained at the beginning of the trial that his "memorie is not good, and the same much decaied since [his] greevous imprisonment, with want of sleepe" (4:34). No doubt Southwell spoke for all of the commissioners (and we can easily imagine his tone of voice) when he said at the end of Throckmorton's verbatim recall of the pertinent wording, "You have a very good memorie" (4:49). Indeed, as only appropriate for a national chronicle,[41] memory becomes during this trial not only a theme but a principle on its own. If the law is to justify itself by its *long* memory, it would be well, the transcript implies by its loving attention to Throckmorton's "very good memorie," that we all had memories as *good* as his. There is a particularly telling statement at the climactic moment of the trial, which, however modestly, ironizes the unequal relationship between the defendant and the Crown. When Chief Justice Bromley completed his summary of all the evidence against Throckmorton, "and either for want of good memorie, or good will, the prisoners answers were in part not recited . . . the prisoner craved *indifferen-cie,* and did help the judges old memorie with his owne recitall" (4:49; italics added).

Indifference

The prisoner had in fact been craving "indifferencie" all along. At the beginning of his defence he had said: "I was minded to have said a few words to the commissioners . . . for their better remembrance of their duties in this place of justice, and concerning direct *indifferencie* to be used towards me" (4:33). When he asked for the statute books, he asserted: "You know it were *indifferent* that I should know and heare the law whereby I am adjudged," and he wheeled in other big guns. Addressing Bromley specifically, he said:

> What time it pleased the queenes majestie, to call you to this honorable office, I did learne of a great personage of hir highnesse privie councell, that amongst other good instructions, hir majestie charged and injoined you to minister the law and justice *indifferentlie* without respect of persons . . . hir highnesse pleasure was, that whatsoever could be brought in the favor of the subject, should be admitted to be heard. (4:45)

And later, when reminding the commissioners of their own arguments in repealing the Henrician treason act, he invited them, and the entire courtroom, to participate in this principle: "And now let us put on *indifferent eyes*" in order to engage in a comparative study of the law under Henry, and the law under his daughter.

For Throckmorton returned to the Marian treason act and its preamble, with its damning admission that the treason laws of her predecessors had been unjust, and suggested that the very commissioners now engaged in his trial were responsible for the language of that preamble:

> To what purpose serveth the statute of repeale the last parlement, where I heard some of you here present, and diverse other of the queenes learned councell, grievouslie inveie against the cruell and bloudie lawes of king Henrie the eight, and against some lawes made in my late sovereigne lord and masters time, king Edward the sixt. Some termed them Dracos lawes, which were written in bloud: some said they were more intollerable than anie laws that Dionysius or anie other tyrant made. In conclusion, as manie men, so manie bitter tearmes and names those lawes had. And moreover, the preface of the same [Marian] statute dooth recite, that for words onelie, manie great personages, and other of good behaviour, have beene most cruellie cast

awaie by these former sanguinolent thirstie lawes, with manie other sugges-
tions for the repeale of the same. (4:52)

In other words, his judges are now cast in the role of mere time-servers,
who have conveniently forgotten their own reforming instincts of a few
months ago. "And now," Throckmorton continued:

> let us put on indifferent eies, and throughlie consider with our selves, as you
> the judges handle the constructions of the statute of Edward the third, with
> your equitie and extentions, whether we be not in much woorse case now
> than we were when those cruell laws [the statutes of Henry VIII and Edward
> VI] yoked us. . . . For those lawes did admonish us, and discover our sinnes
> plainelie unto us, and when a man is warned, he is half armed. These lawes,
> as they be handled, be verie baits to catch us, . . . for at the first sight they as-
> certaine us we be delivered from our old bondage, and by the late repeale the
> last parlement, we live in more securitie. But when it pleaseth the higher
> powers to call anie mans life and saiengs in question, then there be con-
> structions, interpretations, and extentions reserved to the justices and judges
> equitie, that the partie triable, as I am now, shall find himselfe in much
> woorse case than before when those cruell lawes stood in force. (4:52)

The point was to show the jury that when jurisprudence reflects the turn-
ings of the wheel of political power (and of what society can that not occasionally be observed?) nothing is certain. New mercies may turn out to
be new tyrannies in disguise. Even unambiguous statutes may suddenly become pliable under the influence of the so-called judges equitie. And, turning to the jury, he added: "honest men which are to trie my life, consider
these opinions of my life, judges be rather agreeable to the time, than to
the truth: for their judgements be repugnant to their own principle, repugnant to their godlie and best learned predecessors opinions, repugnant I
saie to the proviso in the statute of repeale made in the last parlement." His
final appeal was both to religion and to the civil society: "And in that you
all be *citizens*, I will take my leave of you with S. Paules farewell to the
Ephesians, *citizens* also you be" (4:53; italics added). It was a masterly blend
of political scepticism with ethical fundamentalism, of sharply focused critical legal theory with an appeal to traditional sanctions.

The Trial by Jury

It took the jury about three hours to bring in a verdict of "Not Guilty," to
the unrestrained fury of the commissioners. As Holinshed had stated in his
own preamble to the trial, "with which verdict the judges and councillors

there present were so much offended, that they bound the jurie in the summe of five hundred pounds apeece," to appear before the Star Chamber. On April 21, they appeared before the Star Chamber judges, "from whense after certeine questioning, they were committed to prison, Emanuell Lucar and master Whetston [the two alternates who had been added after Dyer had made his challenges and who had emerged as the most courageous] to the tower, and the other[s] to the Fleet" (4:31) Four of them, under this pressure, submitted and confessed they had erred in their verdict. Many pages later, Holinshed had carefully recorded some information he had found in John Foxe's *Acts and Monuments* (1563), as to the fate of eight of "those honest men that had beene of Throckmortons quest," who refused, though imprisoned, to admit their verdict was wrong. They were called back to the court of Star Chamber, where Lucar "said openlie before all the lords that they had doone in the matter like honest men, and true and faithfull subjects." Not surprisingly, the Star Chamber judges "taking their words in marvellous evill part, judged them worthie to paie excessive fines" (4:64). Five of them were sentenced to pay 1,000 marks apiece, and the intransigent Whetston and Lucar £2,000 apiece. When Abraham Fleming augmented this section of the text in 1587, he added not one but three marginal notes drawing attention to the jury's intimidation: "Eight of maister Throckmorton's jurie appeere in the starchamber"; "The hard judgement of the lords against those eight honest men"; and "Further extremitie against Throckmorton's quest" (4:64). None of his Elizabethan readers could have failed to note, therefore, the significance of the episode. Still later, Holinshed recorded that, just before Christmas 1555, these fines were commuted to more realistic amounts, £220 in some cases and £60 in others, thereby confirming the ritual or intimidatory function (*in terrorem*) of the original penalties.

The Throckmorton jury's resistance to the state's agenda was recognized at the time, in David Loades's words, as "a hostile political demonstration."[42] In Elizabeth's reign, Sir Thomas Smith clearly alluded to Throckmorton's trial without mentioning it by name. In his *De Republica Anglorum*, Smith wrote that he had seen in his time (carefully adding in a parenthesis "not in the reigne of the Queene nowe") "an enquest for pronouncing one not guiltie of treason contrarie to such evidence as was brought in . . . not onely imprisoned for a space but an houge fine set upon their heads, which they were faine to pay"; and he further recorded the public response to this episode: "those doinges were even then of many accounted verie violent, and tyrannical, and contrarie to the libertie and custome of the realme of England."[43]

One would think, therefore, that this case should have acquired some legal-historical status among the historians of the early modern trial by jury; but in fact it has been largely overlooked, if not actually suppressed. Neither Thomas Green nor J. S. Cockburn, the two major authorities on this period, take any significant notice of it.[44] It may be that their emphasis on the large picture leads to their discounting the singular, symbolic instance, the one observed at the time, precisely that for which a cultural historian is most grateful. Yet there seems no doubt that Throckmorton's trial was a signal instance of a defendant's appealing to the jury *within a theory* of the jury trial, as the sign and instrument of the individual's rights before the law, which in turn was nested implicitly in a larger theory of democratic principle. Accentuated by Holinshed's induction of his readers to that same task of supplying "indifferency" or independent judgment, Throckmorton's words would pass through Lilburne's equally successful alliance with the jury in his 1649 trial for treason, and emerge in the mouth of T. J. Wooler in 1817 as plebeian radicalism: "It is your privilege, and a most important one, to stand between the oppressor and the oppressed—the accuser and the accused—it is for a British jury to interpose its aegis for the protection of British liberty."[45]

Reading the Statutes

There is one last area of significance in Throckmorton's trial that requires discussion: the issue of the layman's access to the law, which is obviously connected to the denial of legal counsel. There were, in fact, certain limited circumstances in which counsel was sometimes permitted, when the accused had already himself intuited some procedural irregularity and requested legal clarification. In the *Third Part of the Institutes* Sir Edward Coke had identified these irregularities as follows: the failure to mention an overt act when the indictment concerned compassing the king's death, any inaccuracy in the indictment in respect of time or place or the prisoner's name and rank, a lack of two witnesses at the indictment or the trial, a jury drawn from the wrong place, the application of an irrelevant statute, or there being a general pardon in operation which excused the crime in question.[46] By Coke's standards, Throckmorton should have had access to counsel on three of the above counts.

But he evidently was not prepared to risk refusal, and so had made himself into a legal expert for the occasion, not only "in the parlement house," where he obviously took extensive notes, but probably also during his "eight and fiftie daies" in close prison, where, as he disingenuously told his judges, "I heard nothing but what the birds told me, which did flie over my head" (4:44). It was part of Throckmorton's strategy to pretend ignorance of the law ("I never studied the law, whereof I doo much repent me," 4:49) all the better to surprise his judges with his mastery of it when his request for a reading of the statutes was refused. *The Legend of Sir Nicholas Throckmorton*, however, refers to "the mann who lent mee lawe of late, / To save my life, and putt himselfe in danger."[47] This ploy created much of the comedy in the later part of the trial. "If I had thought you had beene so well furnished in booke cases," said Stanford drily, "I would have beene better provided for you" (4:49), thereby revealing to the audience that the Crown's lawyers had failed to do their homework. And Griffin the attorney stood self-revealed as a whiner in defeat: "I praie you my lords that be the queens commissioners, suffer not the prisoner to use the queenes learned councell thus, I was never interrupted thus in my life, nor I never knew anie thus suffered to talke, as this prisoner is suffered; some of us will come no more at the barre and we be thus handled" (4:49–50).

But in fact the issue went beyond Throckmorton's own preparation for his defence. It gradually becomes clear, in retrospect, that he staged an encounter with his judges over the *public*'s access to the law in more general terms, by emphasizing the importance of the published statutes, which, being in English, were the law's equivalent to a Reformation vernacular scripture. On the judges' part it was made very clear that knowledge of the law by laymen was undesirable altogether, a dangerous impropriety. "I praie you my lords . . . let the statutes be read, as well for the queene, as for me," said Throckmorton, ". . . forasmuch as the statute is in English, men of meaner learning than the justices can understand it, or else how should we know when we offend." "What would you doo with the statute booke?" said Hare, "The jurie doth not require it, they have heard the evidence, and they must upon their conscience trie whether you be guiltie or no, so as the booke needeth not." "You ought not to have anie books read here at your appointment," said Cholmley, "for where dooth arise anie doubt in the law, the judges sit here to informe the court" (4:45–46).

On trial for treason against the Long Parliament in 1649, John Lilburne grasped both the tactical and theoretical advantages of this position. Throughout his two-day trial, he explicitly thematized the problem of the layman's access to the law. He constantly referred to his own reading of such "good old English laws" as were written in English. In accordance with his charge that the Long Parliamentarians were a reincarnation of the Norman Yoke, Lilburne complained: "you come to ensnare and entrap me with unknown niceties and formalities that are locked up in the French and Latin tongue, and cannot be read in English books, they being not expressed in any law of the kingdom, published in our own English tongue: it is not fair play according to the Law of England, plainly in

English expressed in the Petition of Right, and other the good old statute laws of the land" (4:1294). Lilburne was evidently not possessed of Throckmorton's mnemonic powers, and he was in this respect treated with greater latitude, for he was allowed to bring with him into the court bundles of notes, a copy of Coke's *Institutes*, and a statute book, from which he read to the jury the statutes of Edward VI on the need for two witnesses. "Here is the statute-book, let the Jury hear it read," cried Lilburne (4:1396). In contrast, the attorney general warned the rest of the commissioners that to grant Lilburne's demand for legal counsel and a for a copy of the indictment in English "would be a precedent for all future times; by means of which there would never be an end of trials in criminal cases" (4:1309).

Behind this strategy, which Lilburne had learned from Throckmorton, lay the same ancient constitutionalism and a belief that "equall" or "indifferent" laws were fundamental to a more equal and indifferent social structure. But Lilburne rendered their connection visible—by his constant references to Magna Carta and the Petition of Right of 1628, and by his claim that "due process" was as much "the common right of all or any of the people of England, as well as parliament men" (4:1393). In his summation of his defence he reiterated his claim that denial of counsel and of witnesses for the defence meant that his judges "go about to murder" him, "without law and against law." And therefore he commended himself to the protection of his "honest jury and fellow-citizens," who "are the conservators and sole judges of my life, having in them alone the judicial power of the law, as well as fact"; whereas his judges, he extravagantly asserted, were "but cyphers to pronounce the sentence," as well as "the Norman Conqueror's intruders" (4:1395). And, according to Clement Walker, "The People with a loud voice cried, *Amen, Amen,* and gave an extraordinary great hum," causing such unease in the Guildhall that the attending military officer sent for "more fresh companies of foot-soldiers." Huge demonstrations of joy were to follow the verdict of "not Guilty"; "And yet for all his acquittal by the law, his adversaries kept him afterwards so long in prison, that the people wondered, and began to grumble that he was not discharged" (4:1405).

Postscript

After his own acquittal, Throckmorton wisely followed his triumph with an act of submission to the queen, and a request for mercy. The words he used in his submission restate the themes that he (and Holinshed) had throughout been underlining. Throckmorton admitted that some of his talk, though not legally treason, had been on matters *"impertinent* for me a private person to talke of"; and he tactfully declared it had been a fair trial after all. He praised the Lord "for you the magistrats, before whome I have had my triall *indifferentlie* by the law" (4:54–55). Notwithstanding, he too was not released; but was sent back to the Tower, where he remained, attending clemency, for a year. On 18 January 1556, all of the Privy Council went together to the Tower and released all of the political prisoners, including Sir James Croftes, Sir Nicholas Arnold, Sir Edward Warner, Cuthbert Vaughan, and Sir Nicholas Throckmorton himself (4:74). It was a brief moment of clemency, before the burnings began of Cranmer, Latimer, and Ridley.

But there is a supplement to Holinshed's reasons for giving this trial such pride of place in the reign of Mary Tudor. At its conclusion is strange little editorial comment:

> Thus much for sir Nicholas Throckmorton's arreignement, wherein is to be considered, that the repealing of certeine statutes in the last parlement, was the chief matter he had to alledge for his advantage: whereas the repealing of the same statutes was meant notwithstanding for an other purpose (as before you have partlie heard) which statutes effect or the chiefe branches of them have beene since that time againe revived, as by the bookes of the statutes it maie better appeare, to the which I referre the reader. (4:55)

On the one hand, Holinshed seems to be offering his readers a warning against any enjoyment of Throckmorton's escape, a reminder that he was able, and perhaps improperly, to take an advantage of a loophole in the law that had now, under Elizabeth, been properly closed. On the other hand, not only does the mere presence of the trial in the *Chronicles* serve an educational function, the making of knowledgeable citizens and future jurors; but the reader is explicitly directed to that very source of knowledge of the law that Throckmorton's judges wanted to withhold, the "bookes of the statutes" printed in English, which had been appearing both annually and in collections, usually beginning with Magna Carta, from the end of the fifteenth century.[48]

This advice is therefore consistent with the chroniclers' stress throughout on the importance of reading, as one of the essential conditions of the civil society to which their work was a contribution; but whereas access to vernacular Bibles was good for the reformation soul, and those second scriptures, the chronicles, were an invaluable tool in the formation of a latitudinarian perspective, knowledge of the statutes of the realm could be literally a saving knowledge, since, as at least the case of Throckmorton had shown, it could save you from the executioner's block.

Two decades later, Throckmorton must have served as more than a memory of the bad old days of Mary's reign. For the *Chronicles* appeared during that phase of Elizabeth's when the political temper of the times had irrevocably been changed by the papal bull of February 1570, excommunicating the queen and discharging her subjects from obedience toward her. In 1571, accordingly, a new treason act (13 Eliz. I.C.1) made it treason to affirm *by writing* that the queen should not be queen, or that she was an infidel, tyrant, or usurper. In other words, she reinstated the most dangerously elastic provision of her father's notorious act of 1534, with the exception of words that were only spoken. The act goes unmentioned in the *Chronicles* for 1571; for it has already been noticed in Holinshed's reference many pages earlier: "which statutes or the effect of the chiefe branches of them have beene since that time againe revived."

As for Throckmorton himself, he was, as I have said, implicated in the Northern Rebellion, the reprisals for which had been part of the provocation for the papal bull. In January 1572, Thomas Howard, duke of Norfolk, was brought to trial for his part in the rebellion, in circumstances that replicated those of Throckmorton. As Penry Williams described it:

> The play was loaded in favor of the Crown. Norfolk was allowed no access to a lawyer while awaiting trial, and when he did ask to be represented by a lawyer, was refused by the Court. Of all the witnesses who testified against him, only one was actually present in court to have his evidence publicly weighed. The other testimony was read out by prosecuting counsel.[49]

On 2 June 1572, Howard was beheaded. The execution marked materially a change in the prevailing winds, since for this occasion a new scaffold had to be built beside the Tower of London, the previous one being "both rotten and ruinous," because, since "queene Elisabeth having with mercie governed hir commonwealth there was no punishment inflicted there upon anie for the space of fourteene yeares" (4:267). From that time onwards, however, the distinction between the two reigns, especially with regard to punishment for words, would be harder and harder to make.

Part Three

NINE   *Populism*

I n the 1587 edition of the *Chronicles*, in a section subsequently excised by order of the Privy Council, there is a description of the celebrations in London that followed the apprehension of the Babington Plot conspirators. The chronicler (who at this point in the narrative seems to have been Abraham Fleming) puts great emphasis on the popular consensus against the conspirators and claims the occasion as a moment of social harmony, a festival of which the government would approve:

> Beyond this the well affected of the citie did passe certeine degrees: for besides that some wearied themselves with pulling at the bellropes, which were roong both daie and night, as upon the daie of hir maiesties coronation; so other devised a further testification of joie, insomuch that although wood was then at a sore extent of price, yet they spared not their stacks or piles, were the same little or great; but brought (we thinke in conscience) everie house a portion, where fires might conveniently be made and without danger. *Memorandum* that none were more forward herein than *the meaner sort of people*, who rather than they would omit to ad little or much to a fire, being unprovided of fuell, parted with a penie or two to buie a few stiks by retaile. Insomuch that now *by common consent this action grew to be generall*. (4:899–900; italics added)

In this case, the editorial voice wishes the reader especially to note

("Memorandum") the concurrence in these festivities of "the meaner sort of people." This is to be seen, then, as an event of popular culture in the early modern sense of the term "popular," which was usually stigmatic, as in Lord Ellesmere's complaint in the early years of James's reign that "the popular state ever since the begining of his Majesty's gracious and sweet government hath grown big and audacious," a complaint which combined anxiety about the Midlands Rising with irritation at the behavior of the Commons in the fiscal negotiations of 1610.[1] Fleming's account therefore detaches the political idea of "common consent" from its traditional valence—self-determination by the people at large—and transforms it to a less threatening notion. Popular culture and its capacity for producing group action is, we might say, here held harmless: invoked to support the chronicler's claim (at least on the surface of his text) that the nation is united in concern for the safety of the queen and the Protestant religion, and that it benefits from the natural expressions of exuberance of the underclasses. Without this "common consent," which would also, at another level, be demonstrated in the petitions presented by the House of Commons to Elizabeth for the maximum sentence upon Mary, Queen of Scots, the climactic story of the 1587 *Chronicles* will not work.

In "Intentions" I proposed that the chroniclers, while themselves inarguably middle-class, and writing primarily for a middle-class audience, regarded themselves as responsible also for representing the underclasses as a significant component of a diversified society. This inquiry, which I called the anthropological level of the *Chronicles*, engaged the economic problems of the artisanal or peasant classes, as already described in chapter 5. This chapter pursues the representation of the "popular" in the *Chronicles*, and its results might bear comparison with certain assumptions within the field of cultural anthropology, in particular, the theories of "thick description" articulated by Clifford Geertz,[2] an analogy to which I shall return. Many of the episodes or details to which Sir Henry Savile and Edmund Bolton would have objected as "vulgar" or "trivial" have the effect both of thickening the description of the events under inspection with a rich brew of mundane detail, and of showing that popular culture was the medium through which the completely disadvantaged taught each other the techniques of survival. These included a sense of justice as fairness; a larger, more theoretical concept of social and economic egalitarianism; a skeptical penetration of official ideology; local solidarities; literacy when they could get it or, when they could not, the oral transmission of stories that carried popular resistance from one generation to the next; and, most extraordinarily, a kind of black humor.

A systematic reader of the *Chronicles*, one who began at the beginning, would long ago have received a clearer definition of "the meaner sort" from William Harrison's *Description of England.* His chapter "Of Degrees of People in the Commonwealth of England," from which Sir Thomas Smith plagiarized his rather better known sociological analysis,[3] distinguishes four main degrees or classes: gentlemen (a large category that included the aristocracy), citizens or burgesses, yeomen (or minor landowners), and artificers or laborers. When he came to the "fourth and last sort," Harrison further subdivided them into "daie labourers, poore husbandmen, and some retailers (which have no free land), copie holders, and all artificers, as tailers, shomakers, carpenters, brickmakers, masons, &c." (1:275). Later he added to this list "our great swarmes of idle serving men." After congratulating the English on having "no slaves and bondmen" in the system (in the literal sense), he observed that the fourth class "have neither voice nor authoritie in the common wealth, but are to be ruled, and not to rule other: yet they are not altogither neglected, for in cities and corporate townes, for default of yeomen they are faine to make up their inquests of such maner of people." That is to say, the meaner sort may, by default, have some role to play in the polis by way of the jury system, and so receive some minor alleviation of their voicelessness. But it was apparently part of the chroniclers' agenda to allow the fourth class, wherever possible, to speak for themselves, and to make their case for greater consideration, either through instances of active social protest, which the *Chronicles* record with remarkable indifference, or by way of anecdotes that sharply convey, especially by humanizing their protagonists, what kind of justice is available to those at the bottom of society.

To begin with the *Chronicles'* representation of active social protest is to reenter the question raised by Richard Grafton in his rivalry with Stow, as to whether by such representation "the gates [were] rather opened for crooked subjectes to enter into the fielde of Rebellion, then the hedges or gaps of the same stopped."[4] One can certainly state that, quantitatively speaking, the amount of attention given to such events was large, and increased over the life of the project. For the second edition, for example, the editors expanded the account of Jack Cade's rebellion in 1450 by including (from John Stow's personal manuscript copy) the text of the rebels' demands or "articles," and the 1549 uprisings provoked by the Edwardian reformation and Somerset's anti-enclosure policies were greatly expanded by the inclusion, as we shall see, of eyewitness accounts by John Hooker.

But even in the 1577 edition Raphael Holinshed established that, like every other issue of evaluation and judgment in which his readers were invited to participate, the problem of underclass protest was not an issue which could be disposed of in the stigmatic terms assumed by people like Lord Ellesmere, who had argued the traditional wisdom of a crackdown: "It was long ago observed by Livy, *vulgus aut humiliter servit aut superbe dominatur* [The crowd will either serve humbly or govern imperiously]. And it is found daily true, *Plebis importunitas cedendo accenditur* [the importunity of the plebs is increased by yielding to them]."[5] Holinshed and his colleagues, who had themselves been accused by Sir Henry Savile of emerging from the dregs of society, *ex faece plebis,*[6] were apparently less committed to social polarization than to social mediation and negotiation. Within the *Chronicles,* at any rate, the undifferentiated image of the crowd or mob is consistently modified by the appearance of recognizably human protagonists, and plebeian importunity is frequently explained, if not excused, by patient attention to the *causes* of social protest.

Both of these procedures are evident in Holinshed's treatment of what came to be seen as the orginal model of English social protest, whose repetition was, in the minds of government spokesmen, to be avoided at all cost: the 1381 uprising in the reign of Richard II. Holinshed depended for this section of the *Chronicles* primarily on Walsingham's *Historia Anglicana,*[7] almost certainly by way of the edition published by Archbishop Matthew Parker in 1574; and because for much of his account he follows his source almost verbatim, his departures from it can claim a certain significance at the level of intention. Following Walsingham, Holinshed cites three events which might or might not be related, as causes, to the uprising: the "new and strange subsidie" called the poll tax (in the marginal note, "a greevous subsidie") to be levied to support Buckingham's campaign in France; the appointment of Sir Robert Hales as Lord Treasurer, a man "not beloved of the commons"; and, perhaps merely as a coincidence, "about this time" the appearance of Wycliffe as a church reformer. Holinshed differs from Walsingham here only in being more specific about how the tax would apply to women (all those aged sixteen and over), of noting the exclusion only of "beggers certenlie knowne," and of stipulating the amount as four pence, while noting Walsingham's twelve pence in the margin. As in his treatment of Sir John Oldcastle, where the monastic chronicler's hostility to the Lollards was neutralized, Walsingham's view of Wycliffe as "vetus hypocrita, angelus Sathanae" disappears; but Walsingham *was* the source for an overarching theory of causation, in attributing to the commons a larger grievance than even the notorious poll tax, that is, the desire to be free of villenage:

> The commons of the realme sore repining, not onely for the pole grotes that were demanded of them . . . but also (as some write) for that they were sore

oppressed (as they took the matter) by their land-lords, that demanded of them their ancient customes and services, set on by some divelish instinct & persuasion of their owne beastlie intentions, as men not content with the state whereunto they were called, rose in diverse parts of this realme, and assembled togither in companies, purposing to inforce the prince to make them free and to release them of all servitude, whereby they stood as bondmen to their lords and superiors. (2:735)

The reference to "beastlie intentions," while not an exact translation, faithfully transmits to a later age from which villenage has been banished the original narrator's now obsolete political perspective.

Holinshed departed completely, however, from Walsingham when he came to describing how the general and diffused grievances had prepared for a particular and inflammatory occasion. His source here is, ultimately, local knowledge, transmitted through some text that has not survived:

When this rebellion of the commons first began, diverse have written diverslie. One author writeth, that (*as he learned by one that was not farre from the place at that time*) the first beginning should be at Dertford in Kent: for when those pole shillings or rather (as other have) pole grotes, were to be collected, no small murmuring, curssing, and repining among the common people rose about the same, and the more indeed, through the lewd demenour of some undiscreet officers, that were assigned to the gathering thereof, insomuch that one of those officers being appointed to gather up that monie in Dertford aforesaid, came to the house of one John Tiler, that had both servants in his house, and a faire yong maid to his daughter. The officer therefore demanding monie for the said Tiler and for his wife, his servants, and daughter, the wife being at home, and his husband abroad at worke in the towne, made answer that hir daughter was not of age, and therefore she denied to paie for hir.

Now here is to be noted, that this monie was in common speech said to be due for all those that were undergrowne, because that yoonge persons as well of the man as of the womankind, comming to the age of foureteene or fifteene yeares, have commonlie haire growing foorth about those privie parts, which for honesties sake nature hath taught us to cover and keepe secret. The officer therefore not satisfied with the mothers excuse, said he would feele whether hir daughter were of lawfull age or not, and therewith began to misuse the maid, and search further than honestie would have permitted. The mother streightwaies made an outcrie, so that hir husband being in the towne at worke, and hearing of this adoo at his house, came running home with his lathing staffe in his hand, and began to question with the officer, asking who made him so bold to keepe such a rule in his house: the officer being somewhat presumptuous, and highminded, would foorthwith have flowne upon this Tiler; but J. Tiler avoiding the officers blow, raught him such a rap on the pate, that his braines flue out, and so presentlie he died.

Great noise rose about this matter in the streets, and the poore folks being glad, everie man arraied himself to support John Tiler, & *thus the commons drew togither,* and went to Maidestone, and from thence to Blackheath, where their number so increased, that they were reckoned to be thirty thousand. And the said John Tiler tooke upon him to be their cheefe capteine, naming himself Jacke Straw. Others write, that one Thomas Baker of Fobbings was the first that procured the people thus to assemble togither; and that one of the kings servants named John Leg, with three of his fellowes practised to feele yoonge maids whether they were undergrowne (as yee have heard the officer did at Dertford) which dishonest and unseemelie kind of dealing did set the people streight in such a rage and uprore, that they cared not what they did to be revenged of such injuries. (2:735–36; italics added)

The effect of this anecdote apparently runs counter to the earlier note of disapproval that resulted from following Walsingham. Holinshed's "Now here is to be noted" matches the "Memorandum" of Abraham Fleming, as an eyewitness reporting on the popular festivities that marked the capture of the Babington plotters, but here the message is one of social antagonism and sexual outrage. Feeling up teenage girls on the pretext of collecting what has already been designated a "greevous subsidie" does not recommend itself as an image of legitimate government. One would have to be tight-lipped indeed not to feel that some kind of primitive justice was done, or was felt to have been done, when Tiler rises to the defence of his daughter, and his neighbors rise in support of him and his family. This anecdote functions rhetorically as a *captatio benevolentiae* for the uprising as a whole, and not least because Holinshed gives *two* versions of the story, revealing, if not its impeccable qualifications as fact, its dispersal in the popular memory.[8] It is the anecdote that lives on in the cultural memory, all the better for having been recorded in the *Chronicles,* and even as this sympathy is gradually exchanged for recrimination.

As the revolt became more violent, Holinshed's account becomes more critical; but even so there are moments at which he registers a more complex sense of the rebels' motivation, especially as he recounts their vandalization of the house of the duke of Lancaster:

The shamefull spoile which they there made was wonderfull, *and yet the zeale of justice, truth, and upright dealing which they would seeme to shew, was as nice and strange on the other part, speciallie in such kind of misgoverned people:* for in that spoiling of the duke's house, all the jewels, plate, and other rich and sumptuous furniture

which they there found in great plentie, they would not that any man should
fare the better by it a mite, but threw all into the fire, so to be consumed; . . .
One of them having thrust a faire silver peece into his bosome, meaning to conveie it awaie,
was espied of his fellowes, who tooke him, and cast both him and the peece into the fire; saieng
they might not suffer any such thing, sith they professed themselves to be zealous of truth and
justice, and not theeves nor robbers. (2:738)

While the description of the vandalism itself is a close paraphrase of
Walsingham (1:457), the sentences in italics are Holinshed's additions,
whose intention is confirmed by marginal comments: "Strange dealing of
the rebels," and "The justice of the rebels."

On the other hand, Holinshed faithfully translated Walsingham's
protest against the anti-intellectualism of the rebels, in a passage famous
because Shakespeare converted it into an agenda for his Jack Cade:

what wickednesse was it, to compell teachers of children in grammer
schooles to sweare never to instruct any in their art? Againe, could they have
a more mischeefous meaning, than to burne and destroie all old and ancient
monuments, and to murther and dispatch out of the waie all such as were
able to commit to memorie, either any new or old records? For it was dangerous among them to be knowne for one that was lerned, and more dangerous, if any men were found with a penner and inkhorne at his side: for
such seldome or never escaped from them with life. (2:746)

It seems only sensible to assume that in this instance the sixteenth-century
chronicler agreed with the fifteenth-century one on the "mischeefous
meaning" of this different form of vandalism. To one whose profession was
the preservation of the past, this destruction of records must have seemed
incapable of justification.

But we need to locate somewhere *between* these two positions—a guard-
ed sympathy and a shocked antipathy—the effect of Holinshed's recapitu-
lation of the famous sermon of John Ball to the multitude on Blackheath.
For where Walsingham introduced Ball as someone who "taught both the
perverse doctrines of perfidious John Wycliffe, and . . . false insanities"
("Docuit et perversa dogmata perfidi Johannis Wiclyf, . . . et insanias fal-
sas")[9] Holinshed observes merely that "this man had beene a preacher the
space of twentie yeares, *and bicause his doctrine was not according to the religion then*
by the bishops mainteined, he was . . . prohibited to preach in anie church or
chappell" (2:748–49). Driven from the church, Ball proceeded to "set
foorth his doctrine in the streets & fields where he might have audience," a
scenario repeated, as we have already seen in chapter 7, in Holinshed's
story of Sir Roger Acton and his fellow Lollards in 1414. The import of

Ball's prohibition has been subtly altered in the direction of indifferency by
the presence of that humble "then," the sign of ideological change; and if
what was acceptable in religion could change, so presumably could the social doctrine for which Ball had so long been excoriated.

This is what John Ball had spoken on Blackheath, taking as his text the
"common proverbe":

> When Adam delv'd, and Eve span,
> Who was then a gentleman?

and arguing that "from the beginning, all men by nature were created alike,
and that bondage or servitude came in by unjust oppression of naughtie
men":

> For if God would have had anie bondmen from the beginning, he would have
> appointed who should be bond & who free. And therefore he exhorted them
> to consider, that now the time was come appointed to them by God, in
> which they might (if they would) cast off the yoke of bondage, & recover lib-
> ertie. He counselled them therefore to . . . destroie first the great lords of the
> realme, and after the judges and lawiers, questmoongers, and all other whom
> they undertooke to be against the commons, for so might they procure peace
> and suertie to themselves in time to come, if dispatching out of the waie the
> great men, there should be an equalitie in libertie, no difference in degrees of
> nobilitie, but a like dignitie and equall authoritie in all things brought in
> among them. (2:749)

The text of the sermon was taken verbatim from Walsingham; so that were
anyone to object that these were dangerous positions even to articulate in
the late sixteenth century, the chronicler could simply point to his faithful
transmission of a fifteenth-century monastic chronicle.

The most demure assessment we can reach, then, about Holinshed's
representation of the Peasants' Revolt, is that it was inconclusive, but not
irresponsibly so. On the contrary, his reworking of inherited materials
seems to point to a greater interest in causation than his critics have noticed, and, more important, to an investment in the idea of justice, both social and juridical. The total effect is of an analysis less judgmental than
Walsingham's, or rather of a more evenhanded dispersal of judgment
against both sides in the contestation. Although there are moments of sympathy and admiration for the rebels, and more obvious passages of rejection
and repulsion, in sum the story conveighs a message compatible with the
agenda of the *Chronicles* as I have defined it—to assert the complexity of
events and the difficulty of evaluation, not their simplicity. Indeed, this is
how Holinshed summarized it:

To declare the occasion whie such mischeefes happened thus in the realme, we leave to the judgement of those that may conjecture a truth thereof, by conferring the manners of that age & behaviour of all states then, sith they that wrote in those daies, may happilie in that behalfe misse the trueth, in *construing things according to their affections.* But truelie it is to be thought, that the faults, as well in one degree as another, speciallie the sinnes of the whole nation, procured such vengeance to rise, whereby they might be warned of their evill dooings, and seeke to reforme the same in time convenient. (2:751; italics added)

The move to morality at the end in no way cancels the potent advice to the reader to be on the alert for bias in the medieval chroniclers—including class bias, for we have under scrutiny the "behavior of all states *then.*"[10]

This is equally true of Holinshed's treatment of another famous moment of popular disorder over two centuries later, the events of Ill May Day, 1517 (a day notorious among literary scholars by virtue of its *deletion* from the text of the play of *Sir Thomas More*).[11] In this case Holinshed's source was Edward Hall, who may even have witnessed the riot; and we can track Holinshed's intentions by noting that, although his account might be dismissed as a close paraphrase of Hall, he did in fact make significant additions to Hall's narrative; and to make matters more complex still, in 1587 the editor(s) went back to Hall's account to retrieve some passages of emotional force and ideological clarification that Holinshed had originally omitted. If I read their strategy correctly, the view of the *Chronicles'* creators is incompatible with that of modern historians, that Ill May Day was a regrettable case of industrial protectionism driven by xenophobia. They saw it rather as a confrontation between court and city, with the citizens in the disadvantageous position, and as one of the many stories scattered throughout the *Chronicles* about how readily justice is perverted by other powerful interests.

In the London of Henry VIII, we are told, there had been for some time "a great hartburning and malicious grudge amongst the Englishmen of the citie of London against strangers," whose freedom to operate as craftsmen in the city had led to "the great hinderance and impoverishing of the kings liege people" (3:617).[12] The actual riot was ignited, however (as in the 1381 uprising), by a mundane episode involving individuals. Holinshed insists that it was the strangers (in this case, the French) who gave the provocation:

it fortuned that as a carpenter called Williamson had bought two stockdooves in Cheape, and was about to pay for them, a Frenchman tooke them out of his hand, and said they were not meate for a carpenter. Well said the

Englishman I have bought them and now paid for them, and therefore I will have them. Naie said the Frenchman I will have them for my lord the ambassadour. And so for better or woorsse, the Frenchman called the Englishman knave, and went awaie with the stockdooves. (3:617–18)

But there was worse to come. The Frenchman went to his ambassador, and "surmised a complaint against the poore carpenter," who was sent to prison; and when Sir John Baker and others protested against this treatment, the ambassador answered "that by the bodie of God . . . the English knave should lose his life, for he said no Englishman should denie that the Frenchmen required, and other answer had they none" (3:618).

There were several other episodes illustrative of these tensions: but the result was that a certain John Lincoln, whom Hall and Holinshed called a broker, approached a preacher, Henry Standish, to preach a sermon against foreigners, and when Standish refused, Lincoln turned more successfully to Dr. Beale, a canon of St. Mary's Hospital, who on Tuesday in Easter week appeared in the pulpit of the "Spitle" and delivered an incendiary sermon on the economic consequences of uncontrolled foreign business in the city. Holinshed calls it a "pitifull bill," but one containing "much seditious matter" (3:619). On 28 April several young Londoners "piked quarels to certeine strangers. . . . some they did strike, some they buffeted, some they threw in the kennell [gutter]" (3:620). Several men, whose names are given, were imprisoned. A rumor began that on May Day the Londoners would rise and kill all the aliens. Cardinal Wolsey sent for the Lord Mayor to warn him, and after consultation with his own council and with Sir Thomas More it was agreed that there should be a curfew announced on May Day eve. That evening, Sir John Munday, an alderman (whose descendant Anthony Munday was one of the "hands" in the later dramatization of these events), found two young men playing at the bucklers in Cheapside, with a great many onlookers; for, as Holinshed, like Hall, reminded his readers, the curfew had only just been announced, so that many were probably still unaware of it. Munday commanded the game to cease, and when one of them asked why, arrested him. Then all the other apprentices rescued their colleague, "& cried, Prentises and clubs." By eleven that night, there were six or seven hundred persons gathered in Cheapside, and another three hundred in St. Paul's churchyard. Those who had previously been imprisoned were rescued from Newgate, and the riot was on in good earnest. In a famous episode, Sir Thomas More encountered them and attempted to persuade them to disperse; but "from ten or eleven of the clocke, these riotous people continued in their outragious dooings till about three of the clocke, at what time they began to withdraw, and went to their places of resort: and by the waie they were taken by the maior and heads of the citie, and sent some of them to the Tower, some to Newgate, and some to the Counters, to the number of three hundred" (3:621). In other words, the rioters had already exhausted themselves and were on their way home when the arrests were made.

At this point, Holinshed's account began to expand significantly, into areas of analysis that Hall had avoided. Holinshed inserted an explanation of why, against all reason, the disproportionate charge of treason was invoked in the indictments of the rioters. Sir John Fineux, lord chief justice, chose to apply to this situation legislation from the reign of Henry V (2 Henry V.c.6) that, where truces pertained between England and other countries, any attacks on members of those nations would constitute treason. "And note," Holinshed added, "that judge Fineux said, that all such as were parties to the said insurrection, were guiltie of high treason, as well those that did not commit anie robberie, as those that were principall dooers therein" (3:623). And he further extended the reach of the fifteenth-century statute into social control by applying it to breaches of the statute of laborers.

John Bellamy has commented on this astonishing legal interpretation, for which Holinshed seems to be our only informant, as "bad law based on worse history." He assumed it was the king or Wolsey who told the judges that treason was to be charged, but "whoever had the idea of using the statute of 1414 was certainly not well informed historically." Perhaps Fineux knew the weakness of the Crown's case, hence his reference to an insurrection in Kent "made against the statute of labourers," perhaps the act of 1381 (5 Ric. II st. 1.c.6) which had made it treason to initiate the Peasants' Revolt.[13]

Something that Holinshed omitted from his transcription of Hall, but that the 1587 editors *retrieved*, may also bear on the legal issues:

> Now upon examination it could never be prooved of anie meeting, gathering, talking, or conventicle, at anie daie or time before that daie; but that the chance so happened without anie matter prepensed of anie creature saving Lincolne, and never an honest person in maner was taken but onelie he. (3:622; Hall, p. 590)

This, Bellamy suggested, meant that the Crown was seeking evidence of men conspiring together, in the hope of laying a charge of compassing the king's death;[14] but because no evidence could be found, Fineux had to resort to the clearly irrelevant statute of 1414. In addition, we may assume, the issue of class argued against a normal application of the treason law of Edward III; because the only person involved above the level of artisan or

apprentice was Lincoln himself, the participants were assumed to be incapable of rational planning.[15]

The results of this manipulation of the law can now be anticipated.
Returning to Hall, Holinshed described how, on 4 May, the prisoners were
brought through the streets tied in ropes, some men, and some "lads of thirteene yeeres of age," 278 persons in all. All were adjudged guilty of treason
and condemned to be hanged, drawn, and quartered. Eleven pairs of gallows were set up "in diverse places where the offences were doone" (as well,
we now recognize, as to distribute the exemplary spectacle), and the prisoners were there executed "in a most rigorous maner, in the presence of the
lord [Edward] Howard, knight marshall." It is important to recognize that
whereas the tone of pity had been fully established by Hall, it is the justice
of these events that Holinshed brings into question. Yet one of the most
surprising aspects of the *Chronicles'* transmission is that, for the 1587 edition,
the editors went back to Hall for two brief passages previously omitted,
that respectively enhanced the pathos and sharpened the sense of injustice.
Howard, we are told, "shewed no mercie, but extreme crueltie to the poore
yoonglings in their execution: and likewise the dukes servants spake manie
opprobrious words, some bad hang, some bad draw, some bad set the citie
on fire, but all was suffered" (3:624).

The editors also retrieved Lincoln's *words* on receiving sentence: "My
lords, I meant well: for if you knew the mischief that is insued in this realme
by strangers, you would remedie it, & manie times I have complained, and
then I was called a busie fellow: now our Lord have mercie on me" (3:624;
cf. Hall, p. 590). As in the Peasants' Revolt (and several times elsewhere in
the *Chronicles*) violence inflicted on the young is seen as particularly repel-
lent; while emphasis on the actual words spoken by Lincoln extends to the
ordinary London citizen the principle of giving every man leave to tell his
own tale. In this instance, the fact that Lincoln had *not* previously been capable of getting his messsage across to the authorities creates a special kind
of poignancy.

Indeed, this episode supports my theory that the *Chronicles* were pre-
eminently a citizen project. Holinshed's first version already stressed the
different kinds of violence offered to the "city" of London. But for the 1587
text Abraham Fleming, as the marginal note indicates, went back to Hall
and reinstated a curious passage that makes the conflict between court and
city explicit:

> The citie thought the duke [of Norfolk] bare them a grudge for a lewd preest
> of his, which the yeare before was slaine in Cheape, insomuch that he then
> in his furie said; I praie God I maie once have the citizens in my danger! And

likewise the duke thought that they bare him no good will; wherefore he
came into the citie with thirteene hundred men in harnesse to keepe the oier
and determiner. . . . Then proclamations were made, that no women should
come togither to babble and talke, but all men should keepe their wives in
their houses. All the streets that were notable stood full of harnessed men,
which spake manie opprobrious words to the citizens, which greeved them
sore: and if they would have been revenged, the other had the woorsse: for
the citizens were two hundred to one, but like true subjects they suffred pa-
tientlie. (3:622; cf. Hall, pp. 589–90)

With Norfolk as the judge presiding over the trials, his army in the streets,
and his son as the executioner, patience was the only option; but the message hereby delivered was surely more complex than that "true subjects"
will always suffer in silence. The fact that, on 11 May, the king returned to
Greenwich and ordered a stay of the remaining executions can only partially have erased the impact of Ill May Day, a name of ambiguous referent.

These two episodes, from 1381 and 1517 respectively, show how the
Chronicles represented for their late Elizabethan readers the dangerous topic
of popular protest, its causes and consequences. Though striking, they are
not unrepresentative of the *tone* of the *Chronicles* whenever such episodes occurred; and, although Richard Grafton's animus was directed elsewhere,
they might reasonably have aroused his suspicions that this project was insufficiently protective of the institutional "hedges" between different social
strata, and especially designed to keep the popular element under control.
Since my focus here is summary justice, these episodes can also by supplemented by two examples of the workings of martial law; although "martial
law" is actually an oxymoron, since during military actions all due process
was suspended:

In time of this rebellion, a priest that by a butcher dwelling within five miles
of Windsor had been procured to preach in favor of the rebels, and the
butcher (as well for procuring the priest thereto, as for words spoken as he
sold his meat in Windsor) were hanged: the priest on a tree at the foot of
Windsor bridge, and the butcher on a paire of new gallowes set up before the
castell gate, at the end of the same bridge. The words which the butcher
spake were these. When one bad him lesse for the carcase of a sheepe than
he thought he could make of it: Naie by Gods soule (said he) I had rather the
good fellowes of the north had it, and a score more of the best I have, than I
would so sell it. This priest and butcher being accused on a mondaie in the
morning whilest the kings armie was in the field, and the king himselfe lieng
at Windsor, they confessed their faults upon their examinations, and by the

law martiall they were adjudged to death, and suffered as before is mentioned. (3:802)[16]

The source of this anecdote is again the section of the *Chronicles* devoted to the reign of Henry VIII. The context of the episode is the Pilgrimage of Grace, which took place in 1536, and which represented the only major organized threat to the Henrician Reformation. The tone of the anecdote as Holinshed imported it from Hall, and slightly rewrote it, is, I suggest, ambiguous, permitting but not requiring an interpretation favorable to the butcher, or at least interrogating the fairness of the punishment. The "words" which the butcher spoke, conceivably in jest but certainly casually in the course of his daily trade, were scarcely a justification for capital punishment. Even the new treason legislation enacted in 1534, whose severity resided precisely its inclusion of "words" alone, would seem to have required more than this as a pretext for an exemplary execution. It is true, of course, that it was also for "procuring" the priest's sermon (itself only words) that the butcher was executed. But Holinshed's insertion of that legalistic phrase, "for words spoken," intimates that he had in mind precisely that extension of treason to words that was the focus of Sir Nicholas Throckmorton's trial under Mary, and that, though canceled in her reign, had now been reinstated under Elizabeth; whereas Hall had not only introduced the charge of "treason" as if it were inarguable but stated that both priest and butcher "confessed there treason," a rather different matter from "confessed their faults." In fact, as Hall explained, thereby muddying the waters, the butcher was executed not under treason *law* as such, but under "the law mershal," which made no pretence of such distinctions.

Roger Manning, commenting on Hall's version, suggested that "the severity of the punishment may also be related to the fact that [the offence] was committed within the verge (i.e., within twelve miles) of royal palaces while the king's banner was displayed in time of rebellion."[17] In his own use of the word "severity" Manning was recording the *effect* the story had on him; but he nevertheless saw nothing in it to disturb his belief that martial law was taken for granted by the public at large, and only became problematic fifty years later, when it appeared as one of the major grievances in the Petition of Right in 1628.[18] The story as Holinshed told it, however, seems *intended* to produce a meditation on severity; only one of many signs that the *Chronicles* were themselves intentionally a contribution to the long, slow but continuous process of public education on issues of the law, politics, constitutional theory, and social policy more generally.

This inference is confirmed by another anecdote of the workings of martial law that Holinshed inserted into his account of the risings in 1549—the protests generated by the Edwardian Reformation and the social policies of Protector Somerset.

Holinshed provided an evenhanded account of Somerset's proclamation against enclosures, "tending to the benefit and releefe of the poore," but added that "how well soever the setters forth of this proclamation meant . . . yet verelie it turned not to the wished effect, but rather ministred occasion of a foule and dangerous disorder" (3:916). Anti-enclosure riots, he reported, broke out in Somerset, Buckinghamshire, Northamptonshire, Kent, Essex, and Lincolnshire. At the same time a religiously motivated rebellion broke out in Devon and Cornwall, and the *Chronicles* record the "articles" or demands of these rebels, who insisted upon a return in their local churches to the doctrine of transubstantiation. Yet the hedges between religion and the sociopolitical structure of the nation were as arbitrary as those between park and commons, and Holinshed discovered in Richard Grafton's chronicle just the story he needed to make that point—another tale of the workings of martial law in the service of social stabilization.

The tale as so retold has a distinctly Chaucerian flavor: a miller "that had been a great dooer in that rebellion," was consequently being pursued by Sir Anthony Kingston, in order to bring him to justice. "But the miller being thereof warned," Holinshed continued, "called a good tall fellow that he had to his servant, and said unto him:

> I have businesse to go from home, if anie therefore come to aske for me, saie thou art the owner of the mill and . . . that thou hast kept this mill for the space of three years, but in no wise name me.

The inevitable occurs; Kingston arrives to arrest the miller, and finding the servant ready to admit to ownership of the mill, had him hauled away to the nearest tree, saying, "Thou has beene a busie knave, and therefore here thou shalt hang." When the servant, in panic, reclaims his real status, nothing avails:

> Well then, said Sir Anthonie, thou art a false knave to be in two tales, therefore said he, hang him up; and so incontinentlie hanged he was in deed. After he was dead, one that was present told Sir Anthonie; Suerlie sir this was but the millers man. What then, said he, could he ever have doone his maister better service than to hang for him. (3:925–96)

We might be able to infer the social purpose of this real-life fabliau from that "incontinentlie," that puts up its own small resistance to the summary judgements of martial law, not to mention the brutal joke at the end; but the *Chronicles* help the watchful interpreter by adding a marginal note: "This was a hard proceeding, though the partie had been nocent."

Holinshed's fabliau of foxy miller, naive peasant, and callous knight clearly contains some of the black humor that was a crucial ingredient of the popular imagination, even when, as here, the joke is at the peasant's expense and only transmitted by his middle-class chronicler. Neverthless, the *Chronicles* are more than willing to turn the tables, and to register demotic humor at the expense of persons of supposedly dignified status.

Thus in the same section of the history we have just been considering, the uprisings of 1549, there occurs another real-life story showing how religious motives could be complicated by friction between the classes. In 1587 this section received a massive insertion of new material: the place-specific story of the seige of Exeter, as told by John Hooker, whose native territory this was and who wrote as an eyewitness,[19] and included in his account was an anecdote of interest to anyone who follows the adventures of Sir Walter Ralegh, since his father was the troublemaker. "It happened," wrote Hooker:

> that a certeine gentleman named Walter Raleigh dwelling not far from thense, as he was upon a side holie daie riding from his house to Excester, overtooke an old woman going to the parish church of Saint Marie Clift, who had a paire of beads in hir hands, and asked hir what she did with those beads? And entring into further speeches with her concerning religion, which was reformed, & as then by order of law to be put into execution, he did persuade with hir that she should as a good Christian woman and an obedient subject yeeld thereunto; saieng further, that there was a punishment by law appointed against hir, and all such as would not obeie and follow the same, and which would be put in execution upon them. (3:942)

This overzealous behavior on the part of Ralegh senior makes matters considerably worse:

> This woman nothing liking, nor well digesting this matter, went foorth to the parish church, where all the parishioners were then at the service: and being unpatient, and in an agonie with the speeches before passed betweene hir and the gentleman, beginneth to upbraid in the open church verie hard and unseemelie speeches concerning religion, saieng that she was threatned by the gentleman, that except she would leave hir beads, and give over holie bread and holie water, the gentlemen would burne them out of their houses and spoile them, with manie other speeches verie false and untrue, and whereof no talke at all had passed betweene the gentleman and hir. Notwithstanding she had not so soon spoken, but that she was beleeved: and

in all hast like a sort of wasps they fling out of the church, and get them to
the towne which is not far from thense,and there began to intrench and for-
tifie the towne. (3:942)

Ralegh himself was captured and kept prisoner in a local church tower,
"being manie times threatned to be executed to death," but survived. While
I certainly would not claim that Hooker's account *favors* the old woman and
her colleagues, nor that it was *intended* to be comic, his attention to psychological detail (her "agonie" at the conversation with Ralegh) is remarkable.
It seems clear, despite Hooker's statement to the contrary, that no false-
hood is involved in the old woman's account, only exaggeration of Ralegh's
warnings, whose tone—sympathetic, paternalistic, or threatening—we are
left to imagine. That Ralegh was a meddler, and his mildly absurd predicament a form of poetic justice, is certainly one of the possible conclusions.

The most overtly comic section of the *Chronicles*, however, occurs in
Mary Tudor's reign, and in connection with her reversal of the Edwardian
Reformation, her plans for marriage to Philip II of Spain, and her pathetic
imaginary pregnancy. Holinshed himself had recognized the value, in describing these matters, of John Foxe's sardonic account in the *Acts and
Monuments*. From Foxe he took the strategy of making the queen's childless-
ness symbolic, both of the barrenness of the reign and of the emptiness of
official propaganda. The rumors of the birth of an heir were so intense that
bells were rung and bonfires lit, "but in the end, all proved cleane contrarie,
and the joy and expectation of the people utterly frustrate: for shortly it
was fully certified (almost to all men) that the Queene was as then neyther
delivered of childe, nor after was in hope to have any." This, then, was a
false festival (worth remembering when we return to celebrations for the
Babington plotters' apprehension); and Holinshed took from Foxe a telling
paragraph on how popular opinion was not deceived by the bells and the
bonfires. "Of this," he continued, "the people spake diversly. Some sayde,
that the rumor of the Queenes concepcion was spredde for a policie. Some
affirmed that she was with childe, but it miscaried. Some other sayd, that
shee was deceived by a Timpany, or other lyke disease" (1577: 3:1765).[20]
The emphasis on *talk*, and on diversity of opinion among the common people, accords with the program of the *Chronicles* as a whole; and the phrases
signifying reported speech (*some said . . . some other sayd*, etc.) have already
been identified as rhetorical signs of the necessary displacements of social
criticism.

In 1587 this account was heavily expanded by Abraham Fleming, who
spared no opportunity to deride the Catholic queen, not least for her child-
lessness, and returned to the pages of Foxe's *Acts and Monuments* in search of

still more damaging material, augmenting the passage just quoted with another anecdote illustrative of popular scepticism.

> In the midst of this great adoo, there was a simple man (this I speak but upon information) dwelling within foure miles of Barwike, that never had beene before halfe waie to London, which said concerning the bonefire made for queene Maries child; Here is a joifull triumph, but at length all will not prove worth a messe of pottage, as in deed it came to passe. (4:82)

Fleming's point is that the nation was *divided* by the prospect of the Spanish marriage; although "some supposed that this land would have become a golden world," others "were of a contrarie opinion, supposing (as it came to passe indeed) that the peoples minds would be alienated" (4:61); and he strongly implies that those who embraced the new regime were the higher clergy, whereas ordinary folk were wiser. So we are treated (via Foxe) to a sardonic picture of the raising of a crucifix in St. Paul's Cathedral, and how Bishop Bonner "in his roialtie, and all his prebendaries about him . . . annointed the rood with oile in divers places, and after the annointing crept unto it and kissed it." Foxe and Fleming, of course, had intended this ceremony to be read as an act of idolatry; and its parody quickly follows:

> Not long after this, a merrie fellow came into Paules, and spied the rood with Marie and John new set up, wherto (among a great sort of people) he made low curtsie and said: Sir, your maistership is welcome to towne. I had thought to have talked further with your maistership, but that ye be heere clothed in the queenes colours. I hope ye be but a summers bird, for that ye be dressed in white and greene. (4:63)

Here today and gone tomorrow. This is the comic version of the message the *Chronicles* carry in tragic form, as the story of the Tudors unrolls, each determined to erase the traces of their predecessor.

But the most striking episode in this anti-Marian satire is also the most elliptical, the most symbolic, and the least subject to editorial intervention. Although Fleming's own response as a literateur was to insert an Aesopian fable of his own making on the dangers of the queen's marriage,[21] he also slipped into his text another item, this time taken from John Stow, which extends the Aesopian critique in a different direction:

> On the eight of Aprill, then being sundaie, a cat with hir head shorne, and the likeness of a vestment cast over her, with hir fore feet tied togither, and a round peece of paper like a singing cake betwixt them, was hanged on a gallows in Cheape. (4:28)[22]

At the heart of this countercultural message are both theological dispute over the Eucharist, here represented mockingly by "a singing cake" fastened between catspaws, and a demotic antifeminism: the "cat" is assumed to be female, implying also a prostitute (as in cathouse). With great economy the popular satirist had conflated an attack on the Roman Catholic reaction and on the queen herself as a woman whose emotional and sexual needs were driving her into the arms, it was feared, of foreign domination. That it was taken seriously as a protest is demonstrated by the fact that the cat was taken to Bishop Bonner, and he, rather unwisely it appears from this distance, "caused the same to be shewed at Pauls crosse by the preacher doctor Pendleton," thereby spreading its carnival message. Indeed, an alternative version of the story in Foxe's *Acts and Monuments* makes it clear that the joke was taken very seriously indeed. "Whereon rose great evil-will against the city of London; for the queen and the bishops were very angry withal. And therefore the same afternoon there was a proclamation, that whosoever could bring forth the party that did hang up the cat, should have twenty nobles, which reward was afterwards increased to twenty marks; but none could or would earn it."[23] There is a connection, then, between demotic humor, as the vehicle that makes a protest effective by rendering it memorable, and local solidarity, as the broader-based resistance that (as also happened with the rewards offered for the capture of Sir John Oldcastle) runs deeper than economic incentives.

Although the *Chronicles'* interest in the economic health and policy of the nation has already been detailed, that topic is never far from the surface in the representation of popular culture, and it should, therefore, be briefly reconsidered here.

Let me first reduce it to its most elemental level, by returning to John Hooker's account of the 1549 uprisings in the southwest, and particularly to the seige of Exeter, where are we reminded that what runs deeper even than popular resentment or solidarity is the antisocial force of hunger:

> For no force is feared, no lawes observed, no magistrate obeied, nor common societie esteemed, where famine ruleth. For as the poet saith: *Nescit plebs jejuna timere* . . . And albeit there were good store of drie fish, rise, prunes, rasins, and wine, at verie reasonable prices, yet bread which as the prophet saith, *Confirmat cor hominis,* Strengtheneth man's hart, that wanted: neither was anie to be had. And in this extremitie the bakers and housholders were driven to seeke up their old store of puffins and bran, wherewith they in times past were woont to make horsebread, and to feed their swine and poultrie, and this they moulded up in clothes, for otherwise it would not hold togither, and so did bake it up and the people well contented therewith. For (as

Plutarch writeth) *Fames reddit omnia dulcia, nihilque contemnit esuriens:* Hunger
maketh all things sweet, and the hungrie bellie shunneth nothing. (3:952)

While it might be possible to scorn this description as "triviall household
trash," an anthropological perspective must treasure it; not only for the data
on baking in hard times (the Exeter inhabitants would be amused at our
current obsession with bran, and the expensive forms in which it is
processed); not only for the rare word "puffins," which the compilers of the
Oxford English Dictionary encountered only here; but also for the clarity
with which it renders the clash of cultures: the classically educated historian trading in quotations,[24] the life of the mind, yet alert to the recalcitrant
social truth of "the hungrie bellie" elsewhere, a material fact which the
canny bakers know how to assuage, moulding their bran in cloth to make
it, like the social fabric of the beseiged town, "hold togither." We might
infer that Howell intends this as a metaphor; for he explains that the common people would have readily surrendered, had not the magistrates insisted on a rigorously equitable food distribution.

There is a strongly ironic relation, therefore, between this long interpolation in the 1587 edition and Holinshed's previous inclusion, in 1577,
of the complete text of Sir John Cheke's *The Hurt of Sedicion.* Cheke's tract
had been published in the immediate aftermath of the 1549 uprisings and
was presumably intended in part to insulate from the policies of Somerset,
which were thereby discredited, Cheke and the other learned humanists
assembled by Catherine Parr to educate the young king. Cheke's strategy
was to deny validity to both the religious and social causes of the unrest.
Particularly to the Norfolk rebels who had assembled under the leadership
of Robert Ket at Mousehold, and who had held a series of trials of gentlemen under the "Tree of Reformation," Cheke had written as follows:

Ye pretend a common-wealth. How amend ye it? by killing of gentlemen, by
spoiling of gentlemen, by imprisoning of gentlemen? A marvellous tanned
common-wealth. Whie should ye thus hate them? For their riches or for their
rule? . . . In countries some must rule, some must obeie. . . . And therefore not
they that know their own case as everie man doth, but they that understand
the common-welth's state, ought to have in countries the preferment of ruling. (3:989)

But after this standard appeal to irremediable social difference Cheke can-
nily appealed to the economic aspirations of the rebels themselves and invoked the possibility of personal social mobility through the market as the
strongest disincentive against a political readjustment of the power relations. Precisely that which John Ball's sermon had put so starkly as the nec-

essary goal of social protest, then, Cheke's countersermon argues, would prevent each and any of the 1549 protesters from advancing their own prospects and those of their children:

> And to have no gentlemen, bicause ye be none your selves, is to bring down an estate, and to mend none. Would ye have all alike rich: That is the over-throw of labour, and utter decay of worke in this realme. For who will labour more, if when he hath gotten more, the idle shall by lust without right take what him lust from him, under pretense of equalitie with him. . . . If there should be such equalitie, then ye take awaie all hope from yours to come to anie better estate than you now leave them. (3:990)

Holinshed's decision to include Cheke's tract (verbatim) in the rich and complex story of 1549 was, therefore, explicable on at least three grounds. It was compatible with the overall goal of the *Chronicles*, to preserve for pos-terity otherwise ephemeral pamphlets. It was prudential, in the sense that its presence would help to counter criticism such as Grafton had leveled at Stow. And it was intellectually canny, in that Cheke's economic critique of popular egalitarianism had, whatever its motives, a logical force, to which the middle-class readers of the *Chronicles* would be susceptible even as they saw the events of 1549 in more complex human terms.

In my initial description of the protocols of the *Chronicles* I cited the double account of Somerset's execution in 1552, which set against each other the eyewitness accounts of John Stow and John Foxe, each describ-ing the same "hurlie-burlie" among the crowd surrounding the scaffold, yet differently recording the sound of the popular voice speaking in unison. For Stow, who, we remember, rejected a superstitious reading of the great noise caused by the late arrival of militia, the corporate cry was one of prac-tical self-protection ("Awaie, awaie"), for Foxe the martyrologist "most part of them cried out: Jesus save us, Jesus save us." In the penultimate section of this chapter, and before returning to Fleming's account of the public cele-brations that took place in the streets of London in 1586, I want to suggest that the *Chronicles* also display some concern with a theoretical issue that arises whenever one uses terms like "the people," "the plebs," or "the popu-lar voice." That is to say, the procedural problems that the anthropologist faces whenever he attempts to describe a culture other than his own—problems of translation from one gestural language to another—are inten-sified when he moves from the individual, whose behavior he can interro-gate, to the group, about whom he may only generalize. And, as political organizers know to their equal peril, the pulse of popular movements or trends can only be taken by "sampling" the opinions of individuals. Those who compiled the two editions of the *Chronicles* seem to have been alert to the problems of reproducing the popular voice at these levels of abstraction. While they deployed the verbatim principle with confidence in relation to the vocal individual (John Ball, John Lincoln, the old woman telling the story of her confrontation with Ralegh senior, the merry fellow addressing the rood), when it came to representing the voice of the people at large, the speaking crowd, the chroniclers registered various forms of caution, anxiety, or self-consciousness.

Or, at least, they *seem* to; for I myself need to register some mixture of these inhibitions at this point in the argument. The three exhibits that follow are not *examples* in the sense of representing a wider range of conscious or half-conscious articulations of this problem. They are, indeed, unique, and entirely different from each other. Yet each is packed, as it were, with procedural caveats for those who claim to speak for the people at large, or to invoke that concept in the service of their own agendas.

The clearest statement of this issue occurs in the extraordinary block of material that Holinshed inherited from Sir Thomas More. Along with his affinity for More's black humor, and perhaps, as we shall see, his protofeminism, Holinshed would in all probability have welcomed one aspect in particular of More's *History of Richard III,* those scenes in which the Londoners are expected to participate in the formalities invoked to sweeten Richard's usurpation. In these scenes of fifteenth-century history, as retold in the first half of the sixteenth century by More, and replayed by Holinshed in the last quarter of that century, there is displayed an astonishing prolepsis of late-twentieth-century models of analysis: a sceptical account of the connection between state ritual and ideology, offered as evidence for the sceptical penetration of ritual and ideology by ordinary citizens.

More's *History* relates a speech delivered by the duke of Buckingham to the citizens of London—mayor, aldermen, and "commons"—in the Guildhall, persuading them to offer Richard the crown. After all his reasons, which included the destructive effects of Edward IV's conquest, the alleged illegitimacy of his children by virtue of a prior marriage, his adulteries generally, and (a surefire persuasive for such an audience) his abuse of revenue-raising devices, Buckingham looked for a popular consensus. He "looked that the people, whome he hoped that the maior had framed before, should after this proposition made, have cried; King Richard, king Richard." But "all was husht and mute, and not one word answered . . . were it for woonder or feare, or that each looked that other should speake first: not one word was there answered of all the people that stood before, but all was as still as the midnight, not somuch as rowning [whispering] amongest them, by which they might seeme to commune what was best to do."

This *absence* of the popular voice generates a crisis. The duke "rowned unto the maior and said; This is a marvellous obstinate silence," and turning again to the audience, *demanded* an answer. "At these words the people began to whisper among themselves secretly, that their voice was neither lowd nor distinct, but as it were the sound of a swarme of bees," until at last, at the far end of the hall, a group of Richard's servants began to shout "as lowd as their throtes would give; King Richard, king Richard: and threw up their caps in token of joy." The Londoners retained their silence, but the duke and the mayor "wiselie turned it to their purpose, and said it was a goodlie crie, & a joifull, *to heare everie man with one voice, no man saieng naie*" (3:393–94).

Can it be entirely a coincidence that More's swarm of bees (the image of a civil society in transition from one ruler to another) anticipates in the *Chronicles* Hooker's 1549 perception of the Devonshire protesters as a swarm of wasps? With the exception of the production of honey, wasps share their apian cousins' societal structures. At any rate, in the London hive of 1483, the following day was enacted a political drama whose script had been written in advance. The mayor and all the alderman, Buckingham and a large company of knights and gentleman, paid court to Richard at Bainard's castle and begged him to accept the crown. Richard elaborately declined it, citing his conscience. Finally he was persuaded. "With this there was a great shout, crieng; King Richard, king Richard." The *sound* of consensus has been achieved. But, continued More:

> the people departed, talking *diverslie* of the matter, everie man as his fantasie gave him. But much they talked and marvelled of the maner of this dealing, that the matter was on both parts made so strange, as though neither had ever communed with other thereof before, when that themselves wist there was no man so dull that heard them, but he perceived well enough that all the matter was made [prearranged] betweene them. Howbeit some excused that againe, and said all must be doone in good order though: and *men must sometime for the maners sake, not be aknowen what they know* [though it be hard to out-reach the circumspect, wise, & vigilant minded man; as the poet saith:
>
> . . . non facile est tibi
>
> Juvenal: sat 2. Decipere Ulyssem.] (3:396; italics added)

There could scarcely be a better witness against the modern doctrine that ordinary citizens exist within a sealed dome of ideology immune to their cognitive penetration; a witness all the more persuasive by way of its insistence on the diversity of public opinion, some decrying the hypocrisy of the scene (an attitude adopted by Fleming, who added the quotation from Juvenal's second satire) but others excusing it as typical of public rituals and the workings of hegemony. Indeed, More continued (and we have to look carefully to recognize in whose voice he was speaking), we see such rituals continually: in the consecration of a bishop, where the form requires the candidate to twice decline his appointment, and also "in a stage plaie," where

> all the people know right well, that one plaieng the Soldan, is percase a sowter; yet if one should can [know] so little good, to shew out of season what aquaintance he hath with him, and cast him by his owne name while he standeth in his maiestie, one of his tormentors might hap to breake his head (and worthie) for marring of the plaie. *And so they said*, that these matters be kings games, as it were stage plaies, and for the more part plaied upon scaffolds, in which poore men be but the lookers on. And they that wise be will meddle no further. For they that sometime step up, and plaie with them, when they can not plaie their parts, they disorder the plaie, and doo themselves no good. (3:396)

This emphasis on the "theatricality" of politics in church and state is compatible with certain theories of Elizabethan culture formulated today; it is all the more important, therefore, to acknowledge the centrality of *knowingness* in More's account, and that this knowingness (which includes the pretence of naïveté, for "men must sometime for the maners sake, not be aknowen what they know") is attributed to the ordinary London citizens.[25]

Theatricality, or rather an analogy between sociological behavior in the workplace and in the public theaters, is also explicitly an issue in the *Chronicles'* story of the rebuilding of the Dover harbor, already cited in my chapter on economics. Let us look again, in this different context, at that remarkable passage in which Reginald Scot reported on how the workers responded to the hours of work and to the issue of timekeeping, over which, it appears, there was a struggle for control between the workmen themselves and their supervisors. Given the extremely arduous ten-hour day, beginning at five o'clock in the morning, there was evidently a "union" concern for the timeliness of the midday and final breaks; a concern supported by certain vocal rituals generated by the workers themselves:

> And presentlie upon the signe given, there was a generall shout made by all the workers: and wheresoever anie court (cart) was at that instant either emptie or loden, there was it left, till one of the clocke after noone or six of the clocke in the morning, when they returned to their businesse. But by the space of halfe an houre before the flag of libertie was hanged out, all the court drivers entered into a song, wherof although the dittie was barbarous,

and the note rusticall, the matter of no moment, and all but a jest, yet is it not
unworthie of some briefe note of remembrance; because the tune or rather
the noise therof was extraordinarie and (being delivered with the continuall
voice of such a multitude) was verie strange. In this and some other respect,
I will set downe their dittie, the words wherof were these:

> O Harrie hold up thy hat, t'is eleven a clocke,
> and a little, little, little, little past:
> My bow is broke, I would unyoke,
> my foote is sore, I can worke no more.

Here, then, is an another instance of popular culture as consensus, the
workers raising a folk chorus as a warning that their break is imminent, followed by a human equivalent of the factory whistle. In contrast to More's
History, however, the "general shout" is not invoked by the authorities but
part of a sociological negotiation in which the workers, so long as they
work *as* a group, have the dominant position; and as Scot records his own
response to this practice we can tell it makes him uncomfortable. "The tune
or rather the noise therof was extraordinarie and . . . verie strange." As an
anthropologist, he senses he is dealing with an alien culture: "the dittie was
barbarous, and the note rusticall, the matter of no moment, and all but a
jest," a description that comes round at the end to acknowledging the relationship between popular resistance and popular humor. But Scot explicitly located this practice within a broader cultural framework, wherein that
which is "extraordinarie" and at first sight unruly may also be recognizable
as an authentic contribution to the multilayered fabric of civic or citizen
self-representation:

> The song was made and set in Romneie marsh, where their best making is
> making of wals and dikes, and their best setting is to set a needle or a stake
> in a hedge: howbeit *this is a more civill call than the brutish call at the theater for the
> comming awaie of the plaiers to the stage.* (4:865–66)

We can now return, at last, to this chapter's opening gambit, Abraham
Fleming's description of the popular celebrations in London at the discovery of the Babington Plot and the arrest of the conspirators; and we should
surely return as suspicious readers. There seems to be no doubt that
Fleming was straightforward in his intentions, which were to present the
conspiracy in the darkest possible light, to justify the executions in all their
severity, and ultimately to justify the conviction and execution of the
Scottish queen, whose complicity in the plot (he may or may not have
known) had been partially engineered by Sir Francis Walsingham. At the
same time, as we shall see in chapter 11, the historiographical principle of

the *Chronicles* ("to give everie author leave to tell his owne tale") resulted in Fleming's recording in the uncensored text the unpublished or illegally published statements, stories, and poems of the conspirators in the Tower. The effect of *this* imprudent multivocality would have been, at the very least, to further unsettle the readers' sympathy and allegiance. It was scarcely surprising, then, that this section of the text was strenuously pruned in the censored version.

In Fleming's first uncensored account of these festivities, the ritual celebrations, we are told, expanded into a public picnic, which could also be perceived as a sociopolitical eucharist:

> The people . . . did not so staie their inward rejoising; but bringing out their square and round tables into the open streets, like neighbors sitting together, and furnishing the boords with such provision as the present time afforded, made merrie in comelie and honest sort. Where (by the waie) this is noteworthie, that manie times an evill thing doth effectuat a good. For by the breaking out of this conspiracie . . . it so came to passe, that many a privat reconciliation was procured by this mutuall meeting of neighbours between diverse that before had beene at overthwarts and in secret grudge, all which was washed awaie with a cup of merrie go downe for hir sake, that *Secundum Deum est columen salutis nostrae.* (4:900)[26]

In this passage, it is almost impossible to resist the ritual allure of the scene, the impression of verisimilitude, the utopian hypothesis of social harmony, with the queen, the secular redeemer, as the ritual's central object of reverence. But a suspicious reader who looked back at the earlier passage might now observe that when Fleming describes the bellringers as "the well affected of the citie" he unavoidably invokes the question whether there were any citizens not quite so well affected; that in his description of the bonfires to which all wished to contribute a piece of firewood the parenthetical motivation ("we thinke in conscience") makes one wonder what other motivations (social pressure, or simple carnival impulse) might have been operative on such an occasion; and that the sacrificial gestures of "the meaner sort" were memorable (that is, of historical significance) precisely because of economic hardship, because "wood was then at a sore extent of price."

These intimations of strain reappear in a different register when Fleming addresses the problem of verbal testimony, and offers his own ventriloquized version of the popular voice raised in consensus:

> people thronged togither to see the unnaturall beasts that were attached, . . . which how damnable it was, the whisperings, communications, and lowd

speeches of the multitude, pointing at them with the finger of infamie as traitors of singular note (some saieng, Looke, looke, yonder go the errant traitors that would have killed our queene, yonder goe the wretches that would
have burnt our citie, that would have alienated the state of the land, that
would have laid all open unto bloudshed, slaughter, desolation, and spoile:
yonder they go whome heaven above dooth abhorre, the earth below detest,
the sun, moone, and starres be ashamed of, all creatures doo cursse and count
unworthie of breath and life) . . . whome none can pitie without suspicion of
impietie, none lament but with lacke of loialtie, none favorablie speak of but
with great note of ingratitude and privie trecherie? To this effect tended the
interchangable speeches of the people, *all with one voice* disclosing the con-
ceipts of their mind against these eminent traitors. (4:898–99; italics added)

This certainly sounds at first reading like the unimpeachable voice of
hegemony. On second thought, however, it appears that the chronicler
was at least half-conscious of the fictionality of his task—that is to say, the
production of univocality. The quotation that begins with an air of dramatic
realism ("some saieng, Looke, looke . . .") gradually modulates into high-
cultural rhetoric ("yonder they go whome . . . the sun, moone, and starres
be ashamed of") and ends by admitting that unanimity is *required*, since
"none can pitie" the conspirators "without suspicion of impietie . . . none favorablie speak" of them "without great note of ingratitude and privie
trecherie."

And lest we should have any doubt as to how this official version of
popular culture has been constructed, Fleming proceeded, a few pages
later, to show the mechanism at work:

the people were in dailie expectation and desire to heare some report of the
conspirators now by their owne confessions sufficiently convicted: whereupon a preacher at Pauls crosse *was commanded from authoritie*, to deliver some
notice to the assemblie, answerable to the knowledge which he himselfe received by eare at the best hand; namelie, that diverse of the traitors were apprehended, and without anie torture or torment confessed their treasonable
intentions; which were, to murther her majestie, and procure meanes for the
arrivall of forren powers, whereby the land might be overrun, heaven and
earth confounded, and all things turned topsie turvie. (4:909; italics added)

The redefinition of the carnival impulse ("topsie turvie") as apocalypse
("heaven and earth confounded") shows how far the editorial account of
this crisis was incompatible with the demystifying spirit of the *Chronicles*
elsewhere. Whether or not Fleming felt himself "commanded by authoritie," whether he misjudged that mandate and went too far in developing a

punitive rhetoric which discredited itself, whether he understood the gap between that rhetoric and the "facts," he was here evidently struggling, caught between his own anti-Catholic impulses and the anthropological logic of the project as a whole.

In conclusion, I would like to recall, and to wrest to opposite purpose, Levy's words of reproach to the *Chronicles* for putting everything in, no matter how trivial, vulgar, or unworthy, by some standards, it might seem. "Once facts could be established as equal in authenticity," Levy wrote, "they were assumed to be *equal* in all other ways as well."[27] Just so; an egalitarian principle, however, that traditional historiography, often accused of being exclusively concerned with the history of elites, is bound to see rather as *lack* of principle. Cultural history, however, can take comfort from the self-definitions of cultural anthropology, which, in Clifford Geertz's words, is concerned with the following: "construing social expressions on their surface enigmatical"; learning to distinguish between involuntary gestures (a twitch) and conspiratorial signals (a wink); disentangling "a multiplicity of complex conceptual structures, many of them superimposed upon or knotted into one another, which are at once strange, irregular, and inexplicit" (phrases which coincidentally replicate Levy's critique of the *Chronicles*). All of these types of interpretation are justified, finally, by their saving relation to the small things of this world, rather than the large concepts. The anthropological approach to culture is, in Geertz's word, necessarily "microscopic." The cultural anthropologist

> confronts the same grand realities that others—historians, economists, political scientists, sociologists—confront in more fateful settings: Power, Change, Faith, Oppression, Work, Passion, Authority, Beauty, Violence, Love, Prestige; but he confronts them in contexts obscure enough . . . to take the capital letters off them. These all-too-human constancies, "those big words that make us all afraid," take a homely form in such homely contexts. But that is exactly the advantage. There are enough profundities in the world already.[28]

In the *Chronicles*, this microscopic vision recognizes families protecting their teenage girls from sexual harassment, an ethnic struggle over poultry in the marketplace, radical butchers, naive millers' men, dead cats thrown into the street in symbolic fancy dress, mock genuflections at the symbols of church and state, old women "in an agonie" misconstruing the advice of officious gentlemen, puffins and bran baked in cloths to hold the loaves together, workmen singing for their supper, square and round tables brought out into the streets in a public picnic whose motives are, finally, unreadable. As Geertz would say, "another country heard from."[29]

TEN   ❧ *Women*

S hortly after I had committed myself to this project, I was advised that
I had once again chosen a topic that excluded feminist criticism or
scholarship. The huge bulk of Holinshed's *Chronicles*, it was assumed,
would be impervious to what has come to be known as "women's history,"
despite the fact that three of the sixteenth-century sovereigns were women:
Mary Tudor, Mary Stuart, and Elizabeth I. At the socioeconomic, cultural,
or anthropological level, the *Chronicles* would surely be securely male in
their focus, either inadvertently, out of the mental habits of the time, or in
secret or unconscious resistance to the monstrous regiment of women. As
Louis Montrose put it, in a pioneering essay that made considerations of
sex and gender de rigeur for all future discussions of Elizabethan literary
culture, "with one vital exception, all forms of public and domestic authority in Elizabethan England were vested in men: . . . It was inevitable that the
rule of a woman who was unmastered by any man would generate peculiar
tensions within such a `patriarchal' society."[1] But once my attention had
been focused on the representation of women, it quickly became clear that,
like so many of the suppositions about the *Chronicles* that need rethinking,
the world they displayed was by no means simply or unproblematically
"patriarchal" to the chroniclers themselves, whatever the dominant ideology of male superiority or social and legal structures might dictate.

In opening her magisterial study of female "resistance" in Jacobean England, Barbara Lewalski wrote:

> One useful theoretical grid for viewing Jacobean women's resistance is Gramsci's analysis of how a dominant ideology may be contested by subaltern or marginal groups; another is the Marxist concept of negotiation for meaning and power by marginal groups who challenge a hegemonic system. But the most illuminating perspective on their oppositional stances and texts is provided by the recent political upheavals all over Eastern Europe, testifying to the fact that inner resistance and a critical consciousness can develop even while ideological conformity is being rigorously enforced.[2]

Lewalski's grasp of the ways in which women, as a subaltern or marginal population group in the seventeenth century, began to rewrite the male discourses that confined and repressed them is impressive; but what should we make of a discourse—history—so long assumed to have found women invisible that seems to include its own interrogation of that invisibility? Apart from their in-depth studies of the major female players of sixteenth-century history and the hostilities between them (whereby the theme of "Women beware women" rather than men emerges as another kind of corrective), most of the chroniclers show a precise interest in anecdotes revelatory of female resistance, which on the whole they rather seem to admire.

It is in fact hard to discover "patriarchal" sentiments in the *Chronicles*, but where they can be found, they appear to be attributable to Abraham Fleming. Thus Fleming on the relation between protofeminism and disturbances in religious practice in the late fourteenth century:

> In those daies there was a certeine matrone in London, which had one onelie daughter, whome manie daies she instructed and trained up to celebrat the masse, and she set up an altar in hir privie or secret chamber with all the ornaments thereunto belonging, and so she made hir daughter manie daies to attire hir selfe like a priest, and to come to the alter, and after hir maner to celebrate the masse.... This errour a long time lasted, till at last by a certeine neighbour that was secretlie called to such a masse, it was told abroad, and came to the bishops eares, who causing them to appeare before him, talked with them about that errour, and compelled the yoong woman openlie to shew the priestlie shaving of hir haire, whose head was found to be all bare and bald. (2:828)

To this point Fleming, as he himself indicates, was translating from Henry Knighton's fifteenth-century *Chronicon* (2:316–17). But (as if confirming feminist expectations) Fleming proceeded to add to the late-fourteenth-century anecdote a late-sixteenth-century gloss:

It is not to be doubted, but that *in these daies* manie of the female sex be medling in matters impertinent to their degree, and inconvenient to their knowlege; debating & scanning in their privat conventicles of such things as whereabout if they kept silence, it were for their greater commendation; presuming, though not to celebrat a masse, or to make a sacrament; yet to undertake some publike peece of service incident to the ministerie: whose oversawcie rashnesse being bolstered and borne up with abbettors not a few, whether it be by ecclesiasticall discipline corrected, I wot not; but of the uniformed presbiterie I am sure it is lamented. (2:829; italics added)

Nothing could be further from Fleming's emphasis on "over-sawcie rashnesse" and conventionally moralizing tone, however, than the remarkable protofeminist portrait of Elizabeth (Jane) Shore, mistress of Edward IV,[3] that Holinshed imported into his narrative along with the rest of Sir Thomas More's account of Richard III. While one can not place too much emphasis on this portrait's inclusion in the *Chronicles*, its inclusion in More's history of the reign may have encouraged Holinshed and his successors to think more carefully about the role of women in public affairs at all levels. Moreover, because More's portrait of Mistress Shore has suffered a fate parallel to the *Chronicles* as a whole—of being ignored by those to whom it should have been an example (or rather counterexample)—I intend to quote it here virtually in entirety.[4]

"This woman," More had written (in Holinshed's version), "was borne in London, worshipfullie friended, honestlie brought up, and verie well maried, saving somewhat too soone" (3:384). This opening sentence serves a double purpose: a social critique of the practice of marrying off girls in their early teens, and a shield for Elizabeth herself against the conventional moral assumptions that equated Shore with Whore:

But forsomuch as they were coupled yer she were well ripe, she not verie ferventlie loved him, for whom she never longed, which was happilie the thing that the more easilie made hir incline unto the kings appetite, when he required hir. Howbeit the respect of his roialtie, the hope of gaie apparell, ease, and other wanton wealth, was able soone to pearse a soft tender heart.

This tenderness toward female youth (which appeared also in Holinshed's account of the origins in sexual harrassment of the Peasants' Revolt in 1381) is suddenly interrupted, in the 1587 edition of the *Chronicles*, by the intrusive moral voice of Fleming:

so that she became flexible and pliant to the kings appetite and will; being so blinded with the bright glorie of the present courtlie braverie which shee injoied, that she utterlie forgat how excellent a treasure good name and fame is, and of what incomparable sweetnesse, even by the judgement of him, whose match for wisdome the world never bred up, saieng:

Sunt optanda magis purae bona nomina famae,
Nobilis unguenti quam pretiosus odor. (Ecclesiastes 7:1)

More, however, had a more urbane approach to the way a beautiful woman is passed from hand to hand (remember Marilyn Monroe) in the world of high-level politics: "But when the king had *abused* hir," he continued, "anon hir husband (as he was an honest man, and one that could [i.e., knew] his good, not presuming to touch a kings concubine) left hir up to him altogither. When the king died, the lord chamberleine tooke hir, which in the kings daies, albeit he was sore inamoured upon hir, yet he forbare hir; ether for reverence, or for a certaine friendlie faithfulnesse." The attribution of blame, which comes so easily to Fleming, is appropriately modified by More for both men and woman, but especially for her.[5] That later readers saw this intention is clear from the 1563 edition of the *Mirror for Magistrates*, where the tragedy of "Shore's wife, Edwarde the fowerthes concubine" is evidently an expansion of the attitudes and language of More's *History*, now placed in Elizabeth's own mouth as self-defence:

But cleare from blame my frendes can not be found,
Before my time my youth they did abuse:
In maryage, a prentyse was I bound,
When that meere love I knewe not howe to use.
[...]
Who is in fault? the offendour yea or no,
Or they that are the cause of all this wo?
[...]
What nede I more to cleare my selfe to much?
A kyng me wanne, and had me at his call:
His royall state, his pryncely grace was such,
The hope of will (that women seeke for all,)
The ease and wealth, the gyftes whych were not smal,
Besieged me so strongly rounde aboute,
My power was weake, I could not holde him out.[6]

After excuse for human frailty comes a different kind of tenderness, this time for the mortal body:

Proper she was and faire; nothing in hir bodie that you would have changed, but if ye would have wished hir somewhat higher. Thus saie they that knew hir in hir youth. Albeit some that now see hir (for yet she liveth) deem hir never to have beene well visaged: whose judgement seemeth me somewhat like, as though men should gesse the beautie of one long before departed by hir scalpe taken out of the charnell house. For now [1587 marginal note: Meaning when this storie was written] is she old, leane, withered and dried up, nothing left but rivelled skin and hard bone. And yet being even such, who so well advise hir visage, might gesse and devise, which parts how filled would make it a faire face.

Why would More, writing ca. 1513, have cared so much for Mistress Shore, who would have been in her late fifties ("yet she liveth") when this tribute was written. Because she was, like him, distinguished for her wit:

Yet delighted not men so much in her beautie, as in hir pleasant behavior. *For a proper wit had she, and could both read well and write, merrie in companie, readie and quicke of answer,* neither mute, nor full of bable, sometime tawnting without displeasure, and not without disport. The king would saie that he had three concubins, which in three diverse properties diverslie excelled. One the merriest, another the wiliest, the third the holiest harlot in his realme, as one whome no man could get out of the church lightlie to any place, but it were to his bed. The other two were somewhat greater personages, and nathelesse of their humilitie content to be namelesse, and to forbeare the praise of those properties: but the merriest was this Shores wife, in whom the king therefore tooke speciall pleasure. For manie he had, but hir he loved.

In the Latin version of More's *History,* this praise of Elizabeth's wit is keyed to More's own values by a pun on his own name: "ingenio tamen adeo festivo, ac *moribus* tanta comitate conditis fuit, ut magis propter *morum* sanitatem, quam oris pulchritudinem amanda videretur."[7]

But even more important than Shore's wit is the political role that she played as the king's favorite mistress. Unlike Edward, who had "abused" her, she never, More wrote, "abused [her power] to anie mans hurt, but to manie a mans comfort and releefe":

Where the king tooke displeasure, shee would mitigate and appease his mind: where men were out of favour, she would bring them in his grace. For manie that had highlie offended she obtained pardon. Of great forfeitures she gat men remission. Finallie, in many weightie sutes she stood manie a man in great stead, either for none or verie small rewards, and those rather gaie than rich; either that she was content with the deed it selfe well doone; or for that she delighted to be sued unto, and to shew what she was able to doo with the king; or for that wanton women and wealthie be not alwaies covetous.

To have used her sexual influence to mitigate the ferocity of late feudal despotism was, for More, justification for a life irregular by conventional moral standards. Alison Hanham could not understand the importance of this portrait in the *History*,[8] but in fact More himself supplies its rationale as a correction to a conventional *res gestae* historiography:

> I doubt not some shall think this woman too slight a thing to be written of, and set among the remembrances of great matters; which they shall speciallie thinke, that happilie shall esteeme hir onelie by that they now see hir. But me seemeth the chance so much the more worthie to be remembred, in how much she is now in the more beggerlie condition, unfreended and worne out of acquaintance, after good substance, after as great favour with the prince, after as great sute and seeking to with all those, that those daies had businesse to speed, as manie other men were in their times, which be now famous onelie by the infamie of their ill deeds. Hir dooings were not much lesse, albeit they be much lesse remembred, bicause they were not so evill. For men use if they have an evill turne, to write it in marble: and who so dooth us a good turne, we write it in dust, which is not worst prooved by hir: for at this daie she beggeth of manie at this daie living, that at this daie had begged if she had not beene. (3:384–85)

Writings in marble for the "evill" male imprint upon history; writings in the dust for the female benefactor. More's attempt to alter the balance in favor of the "proper wit" who could herself "both read well, and write" has not been entirely successful. The attention of too many of his modern readers has been distracted by other issues, especially, of course, the reliability of his *History* with respect to the character of Richard III.

But in order to claim that More's defense of Shore was intentionally absorbed into the *Chronicles*' agenda and even, perhaps, an influence upon it, she would need to be supported by other salient examples. One of the most salient must surely be Holinshed's treatment of the British queen Voadicea as a heroine of the ancient constitution, supported in the 1577 edition by a striking woodcut apparently designed for the purpose; not least because John Milton, in the history of Britain that he began in the late 1640s, violently attacked her as feminist monster. Milton's own views of the ancient constitution, which I shall cite in "Conclusions," excluded the contributions of women. His insults are worth repeating for contrast, and also because they happen to supply an *ecphrasis* of the 1577 illustration:

> a Woeman also was thir Commander in Chief. For Boadicea and her Daughters ride about in a Chariot, telling the tall Champions as a great encouragement, that with the Britans it was usual for Woemen to be thir

Leaders. A deal of other rondness they put into her mouth, not worth recital; how she was lash'd, how her Daughters were handl'd, things worthier silence, retirment, and a Vail, then for a Woeman to repeat, as don to hir own person, or to hear repeated before an host of men. *The Greek Historian* setts her in the field on a high heap of Turves, in a loose-bodied Gown declaming, a Spear in her hand, a Hare in her bosome, which after a long circumlocution she was to let slip among them for lucks sake. . . . And this they do out of a vanity, hoping to embellish and set out thir Historie with the strangness of our manners, not careing in the mean while to brand us with the rankest note of Barbarism, as if in Britain Woemen were Men, and Men Woemen.[9]

Another salient example, not least since I began with the contrast between More and Abraham Fleming, is an interpolation by which Fleming expanded the *Chronicles'* account of Lady Jane Grey. For the 1587 edition Fleming apparently decided to enhance his polemic against Mary Tudor by rounding out the character of her female victim. As elsewhere in expanding on Holinshed's account of Mary's reign, he turned to Foxe's *Acts and Monuments* and produced the story of how Lady Jane had lost Mary's sympathy some years before they became rivals for the throne, by casually demonstrating disbelief in the Real Presence in the Eucharist. "Touching this ladie Jane in the high commendation of her goodlie mind," wrote Fleming, "I find this report in maister Foxes appendix":

namelie that being on a time when she was verie yoong at Newhall in Essex at the ladie Maries, was by one ladie Anne Wharton desired to walke, and they passing by the chapell, the ladie Wharton made low curtsie to the popish sacrament hanging on the altar: Which when the ladie Jane saw [she] marvelled why she did so, and asked hir whether the ladie Marie were there or not? [i.e., watching them] Unto whome the ladie Wharton answered no, but she said that she made hir curtsie to him that made us all. Why quoth the ladie Jane, *how can he be there that made us all, and the baker made him.* This hir answer comming to the ladie Maries eares, she did never love hir after, as is credibly reported. (4:23; italics added)

Fleming's selection of this anecdote, hidden away in Foxe's appendix, to characterize Jane's independence of spirit, suggests a more complicated division of his sympathy than his other remarks on women would lead one to expect. As a Protestant polemicist, he *could* have chosen the more solemn dialogue between her and Dr. Feckenham, Queen Mary's personal confessor, whose mission was to "reduce" her to Catholicism before her execution; instead we have another story of a young girl abused (though this time by an older woman): another instance of female wit, or at least of female playfulness.

In summing up Mary's reign and providing a catalog of the "learned men" who distinguished the reign and sometimes suffered for it, Holinshed had noted that "Jane Dudleie daughter unto Henrie Greie duke of Suffolke, wrote diverse things highlie to her commendation, of whome yee have heard more before heere in this historie" (4:153). Not only did she write, but her writings were published, posthumously. In 1554, immediately after her execution, there appeared a small collection of what she had written in the Tower, under the title *Here in this booke ye have a godly epistle made by a faithful Christian,* including several letters, a prayer, and the account of her debate with Feckenham, which she may or may not have written up herself. Other sixteenth-century editions, and one in 1615, were published at home and abroad, and Foxe had included Lady Jane's writings in the *Acts and Monuments.* John King considered these publications "the most powerful contemporary Protestant attack on the Marian regime."[10] If so, it was surely *because* Lady Jane was atypical as a Protestant martyr that her image worked so well for her supporters.

Female resistance does not, however, have to be intellectual to register in the *Chronicles.* In Holinshed's history of Scotland there is an account of the duke of Albany's plan to murder the duke of Rothsey by starvation. "It is said," wrote Holinshed:

> that a woman understanding the duke of Albanies intention, and taking ruth of the others pitifull case, found meanes to let meale fall downe thorough a rift of the loft of that tower wherein he was inclosed, by meanes whereof his life was certaine daies susteined; but after this was once knowen, incontinentlie was the woman made awaie. On the same manner, another woman through a long reed fed him with milke of hir owne brests, and was likewise dispatched as soone as hir dooings were perceived. (5:405)

Another instance of female protectiveness leading to heroism occurs as an attempt to avert the murder of James I. When the assassins arrived, "not without great noise & rumbling, a yoong virgin named Katharine Dowglasse (that was after maried to Alexander Lovell of Bolunnie) got to the doore, and shut it:

> but because the barre was awaie that should have made it fast, she thrust hir arme in the place where the bar should have passed: she was but yoong, and hir bones not strong, but rather tender as a gristle, and therefore hir arme was soone crasht in sunder, and the doore broken up by force. (5:425)

Katherine Douglas's arm, "tender as a gristle," and Elizabeth Shore's "soft tender heart" are connected by Holinshed's historical tenderness for the young woman whose toughness manifests itself in complex proportion to her vulnerability.

Not all the resiliant women in the *Chronicles* are young. Once again, we have the inconsistent Abraham Fleming to thank for expanding the story of Henry VIII's divorce from Catherine of Aragon in a way that dramatizes female defiance. Though derived verbatim from Hall, Queen Catherine's response to the verdict of the French universities that her marriage was invalid resounds with dignity and rectitude:

> And as to the determination of the universitie, I am a woman, and lacke wit and learning to answer to them, but to God I commit the judgement of that, whether they have doone justlie or parciallie: for this I am sure, that neither the kings father, nor my father would have condescended to our marriage, if it had beene declared to be unlawfull. . . . And this shall be your answer: that I saie I am his lawfull wife, and to him lawfullie married, and by the order of holie church I was to him espoused as his true wife . . . and in that point I will abide till the court of Rome, which was privie to the beginning, have made thereof a determination, and finall ending.

"With this answer," Fleming/Hall recorded, "the lords departed to the king, which was sorie to heare of hir wilfull opinion, and in especiall that she more trusted in the popes law, than in keeping the precepts of God" (3:772). But this is an occasion for female solidarity. "When these determinations were published, all wise men in the realme much abhorred that marriage: but women, and such as were more wilfull than wise or learned, spake against that determination, and said that the universities were corrupt and intised so to doo, which is not to be thought" (3:772). The "wilfulness" of the queen is shared by women generally. Support for them against the pompous machinery of male expert opinion is, if not invited, *permitted;* not only by Queen Catharine's effective self-defence but also by that ambiguously located final clause "which is not to be thought," semantically pendant between women's wilfulness (in being so suspicious) and the real possibility of academic corruption, which can no longer be unthinkable once the women have put it into our heads.[11]

Sometimes, however, the chroniclers insert a story that witnesses to the victimization of women without the narrative consolation of their resistance or outright heroism. In the following anecdote, inserted by John Hooker into his section of the Irish history, the meaning of the story apparently resides in the complicity of women in military violence and deceit. This moral is pointed by repetition; but the asymmetry of the results again supports the inference that the spirit of the *Chronicles* is generous toward young women. The story relates to the baron of Lexna's campaign to rid his domains of all English garrisons. Focusing on the eight-man garrison of Lesconile, he conceived the following stratagem:

> He laid verie close & tectlie a companie of his men in an old house fast by the castell, & then he practised with an old woman, which was woont everie morning to bring a great basket of coles or turffe into the ward, that as soone as she was between the two gates of the castell, she should let fall her basket and crie out: which she did. . . . The companie foorthwith lieng in the said old house came, and the ward being not able to draw unto them the utter iron door, nor to shut fast the inner doore, the enimie entred, tooke the castell, killed all the ward, and cast them over the wals. (6:447)

"The good successe of this stratagem," as Hooker put it, encouraged Lexna to try another version of it on the garrison at Adnegh. Assuming "that hungrie soldiors would be contented to accept anie courtesie, he procured a yoong harlot, who was somewhat snowtfaire, to go to the castell, pretending some injurie to have beene doone to hir, and to humble hirselfe to the capteins devotion, being supposed that he by these meanes would fall into the liking and fantasieng of hir, and so would retaine hir." Repetition, however, has its own pitfalls. The captain of the garrison, "not forgetting the late former practise at Lesconile," received the young woman into the castle, but "so handled the matter with this harlot," a statement of considerable ambiguity, "that he in the end found out all the devise, and foorthwith he carried hir up unto the top of the castell and cast hir over the wals, where with the fall she was crushed and died." (6:448) It is clear that Hooker has neither the leisure nor the inclination to meditate, like More, on the problems of justice as fairness in relation to women. It is equally clear that young harlots who have the bad luck to be "somewhat snowtfaire" in the vicinity of a territorial struggle are to be given at least the support of an ironically and effectively structured narrative.

This story of old hag and young harlot leads, however, to the more troubling topic of witchcraft, to which on the whole the *Chronicles* paid remarkably little attention, given what we have subsequently learned about the intensity with which witchcraft was criminalized during the period of their compilation. According to Keith Thomas, Home Circuit trials for witchcraft "were at their zenith" during Elizabeth's reign, "when 455 out of the 790 known indictments were made, the majority during the 1580s and 1590s." And, he added, "it is probable that there were more trials everywhere under Elizabeth than during the whole of the subsequent century."[12] Holinshed did not, however, record the passing of the 1563 statute[13] making it a felony to invoke evil spirits for any purpose, whether or not *maleficium*, damage to others, was charged. His account of 1563 was almost completely devoted to a detailed description of the queen's campaign, headed by Ambrose Dudley, earl of Warwick, and entirely unsuccessful in the outcome, to protect the Normandy towns endangered by the forces of the Guise.

There is a natural temptation, especially among literary critics, to explain the witchcraft craze in England as an expression of misogyny.[14] That the victims of witchcraft prosecutions were overwhelmingly female (as also old and from the lowest social strata) is uncontested.[15] Keith Thomas, who made the most persistent inquiry into the causes of these events, in the process discounting the influence of either Catholics or Protestants as a political force affecting the nation's jurisprudence, also eschewed sexual politics as an explanation, and preferred a materialist-psychological view: a combination of religious depression (caused by the withdrawal of Catholicism's psychological supports); extreme poverty, especially on the part of those who became the victims of witchcraft trials, and who may have annoyed or embarrassed their neighbors by begging; the general inadequacy of medicine; and the "tyranny of local opinion," especially in rural environments, as to what constituted socially acceptable behavior. On the other hand he determined no correlation between "the chronology of witch-persecution and such general events as the incidence of plague, famine, unemployment or price fluctuations."[16] The misfortunes for which superstitious people continued to blame their neighbors remained the same as they had been throughout the Middle Ages—the death or sickness of themselves or their children or their animals. Thomas remained committed to the view that the trials were fueled primarily by the same fears and misfortunes as in the past, and that witch-persecution was an essentially grassroots phenomenon, not one created by either churchmen or lawyers, thus leaving himself finally with no very satisfactory explanation as to why such trials should have dramatically increased in the period under review. And a central part of his argument was that the legal machinery—that statutes that made prosecution by the state available as an option—was not to blame.[17]

The one witchcraft prosecution that is given substantial coverage in the *Chronicles* throws doubt on that last presumption. The case permits us also to raise the specter of a certain type of misogyny, visible to the chroniclers, and seen by them as one unfortunate strand of the complex injustice done under the auspices of the Elizabethan witchcraft statute. The case is that of Joan Cason, tried on 19 April 1586, in the town of Feversham, in Kent, before Thomas Barming, mayor of Feversham, because Feversham was a Cinque Port, outside the normal jurisdiction of sessions and assizes.[18]

Joan Cason was a widow, "late the wife of one Freeman," and accused of having bewitched a three-year old girl, Jane Cook, who subsequently "languished and died." Seven women and one man gave evidence against her, who "though they were all verie poore people, yet were they the rather admitted to accuse hir, for that they were hir neere neighbors, and hir offense verie odious" (4:391).

This section of the *Chronicles*, probably compiled by Abraham Fleming, here depends for its information upon "The note of John Waller," who may have been the person mentioned by Anthony à Wood as an Oxford undergraduate magician.[19] The role of the chronicler is therefore neutralized by the protocol of verbatim rerecording. If we wish to determine the sympathies of Waller, this first sentence is ambivalent; for its sense of socioeconomic conditioning (*"though they were all verie poore people"*) suggests *both* that the poor would normally be expected to support each other *and* that in this instance Cason's neighbors were genuinely convinced of the heinousness of her offence. At this stage there is nothing to contradict the classic accounts of witchcraft prosecutions and their motives. But there is not only more to follow, but, thanks to a coincidence, evidence from another source suggesting that Abraham Fleming himself was not neutral in his interest.

In 1584, two years before the second edition of the *Chronicles* was sent to press, Reginald Scot published his *Discoverie of Witchcraft*, a skeptical account of the witchcraft craze designed to counter the influence of the continental writers, Father James Sprenger, one of the authors of the 1490 *Malleus Maleficarum*, and Jean Bodin, whose *De Magorum Daemonomania* derived from the *Malleus*. We have encountered Reginald Scot before, as himself the author of the "Note" on the rebuilding of the port of Dover, and as the business administrator for his cousin, Sir Thomas Scot, whose genius it was to build both the seawalls and the socioindustrial fabric of the Dover enterprise. In 1588 Reginald Scot sat as member of Parliament for New Romney in Kent and may himself have had legal training and served as a justice of the peace. The *Discoverie* is lavishly illustrated with literary examples, many of them taken from the classical poets, Virgil, Ovid, Lucretius, and others, such as the Latin verses of the *Agnus Dei*, examples of Catholic ritual. In most instances these Latin illustrations of centuries of superstition (to whose demystification Scot devoted such energy) are provided with English verse translations by none other (the margins inform us) than Abraham Fleming.[20] It seems clear that Scot and Fleming must have worked together on this project, in a manner that implies conceptual collaboration. They certainly shared an anti-Catholic fervor.

Scot's approach to witchcraft is a remarkable anticipation of the materialist approach of Keith Thomas, with whom he shares the perception of why women would confess to *maleficia* they manifestly could not have accomplished. Because Scot himself can qualify as one of the subsidiary "authors" of the 1587 *Chronicles*, it is worth pausing to examine his grasp of the psychosocial complex involved in the so-called confessions. In chapter 3 of the *Discoverie*, "Who they be that are called witches, with a manifest declaration of the cause that mooveth men so commonlie to thinke, and witches themselves to beleeve that they can hurt children, cattell, &c." Scot delivered a devastating analysis of the manner in which the law, thanks to the 1563 statute, has become complicit with poverty and ignorance in a massive exercise in credulity and injustice:

> One sort of such as are said to be witches, are women which be commonly old, lame, bleare-eied, pale, fowle, and full of wrinkles; poore, sullen, superstitious, and papists; or such as knowe no religion: in whose drousie minds the divell hath goten a fine seat; so as, what mischeefe, mischance, calamitie, or slaughter is brought to passe, they are easily persuaded the same is doone by themselves. . . . They are leane and deformed, shewing melancholie in their faces, to the horror of all that see them. . . .
>
> These miserable wretches are so odious unto all their neighbors, and so feared, that few dare offend them, or denie them anie thing they aske: whereby they take upon them; yea, and sometimes thinke, that they can doo such things as are beyond the abilitie of humane nature. These go from house to house, and from doore to doore for a pot full of milke, yest, drinke, pottage, or some such releefe; without the which they could hardlie live. . . .
>
> It falleth out many times, that neither their necessities, nor their expectation is answered or served, in those places where they beg or borrowe; but rather their lewdnesse is by their neighbors reprooved . . . so as sometimes she cursseth one, and sometimes another. . . . Thus in processe of time they have all displeased hir, and she hath wished evill lucke unto them all; perhaps with curses and imprecations made in forme. Doubtlesse (at length) some of hir neighbors die, or fall sicke; or some of their children are visited with diseases that vex them strangelie. . . . Which by ignorant persons are supposed to be the vengeance of witches. . . .
>
> The witch on the other side expecting hir neighbours mischances, and seeing things sometimes come to passe according to hir wishes, cursses, and incantations (for Bodin himselfe confesseth, that not above two in a hundred of the witchings or wishings take effect) *being called before a Justice, by due examination of the circumstances is driven to see hir imprecations and desires, and hir neighbors harmes and losses to concurre, and as it were to take effect:* and so confesseth that she (as a goddes) hath brought such things to passe. Wherein not onelie she, but the accuser, and also the Justice are fowlie deceived and abused.[21]

In fact, Scot takes up expressly the question of the law's responsibility for such abuses. Although he suggests that the Henrician and the Elizabethan statutes may have qualified the "old rigor" of the Catholic church, they have left intact the *concept* of witchcraft: "the estimation of the omnipotencie of their words and charmes seemeth in those statutes to be somewhat mainteined, as a matter hitherto generallie received; and not yet so looked into, as that it is refuted and decided."[22] Scot was clearly unwilling to criticize the statute and its makers too sharply, and added tactfully, "Most certaine it is, that in what point soever anie of these extremeties . . . be mitigated, it is thorough the goodnesse of the Queenes Majestie, and hir excellent magistrates placed among us" (p. 37).

In the case of Joan Cason (not to mention the 21% of accused persons who were convicted and hanged on Elizabeth's Home Circuit in 1587)[23] such mitigation did not occur. Indeed, the chronicler's narrative gradually reveals that the case is introduced as an example of injustice, and one that, while it may be rendered more intelligible by Scot's *Discoverie* appearing just two years earlier, is still more shocking than the examples he gives, since its victim did not illustrate any of the malevolence of the typical rural scapegoat. Nor does the ignorance and superstition required to produce injustice arise from the grass-roots level of the community. On the contrary, it is external interference.

The first deposition in the case was made by Sara Cooke, mother of the dead child:

> that after hir said child had beene sicke, languishing by the space of thirteene daies, a travellor came into hir house, to the end to drinke a pot of ale (for she kept an alehouse) who seeing the lamentable case and pitious griefe of the child, called hir unto him saieng; Hostesse, I take it that your child is bewitched. Whereunto she answered, that she for hir part knew of no such matter.

Note that the idea of bewitchment is imported into the community by a stranger (male), and that it carries authority for precisely that reason. The traveler proposes that Cooke take a tile from over the lodging of "the partie suspected," and place it in the fire, and if that person has bewitched the child, the fire "will sparkle and flie round about the cradle." And she, "conceiving that travellors have good experience in such matters," proceeded to make the test. The tile stolen from Joan Cason's house, though not taken, Waller reported, "from over her lodging," did indeed send sparks flying out of the fireplace and around the cradle, which happened to be placed beside the fire! Suspicions were confirmed by the fact that Cason shortly after entered the Cookes' house to ask after the sick child, who gazed up at her (having not opened her eyes all the previous night), and died four hours later. So, Sara Cooke continued in her deposition, "she thought it might plainlie appeare to the jurie, that the said Jone had betwitched the child to death."

Seven of her neighbors also gave evidence; but this had nothing to do with the death of the child, and was all focused on "a little thing like a rat (but more reddish) having a brode taile, which some of them had seene, and some had heard of." This, of course, was the necessary "familiar," necessary to establish in the minds of the jury a suspicion of supernatural dealings.

The prisoner, however, unlike the many old women who confessed to a *maleficium* for the reasons Scot had analyzed two years earlier, steadfastly *refused* to admit any curse or ill will, "anie thing doone, or purposed by hir to have beene doone in this behalfe" (4:392). (She had, after all, visited the child out of neighborly solicitousness.) She firmly continued to assert herself not guilty; and she gave examples of the malice her neighbors held toward her, "reciting also certaine controversies betwixt hir and them, wherein they had doone hir open wrong." In fact, she satisfied "the bench and all the jurie touching hir innocence for the killing of hir child." However, at this point something went seriously wrong with her testimony (which would never have occurred, we may be sure, had she received proper legal advice). Joan Cason admitted that "a little vermin, being of colour reddish, of stature lesse than a rat . . . did diverse yeares since (*but not latelie*) haunt her house, and manie other houses in the towne":

and further, that she (*as she imagined*) heard it crie sometimes; Go to, go to, go to; sometimes, Sicke sicke; sometimes, Come, come. Whereby she gathered, that it charged hir to see hir maister Masons will performed; which she had not executed according to the confidence he had in hir; to the trouble of hir conscience, and vexation of her mind. And she honestlie confessed, that he had the use of hir bodie verie dishonestlie, whilest she was wife to hir husband Freeman. (4:392)

A guilty conscience, for personal matters quite irrelevant to the charge at hand, made Joan Cason susceptible to the same superstitions as those that her neighbors invoked against her. The existence of her "familiar," despite the fact that the creature was ubiquitous in her town, is therefore taken to be established by her own "confession." The chronicler, however, reveals his scepticism in his asides ("as she imagined"); and the jury were themselves, if not sceptical, sympathetic: "being loth to condemne hir of witchcraft, which they knew to be a fellonie, they aquitted hir thereof, and found hir giltie upon the said statute, for invocation of wicked spirits; thinking therefore to have procured her punishment by pillorie, or imprisonment, and to have saved hir from the gallowes."

But the story is not to have a happy ending. For after Mayor Barming had pronounced the verdict, with the appropriate moralizations ("render most humble thanks to God and the queene, and hereafter . . . beware that you give no such occasions of offense againe"), there is another intervention from outside the community:

> A gentleman (being a lawyer, and of counsell with the towne, sitting upon the bench with the maior, to assist, or rather to direct him in the course of law and justice) hearing this mild judgement to proceed out of the maiors mouth, stept unto him, and told him, that (under correction) he thought him to erre in the principall point of his sentence (that is to saie) that instead of life he should have pronounced death; because invocation of wicked spirits was made fellonie by the statute whereupon she was arreigned. (4:893)

The mayor thereupon reversed his sentence, despite the fact that, as the *Chronicles* proceed to explain, a mistrial has obviously occurred; "because there was no matter of invocation given in evidence against hir, nor proved in or by anie accusation, whereby the jurie might have anie colour to condemne hir therfore." The jurors, in their well-meaning ignorance, misunderstood what verdict was possible; the mayor failed to correct them; and the interfering lawyer (supposedly expert) corrected judge and jury only in the direction of unjust severity. Given the direction of the narrative itself, it seems reasonable to hear an intense irony in the chronicler's own self-correction: the lawyer is there "to assist, *or rather to direct him* in the course of law and justice."

Everyone knew that something had gone wrong; but their only response was to stay the execution for three days, during which time preachers attempted to persuade Joan Cason to confess to the invocation of wicked spirits, in order to clean up the record. "But no persuasion could prevaile, to make hir acknowledge anie other criminall offense, but hir lewd life and adulterous conversation" with Mason, and that when he died she had abused his trust in her with respect to the terms of his will. She went to the gallows still berating herself for this conflicted relationship, for which, she said, "the judgement of God was in such measure laid upon her." And so, the chronicler concluded, she made "so godlie and penitent an end, that manie now lamented hir death, which were (before) hir utter enemies. Yea some wished hir alive after she was hanged, that cried out for the hangman when she was alive: but she should have beene more beholding unto them that had kept hir from the gallows, than to such as would have cut the rope when she was strangled" (4:893).

What role did Cason's adultery play in this mockery of justice? The story provides no editorial guidance; but neither is there a trace of a male moralizing voice, outside of Mayor Barming's initial sentencing. With Reginald Scot's subtle analysis of the so-called confessions in hand, we might infer that what happened to Joan Cason was analogous psychologically to the responses of the old scolds who thought they saw their maledictions take effect. "Being called before a Justice, by due examination of the circumstances," Cason is driven to search her conscience for guilt, and unsurprisingly she finds it. Her community is therefore able to *feel* her guilty of something deserving a ritual punishment.

That there was a sexual component (as distinct from a gendered prejudice) in antiwitch propaganda is attested by Scot's *Discoverie*. He cites with derision from Leonardus Vairus' *De fascino* (1589) an argument as to why "women are oftener found to be witches than men":

> For (saith he) they have such an unbrideled force of furie and concupiscence naturallie, that by no means it is possible for them to temper or moderate the same . . . and they are so troubled with evill humors, that out go their venomous exhalations, ingendred thorough their ilfavoured diet, and increased by meanes of their pernicious excrements, which they expell. (p. 236)

"And if this were true," Scot concluded sardonically of this essentialism, "honest women maie be witches, in despight of all inquisitors: neither can anie avoid being a witch, except shee locke hir selfe up in a chamber" (p. 237).

But the *Chronicles* seem not only to avoid such essentialism, but to insist on their readers understanding that injustice is not gender-specific. Indeed, the story of Joan Cason is followed by another anecdote deliberately misplaced chronologically (since it belonged to the year 1547) on the grounds that both tales illustrate "one kind of government, for they are of the [Cinque] ports." The editor, presumably still Fleming, himself draws an analogy between Joan Cason and one Mr. Foule of Rye; and he echoes the words of Holinshed in introducing the trial of Sir Nicholas Throckmorton: "Which storie being not altogither impertinent, . . . I thought it not unfit to be in this place inserted." The story of Mr. Foule seems a fitting ending to my own discussion of women in the *Chronicles*, not only because in this version of male-female contestation the husband loses, but also because, in contrast to the tragedy of Joan Cason, its tone is unmistakably comic:

> There haunted to the house of this Foule, in respect of the good will he bare his wife, a little honest man, whose name I will not discover, who committed unto hir custodie a bag of monie, amounting to the sum of ten pounds stear-

ling. Fouls wife locked it up in hir cupboord. Howbeit, she handled not the matter so covertlie, but hir covert baron espied it, and (in hir absence) either picked or brake open the locke, and tooke out the monie; wherewith afterwards he plaied the good fellow all the daies of life. For immediatelie his wife accused him (not of subtill dealing) but of plaine theft, regarding more hir friends losse, than hir husbands life. Hereupon the maior of Rie (at the next sessions) caused him to be indicted and arreigned, and being convinced of the fact, he was condemned and adjudged to death. For whose better execution, there was presentlie a new paire of gallowes erected, whereupon without further delaie he was hanged untill he was dead; which gallowes hath beene ever since called by the name of Fouls mare. And now he cared not so much for the maior, as the maior did for him. For Foule was skant cold, but manie murmured at the maior's hastie proceedings; which moved them to doubt and whisper, that Fouls fault was no fellonie. (4:893–94)

The zest with which this tale is told (to this point) belongs to the genre of the fabliau. It has a secret, sexual subtext; and it is packed with jokes, whose point is increased by alliteration. "He plaied the good fellow all the daies of his life" plays right into the announcement of Foul's speedy execution; his very name is an emblem of foul play; and the relation between "Foul's Mare" and the mayor who placed him on it is almost too good to believe. One would be tempted to read this an etiological fable, folk-embroidery on a local placename, or a modern marital satire ("Foul, his wife, the mayor and Foul's mare") were it not for what follows:

> But now the maior (although it be said that portsmen maie tell their tale twise) could not now devise, how (Foule being dead) he might reverse this *foule* sentence. Neverthelesse, he sent up with all speed to one maister Ramseie of Greies Inne, who was of counsell with the towne, to learne what the law was in that case: who having fully weied and conceived thereof, told the partie directlie, that the matter was without the compasse of fellonie. Whie sir (quoth the messenger) goodman Foule is alreadie hanged. . . . But what was he for a man (said maister Ramsie?) A bad fellow (said the messenger). Well (quoth he) go thou thie waies home, and then there is but one knave out of the waie. (4:894; italics added)

This tale does have a moral, but it is not, perhaps, the one the reader has been led to expect by its earlier comedic, parodic tone. "Such conclusions," the continuator wrote, "are manie times made in the ports, who sometimes use the privilege of their liberties, not as they ought, but as they list, seldome times applieng their authoritie to so good purposes as they might: for commonlie they use more circumspection in their expenses, than in their sentences" (4:894). This tale offered its Elizabethan readers an unofficial view of the nation's decentralized system of justice that the ordinary citizen could grasp in all its human fallibility; even or especially as he laughed.

In Francis Peck's *Desiderata Curiosa*, the source of much intriguing information about what happened to the 1587 edition after its first appearance, there appears the following note of a manuscript once owned by Abraham Fleming, and now lost:

> An Epitaph upon the Death of the famous & renowned Knight Sir Thomas
> Scot . . . with divers Historical Notes. The whole written by Mr. Reynold
> Scot (Author of the Discovery of Witchcraft) & sent, as thought, to be in-
> serted in the late new Edition of Holinshed; *but not permitted*. A curious
> Thing.[24]

This tantalizing little mystery not only connects the two Scots, Fleming, witches, and the Dover workmen, but points forward to the topic of my last chapter: the conditions of limited permission or partial restraint under which the *Chronicles* were constructed and which, according to this note of Peck's, were in operation at more than one stage of the process. But more to the point still is the fact that *both* of these stories, that of Joan Cason and Goodman Foule, were *removed* from the text during its 1587 castration. This might have been due to their proximity to the dangerous passage about Scotland; but considering the care with which the censored text was reconstructed, it seems more likely that a decision was taken that they, too, contained matter unsuitable for public scrutiny. Like their protagonists, the anecdotes of Cason and Foule joined the ranks of the "disappeared," which, by the preposterous logic of censorship, is the strongest proof of their significance.

ELEVEN   𝕾 *Censorship*

I began this project by taking issue with Stephen Booth's statement that "we care about *Holinshed's Chronicles* because Shakespeare read them."[1] I end it by contesting his statement that the "castration" of the 1587 edition was unintelligible to modern readers. More precisely, he said: "There are no common denominators among the materials removed and there is nothing in any of the excised pages that looks obviously dangerous to governmental policy."[2] Others have partially disagreed. Different hypotheses have been adduced to explain why, for example, the material on the Sidney family or Leicester's visit to the Netherlands was not just deleted but carefully condensed.[3] My own argument goes a good deal further, both in assuming the reasonableness of the Privy Council's action—there was reason to fear that the uncensored text could produce the wrong sort of reaction among sections of the public—and its inefficacy—they failed to notice those parts of the project prior to the "Continuation" that were equally obnoxious to governmental policy and prestige. In addition, I propose that the chroniclers continually *thematized* the problem of censorship as the obverse of their belief (which they held with unequal conviction and with different kinds of exceptions) in freedom of the press, the right to know, and liberty at least of conscience.

The subtlety by which the *Chronicles* deal with censorship as a fact of life and an obstacle in their course is brilliantly displayed in the two following extracts, both of them added by Abraham Fleming for the second edition, and taken from the 1580 edition of Stow's *Chronicle*. To the first, however, Fleming appended a characteristic moral, which makes it more easily recognizable as an anecdote precisely about censorship, although in an oral and partly archaic domain:

> Also this yeare [1476] Thomas Burdet an esquier of Arrow in Warwikeshire, sonne to sir Nicholas Burdet (who was great butler of Normandie in Henrie the sixt daies) was beheaded for a word spoken in this sort. King Edward in his progresse hunted in Thomas Burdets parke at Arrow, and slue manie of his deere, amongst the which was a white bucke, whereof Thomas Burdet made great account. And therefore when he understood thereof, he wished the buckes head in his bellie that mooved the king to kill it. Which tale being told to the king, Burdet was apprehended and accused of treason, for wishing the buckes head (hornes and all) in the kings bellie: he was condemned, drawne from the Tower of London to Tiburne, and there beheaded, and then buried in the Greie friers church at London. [Wherefore it is good counsell that the wiseman giveth, saieng: Keepe thy toong & keepe thy life, for manie times we see, that speech offendeth & procureth mischeefe, where silence is author neither of the one nor the other, as it is trulie and in praise of silence spoken by the poet: nulli tacuisse nocet, nocet esse loquutum.] (3:345; cf. Stow, p. 747)

> [It raigned blood]
> The noble science of Printing was about this time found in Germanie at Magunce by one John Cuthembergus a knight: one Conradus an Almaine brought it into Rome: William Caxton of London mercer brought it into England about the yeare 1471: and first practised the same in the abbie of saint Peter at Westminster; after which time it was likewise practised in the abbies of S. Augustine at Canturburie, saint Albons, and other monasteries of England. In a little towne in Bedfordshire there fell a bloudie raine, whereof the red drops appeered in sheets, the which a woman had hanged out for to drie. (3:250; cf. Stow, pp. 686, 687)

The first anecdote depends for its power on understatement—that is, before Abraham Fleming manhandled it into serving a generalized moral. The buck's head "horns and all" in the king's belly is a Dantesque punishment envisaged by the subject whose totemic animal, white as snow, was sacrificed to royal greed and carelessness; and Edward, by applying the curse to himself, extended that rapacity into the political sphere. There are imaginative energies here that we no longer really understand, and that are poorly rendered as psychological complexities or the day-to-day vagaries of feudalism.

The second statement actually preceded the first chronologically, yet it clearly stands in the narrative, all the more clearly for being an interpolation, as a mark of the transition to a print culture. Does this make the world more recognizable, less archaic? Well, not exactly. Although it contains no *statement* about censorship, still less any moralization, much is implied, and none of it reassuring. After the arrival of the noble science, the injunction to keep silence acquires a different valence, intimated in the startling proximity between printer's ink on paper and the bloody rain on the white sheets. Who is to say whether this was or was not intended to suggest a causal connection between publication and persecution, whose conjunction would become increasingly frequent as the fifteenth century gave way to the sixteenth?

In this chapter I shall offer a conceptual framework to embrace three hitherto unconnected matters. The first of these are the examples we have already seen of constraints on freedom of thought and expression recorded by Holinshed and his colleagues: John Badby's burning for Lollardry in 1410; John Roo's imprisonment in 1527 by Cardinal Wolsey for his political morality play; the butcher's execution under martial law during the Northern Rebellion for "words spoken" as he sold his meat at Windsor; Sir Nicholas Throckmorton's narrow escape in 1554 from the charge of treason by "words only"; and William Harrison's defence of the prophesyings suppressed by Elizabeth. In the otherwise quite different spheres, then, of ecclesiastical regulation, criminal law, and control over both popular culture and courtly (literary) culture, paradigmatic events involving punishment serve to mark the contested boundary between the "state" and individual self-determination, with its inevitable dependence on literacy, education, freedom of speech, and access to other media of persuasion. This boundary was, thanks to the history of the Reformation in England and the unmanageable spread of print, increasingly difficult for the state to police; and by putting its giant presence on the line, the *Chronicles* attempted to move it in the direction we now take for granted as modernity.

Such instances should be seen in the context of the second group of signs pointing to a problem of censorship: those prefatory and procedural remarks cited in chapter 1, statements by Stanyhurst, Hooker (speaking through Giraldus), and Holinshed himself, on the dangerous task that the historian sets himself whenever he embarks on the prehistory of his own place and time. Within the general problematic of citizenship and individual autonomy, history writing in the early modern period held both an extremely exposed and a slightly privileged position, about which we now have a good deal of information, both hard and inferential. Although I earlier mentioned Polydore Vergil's *Anglica Historia*, for example, as an example of a history written under royal patronage to legitimate the early Tudors, Vergil's modern editor Denys Hay has detected self-censorship in the work's publication history. That the first edition, though written between 1521 and 1524, was not in fact published until 1534 suggested to Hay that the role of royal historian was as uncomfortable as Giraldus had perceived it to be in the late twelfth century; although the entire project was commissioned by Henry VIII, it was not until Mary's reign that Vergil apparently dared to publish an edition that included an account of her father's. Clearly, the "weathercock" religion of the early sixteenth century could only have exacerbated that kind of vulnerability.[4]

We could follow this line of thought through similar facts about Edward Hall's *Union of the two noble & illustre famelies*, which avoided dealing with Richard II's deposition and the constitutional challenges it posed by beginning the story with the reign of Henry IV, not to mention the work's breaking off in 1540, yet remaining unpublished until 1548, a fact that the *Dictionary of National Biography* read as showing that "the office of royal panegyrist [was] beset with difficulties and dangers." Whatever degree of self-censorship affected Hall, it is certainly to my point that in 1555 Mary Tudor's proclamation enforcing a previous statute against heresy and "Prohibiting Seditious and Heretical Books" lists among the books now forbidden the works of Hugh Latimer, John Bale, William Tyndale, Thomas Cranmer, Miles Coverdale, "and the book commonly called *Hall's Chronicles*."[5] Hall thus suffered posthumously from the impact of "weathercock religion" on the various governments' relations with the press; a predicament that he shared with Robert Fabian, whose chronicle was censored, not by the Crown, but by John Kingston, its printer-continuator, who removed from it any material that would be offensive in post-Reformation England, such as most of the contest between Henry and Archbishop Becket, and Fabian's enthusiasm for the burning of John Badby.[6]

These earlier instances from within the practice of historiography allow us to make better-informed guesses about the third matter hitherto only alluded to, the well-documented though still somewhat mysterious affair of the censorship of the *Chronicles* themselves. The second edition appeared in the booksellers in mid-January, 1587. On 1 February 1587, the Privy Council wrote to John Whitgift, archbishop of Canterbury, ordering him to halt the distribution and sale of the work, and to oversee its revision. The text of this letter is full of information, and yet we could wish for more:

wheras ther is lately published a new booke of the Chronicles of England divided into twoo volumes or partes, in the end of which ther are added, as an
augmentation to Hollingsheads Chronicles, sondry thinges which we wish
had bene better considered; forasmuch as the same booke doth allso con-
teyne reporte of matters of later yeeres that concern the State, and are not
therfore meete to be published in such sorte as they are delyvered, the same
allso required to be reformid, their Lordships have thought good to require
his Lordship fourthwith to take order for the staye of furder sale and uttering
of the same bookes untill they shall be reviewed and reformyd; for the better examinacion of which thinges theyr Lordships wishe him to commytt and
devide the volumes and partes of the saide books to the consideracion of Mr.
Randolph and Mr. H. Killegrew, with Mr. Doctour Hammond, or to som
such other persons as his Lordship shall think meeete for this purpose for the
more speed to be used in the reformacion of the same, the rather allso for
that there is inserted such mention of matter touching the King of Scottes as
may give him cause of offence.[7]

As Anne Castanian summarized the situation, it seems to have been more
tactfully handled, despite the overheated political climate created by the
Babington Plot, than anyone could manage in the equally fraught context
of 1599: "The members of the Council may have known, when they sent
this letter, that they were about to give the King of Scots another cause for
offense. During the course *of this same day*, Queen Elizabeth ordered
Secretary Davison to deliver Mary Stewart's signed death warrant to be
sealed with the great seal, thus setting in motion the official procedures
that resulted in her execution on February 8."[8]

Despite this tension, Castanien continued,

the expurgation of the *Chronicles* was apparently carried out without dramatic incidents of search, seizure or punishment that would have brought it
forcefully to the attention of the public or contributed to the survival of
more information about the event. There is no record of interviews with the
offending publishers and authors or of the imposition of penalties other than
inconvenience, expense, embarrassment or irritation. . . . So far as is known,
the corrected volumes were distributed to the public without arousing
curiosity as to the cause or effects of the expurgation. (pp. 11–13)

It was only at the beginning of the eighteenth century that antiquarian
scholars became curious about the fact that the surviving copies bore traces
of interference in the pagination, and that some had been, in fact, incom-
pletely expurgated.[9]

The fact that the chroniclers peppered their story with telling instances of freedom of speech denied and punished must surely be linked to that actual censorship of their own project, which partly justified the warnings they had transmitted about the dangerous discipline in which they were engaged. Would it have been true, as Castanien argued, that they merely shrugged their shoulders when the decision to "castrate" came down, observing perhaps that very much worse could have happened? Was the mildness of the discipline the result of a desire on the part of the government to avoid creating a *succès de scandale*, as happened in the next decade with Sir John Hayward's *History of Henry IIII*? Was it rather in recognition that the project had considerable public merits, in relation to which the errors announced by the Privy Council seemed minor and correctible? Or was it that the Council had not, in fact, read carefully enough, and so were able to believe, not having inspected the supplements to material already published, that the breaches in decorum could be construed as overenthusiastic loyalty and nationalism? We will obviously never be able to answer those questions with confidence; but looking more closely at the thematics of censorship in the *Chronicles* may tell us more about what did and did not happen in the spring of 1587 than scholarship has so far accomplished.

Late Medieval Censorship

The chroniclers managed to keep their own predicament in view of the reader throughout the entire project by making the unfreedom of speech itself a matter of public record; and while some of these records are merely the bleak notices of charges laid and punishments inflicted, there are several anecdotes of censorship in which the authorities do not always get the best of the confrontation. As we saw in chapter 7, part of Sir John Oldcastle's challenge to Henry V and his church consisted in the highly efficient dissemination of Wycliffite pamphlets and little "bills" countering official propaganda. Stow's *Chronicle* had recorded one consequence of the 1416 legislation criminalizing the distribution and possession of books in English: "John Benet Woolman who had in London scattered scedules ful of sedition, was drawne, hanged and beheaded on Michaelmas day" (p. 597). Holinshed, however, ignored this item, preferring one for 1417 which he found in Walsingham,[10] and which stands instead for a successful defiance:

> The king kept his Christmasse at Killingworth, and the morrow after Christmasse daie were certeine writings cast abroad, in great mens houses, and almost in everie inne within the townes of S. Albons, Northampton, and Reading, conteining sharpe reproofes against all estates of the church, and it could not be knowne from whence those writings came, nor who was the author of them. (3:88)

Dispersal of "libels" on this scale implies the existence of secular scriptoria operating underground, perhaps in some knightly household. Anne Hudson has stated that it was common practice in Bohemia to produce multiple texts by dictation to a group of scribes, and there is no reason to suppose that this practice did not occur in England.[11] Holinshed's translation, as usual, discards Walsingham's malice toward the "scedulae Lollardorum venenosae" and cheerfully expands on his dry "auctorem nullo sciente," which becomes a sign of official frustration: "It could not be knowne from whence those writings came, nor who was the author of them." Without, of course, saying so, the success of the operation, both at the level of production and distribution, establishes a premise, which we will find repeated over and over again in the *Chronicles*, that despite the bloody sheets and the roll call of victims, in the light of the *longue durée* censorship does not work.

It is partly thanks to the chroniclers themselves that this message survived the castrations of 1587. And the first major example of what was successfully hidden in the pre-"Continuation" sections of the *Chronicles* comes from that transitional phase when a manuscript culture behaves like the culture of print *avant la lettre*. In 1458, in the reign of Henry VI, Holinshed recorded that Reginald Pecock, bishop of Chichester, had all his books burned at Paul's Cross, and "himselfe commanded to keep his owne house during his naturall life." Pecock was forced to abjure his doctrines, which had in fact been developed as a rational defence against Lollardry, and had offended the church authorities by putting too great a weight on reason and too little on Scripture and church authority. He had also offended by writing too much, by "publishing" his works in manuscript, and especially by writing in English. He believed that because the laity had been seduced by books "in her modiris langage" they must be reclaimed in the same medium.[12] He apparently did not realize that this exercise allied him with his antagonists on the crucial question of whether lay literacy should be encouraged or suppressed; and it has subsequently been realized that many of his quotations from Scripture were actually derived from the second version of the Lollard Bible.[13] Although his membership in the Suffolk party at court does not seem to have contributed to his troubles,[14] Pecock was both extremely vain (and thus unfortunately named) and lacking in proper deference. When passages from the Church fathers had been cited against him, he had been known to say, "Pooh! Pooh!"[15] Toward the close of 1457, when Henry VI held a council at Westminster, the hostility that Pecock's earlier pronouncements had generated was so widely expressed that he was expelled from the council and summoned to appear before a special tribunal chaired by Bourchier, archbishop of Canterbury. The result of his trial was, first, his formal abjuration, the choice that he preferred to degradation and incineration.[16] As one of his opponents put it, *sic deplumatus pavo fuit,* the peacock was stripped of his plumage.[17]

Pecock's *Repressor of Overmuch Blaming the Clergy* has not unreasonably been compared to Hooker's *Laws of Ecclesiastical Polity,* developed to counter Puritan arguments in the early 1590s.[18] The *Repressor,* for example, contains an elaborate defence against Lollard arguments for disendowment, and it is only in that context that he admits that not all clerics deserve their possessions, thereby momentarily sounding like William Harrison.[19] By the same token, he attacked the Lollard dependence on the text of Scripture, arguing that while the Bible provides the grounds of faith it does not decree ecclesiastical practice, for which reason, via "the helpe of weel leerned clerkis," is a perfectly adequate source.[20] It is true that Pecock's own reasoning led him into suspect arguments such as the *theoretical* fallibility of general councils,[21] and that his antiliteralism with respect to the biblical text produced the curiously recessive position that Christian truth *preceded* its inscription or even articulation by Christ and his apostles.[22]

No Elizabethan reader, however, could possibly have guessed these complex facts from the paraphrase of his opinions offered in the *Chronicles,* itself both a document in defiance of censorship and, in its archeological layerings, a proof that in certain situations the chroniclers could censor each other or themselves. I shall cite first the story as it finally appeared in 1587. Pecock was arraigned, we are told, because

> that he (verie well learned, and better stomached) began to moove questions, not privilie but openlie, in the universities, concerning the annates, Peter pence, and other jurisdictions & authorities, which the pope usurped; and not onelie put foorth such questions, but declared his mind and opinion in the same. *Some saie* he held that spirituall persons by Gods law ought to have no temporall possessions, nor that personall tithes by Gods law were due [*nor that christian men were to beleeve in the catholike church, nor in the communion of saints, but to beleeve that a catholike church and a communion of saints there is*] and that he held how the universall church might erre in matters of faith; and that it is not of necessitie to beleeve all that which is ordeined by generall councels, nor all that which they call the universall church ought to be allowed and holden of all christian people.
>
> *Moreover, that it was meet to everie man to understand the scriptures in the true and plaine sense, & none bound to glosses of anie other sense, upon anie necessitie of salvation.* (3:245; italics added)

In this account of Pecock's supposed opinions, the first section, prior to the italicized passages, derived from Hall's *Union*—with one important exception. The phrase "jurisdictions & authorities, which the pope *usurped,*" was by Hall represented neutrally as "appertyning to the see of Rome,"[23] and in 1577 Holinshed had transcribed this as "appertyning to the Bishop of Rome" (p. 1291). It was left to the 1587 reviser to add the Protestant charge of papal usurpation, thereby producing the exact converse of what Pecock had actually argued.[24]

The next, italicized section consists of a revised version of what Holinshed had originally written in 1577, citing John Whethamstede, abbot of St. Albans, as his source, who had himself cited Pecock's formal abjuration. Pecock's alleged opinion "that it was not needfull to believe that Christ after his passion did descend into hell" disappeared from the second edition; and where in 1587 Pecock was supposed to believe "that it was *meet* to everie man to understand the scriptures in the *true and plaine sense*," and to ignore "glosses," in 1577 he was said to have believed "that it was *lawfull* to everie man to understande the scriptures in the *literall* sense, and that none is bounde to cleave unto any other sense." This relation between the "lawfull" and the "literall" I would be tempted to see as characteristic of Raphael Holinshed, were it not for the fact that Holinshed was himself translating literally from Pecock's abjuration, as reproduced in Whethamstede's chronicle (the only one of the early sources that includes this opinion, so crucial for the development of Protestant hermeneutics).[25] It is hard to see what significance its revision would have had; what is significant is that such careful revision was thought requisite. In both versions, emphasis falls on the contested relation of the individual (and the individual as reader) to the church as an institution. By a perverse combination of those beliefs that Pecock was forced to confess to in his abjuration with those he was never accused of and in fact argued strenuously against, the *Chronicles* had managed to produce, and reprint, a manifesto of Protestant reformist thought. Ironically, they censored Pecock themselves in order to demonstrate that official censorship will usually be proved wrongheaded by the next generation. It could scarcely have escaped an Elizabethan reader in either 1577 or 1587 that Pecock's beliefs as so represented were scarcely compatible with the Elizabethan Act of Uniformity and especially not with Whitgift's campaign from 1583 onwards to enforce uniformity at whatever cost to consensus.

This perverse interpretation of Pecock's case by the chroniclers seems unlikely to have been accidental. Just in case his readers might want to refer to Pecock's thought in their own ecclesiastical environment, Abraham Fleming directed them to John Stow's *Chronicle* (1580) for a "larger report," adding the confessional opening of Pecock's abjuration, and, from the same source, a convenient list of his books, which, significantly, had to be burned twice by the University of Oxford; once in 1457 and again 1476:

1. *Of Christian religion;* 2. *Of matrimonie;* 3. *Just expressing of holie scripture, divided into three parts;* 4. *The donet of Christian religion;* 5. *The follower of the donet;* 6. *The booke of faith;* 7. *The booke filling the foure tables;* 8. *The booke of worshipping;* 9. *The provoker of christian men;* 10. *The booke of councell.*[26]

Note the omission of the *Repressor* from this list. The fifteenth-century manuscript of the *Repressor* now in Cambridge University Library (Kk.iv.26) was once owned by Stow, who added a catalog of Pecock's works as referred to therein at the beginning of the manuscript and a note, "So sayth John Stowe," at the end.[27] We might infer, therefore, that Stow had read the *Repressor* with some care; that he knew of its arguments against clerical disendowment and a rigorously literalist exegetics; and that he chose to exclude the *Repressor* from his catalog of Pecock's works lest its discovery should undermine the picture of the renegade bishop that the Elizabethan chroniclers wished to perpetuate.

I take this story and its treatment by the chroniclers as paradigmatic of their own theory of censorship and how it was to be combatted. First, the care with which the account was constructed and reconstructed over a decade, the attention to verbal detail, suggests that its message was critical to the project. Second, the protocol of verbatim reporting, even or especially in the perverse form it here assumes, acquires in a case of censorship an unusual frisson; for what the chroniclers are reporting, publishing, rescuing for future readers to consider, are precisely the opinions that have been forbidden, abjured, and publicly burned to prevent their further circulation. True, the chroniclers at one level have reason to believe that a victim of fifteenth-century ecclesiastical censorship would be honored in a sixteenth-century Protestant environment; but this same strategy will be used again in a situation where the ideological tables have been turned, and it is the words of Roman Catholic speakers that are denied legal publication. Finally, it is worth noting that Pecock's story appears, in the 1587 edition, just a few paragraphs before the announcement of the arrival of printing in England.

Certainly one of the most striking episodes thematizing censorship occurs in the short reign of Richard III—the execution of the poet William Collingbourne for writing a brief Aesopian satire on the king and his administration. That, at least, was the story as Holinshed found it in Hall:

[Richard] must also extend his bloudie furie against a poore gentleman called Collingborne, for making a small rime of three of his unfortunate councellors, which were the lord Lovell, sir Richard Ratcliffe his mischeevous minion, and sir William Catesbie his secret seducer, which meeter or rime was thus framed:

The Cat, the Rat, and Lovell our dog,
Rule all England under a hog.

Meaning by the hog, the dreadfull wild boare, which was the king[s] cogni-
sance. But bicause the first line ended in dog, the metrician could not (observing the regiments of meeter) end the second verse in boare, but called
the boare an hog. This poeticall schoolemaister, corrector of breefs and
longs, caused Collingborne to be abbreviated shorter by the head, and to be
divided into four quarters. (3:422)

We can recognize Hall's black humor in this story of imprudent prosody
leading to bodily sectioning.

It is, above all, a story of *literary* censorship; and upon it the *Mirror for
Magistrates* based its "tragedy" of Collingbourne, which contains a classic
statement both of the hermeneutics of censorship and of the principle of
the "ancient liberty" of imaginative literature to intervene with immunity in
affairs of state, so long as its critique was sufficiently covert or sufficiently
humorous. "I thought the freedome of the auncient tymes," wrote the fictional Collingbourne, "Stoode styll in force. *Ridentem dicere verum / Quis
vetat?*"[28] The poem, published for the first time in 1561, was clearly a document in the program to make historiography serve political theory; for
what Collingbourne defines as "the Poetes auncient liberties"[29] were obviously connected to the ancient liberty asserted in those parts of the
Chronicles that define a new or renewed constitutionalism. When Baldwin
and his colleagues added their interpretation and evaluation of the poem,
in what must surely have been seen as an address to Elizabeth, the larger
political implications of censorship are made unavoidable:

> Gods blessing on his heart that made thys (sayd one) *specially for revivinge our
> auncient liberties.* And I pray god it may take suche place with the Magistrates,
> that they maye ratifie our olde freedome, Amen (quoth another) For that
> shalbe a meane bothe to staye and upholde them selves from fallyng: and
> also to preserve many kinde, true, zealous, and well meaning mindes from
> slaughter and infamie. If kyng Richard and his counsayloures had allowed, or
> at the least but wynked at sum such wits, what great commodities myght
> they have taken thereby. [For] they should have knowen what the people
> myslyked and grudged at . . . & so mought have found meane, eyther by
> amendment (whyche is best) or by some other pollicie to have stayed the
> peoples grudge: the forerunner commonly of Rulers destructions. *Vox populi,
> vox dei,* in this case is not so famous a proverb as true.[30]

But Holinshed, who himself contributed the tragedy of Sir Nicholas
Burdet to the *Mirror*[31] and would surely have been aware of Collingbourne's

importance in *its* historiographical program, was not content to leave this story in Hall's ironic hands, nor to leave it as a story of literary censorship alone. He also, characteristically, wished to look further into the legal aspects of the case. "Here it is to be noted," he wrote, "that *beside the rime which is reported by some to be the onelie cause* for which this gentleman suffered, I find in a register booke of indictements concerning fellonies and treasons . . . that the said Collingborne (by the name of William Collingborne) late of Lidyard in the countie of Wilshire esquier, and other his associats were indicted in London." The charge was that, on or about 10 July 1484, they had communicated with Henry, earl of Richmond, in Brittany and attempted to arrange his return the following spring; and that on 18 July Collingbourne had "devised certeine bils and writing in rime, to the end that the same being published, might stir the people to a commotion against the king" (3:422–23; italics added). The indictment also stated that Collingbourne had fastened his rhyme "upon diverse doores of the cathedrall church of saint Paule, for the more speedie furthering of his intended purpose," and the *Great Chronicle of London* indicated a still wider distribution.[32] In any case, Holinshed remained sceptical of the indictment: "But whether he was giltie in part or in all, I have not to saie." The result of adding this was, presumably, to show that Collingbourne's execution made legal sense only if the notorious rhyme was placed in the larger context of organized resistance to Richard; but also that, like the expression of religious belief, theoretical liberalism may here have been unjustly prosecuted on a trumped-up charge of treason.

Early Tudor Censorship

Not all symbolic challenges to authority were textual at the point of origin, in the sense of transmitting a critique through "words only," although of course they became textual at the point where they entered the *Chronicles*. Visual images could also be subject to revision or erasure. It is useful here to recall Stanyhurst's metaphor for his work as historian of Ireland, his anecdote of "one Dolie, a peintor of Oxford," his omission (from his painterly commission) of the tenth commandment, and his cheeky defence of his work, to the effect that the mural matched his employer's moral deficiency. Among the materials on the reign of Mary Tudor that Abraham Fleming appropriated from Foxe's *Acts and Monuments* was another anecdote about painterly impudence. It occurs in the context of the pageants set up in London to celebrate the queen's marriage to Philip of Spain; where, among the spectacles which, wrote Fleming, "for the vaine ostentation of flatterie [he would] overpasse," there was notably a painted icon on the "conduit in Gratious street," showing the nine worthies of England, with Henry VIII represented as one of the nine:

> He was painted in harnesse having in one hand a sword, and in the other hand a booke, whereupon was written Verbum Dei, delivering the same booke (as it were) to his sonne king Edward, who was painted in a corner by him. But hereupon was no small matter made, for the bishop of Winchester lord chancellor, sent for the painter, and not onelie called him knave for painting a booke in king Henries hand, and speciallie for writing thereupon Verbum Dei: but also ranke traitor and villen, saieng to him that he should rather have put the booke into the queenes hand (who was also painted there) for that she had reformed the church and religion, with other things according to the pure and sincere word of God indeed. The painter answered and said, that if he had knowne that that had beene the matter wherefore his lordship sent for him, he could have remedied it, and not have troubled his lordship. The bishop answered and said, that it was the queenes majesties will and commandment, that he should send for him; and so commanding him to wipe out the booke and Verbum Dei too: he sent him home. So the painter departed, but fearing least he should leave some part either of the booke, or of Verbum Dei, in King Henries hand: he wiped away a peece of his fingers withall (4:62–63)

Everything in this narrative bespeaks an intentional irony: the confrontation between the uptight bishop (Stephen Gardiner, whom Mary had rewarded for his sufferings under Edward by making him Lord Chancellor) and the matter-of-fact painter (who was, of course, an artisanal sign painter rather than an artist); the relation between a seemingly trivial detail in the iconography of church and state, and the huge symbolic importance attached to it; the cynicism discernible in the colloquial syntax ("commanding him to wipe out the booke and Verbum Dei too") from which the reader may recognize that the Word of God has indeed become a mere prop in the hands of competing regimes; and the comic materialism of the story's conclusion. In the alternative version of this story that appears in the *Chronicle of Queen Jane*, a contemporary diary of which John Stow possessed a manuscript, the anecdote concludes slightly differently, with the painter substituting for the Bible a pair of gloves, a detail which transforms comic materialism into social satire; and the fact that this is a story *about* censorship in the popular arts is oddly accentuated by the fact that the entire passage is crossed out, as if, wrote J. G. Nichols in his edition, "the writer had been fearful of retaining it."[33]

Like so much else in the chroniclers' treatment of the reign of Mary Tudor, this is one of those stories that, as I promised, redeem the bitter history of censorship by making the authorities the butt of the joke. This is also true of the finest and funniest anecdote of the history of surreptitious printing, one that was itself secreted within the seemingly digressive catalog of the bishops of Exeter, compiled by John Hooker, which appears mysteriously in the place of almost all events of the troublesome year 1579—the year of Elizabeth's plans to marry the French duc d'Alençon, and of John Stubbs' challenge to those plans in *The Gaping Gulf,* an event in the annals of censorship with which most literary scholars of the sixteenth century are, if anything, all too familiar. It was no doubt the course of prudence for Fleming and his colleagues to avoid any mention of these events. Nevertheless, the catalog of bishops from the year 905 onwards, which was inserted where 1579 failed to register, tells its own story about censorship and how it can be self-defeating. The story occurs in the biography of Miles Coverdale, who is presented as a pioneer of English Protestantism, and hence as both victim and survivor of episcopal repression during Henry's reign. "He was one of the first," wrote Hooker:

> which professed the gospell in this land in the time of king Henrie the eight, he translated the bible out of the Hebrue, into English, and wrote sundrie bookes upon the scriptures. Which doctrine being verie new and strange in those daies, and he verie streightlie pursued by the bishops made his escape, and passed over into low Germanie, where he printed the bibles of his translation and sent them over into England, and therof made his gaine wherby he lived.

The heart of the story, however, resides in the ironic anecdote whereby John Stokesley, who succeeded Cuthbert Tunstall as bishop of London in 1536, sought to suppress Coverdale's Bibles, but was actually inveigled into financing his adversary:

> [he] made inquirie where they were to be sold, and bought them all up; supposing that by this meanes no more bibles would be had: but contrary to his expectation it fell out otherwise. For the same monie which the bishop gave for these bookes, was sent over by the merchant unto this Coverdale, and by that meanes he was of that wealth and abilitie, that he imprinted as manie more and sent them over into England. (4:422)

This story is the twin of a more richly developed anecdote told by Hall about William Tyndale's New Testament. In this story, which took place a decade earlier than the Stokesley-Coverdale incident, the bishop of London was then Tunstall and the cunning merchant was Augustine Packington, who offered to procure for Tunstall the entire printing of Tyndale's New Testament:

> The Bishop thinking that he had God by the too, when in deede he had (as
> after he thought) the Devell by the fist, saied, gentle Master Packington, do
> your diligence and get them and with all my harte I will paie for them, what-
> soever thei cost you, for the bokes are erroneous and naughtes and I entend
> surely to destroy them all, and to burne theim at Paules Crosse.[34]

When Packington explained the deal to Tyndale, he exclaimed, "I am the
gladder . . . for these two benefites shall come thereof, I shall get money of
hym for these bokes, to bring my self out of debt (and the whole world
shall cry out upon the burning of Goddes worde). And the overplus of the
money, that shall remain to me, shall make me more studious, to correct
thesaid New Testament, and so newly to Imprint thesame once again. . . .
And so forward went the bargain, the bishop had the bokes, Packyngton
had the thankes, and Tyndale had the money."[35]

When Tunstall subsequently observed that the *new* New Testaments
were being imported thick and fast into England, he sent for Packington,
who pointed out that this was a second imprint, and that the bishop would
never be sure to have stopped the flow until he had also purchased the
frames and the print! "The bishop smiled at him and said, well Packyngton
well, and so ended this matter." This story, insulated from Tyndale's execution for heresy in the Low Countries in 1536, remains a comedy; and it
seems to support the modern estimation of Tunstall as a moderate, who
hoped by burning Bibles to avoid the need for burning heretics.

Yet the relationship between the two tales, like that of the two versions of the sexual harrassment of teenage girls in 1381, is problematic. Did
both incidents "really" happen, and if so, did Coverdale and his anonymous
merchant learn their strategy from the earlier episode? Or should the repetition (in a less detailed, less colorful style, with one of the three agents
unidentified) be attributed to the formulaic character of popular legend?
Whereas Edward Hall, the source of the Tyndale/Tunstall anecdote, would
have been a contemporary witness, John Hooker, whose catalog of the
bishops of Exeter was separately published in 1584, was only ten years old
when the Coverdale/Stokesley episode was supposed to have occurred. Yet
as an employee of Coverdale in the early 1550s, he could certainly have
heard it on the best authority. Credibility is also strained by the fact that
Coverdale's translation of the Bible was dedicated to Henry VIII, that he
was probably encouraged by Cromwell to produce it, and that it was not
banned until the proclamation of 1546, which, after the execution of Anne
Askew, swept into one huge forbidding embrace both Tyndale's and
Coverdale's Bibles, along with Bale's *Breefe Chronicle of Sir John Oldcastle*, and
the works of Wycliffe, Frith, Joye, Turner, Barnes, etc.[36] On the other

hand, the story is compatible with Stokesley's reputation as a strenuously persecuting bishop in conflict with Cromwell on that score, and responsible for turning John Frith over to execution in 1533. Its credibility, rather than the converse, may be supported by the existence of a *third* story of a bishop attempting to buy up Bibles, in this case Archbishop William Warham, who attempted to acquire foreign stock of Tyndale's New Testament in 1526.[37]

Pre-Elizabethan Censorship Mechanisms

In order to understand the strategy of the chroniclers, or to understand their methods as strategy, we need to acquire some perspective on the temper of Elizabeth's reign with respect to the control of the press. While this topic is to some degree inextricable from that of control of dissent more generally, a problem far too large to be even summarized here, a good deal can be learned merely by presenting a calendar of events in which "words" or the public expression of dissent were criminalized; for the clustering of those events in the later part of the reign, to which the two editions of the *Chronicles* belong, must have affected the chroniclers' sense of what their own contribution to Elizabethan culture and public consciousness could or should be.

The evolution of censorship law under Elizabeth's immediate predecessors has been deftly summarized by D. M. Loades.[38] Although he narrows his definition of censorship strictly, as I do not, to control of the press, as distinct from the episodes already mentioned above where a pre-print culture anticipates the multiplication and distribution, and therefore argues that formal censorship does not begin in England until the early 1520s, when Luther's books were burned at Paul's Cross, he draws valuable distinctions between the strategies of the first three Tudor monarchs with respect to restraints upon published debate, especially in the religious arena. Henry VIII's interest in control of the press began with religion but was intensified by the issue of his divorce, and, as Loades put it, "for the rest of his reign the king was fighting this battle on two fronts, against the Lutherans—to whom his objections were purely theological—and against the papists to whom they were mainly political."[39] In 1524 the bishop of London had ordered that no new book was to be imported without episcopal license, and in 1529 and 1530 royal proclamations confirmed this order and condemned nineteen books as heretical. The Church and the Crown collaborated in a series of prosecutions, and Richard Bayfield was burned for heresy in December in 1531. It was in reaction to the Pilgrimage of Grace in 1536, however, that Henry ordered, by a proclamation of 1538, a complete ban on the importation of books in English printed abroad. More important, he invented at the same time the system of licensing by some of the Privy Council, or prior restraint of the press, which with certain modifications (as to the identity of the licensers) would remain in force until the end of the seventeenth century. In 1543 a parliamentary statute (34/35 Hen. VIII, c.1) decreed that any printer or bookseller producing or distributing any of the forbidden titles would be subject to three months' imprisonment and a fine of 10 pounds per book, which on a second offence would become imprisonment for life and forfeiture of all their goods. A proclamation of July 1546 repeated the provisions of earlier ones, established an Index of eleven forbidden Protestant authors, and required that every book bear the names of its author, its printer, and the date of publication. Loades makes the point that, Henry's "awesome personality" notwithstanding, the very repetition of these proclamations implies that enforcement was ragged at best, and he finds very little evidence that printers encountered serious difficulties.[40] But one might argue in addition that this last provision of 1546 was a double-edged sword; not only did it provoke its own high-spirited flouting, as the continued production of anonymous, semianonymous or pseudonymous works with fictional imprints throughout the century bear witness, but it may well have created, as a by-product of discouraging anonymity, a sense of individual responsibility for one's ideas in a way that developed self-determination.

When the young king Edward VI succeeded, his councillors initially continued the policy of control where possible. In August 1549 the Council determined that all English books were to be examined by "Mr. Secretary Peter, Mr. Secretary [Sir Thomas] Smith, and Mr. [William] Cicill, or the one of them."[41] This indicated a further shift toward the secularization of censorship *regulation*, as distinct from its purpose. Nevertheless, when Protector Somerset was arrested in October 1549 for responsibility for the risings of that year, the Council had to offer 100 crowns reward for information leading to the arrest of those who had distributed bills and letters in his support—a historical reprise of "publishing" events in the story of Sir John Oldcastle more than a century earlier. Again, the repetition of proclamations in 1550 and 1551 was a sign of their inefficacy, the later admitting ruefully that "notwithstanding the good order taken for the Church . . . Divers Printers, Booksellers and Players of Interludes do . . . whatsoever any light and fantastical head doth invent."[42]

The legend of Mary Tudor's reign as the century's low point from a libertarian perspective was largely constructed by John Foxe. According to Loades, "illicit publishing in London was continuous, and defied all efforts to suppress it."[43] In addition to the *Copye of a letter sent by John Bradforthe*, and the pamphlets and ballads celebrating Lady Jane Grey, we can imagine the original of Holinshed's account of the trial of Sir Nicholas Throckmorton circulating in pamphlet form. Again the regime proceeded by proclamation, in July 1553 and March 1554; but in January 1555, in the wake of the Throckmorton trial, Mary introduced through Parliament a new development, whereby slander against herself and King Philip became a felony, and its publication, if incapable of being brought within the ancient treason statute of 1352, was also a felony and punishable by loss of the right hand. In June 1555 a further proclamation revived the terrible statute *de heretico comburendo*, and extended the idea of a national Index, as Henry had pioneered it, by listing the names of twenty-four Protestant writers, along with Edward Hall's *Union*.[44] As the short reign drew to its unhappy end, on 6 June 1558 the Council proclaimed the death penalty by, of all things, martial law, for the mere possession of any heretical or treasonable book, whether imported from abroad or printed at home.[45] Yet despite all this threatening, as Loades points out, only eighteen persons were examined and imprisoned by the Council during this period, and there was a noticeable pattern of delay in bringing them to trial, release without further process, or actual pardon.

The one successful strategy for press control developed in Mary's reign, though its connection to control for ideological *content* may not have been understood at the time, was the system of collaboration with the Stationers' Company introduced by charter in 1557, whereby the Company received an effective monopoly over printing, which was thereby restricted to London. As Elizabeth developed this system, within that large monopoly were dozens of smaller ones acquired by individual printers over books or classes of books directly from the queen herself, a system of privileges or patents reinforced by a Star Chamber decree of 1567. The principle here, restated in 1583, was anticompetitive: it was "not meet that sondrye men should print one book."[46] At the interrogation of Robert Robinson in 1585 for challenging that principle, the defendant's counterprinciple was recorded as follows:

> he saith he doth verily thinke that it were best for the company of Stacioners of which company this defendant is one if the imprinting of bokes might be common and that it weare lawfull for every man that wolde to imprynt the *accedence or gramer* and such like bokes. . . . for that if it so were that then the poorer sorte of prynters should be better able to lyve than they nowe are havyng servyd ther tyme to be free of that companye as also for that he thinketh these bookes woulde be solde for lesse price to her Maiesties Subjectes than the same nowe are.[47]

As David Loades has argued, it is important not to confuse the Stationers' interests with those of the Crown, but neither were they entirely distinct. While the Company did not become "the subservient agent of government censorship,"[48] the new arrangements substituted for that rather crude relationship the more elastic one of self-regulation well motivated by economic interest. Surely the private monopolies helped to simplify supervision. Indeed, in 1586 Robert Bourne and Henry Jefferson argued cogently that there had developed a confusion between censorship proper and internal regulation of the press via the monopoly system. Given the number of special privileges, "there is almost no liberty lefte for printinge but for ballettes and toyes and such like, which might with better reason be prohibited," and that "the true meaning" of the Star Chamber decree of 1567 was "to restrayne the prynting of bookes not fitt to be prynted, and not to restrayne somme personnes from printing of thinges that are lawfull and fitt to be prynted, and to gyve liberty to somme one or two others only to printe the same, being . . . neither profitable to the comon wealth, nor agreeing with equity."[49]

And perhaps one should here mention John Wolfe, who had larger ideas still, conflating antimonopoly fervor with civil libertarianism and reminding his colleagues and other citizens that there were deep connections between freedom of the press and the spiritual principles of the Reformation. Wolfe became the leader of a group of piratical printers agitating against the Stationers' Company monopoly over printing, but whose agenda had larger political dimensions. They "stood upon this point that they were freemen, and might print all lawfull bokes notwithstanding any comaundement of the Quene, and that the Quenes comaundementes in this case were no lawe, nor warranted by lawe." "Tush," Wolfe was reported to have said, "Luther was but one man, and reformed all the world for religion, and I am that one man, that must and will reforme the governement of this trade."[50] Wolfe was, therefore, an agent provocateur in a larger political context. When the authorities tried to tame him by throwing him into prison, he petitioned Burghley and Walsingham and encouraged his colleagues to organize more widely. They retained lawyers and set up a distribution system for the sale of their pirated books outside of London. And they "incensed the meaner sort of people throughout the City . . . [so] that it became a common talk in Alehouses, tavernes and such like places, whereupon issued dangerous and undutifull speaches of her Majesties most gracious government." According to S. L. Goldberg, "it took a second imprisonment and a raid on his secret presses to make Wolfe willing to be bought out by the Company in 1583."[51] But if Wolfe was bought out of piracy, he was not necessarily tamed. As his role in printing Hayward's notorious *History of Henry IIII* suggests, the very certainty of financial gain from such a project implied a prior assessment of its potential for political provocation.[52]

Elizabethan Censorship

But this is to leap ahead. My purpose here, in retailing the prehistory of the Elizabethan censorship system, is to show both what legal structures Elizabeth inherited from the other members of her family, and to raise the important question of how the temper of her reign compared with theirs. And here I must depart from David Loades, to whom much of the previous section has been indebted; for his account of sixteenth-century censorship was teleological in the sense that Elizabeth was held immune from the impotence of her predecessors. Loades recirculated the counterlegend that was constructed on her behalf and in contrast to her sister's, not by John Foxe, but by modern historians and literary historians. According to Loades, "Elizabeth realized that by persuasion, concession, and if necessary subterfuge, she had to mobilize a broad measure of support among her subjects. She therefore paraded her respect for their prejudices, and won their affection by an instinctive sympathy which allowed her frequently to ignore their wishes." In this process she used the popular press as "a sort of thermometer for the political temperature of England," precisely that which William Baldwin and his colleagues in the *Mirror* had recommended; and, concluded Loades, she succeeded, because of her government's ability "to read the signs aright, and administer suitable tonics and sedatives. More drastic measures of control were repeatedly proved impracticable."[53]

In the rest of this chapter I shall argue, first, that this is entirely too benign an account of Elizabeth's censorship, which was a good deal stronger on enforcement, and more closely resembled her sister's (including the use of the same legislation) than is popularly believed; and second, that it was part of the agenda of Holinshed's *Chronicles*, especially of the second edition, to make this perception possible—even though, implausible though this proposition may at first appear, the strategy adopted by the chroniclers was to keep silent about some of the most notorious cases of censorship, and to appear to be themselves willing to "administer suitable tonics and sedatives."

When Elizabeth succeeded to the throne in 1559 the Crown promptly issued a set of *Injunctions to the Clergy*, extending the licensing requirement and the machinery it required. The government now required all books and papers printed in England or abroad, in any language, to be submitted for official scrutiny before publication or distribution. The queen was to be the first authority for licensing, followed by any six members of the Privy Council, the archbishops of Canterbury and York, the bishop of London, and the chancellors of the universities. The ecclesiastical commission for London, which included common and civil laywers and businessmen as well as clergymen, were to be responsible for approving books on religion or politics, pamphlets, plays, and ballads.[54] There seem, however, to have been almost no significant complaints by writers about this system (unless we count the *Mirror for Magistrates*' tragedy of Collingbourne, published in 1561, as precisely that), and no significant cases of censorship from the first decade of the reign; none, at any rate, that the *Chronicles* chose to record.[55]

In 1570, however, everything changed. Elizabeth was excommunicated by the pope. Holinshed reported this event rather tersely: "the five and twentith of Maie in the morning was found hanging on the bishop of Londons palace gate in Pauls churchyard, a bull which latelie had beene sent from Rome, conteining diverse horrible treasons against the queens majestie: for the which one John Felton was shortlie after apprehended, and committed to the tower of London" (4:252). And for the second edition Fleming decided to add "some rorings" of the papal bull, as he had gathered them "out of one that I am sure had a conscience to tell the truth": that is to say, a collection of the most offensive sentences culled from the bull at large, accompanied by a colorful and expansive translation. One might be tempted to ask why Fleming chose to recycle such statements in print, when Felton had been imprisoned for posting them in a single location, and why he had selected matters extraneous to the religious conflict per se. For example, the *Chronicles*' readers now had access to the complaint that the queen "hath remooved the noble men of England from the kings councell. She hath made hir councell of poore, darke, beggerlie fellows, and hath placed them over the people" (4:252). This sounds more like political satire against the *regnum cecilianum* than the outraged support of the Protestant subject.

In 1571 a new treason act (13 Eliz. I.c.1) made it treason to affirm *by writing* that the queen should not be queen, or that she was an infidel, tyrant, or usurper. This goes unmentioned for 1571, but it was, as I have shown, alluded to in Holinshed's final words on the trial of Sir Nicholas Throckmorton (4:55). On 28 November 1572 John Hall and Oswald Wilkinson were executed for treason under the new act; but this fact, along with every other event for 1572, was preempted by several of Francis Thynne's catalogs.

On 11 June 1573 the Crown issued a proclamation ordering the surrender of all copies of the *Admonitions to the Parliament*. This indicates that the crackdown was to be extended from Catholic to Puritan dissent. The text of the proclamation, which also covered the *Second Admonition* published anonymously by Thomas Cartwright, required "all and every printer, stationer, bookbinder, merchant, and all other men . . . who hath in their custody any of the said books to bring in the same to the bishop of the diocese, or to one of her highness' Privy Council, . . . upon pain of imprisonment, and her highness' further displeasure.⁵⁶ And on 7 July 1573 John Field and Thomas Wilcox were imprisoned for authorship of the *Admonition to Parliament*, which they subsequently acknowledged. Although several indictments and executions are mentioned for this year, *these* facts go unrecorded. Thereafter other proclamations would seem to suggest that Elizabeth experienced the same difficulties in monitoring the press as had her father and her sister. On 28 September 1573 was proclaimed an order for the "Destruction of Seditious Books," primarily aimed at *A Treatise of Treasons* (Louvain, 1572), which had itself aimed at Burghley as the architect of Elizabethan religious policy. The authors of the "said books and libels" are declared to be "obstinate traitors against her majesty's person, estate, and dignity."⁵⁷ And on 26 March 1576 another proclamation offered "Rewards for Information on Libels against the Queen."⁵⁸

These were the events of the 1570s that preceded the first edition of the *Chronicles*. In the intervening decade before the second edition appeared, there occurred one of the best known cases of Elizabethan censorship, to which, once more, Fleming paid a respectful silence. John Stubbs published his *Gaping Gulf*, a pamphlet advising the queen against marriage with the French duc d'Alençon. On 13 October 1579 Stubbs was convicted under the law of seditious libel, and he, his printer and his bookseller, were condemned to lose their right hands. A royal proclamation dated 27 September 1579 denounced the book for, among other things, misleading the "simpler sort," by "offering to every most meanest person of judgement by these kind of popular libels authority to argue and determine in every blind corner at their several wills of the affairs of public estate."⁵⁹

William Camden, in his *Annals*, gave a powerful rendering of this event, which, being published after Elizabeth's death, could afford to be explicit. Not only did Camden record the case of Stubbs in a manner designed to draw his reader's sympathy, but he evinced an interest in the interpretation of the statutes, and in justice as fairness, such that we might imagine he had learned it from Raphael Holinshed:

> Since that she begunne to bee the more displeased with Puritans than she had been before-time, perswading herselfe that [Stubbs' pamphlet] had not passed without their privitie: and within a few dayes after, John Stubbes of Lincolnes Inn, a zealous professor of Religion, the Author of this Relative Pamphlet (whose Sister Thomas Cartwright the arch-Puritan had maried) William Page

the disperser of the Copies, and Singleton the Printer were apprehended: against whom sentence was given that their right hands should be cut off by a law in the time of Philip and Marie, against the Authors of Seditious Writings, and those that disperse them. Some Lawyers storming hereat, said the judgement was erroneous, and fetcht from a false observation of the time, wherein the Statute was made, that it was onely temporarie, and that (Queene Marie dying) it dyed with her. Of the which Lawyers, one Dalton for his clamorous speeches was committed to prison, and Monson a Judge of the Common-pleas, was sharply rebuked, and his place taken from him, after that Sir Chr. Wray chiefe Justice of England had made it manifest by Law, that in that Statute were was no errour of time, but the Act was made against such as should put forth, or divulge any seditious writing against the King; and that the King of England never dyed; yea, that Statute likewise in the first yeare of Queen Elizabeth was revived again to the Queene and her Heires for ever.[60]

"Not long after," Camden continued (adopting the eyewitness protocol of the *Chronicles* along with their sympathies):

upon a Stage set up on the Market-place at Westminster, Stubbes and Page had their right hands cut off by the blow of a Butchers knife, with a Mallet strucke through their wrests. The Printer had his Pardon. *I can remember* that standing by John Stubbes, so soone as his right hand was off, put off his hat with the left, and cryed aloud, God save the Queene. The people round about him stood mute, whether stricken with feare of the first sight of this strange kind of punishment, or for commiseration of the man whom they reputed honest, or out of a secret inward repining they had at this marriage, which they suspected would be dangerous to Religion. (italics added)

In 1581, there was passed an act "against Seditious Words or Rumors" (23 Eliz. I.c.2) which made it a felony to spread papers or pamphlets containing slanderous words or rumors of rebellion, and raised the penalty from loss of the right hand to capital punishment. On 12 October 1585 yet another royal proclamation ordered the "Suppression of Books Defacing True Religion, Slandering Administration of Justice, Endangering Queen's Title, etc."[61] And the following year Thomas Allfield was executed as a felon for importing and distributing Cardinal Allen's *Modest Defence of the English Catholics*. The *Chronicles* reported: "On the fift daie of Julie Thomas Awfeld a seminarie priest, and Thomas Weblie diar, were arreigned at the sessions hall in the Old bailie, found guiltie, condemned, and had judgement as fellons to be hanged: for publishing bokes conteining false, seditious, and slanderous matter, to the defamation of our sovereigne ladie the queene, and to the excitation of insurrection and rebellion" (4:620).

If one simply reads these later sections of the *Chronicles* for what they
do include (without adding the list of victims in Allen's *Defence* or other
sources), the repeated evidence of state violence is unavoidable. Whatever
they omit, moreover, and for whatever reasons, they remain true in the
matter of the history of censorship to the anthropological branch of the
project, with the inference that the state deals unreasonably harshly with
the smallest of the fry it could catch in its net, perhaps because the bigger
fish, like Cardinal Allen himself, were beyond its reach.

The Babington Plot

The last phase of the *Chronicles* was rendered peculiarly barbarous, even after
this preparation, by a long account of the Babington Plot, or rather of the
apprehension and execution of the foolish young men who had secretly
communicated with Mary, Queen of Scots, and may well have been encouraged to do so in order to render Mary ultimately destructible.[62] That is
to say, it *was* a long account before the 1587 censorship, after which the
episode was hugely reduced in scale and color. The plot was "discovered" by
Walsingham's agents in July 1586, and the conspirators were duly executed
with the fullest degree of cruelty permitted by the law. Needless to say,
Abraham Fleming, who claimed responsibility for this section of the text in
an unusually possessive marginal note,[63] formally adopted the position that
the conspiracy was diabolical, and that the rigors of the law were acceptable. But the protocols he inherited from Holinshed of multivocality and
verbatim reporting, as well as his own literary proclivities, had very interesting consequences for the recording process. Like Holinshed, who so
carefully represented both the case of Sir Nicholas Throckmorton and that
of his "honest" jurors, Fleming offered (before the censorship occurred) a
multivocal approach to the Babington Plot; for he decided to include the
"literary" responses to their predicament of the Babington conspirators.[64]
Waiting in the Tower for their execution, those young men "occupied their
wits in dolorous devises, bemoning their miseries, of the like stampe to this
here annexed, savouring more of prophane poetrie than christianitie, of fansie than religion." There followed in the uncensored text the poem we now
know as "Tichborne's Elegie," identified in the margin as "written with his
owne hand in the Tower before his execution, printed by John Wolfe 1586":

> My prime of youth is but a frost of cares,
> My feast of joie is but a dish of paine:
> My crop of corne is but a field of tares,
> And all my good is but vaine hope of gaine:

> The daie is past, and yet I saw no sun,
> And now I live, and now my life is doone.
> My tale was heard, and yet it was not told,
>
> My fruit is falne, and yet my leaves are greene:
> My youth is spent, and yet I am not old,
> I saw the world, and yet I was not seene:
> My thread is cut, and yet it is not spun,
> And now I live, and now my life is doone. (4:911)

This poem, of which I quote two of the three stanzas, has been celebrated as one of the most moving of the era's meditations on death,[65] not least because of its formal rigidities as an expression of the ultimate personal crisis. The short story of the young man whose life is about to be taken rings out with clear pathos, despite the fact that, as he tells us in the only unconventional line in the poem, his "tale was heard, and yet it was not told." Not told, that is, as he would have told it.

The poem's appearance in the national archive was, therefore, surely peculiar, as was the specification of the elegy's previous printing by John Wolfe. Ostensibly, Wolfe had published Tichborne's elegy in order to reject it, in a pamphlet dutifully entitled *Verses of Prayse and Joye, Written upon her Maiesties preservation. Whereunto is annexed Tychborne's lamentation, written in the Towre with his owne hand, and an aunswere to the same* (1586); but the effect of such a strategy (an answer to the poem requires the publication of that which is to be refuted) was itself formally dialogic. For the 1587 *Chronicles* to enter Wolfe's name, recently notorious as a campaigner for a freer press, in the public record, and to associate him with the Babington conspirators' desire for self-expression was, to say the least, to introduce voices in counterpoint to the official view.

But there is more. Babington himself, so the chronicler tells us, managed to distribute to friends outside the Tower certain poems, which were apparently printed illegally: "the copies are common (yet never authorised for the print)." His objective might have been to appeal for royal clemency on account of his rank; but it was surely also, as the act of publication implies, an appeal for popular sympathy. And Fleming proceeded to describe one of these illegal documents, which obviously spoke to his own interest in the Aesopian fable:

> to procure the speedier commiseration (in his fansie) he falleth into a familiar tale of a certaine man, that having a great flocke of sheepe, mooved either with a sheepish unruliness, or for his better commoditie, threatened everie daie by one and one to dispatch them all: which he dailie performed accord-

ing to his promise, untill such time as the terror of his accustomed butcherie strake the whole flocke into such a fear, as whensoever he came and held up his knife, advising at that instant but the slaughter of one, the whole number of them would quake, fearing each one his particular chance. Which tale he applieth to himself, being one of the brutish herde (as he confesseth) that for their disordinat behaviour the law justlie condemneth, and threatneth to dispatch one after another. (4:912)

This extraordinary insert was marked out for readerly interest, indeed, literary attention, by the marginal gloss "A fable or tale which Babington applieth to his present case of wretchednesse." Whatever Fleming's conscious intention in so permitting the forbidden material a second circulation, the effect would surely have been to permit readers to experience precisely that "commiseration" the fable was intended to promote.

Fleming noted that this was "a familiar tale." In fact, it was a remarkable adaptation of the Aesopian fable of *The Sheep and the Butcher*, which appeared in the ubiquitous editions descended from Steinhöwel's (and hence also in Caxton's fifteenth-century English translation) with a woodcut showing the butcher cutting the throat of one sheep while the rest of the flock look on. The moral of the original fable was that personal safety depends on group solidarity, and of the tragedy that results when, like sheep, men fail to unite in resistance to a seemingly irresistible power. Babington, through the voice of the chronicler, intelligently rewrote the old fable so as to add to its ancient message of sympathy for the too-passive sheep an unmistakable indictment of the psychology of repression. His brilliant conception of how the shepherd terrifies his flock into submission by a daily, ritual execution of òne of their number was a genuine insight into the Elizabethan theory of public executions as, literally, exemplary ritual.

Despite the editorial comment, the story transmits its own message. A sheepish "unrulinesse" (which is only one of the two motives offered, the other being "better commoditie") scarcely justifies such "accustomed butcherie" as indeed, common sense asserts, must surely work *against* the economy of sheep farming; while the plot of the fable must have punched a large hole through the ideal of a peaceful pastoral world, with the queen at its center, that courtly poets had already established as typically "Elizabethan." And if the reader of the *Chronicles* (the ideal reader whom, we have posited, remembered what he had read before) could recall Sir Thomas More's fable of Wolsey as the "great wedder" "which the good sheepheard sendeth from the good sheepe" (3:743–44: 1529), or George Stadlow's reference (via Fabian via Foxe) to Edward VI as "our high shepheard" whose wrath means death (3:1018: 1549), or Sir John Cheke's rebuke to the rebels of the same year ("ye that ought to be like sheepe to your king, who ought to be like a sheepeheard unto you"; 3:993), or the unnamed Grimsby shepherd who drowned attempting to save his master's sheep from the floods (4:356: 1570), the ironies of political representation would have been more apparent still.

A few pages later, marking the spot with another marginal gloss ("A prettie apolog allusorie to the present case of malcontents") Fleming proceeded himself to rewrite for the occasion the ancient Aesopian fable of *The Frogs Desiring a King*:

> God make prince and people of one mind, and plant in all subjects a reverend regard of obedience and contentment of present estate, supported with justice and religion: least longing after novelties, it fare with them as with the frogs, who living at libertie in lakes and ponds, would needs (as misliking their present intercommunitie of life) with one consent sue to Jupiter for a king, and so did. (4:922)

Again, he delivered the official position editorially. At the end of the all-too-familiar story, when the too-passive log has been replaced by the too-active stork or heron, the frogs, "seeing their new king so ravenouslie gobling up their fellowes, lamentablie weeping besought Jupiter to deliver them from the throte of that dragon and tyrant. But he . . . made them a flat answer, that (will they nill they) the herne should rule over them." "Whereby we are taught," the chronicler concluded, "to be content when we are well and to make much of good queene Elizabeth, by whom we enjoie life and libertie" (4:922).

The Frogs Desiring a King has had a long political history of its own, perhaps precisely because its venerable plot has always beeń too complicated for unambiguous application.[66] On the one hand it appears to argue for a divinely sanctioned monarchy, and the required obedience of subjects no matter how harsh the rule; on the other it implies a contractual relationship, whereby the frogs freely brought monarchy upon themselves. In fact, Fleming made matters worse than in simpler versions of the fable, by emphasising the earlier, republican state of the frogs, "living at libertie in lakes and ponds" or "intercommunitie" (a word here used for the first time in the vernacular) and moving to petition "with one consent." All of this computes with the parliamentarianism of the *Chronicles* as a whole and jars with the "libertie" that is said to derive from Elizabeth's rule. The two fables speak to each other, moreover, precisely in dramatizing the sequential execution of the powerless; and neither of the rationales they supply is any more persuasive than Fleming's excessive justification ("our severitie is clemencie," 4:922) of the string of executions that follow.

I have already suggested, in "Populism," the complexity of Fleming's intentions at this point in his narrative, and the impossibility of determining to what extent his loyalty to queen and country was both enhanced by his anti-Catholicism and confused by his years of work with the *Chronicles,* and their overall commitment to latitudinarianism. Proof of the *effect* of these remarkable materials on a late-sixteenth-century reader resides, however, in what happened to them. In place of the long account of the Babington Plot the censored text offered only a brief summary of events, now disproportionately dominated by the dutiful "oration of maister James Dalton one of the councillors of the citie of London." Anne Castanien believed that the revised account, which begins with a paragraph marginally attributed to Stow, was all Stow's work. "The exhortations," she observed, "are gone, and all the expressions of horror and revulsion. . . . None of this text contains any defence of the severity of the executions of the first day, nor does it make clear the fact that these executions were carried out with such severity."[67] She concluded, however, that the revision, though set in motion by the need to avoid offence to King James, was here conducted in the interests of moving closer to "modern historical practice." "It is difficult to suppose," she concluded, "that government censors were anxious to bring about this kind of amendment in the text." I find this conclusion unpersuasive, not least because it is governed by precisely those biases against the *Chronicles'* style of historiography with which I began, and because the castration of the Plot matches *for its interest* the disappearance of the stories of Joan Cason and Goodman Foule, the contraction of praise for the Sidneys, father and son, of Leicester's entertainment in the Low Countries, and those catalogs of Thynne's which, Castanien acknowledged, might have been used for "attacks on episcopacy or for forming a body of opinion opposing the established church organization" (p. 309). All of these materials become significant (and hence their removal becomes intelligible) in the light of our knowledge about the tensions in the Elizabethan regime during the period of the "second reign," as well as in the light of the chroniclers' agenda in the project as a whole. Besides, not all of what survived can readily be attributed to Stow. Tichbourne's elegy disappeared, as did Babington's version of *The Sheep and the Butcher;* but that other sign of Fleming's interest in fables, *The Frogs Desiring a King,* no longer dangerously reverberating with its predecessor, was retained.

Finally, let me return to the rather bland account provided by Castanien of the consequences to the individual chroniclers of the 1587 "castrations," consequences which she restricted to "inconvenience, expense, embarrassment or irritation."[68] While she noted that John Stow expressed "a mild complaint" in his *Summarie of the English Chronicles* (1590), she ascribes to Thynne an unsigned apology directed to the earl of Shrewsbury, and added: "The apology shows no resentment; Thynne expressed willingness to rectify his mistakes and furnished a revised paragraph, though it did not make its way into the amended text."

I would like to believe that, despite his own humiliation in 1587, Thynne chose to imitate Grindal in "standing upon the defense of his cause" through the unlikely medium of literary history; that is to say, a defence of his father's edition of Chaucer, in which Francis implied the same principle of literature's ancient liberty as the *Mirror for Magistrates* had put into the mouth of Collingbourne. The defence of William Thynne against Thomas Speight's criticisms takes up the question of whether the Lollard "Pilgrim's Tale" was spurious; but Thynne defends its canonicity, and hence his father's editorial wisdom, not on the grounds of its Chaucerian character or its likely date of composition (the tale mentions Perkin Warbeck) but by impugning those who attempted to suppress it. Thynne includes in his *Animadversions* against Speight a long anecdote about his fathers' dealings with the clergy and Henry VIII on this matter, which not only serves to carry his father's radical Protestant agenda forward to the end of the sixteenth century, but surely also his own views on Whitgift's campaign to control the contemporary press. The "Pilgrim's Tale," he wrote, was "a thing more odious to the Clergye, then the speche of the plowmanne":

> In this tale did Chaucer most bitterlye enveye against the pride, state, covetousnes, and extorcione of the Bysshoppes, their officialls, Archdeacons, vicars generalls, comissaryes, and other officers of the spirituall courte. . . . This tale, when king henrye the eighte had redde, he called my father unto hym, sayinge, "William Thynne! I dobte this will not be allowed; for I suspecte the Byshoppes will call the in questione for yt." to whome my father, beinge in greate favore with his prince, (as manye yet lyvinge canne testyfye,) sayd, "yf your grace be not offended, I hoope to be protected by you:" whereuppon the kinge bydd hym goo his waye, and feare not. All which not withstandinge, my father was called in questione by the Bysshoppes, and heaved at by cardinall Wolseye, his olde enymye, for manye causes, but mostly for that my father had furthered Skelton to publishe his "Collen Cloute" againste the Cardinall, the most parte of whiche Booke was compiled in my fathers howse at Erithe in Kente. But for all my fathers frendes, the Cardinalls perswadinge auctorytye was so greate withe the kinge, that thoughe by the kinges favor my father escaped bodely daunger, yet the Cardinall caused the kinge so much to myslyke of that tale, that chaucer must be newe printed, and that discourse of the pilgrymes tale left oute; and so beinge printed agayne, some thynges were forsed to be omitted, and the

plowmans tale (supposed, but untrulye, to be made by olde Sir Thomas Wyatt, father to hym which was executed in the first yere of Quene Marye, and not by Chaucer) with muche ado permitted to passe with the reste;[69] in suche sorte that in one open parliamente (as I have herde Sir John Thynne reporte, beinge then a member of the howse,) when talke was had of Bookes to be forbidden, Chaucer had there for ever byn condempned, had yt not byn that his woorkes had byn counted but fables.[70]

The effect of this anecdote, with its seeming weakness for gossip and digression, is to enroll Thynne himself in a league of heroic writers (Chaucer, Skelton, the Thynnes, father and son) and activists (Henry VIII, the Wyatts, father and son) that stretches from the end of the fourteenth century to the end of the sixteenth century the story of resistance to clerical oppression.[71] The point that Chaucer's works were exempted because they were "counted but fables" drives home the bitter experience of the antiquarian, who attempts to deliver the truth.

TWELVE   ℬ *Readers*

T he preceding chapters have told a story of intentions, both of the individual chroniclers and of the "syndicate" they formed over time. Its persuasiveness will not be enhanced by my merely repeating at the end the claims I made at the beginning. In conclusion, however, I offer a mode of proof—reception history—appropriate for a cultural historian, however limited the resources for it must necessarily be. There are records of how the *Chronicles* were read in their own time and in the next century, a question which brings us back to the report of their supposedly rapid obsolescence and devaluation at the end of the sixteenth century.

The most important claim for this obsolescence has been made by D. R. Woolf, important in that it is based on new research into publishing habits rather than upon old assumptions and teleology. In an article that considerably qualifies the teleology implied in his later published monograph, Woolf decided to investigate the "decay of the chronicle from its former stature as a living, growing genre into a remnant of the past," and suggested that it was caused primarily by technological and social change, and that "the advent of humanist historical writing . . . was not so much a cause of the chronicle's demise as another consequence" of these factors. The chronicle, he added, "did not so much decay as *dissolve* into a variety of genres, such as almanacs (information); newsbooks, diurnals, and finally newspapers (communication); antiquarian and classically modelled histories (historical); diaries, biographies and autobiographies (commemorative); and historical drama, verse, and prose fiction."[1] While Woolf does not distinguish at all between Holinshed's *Chronicles* and their predecessors, except to imply that their great size rendered them even more vulnerable to the demand for smaller, cheaper and more portable products, his comments, like F. J. Levy's, can be turned to the support of my thesis, by foregrounding how clearly Holinshed and his colleagues and successors believed in *combining* these functions, and thereby creating what we today call a *cultural* history of Britain.

Like Levy, Woolf cites several negative comments about the chronicles. There is Thomas Nashe's warning against "lay chronigraphers, that write of nothing but of mayors and sheriefs, and the dere yere, and the great frost,"[2] a comment that applies much better to John Stow, and the Stow-derived materials in the *Chronicles*, than it does to the whole. There is Gabriel Harvey's querulous marginal note to Livy's *Romanae Historia Principis*, complaining of the "many asses who dare to compile histories, chronicles, annals, commentaries . . . Grafton, Stow, Holinshed, and a few others like them who are not cognizant of law or politics, nor of the art of depicting character, nor are they in any way learned."[3] There is Ben Jonson, whose *News from the New World Discovered in the Moon*, a court masque of January 1620, provides (as one would expect from the most ostentatiously neoclassical writer of the Jacobean era) a caricature of the chronicler as the man who stuffs in trivial details. There is Sir Henry Savile, whose "contempt for the low social origins of many annalists" Woolf has also noticed; and, perhaps most significantly, there is Sir Thomas Egerton, Lord Ellesmere, who in 1608 refused to cite evidence from Richard II's reign during the debate on the case of the post-nati, because "some of our chroniclers doe talke idely [of the reign] and understand little." This last comment does indeed bear relation to Holinshed's careful and tendentious treatment of that reign, to which, as we shall see, other readers paid equally careful attention. But, as Woolf himself observes, such comments do not necessarily suggest a declining interest in the tales that the chronicler told or the information he made available. On the contrary, "It is undeniable," he concluded, that the second half of the century witnessed an enormous expansion in the public . . . interest in the past, particularly within the urban environment. It is probably truer to say that the chronicle disappeared because supply could not keep up with demand—and demand turned elsewhere for satisfaction."[4] At the same time it appears that the economics of publishing allowed for only one really large-scale history at a time; a fact which accounts for the complaints of John Stow that I cited in my opening chapter.

We must grant, of course, that Holinshed's *Chronicles* were not (despite the appeal of Clement Walker in 1649) republished in the seventeenth century. This does not mean, however, that they were not read. In fact, if I am correct in describing one of the central motives of the chroniclers as being the creation, and preservation in print, of a complex national archive, they would scarcely have been disappointed to learn that their work became in the following century (after the topicality of the "Continuation" was no longer an appeal to a popular audience) a scholarly work of reference. Not, as we shall see, that topicality ceased to be an attraction, as different historical circumstances suddenly required arguments from the past. But the simplest conclusion to be drawn from a survey of consumers (as fallible, naturally, as all such surveys must be) is that the *Chronicles* continued to be read, until at least the middle of the seventeenth century, for many different reasons, and to satisfy all of the categories of demand outlined by Woolf above.

From an early stage, the casual use of references to the *Chronicles*, or to Holinshed as their "author," implies that the work had acquired some of the status desired for it by Abraham Fleming, if not carrying credit "next unto the holie scripture," at least being required for cultural literacy. We could add to Woolf's citation from Nashe his comment in *Have with You to Saffron-Walden* (1596) where he made fun at Gabriel Harvey's expense by claiming that "hee hath vowd . . . to discover and search foorth certaine rare Mathematicall Experimentes; as for example, that of tying a flea in a chaine, (put in the last edition of the great Chronicle)" and pretended that Harvey planned to make his living "by carrying that Flea, like a monster, up and down the countrey, teaching it to doo trickes."[5] But four years earlier, in *Foure Letters Confuted* (1592), Nashe had used the *Chronicles* as an arbiter of commonsense against the Harvey family. "The other night," he claims, he found a critical account of Richard Harvey's *Astrologicall discourse* on the imminent conjunction of Saturn and Jupiter (1583) which provoked, among other disturbances, an official answer by John Aylmer, bishop of London, in a sermon at Paul's Cross.[6] "The common sort of people," wrote Nashe, supposedly quoting the *Chronicles*, "were almost driv'n out of their wits, and knew not what to doe: but when no such thing hapned, they fell to their former securitie, and condemned the discourser of extreame madnesse and follie."[7]

I have already mentioned that the poet Edmund Spenser owned a copy, and he used it assiduously for the antiquarian parts of *The Faerie Queene* (1590); but a decade before that he and Gabriel Harvey, his Cambridge friend and mentor, had published a section of their correspondence that twice mentions Spenser's debt to Holinshed as if it were a matter that would reciprocally dignify each. (In the same year, 1580, Harvey replaced

Spenser, who seems to have been hastily dispatched to Ireland, as secretary to the earl of Leicester.)[8] Spenser refers to a poem he is writing, the "Epithalamion Thamesis" (later probably incorporated into the fourth book of his epic) as a topographical endeavor:

> in setting forth the marriage of the Thames I shew his first beginning and off-spring, and all the Countrey that he passeth thorough, and also describe all the Rivers throughout Englande whyche came to this Wedding, and their righte names, and right passage, &c. A worke, beleeve me, of much labour, wherein not withstanding Master Holinshed hath muche furthered and advantaged me, who therein hath bestowed singular paines in searching oute their firste heades and sources, and also in tracing and dogging oute all their course til they fall into the Sea.[9]

And in a later letter Harvey refers to the same work in progress as something to be admired, "both Master Collinshead and M. Hollinshead too being togither therein," a joke that depends as much on knowledge of the *Chronicles* as it does on the reference to Spenser's pseudonym in *The Shepheardes Calendar*. Harvey himself had mixed feelings about the *Chronicles*. In one of his attacks on Thomas Nashe, *Pierce's Superogation*, printed by John Wolfe in 1593, he referred to his previous mockery of "Eldertons ballatinge, Gascoigne's sonnettinge, Greenes pamphletting, Martins libelling, Holinsheads engrosing,"[10] which combines the complaint about the sheer bulk of the *Chronicles* with one of the agricultural abuses listed by William Harrison—buying up all the available grain in order to control the market. But a few pages later Harvey rendered an apology:

> Let every man in his degree enjoy his due; and . . . be respected according to the uttermost extent of his publique service or private industry . . . Our late writers are as they are. . . . In Grafton, Holinshed, and Stow . . . in an hundred such vulgar writers many things are commendable, divers things notable, somethings excellent. (2:280)

For Samuel Daniel, himself a historian, the list is longer and the respect greater. In preparing his own prose *Collection of the History of England*, first published for private circulation in 1612, and dedicated to Robert Carr, then viscount Rochester, Daniel explained to the reader "whence I had my furniture," and for the lives of the first three Edwards declared his debts to "Froissart and Walsingham, with such Collections as by Polydore Virgile, Fabian, Grafton, Hall, Holingshead, Stow and Speed, diligent and Famous Travailors in the search of our History."[11] Although it has long been assumed that Daniel derived the new hands-off historiography he developed for this work (as compared to his deeply meditative verse account of the fifteenth-century *Civil Wars*) from Jean Bodin, it now seems possible that he learned something from Holinshed of the virtue of merely "sowing it together:

> holding it fittest and best agreeing with Integrity (the chiefest duty of a Writer) to leave things to their owne Fame, and the Censure thereof to the Reader, as being his part rather then mine, who am onely to recite things done, not to rule them. (4:83)

Indeed, although Daniel explicitly rejects the theory of the ancient constitution as pre-Norman, it appears that he followed Holinshed's discussions of this topic with great attention. He mentions how Voadicea incited her followers to "that noble, and manly worke of liberty: which to recover, she protests to hold her selfe there, but as one of the vulgar" (4:93). He notes the beginning of parliaments, "where Princes keepe within their circles to the good of their people," in the reign of Henry I (4:211). And he devoted disproportionate space to the legal innovations of the Conqueror, including a strenuous critique of the imposition of law French:

> The agreeved Lords, and sadde people of England, tender their humble petition, Beseeching him in regard of his oath made at his Coronation: And by the soule of Saint Edward, from whom he had the Crowne and Kingdom: under whose Lawes they were borne and bred; that he would not adde that misery, to deliver them up to be judged by a strange Law they understood not. And so earnestly they wrought, that hee was pleased to confirme that by his Charter, which he had twice fore-promised by his Oath: And gave commaundement unto his Justiciaries to see those Lawes of Saint Edward (so called, not that he made them but collected them out of Merchen-Law, Dane-Law, and Westsex-Law) To bee inviolably observed throughout the Kingdome. And yet notwithstanding this confirmation, and the Charters afterward granted by Henry the first, Henry the second and King John, to the same effect; there followed a great innovation both in the Lawes and government in England, So that this seemes rather to bee done to acquiet the people, with a shew of the Continuation of their ancient customes and liberties, then that they enjoyed them in effect. For the little conformitie betweene them of former times, and these that followed upon this change of State, shew from what head they sprang. And though there might bee some veynes issuing from former originals, yet the maine streame of our Common law, with the practise thereof, flowed out of Normandy, notwithstanding all objections can bee made to the contrary . . . and to strive to looke beyond this, is to looke into an uncertaine Vastnesse, beyond our discerning. Nor can it detract from the glory of good Customes, if they bring but a pedigree of 600 yeares to approve

their gentility; seeing it is the equity, and not the Antiquity of lawes, that makes them venerable. . . . But this alteration of the Lawes of England bred most heavie doleancies, not onely in this Kings time, but long after: For whereas before, those Lawes they had, were written in their owne tongue intelligible to all; now are they translated into Latine and French, and practized wholly in the Norman forme and Languages . . . nor have we now, other marke of our subjection and invassalage from Normandie, but onely that, and that still speakes French to us in England. (4:165–67)

Since this version of English history was written for, and invoked the patronage of, the Jacobean court, and under a king who claimed his authority in part from the Conqueror, it is remarkable to see how defiantly Daniel has kept the spirit of Holinshed's constitutionalism, while discarding its improbable extensions into time immemorial.

In their definition of "reading" as practiced by early modern intellectuals such as Harvey (and this would apply equally to all the names I have mentioned so far) Lisa Jardine and Anthony Grafton sought to give the term a more active or "transactional" sense, and aimed for a more diverse theory of what reading was good for:

> the transactional model of reading which we use assumes that a single text may give rise to a plurality of possible responses, not a tidily univocal interpretation. Historians of reading have been inclined to settle for rather simple models for the reading practices of definable social groups and to locate sharp moments of transition when one set of practices yields to another.[12]

In the case of Harvey, product of a prominent Saffron Walden burgher family, university praelector of rhetoric, later LL.B and Doctor of Civil Law at Oxford, and with connections to the Leicester-Sidney circle, the transactional model of reading *classical* history (Livy) appears to have been inflected with a generalized political concern that may well have had career objectives behind it; yet Harvey's reading of the *Chronicles* does not have that valence. Samuel Daniel evidently read his "Holinshed" differently. Yet he belonged to the same social group, in the 1590s becoming a protégé of the Sidney circle via Mary, countess of Pembroke, and under James I a writer of court masques. He was also suspected of being an apologist (through dramatic fiction) for another reader of the *Chronicles*: Robert Devereux, earl of Essex, after his execution for treason in 1601.[13] How do these middle-class readers with court connections compare with William Whiteway, the Dorchester citizen discovered by David Underdown, whose prosperous civic status, devout Puritanism, political views, and patterns of reading are recorded in his diary and commonplace book?

Daniel's *Collection* first appeared in 1612, toward the end of the first decade of James's reign. It is therefore the work of an old Elizabethan, coming to terms with the new regime, and with the same mixed feelings, perhaps, as John Donne, whose gibe at the *Chronicles* did probably *not* represent his actual feelings. Whiteway's diary begins in 1618, at the outset of the Thirty Years War, and his first major entry records the appearance of the comet of 1618, which, like Richard Harvey on the conjunction of Saturn and Jupiter in 1583, he took to presage alarming changes in the world.[14] It ends in the 1630s, when the rise of Archbishop Laud in the Caroline heavens also presaged alarming consequences.

Whiteway was an avid reader of English history, including historians with dubious reputations. He owned Sir Walter Ralegh's *History of the World* (banned by King James in 1614), George Buchanan's *History of Scotland*, Bacon's *History of King Henry VII*, Camden's *Britannia*, Stow, Speed, and Holinshed. According to Underdown, Whiteway contemplated writing a history of England in his own time, a risky undertaking, given his views, which were ancient constitutionalist and anti-Laudian. He drew up a list of "Materials for the History of the Reigns of K. J[ames] and K. C[harles]."[15] Elected to the 1626 parliament, which vigorously pursued impeachment proceedings against George Villiers, duke of Buckingham, Whiteway carefully copied into his commonplace book the texts of several libels against the duke.[16] He saw the Petition of Right of 1628 as being "for the expression of our liberties," and the passage of Sir John Eliot's resolutions against tonnage and poundage in the next session—the last Caroline parliament before the civil war—as the "articles of liberty."[17]

Whiteway's commonplace book, Cambridge University Library MS. Dd.xi.73, also contains his personal selection from the 1587 edition of Holinshed's *Chronicles*, which he apparently read in 1633, the year of Laud's ascension to the archbishopric.

Whiteway started his reading of the *Chronicles* where, I have assumed, most readers would begin, with William Harrison's *Description of England*, and culled from that heterogeneous source lists of legal terms, types of guns, information about hot springs, fish, and deer. However, his eyes were equally sharp for Holinshed's ancient constitutionalism. One of his very few notes on the medieval section of the *Chronicles* reads: "K. Edward the 3 befor the Conquest, instituted the lawes now called the Common Lawes; they were for the most part made befor by K. Edgar and now restored by St. Edward" (f. 176v). From the Irish section he compiled a list of the governors of Ireland, and then extracted from John Hooker's *Order and Usage* the following crucial statement of the importance of the House of Commons, precisely that which had rendered the Ricardian *Modus tenendi* tendentious: "If the lords of the Parlement be [not] present the King & the Commons may make lawes 127b. But the King & Lords cannot do so without consent of the Commons" (f. 178v). In his reading of the Scottish history, Whiteway became fascinated by Francis Thynne's account of the most recent struggles between King James and the Presbyterian general assembly, recording among other episodes that in 1586 "the King was overruled & the Presbytery established in Scotland by a generall assembly," which, having excommunicated Patrick Adamson, archbishop of Edinburgh, would not reinstate him "for all the Kings mediation, until he did submit unto them & promise to be conformable to their orders."[18]

Whiteway, then, was one of those Puritan-minded country burgesses whose significance as a group and whose capacity for political thought have been devalued by revisionist history. His interest in the *Chronicles* in the 1630s would, according to the traditional story of their displacement by newer and more coherent historiographical models, appear to be retrograde. In my story he might appear, on the contrary, to be exactly the sort of reader Holinshed and his colleagues had in mind. Place Whiteway beside Sir Edward Coke, and the reception history of the *Chronicles* becomes more interesting still. Whiteway died in 1635 and Coke in 1634, having managed in his seventies to complete his last act of defiance of the Stuart monarchy, the four parts of his *Institutes*. Removed from the Bench in 1616 by King James for refusing to amend his *Reports*, he transferred his energies to Parliament, where, as Richard Helgerson remarked, "he caused the crown no less annoyance than he had as a judge."[19] Dismissed from the council in 1621 and briefly imprisoned on a charge of treason, Coke was one of the leading promoters of the 1628 Petition of Right. In that year appeared also the first part of his *Institutes*, his commentary on Littleton's *Tenures*. Parts 2, 3, and 4, however, were suppressed by King Charles in 1631, and were only published posthumously by order of the Long Parliament. As Lord Holland wrote to Dudley Carlton, now viscount Dorchester, "the king fears somewhat may be to the prejudice of his prerogative, for [Coke] is held too great an oracle amongst the people."[20]

Helgerson decided (as he ironically puts it) to "respect King Charles's censorship" and concentrate only on the first part of the *Institutes*.[21] But for the present purpose, the suppressed volumes are the ones germane, for they show that Holinshed's *Chronicles* were still alive as a source of historical jurisprudence in the early 1630s. We know that Coke owned *three* copies of the 1587 *Chronicles*, or rather one complete copy and two of the English section of the history.[22] He seems, however, to have only cited from the latter. Although some of his allusions seem casual or coincidental, some striking patterns of interest emerge.

In the Fourth Part of the *Institutes*, under the heading "Of the High Court of Parliament," Coke twice cited the *Chronicles* on the topic of excessive taxation, most interestingly in the case of the uprising of clothworkers in Suffolk in response to Cardinal Wolsey's exactions (discussed above in chapter 9).[23] He does not, however, associate the *Chronicles* with the *Modus tenendi parliamentum* (pp. 12–14). Instead, his attention seems to have been attracted by Holinshed's other most important legal focus, the law governing treason, perhaps not surprisingly in view of Coke's own experiences. In the third part of the *Institutes*, under the heading of "Treason," an early marginal note refers to "Dier, in Sir N. Throgmortons Case," on conspiracy to levy war (p. 9). But this is merely the signpost revealing Coke's critique of any law permitting treason for words alone.

He mentions "the laws that made words treason, now all repealed or expired" (p. 14). One of these was the Elizabethan statute of 1572 (13 Eliz. I.c.1) (discussed in chapter 11), whereby "if any within the Realme or without should compasse, imagine, invent, devise or intend to levie war aganst her Majesty, and the same declare by writing, or word, & that should be High Treason" (p. 10). When the Long Parliament saw to the publication of the later parts of the *Institutes*, someone with hindsight rendered this critique extremely, if carelessly, topical, by alluding to the famous case of 1637, when Henry Burton, John Bastwick, and William Prynne were arrested for seditious publications, and, in the early stages of the indictment, an attempt was made to charge them with treason: "and upon that law, Bradshaw [i.e., Bastwick], Burton, and others, were attainted of High Treason, for conspiracy only to levie war. But it was resolved by all the Justices, that it was no treason within the Statute of 25 Eliz.3 as hath been said" (p. 10). In his section on "Petit Treason" Coke in fact looped back to the topic of high treason, and, like Throckmorton, praised Mary's treason act for clearing away the confusions in the law:

> Before this Act so many treasons had been made . . . as not only the ignorant and unlearned people, but also learned and expert men were many times trapped and snared: and sometimes treasons made or declared in one kings time, were abrogated in another kings time. (p. 11)

And he also, in the guise of defending the English denial of counsel, provided a trenchant attack upon it, in Throckmorton's own language of indifferency:

> First, that the testimonies and the proofs of the offence ought to be so clear and manifest, as there can be no defence of it. Secondly, the Court ought to be in stead of councell for the prisoner, to see that nothing be urged against

him contrary to law and right. . . . And to the end that the triall may be the
more *indifferent*, seeing that the safety of the prisoner consisteth in the *indifferency* of the Court, the Judges ought not to deliver their opinions before hand
of any criminall case . . . For how can they be *indifferent*, who have delivered
their opinions beforehand without hearing of the party, when a small addition, or subtraction may alter the case. (p. 11)

A marginal note points out that "In Scotland in all criminall cases, yea in
cases of High Treason, Pars rea may have Councell learned."

My penultimate example of how the *Chronicles* were read in the seventeenth century is again a member of the middle class: John Milton, scriven-
er's son, Cambridge-educated writer-intellectual, who, having returned to
London after his continental tour at the end of 1639, began to keep a commonplace book. Into this book Milton copied over a hundred references
from the 1587 edition of "Holinshed's" *Chronicles*, with by far the largest proportion clustered in the "political" section of the standard triple index (the
other two sections being "moral" and "domestic.") These were to become his
notes for the series of polemical pamphlets written later during the civil war
and republican period. Under the entry "Laws" Milton entered sixteen references to early kings who had been law reformers or the opposite, or who
had sworn to restore the ancient rights and liberties, as, for example:

> Edward the Confessor reduc't the laws to fewer, pick't them, and set them
> out under name of the common law. Holin.Book 8.c 4. . . . K.John vid.
> Subditus. promiseth to abolish the unjust laws of the Normans and to restore
> the laws of K.Edward. Holinsh. p 28.[24]

Among twenty-one items under "Subject," cross-referenced with "King,"
Milton observed that "to say that the lives and goods of the subjects are in
the hands of the K. and at his disposition is an article against Ri. 2. i parl. a
thing ther said to be most tyrannous and unprincely.Holinsh. 503" (1:446).
He noted also the events of 1386, when Parliament sent representatives to
Richard II to remind him that if he absented himself for forty days, not
being sick, "it was greatlie to their discomfort." (1:449), a topic (royal ab-
senteeism) he returned to in 1649, when defending the execution of
Charles I.[25]

In the commonplace book, Richard II became prominent again under
Milton's heading "The Tyrant," most significantly, in relation to "the deposing of a tirant and proceeding against him. Richard the 2d was not only
depos'd by parliament, but sute made by the commons that ' he might have
judgement decreed against him' to avoid furder mischeif in the realm.
Holinsh. 512" (1:455).

Under "Property and Taxes" Richard is mentioned as "a farmer of his kingdom. Holin. 496" (1:481). And, like Coke, Milton's attention was attracted by the uprisings caused in 1525 by Cardinal Wolsey's exactions, which are mentioned on three separate occasions (1:482, 486, 487), the last (under the heading of "Official Robbery or Extortion") carrying the flavor of popular protest:

> Commotion for these reasons want not a stout captain as a plebeian wittily answerd the duke of norfolk (sent against the commons in Suffolk and asking who was thire captain) that Poverty was thire captain with his cozin Necessity. Holin. p 891.

It is pleasant to hear that Milton appreciated the demotic wit of this anecdote, and suggestive to discover that in 1641 comparisons were made between Wolsey and Archbishop Laud.[26]

We can even extend the readership of the *Chronicles* into the eighteenth century, and across the Atlantic, by way of Thomas Hollis, the idealistic Whig book-collector and promoter of liberal publications. Hollis's donations to American libraries, especially to Harvard, may well have fostered the American revolution, though his claim was always to mediate the disputes between Britain and its American colonies. When Brand Hollis, Thomas's heir, compiled his benefactor's *Memoirs* and had them privately printed in two handsome volumes in 1780, he sent a copy to Benjamin Franklin, who wrote back expressing his admiration for Hollis and the special kind of influence that, as only a private scholar, he had exerted.[27] Thomas Hollis probably did more, singlehandedly, to discover and restore to public use what we may now call the liberal canon of early modern political writings than anyone before or since. John Milton was one of his heroes; among his preparations for a new edition of Milton's prose works was a commonplace booklet on the doctrine "of bridling Kings," inserted into his copy of *Eikonoklastes*, and printed in the *Memoirs*. It included, among others, the sixteenth-century monarchomachs, Hotman, Buchanan, and the *Vindiciae contra Tyrannos*; Andrew Marvell's *Account of the Growth of Popery and Arbitrary Government*, and Ludlow's *Memoirs*; five selections from Locke's *Two Treatises*; Lord Molesworth's preface to his translation of Hotman; *Cato's Letters*; the American Jonathan Mayhew's 1750 *Discourse on unlimited Submission*, preached on the anniversary of Charles I's execution; and the following, less expected entry:

> Raphael Holinshed, cap. VIII, vol. 1, p. 173. This (the Parliament) House hath the most high and absolute power of the realme; for thereby Kings and mighty Princes have from time to time been deposed from their thrones, and

laws are enacted and abrogated, offenders of all sorts punished, and corrupted religion either disannulled or reformed. It is the head and body of all the
Realme, and the place where every particular man is intended to be present,
if not by himself, yet by his advocate and attorney; for this cause any thing
that is there enacted is not to be withstood, but obeyed of all men, without
contradiction or grudge. (2:774)

This relocation, in a history of political thought from the Middle Ages
through to the era of the Stamp Act, of William Harrison's provocative
opening to his chapter on Parliament, confirms the interpretation offered
in this study of Harrison's intentions and their place in the *Chronicles* as a
whole.[28]

But let me end by giving credit where credit is mostly due. It should
not be forgotten that the compilers of "Holinshed's" *Chronicles* were themselves extremely intelligent readers of preceding chronicles, and that they
aimed to improve and guide their own readers in the rather special art and
mental agility that this practice required. I trust that by this time I have persuaded some of my own readers how carefully they constructed their massive archive: as one in which the main ("official") story of reigns and battles
(though in three kingdoms) continued its mighty way, but deliberately
modified and interrogated by other kinds of material and perspectives.
Sometimes they carefully noted the insertion of materials that others might
deem digressive, but denied the charge of absent-mindedness (or engrossing) by the presence of markers: "In the meantime," "But to return," "And
now to our present history again." Sometimes they counted on the shock
value of contrast: of expensive courtly entertainments with the brutal executions of commoners, of the ritual reinstatement of the rood in St. Paul's
Cathedral with the street appearance of a dead cat in papist fancy dress.
Sometimes they carefully corrected the mistakes of their predecessors; al-
ternatively they stated their wish to have the reader contemplate the multiplication of *versions* of history, as, for example, of how preciely Richard II
died.

But perhaps no passage could better illustrate the subtle instruction the
chroniclers gave their readers than the following, seemingly unnecessary,
item inserted by Abraham Fleming for the 1587 edition for the year 1444.
For this he went back to Fabian and *Polychronicon*, and marked his activities
carefully in the margin:

On Candlemasse eeve this yeere by lightning . . . Paules steeple was set on
fier. . . . This steeple hath diverse times beene overthrowne and defaced,
partlie by winds, and partlie by lightning, *as may be observed in the reading of this
volume*: yea when the staff hath beene repared by the choisest workemen, and

of the substantiallest stuffe, and all meanes (that stood with the deepe devise of man) used to make it so sure that it might continue, as a monument of perpetuitie for posteritie, to woonder at and admire. *But to returne to the historie.* (3:206; italics added)

Not only does this passage advise the reader to look forward and back through "this volume" for other occurrences of damage to the steeple; by framing the damage to the steeple as an insert in "the historie" it seems cunningly to remind that same competent reader to remember Fleming's analogies *between* the two parallel enterprises, of building and rebuilding the church and the nation. At the beginning of the "Continuation," Fleming had appealed to the "mind indifferentlie free" as the basis of a new historiography, which would permit the *Chronicles* to "approach next in truth to the sacred and inviolable scripture, and their use not onelie growe more common, but of greater account." Here in this seemingly casual observation about yet one more natural disaster, Fleming permits a less optimistic prognosis—both for the steeple and for the history that surrounds it. Yet the language with which he mourns the defeating of human efforts also celebrates those efforts ("the choisest workemen," "the substantiallest stuffe," "the deepe devise of man," "a monument of perpetuitie for posteritie, to woonder at and admire") in terms that remain applicable to the *Chronicles*, no matter what happened to the economics of publishing or the fashions of historical evaluation.

ॐ *Notes*

Preface

1. Here, and throughout unless otherwise specified, I cite from *Holinshed's Chronicles*, ed. Henry Ellis, 6 vols. (London, 1807–8; repr. with an introduction by Vernon Snow, New York, 1965), 1:766; 4:341.

2. John Bale, *A brefe Chronycle concerning the examination and death of the Blessed martir of Christ, Sir John Oldecastell the Lord Cobham* (Antwerp, 1544), A5v; italics added.

3. This meaning of "indifference" existed in the sixteenth century side by side with the related meaning, "not mattering either way, not essential." The latter emphasis emerged as a theological category of "things indifferent to salvation" (*adiophora*) in the theory of Erasmus or Melanchthon, and became central in the ecclesiastical pamphlet wars of the 1640s and 1670s. For an analogous, if ironic, example of the former meaning (impartiality or fairness), see Sir Thomas More, *Apology* (1533), in *Works*, vol. 9, ed. J. B. Trapp (New Haven, 1979), where More complains that the author of *A treatise concernynge the division betwene the spirytualitie and temporalitie* (1532?), now identified as Christopher St. German, "sheweth . . . that the grudge is borne by the temporaltye and the causes and occasions therof growen and gyven in effecte all by the spyrytualtye. Whyche handelyng is not as me thinketh very myche indyfferent" (p. 55).

4. J. G. A. Pocock, *The Ancient Constitution and the Feudal Law: A Study of English Historical Thought in the Seventeenth Century* (Cambridge, 1957; repr. 1987).

5. Compare Joyce Appleby, *Liberalism and Republicanism in the Historical Imagination* (Cambridge, Mass., 1992), pp. 1–33. In this title essay, Appleby shrewdly identifies the shifts in historiographical fashion in the United States without fully extricating herself from the "progressivist" or materialist definition of liberalism. The result is a mysterious *contrast* between American historians' "bad" liberalism and the "classical republicanism" rediscovered by Pocock, with its interest in disinterestedness. Yet by the end of her essay, Appleby concludes: "Freed from the burden of explaining American origins, the values of liberalism have much to commend them," provided that "a hatred of injustice, once premised on the concept of inalienable natural rights," can learn to coexist with an understanding of cultural differences (p. 33).

6. John Rawls, *A Theory of Justice* (Cambridge, Mass., 1971).

7. Rawls, *Political Liberalism* (New York, 1993), xxii.

8. Arthur Ferguson, *The Articulate Citizen and the English Renaissance* (Durham, N.C., 1965).

9. Collinson, *De Republica Anglorum, Or, History with the Politics Put Back* (Cambridge, 1990), pp. 23–24.

10. C. L. Kingsford, *English Historical Literature in the Fifteenth Century* (Oxford, 1913), p. 274.

11. Because this is only one of many arguments, and because of their relative inaccessability, I have chosen not to cite the 1577 and 1587 editions throughout. Since the 1807–8 edition and its reprint represent the 1587 edition (uncensored), all citations will be to 1807, with occasional comparisons with 1577.

12. Anne Castanien, "Censorship and Historiography in Elizabethan England: The Expurgation of Holinshed's *Chronicles*," unpublished Ph.D dissertation, University of California, Davis, 1970.

Chapter One: Intentions

1. In *The Annales of England . . . untill this present yeare 1605* (London, 1605), p. 1438: "To the reader," Stow speaks of "a farre larger Volume (long since by me laboured, at the request and commandment of the reverend Father Matthew Parker Archbishop of Canterbury) but he then deceasing, my worke was prevented, by Printing & reprinting (without warrant, or well liking) of Raigne Wolfes collection, and other late commers, by the name of Raphael Hollinshead his Chronicles."

2. Stephen Booth, *The Book Called Holinshed's Chronicles* (San Francisco, 1968), p. 72.

3. See Levy, *Tudor Historical Thought* (San Marino, 1967), p. 168. I wish, however, to express my personal gratitude to Levy, who has generously admitted that, at least in this one area, his pioneering study, to date our definitive account of sixteenth-century historiography, might be due for revision.

4. Ibid., pp. 183–84.

5. Levy, "Holinshed in Context," MLA Convention, 1987. I am grateful for having been able to see this paper, and push against it.

6. Edmund Bolton, *Hypercritica; or A Rule of Judgement, for writing, or reading our Historys* (Oxford, 1722), repr. in Joseph Hazlewood, ed., *Ancient Critical Essays*, 2 vols. (London, 1815), 2:237.

7. E. M. W. Tillyard, *Shakespeare's History Plays* (London, 1944; repr. 1980).

8. D. R. Woolf, *The Idea of History in Early Stuart England* (Toronto, 1990). Woolf uses this conception as the primitive model against which his more modern practitioners can be appreciated. Holinshed, he maintained, "had described the fall of the house of York as the product of divine revenge on its bloodshed in the Wars of the Roses," and he drew no distinction between Holinshed, Hall, and the Tudor playwrights, for all of whom "Henry VII's victory and the Tudor dynasty appeared as inevitable as the coming of spring after a harsh winter" (pp. 9–10). In fact, even Hall's *Union* habitually reports events incapable of absorption by such an ideology; and even the *Dictionary of National Biography*, scarcely the product of suspicious readers, hypothesized that Hall left the work unfinished because he found "the office of royal panegyrist beset with difficulties and dangers."

9. *Holinshed's Chronicles*, 4:121. Compare Francis Thynne's more ironic account of the same reversals, in his catalog of archbishops: "King Edward the sixt being thus

dead, his sister Marie obtained the crowne, made alteration of religion, set the before imprisoned bishops at libertie, restored them unto their see, and displaced other appointed thereunto in hir brothers time. Which bishops having now the sword in their hand, and full authoritie, stretched the same to the execution of their lawes, burning some, banishing others, and imprisoning the third sort: whereof, some were in life reserved untill the government of queene Elizabeth, and after advanced to places of great honor" (4:742).

10. Evidently, I disagree completely with Phyllis Rackin, *Stages of History: Shakespeare's English Chronicles* (Ithaca, 1990), p. 25: "The univocal form of history writing conflated providential moralizing with pragmatic skepticism, the dynastic ideology implicit in Holinshed's chronicle structure with the new conception of the nation implicit in Harrison's chorography. . . . Monologic, it obscured the differences between the disparate authorial voices, opposed discursive positions, divergent accounts, and contradictory interpretations that were incorporated into the historiographic text. The polyphonic form of theatrical performance enacted them."

11. Two possible references to Holinshed, both intriguing, have recently surfaced in the newly calendered *State Papers Domestic Edward VI: 1547–1553*, rev. ed. C. S. Knighton (London, 1992). The first is a letter from William Rogers to Sir Thomas Smith, on 29 May 1549, from Cambridge: "I have sent you by this bearer, Mr. Holinshed, six pairs of double gloves" (p. 251). The letter proceeds to discuss the university's reception of injunctions regarding the Edwardian reformation. The other possible reference occurs in the Memoranda of William Cecil (#594), dated 1552, which refer separately to "R. Wolfe. *Charta variosa*," "Mr. Throckmorton," and "Hollyngshed." Mysteriously, the index to the Calendar glosses Holinshed's name as "prisoner."

12. Peter Blayney, *The Bookshops in Paul's Cross Churchyard* (London, 1990), pp. 18–20, presents new information about Wolfe's importance as a central figure in publishing and bookselling. He is surely mistaken, however, when he claims that Wolfe "had compiled most of [the *Chronicles*] himself" (p. 30) unless by compiling one means merely collecting the earlier books and manuscripts that were used as sources. Holinshed may have been employed originally as translator, but his role seems to have expanded to that of editor-writer. In describing the relationship in his dedication to Burghley, Holinshed, who could never be accused of self-promotion, describes a long-term partnership: "amongst other whome he purposed to use for performance of his entent in that behalfe, he procured me to take in hande the collection of those Histories, and having proceeded so far in the same, as little wanted to the accomplishment of that long promised worke, it pleased God to call him to his mercie, after xxv years travell spent therein, so that by his untimely deceasse, no hope remayned to see that performed, whiche *we had so long travayled about*." That "we" should be taken seriously. It was the loss of Wolfe's considerable financial backing, soon to be restored by his inheritors, that Holinshed points to as the cause of such threatened incompletion.

13. *Holinshed's Chronicles*, introduction by Vernon Snow (repr. New York, 1965), viii, n. 25.

14. Stephen Booth, *The Book Called Holinshed's Chronicles*, pp. 61–71. He based his assessment on the arguments of Sarah C. Dodson, "Abraham Fleming, Writer and Editor," *University of Texas Studies in English* 34 (1955), 51–66, and William E. Miller, "Abraham Fleming: Editor of Shakespeare's Holinshed," *Texas Studies in Literature and Language* 1 (1959), 89–100. Booth, in turn, was followed by Anne Castanien, "Censorship and Historiography in Elizabethan England: The Expurgation of Holinshed's *Chronicles*," unpublished Ph.D. dissertation, University of California, Davis, 1970, who believed that Fleming was, in effect, the editor of the 1587 text throughout, both before and after the censorship.

15. Elizabeth Story Donno," Some Aspects of Shakespeare's Holinshed," *Huntington Library Quarterly* 50 (1987), p. 231. Snow also believed that "the extended narrative" (of the English "Continuation") was written by John Stow.

16. John Stow, *The Annales of England . . . untill this present yeare 1605* (London, 1605), pp. 1184, 1240.

17. For Stanyhurst's biography, see Colm Lennon, *Richard Stanihurst the Dubliner 1547–1618* (Blackrock, County Dublin, 1981).

18. The tone of Stow's *Summarie* was carefully calculated to distinguish it, as a book that many could afford, from the larger *Chronicle* of 1580, also dedicated to Leicester. See the *Summarie's* "To the Reader": Divers wryters of hystories write dyversly . . . Amongst whom, good Reader, I crave to have place, and desyre roome in the lower part of this table. For I use thee in this my booke as some symple feaster, that beynge not able of his owne coste to feast his guestes sufficientely, is fayne to bee frended of his neyghboures, and to sette before them suche dishes as he hath gotten of others. . . . So that of their great plenty, I might wel take some what to hyde my povertie." Nevertheless, Stow continued, the work is not devoid of original scholarship; and "though it be written homely, yet it is not (as I trust) written untruly."

19. A copy of the printed Letters Patent is bound into Harley MS. 367, fol. 10, no. 8. See also John Strype, ed., *Survey of London* (London, 1720), 1:xi, xiii.

20. Holinshed shaped his dedication to Burghley to explain how he was first induced to undertake so huge a project, "although the cause that moved me thereto hath (in part) yer this beene signified unto your good Lordship," which indicates that Burghley has not commissioned the project. Burghley did, however, have an interest in Christopher Saxton's maps, originally destined for inclusion in the *Chronicles*. For Saxton and his patron Thomas Seckford, see Ifor Evans and Heather Lawrence, *Christopher Saxton Elizabethan Map-Maker* (London, 1979), especially pp. 7–11. See also the inference drawn by Sarah Tyacke and John Huddy, *Christopher Saxton and Tudor Map-Making* (London, 1980), p. 25, that the "administrative assistance and rewards" Saxton received from the Crown mean that the survey and publication of the maps "had the backing of the central government."

21. *Acts of the Privy Council, 1587*, ed. J. R. Dasent (London, 1890–1907), pp. 114–15. See also "Censorship and Historiography," p. 91.

22. Miller and Power, eds. *Holinshed's Irish Chronicle* (Dublin, 1979), xvi–xvii.

23. Castanien (p. 93, n. 12) thought it "remotely possible" that the Irish history could have been sold as a separate work. It bore a title page of its own, and its separate index followed the text immediately.

24. At the end of his continuation of the Scottish history, Francis Thynne complained: "I protest to thee that both the histories of England and Scotland were halfe printed before I set pen to paper to enter into the augmentation or continuation of anie of them, as by the inserting of those things which I have doone maie well appeare" (5:756). This suggests that there was a radical change of plan for the second edition, perhaps developed after the 1584 license was granted.

25. Although "control" here appears to be used in the sense of "correct," and the "danger" is that of running into error, the word is still anxiogenic.

26. Compare Woolf, who generously adopts my arguments from *Censorship and Interpretation* (Madison, 1984; repr. 1990): "there existed by 1600 an identifiable 'corridor' or safe zone of correct opinion about the past, . . . a corridor policed partly by external authorities such as church and crown but mainly by historians themselves, through a process which looks very much like a collective version of that self-censorship ascribed . . . to poets and dramatists" (*Idea of History*, p. 32).

27. Essex's copy was slightly more expensive than the single-volume Shakespeare First Folio (1623) at 20s., and a bargain compared to the folio King James version of the Bible (1616), 40s. bound, 25s. unbound. See Francis R. Johnson, "Notes on English Retail Book-prices, 1550–1640," *The Library*, 5th series, 5 (1950), 83–112, especially pp. 91–92.

28. See E. S. Leedham-Green, *Books in Cambridge Inventories*, 2 vols. (Cambridge, 1986), 1:467, nos. 2050–52; 1:354, no. 109.

29. See Spenser, *Prose Works*, ed. Rudolf Gottfried (Baltimore, 1949), p. 266.

30. Jack Hexter, "The Myth of the Middle Class in Tudor England," in his *Reappraisals in History: New Views on History and Society in Early Modern Europe* (Chicago and London, 1961, 1979), pp. 71–116. There is increasing resistance to Hexter's demolition of the Tudor middle class. See Jonathan Barry and Christopher Brooks, eds., *The Middling Sort of People: Culture, Society and Politics in England, 1550–1800* (London, 1993) and Theodore Leinwand, "Shakespeare and the Middling Sort," *Shakespeare Quarterly* 44 (1993), 284–303, which places literary questions in a rich network of social history.

31. Ibid., p. 102; citing *Tudor Economic Documents*, 2:326 (an inaccurate footnote; p. 326 refers to a certificate of beggars.)

32. Ibid., p. 113.

33. Not all modern historians accept that Somerset was genuinely committed to social reform. Throughout, I cite historical evaluations as the *Chronicles* present them, whether or not they match later assessments.

34. For the civic prudence and religious latitudinarianism of the London City governors as a social group, see Frank Freeman Foster, *The Politics of Stability: A Portrait of the Rulers in Elizabethan London* (London, 1977), pp. 5, 122–25. Note the use of the term "indifferent" to indicate neutrality in religion in 1564 (p. 122), and his de-

finition of a "rulers' ethic" that translated the doctrine of election into secular terms. See also Ian W. Archer, *The Pursuit of Stability: Social Relations in Elizabethan London* (Cambridge, 1991), p. 259. "[The] identification of this group with their regime was still partial and conditional. Many of the men of middling status who wielded power in local government and the companies sympathised with the grievances of the craftsmen . . . and their attitudes towards the poor were shaped by the awareness of the transitory nature of their own business fortunes."

35. Jürgen Habermas, "The Normative Content of Modernity," in *The Philosophical Discourse of Modernity,* trans. Frederick Lawrence (Cambridge, Mass., 1987), p. 363.

36. F. J. Levy has suggested to me that Bolton and Savile would assume that the middle class should neither write nor read history because thereby *arcana imperii* might be revealed to those who had no business with such matters.

Chapter Two: Authors

1. Roger Williams, "Christenings make not Christians," in *Complete Writings*, 7 vols. (New York, 1963), 7:36. The pamphlet was published in 1645 as an argument against the Massachusetts Puritans and their hold on the New World; but Williams pointed, by analogy, at the insincerity, the political motivation, of England's unstable religious history at home, which unfortunately was transportable to the New World. I owe this reference to Thomas Scanlan.

2. This passage is based on the *Chronicle of Queen Jane,* a manuscript diary, Harley MS 194, which was owned by John Stow, and whose main focus is Wyatt's rebellion, to which the diarist is noticeably sympathetic. Material from it was included in Stow's *Annals,* as also in the *Chronicles.* See *The Chronicle of Queen Jane, and of Two Years of Queen Mary,* ed. J. G. Nichols (London, 1850), p. 59. This source gives, however, different figures: 400 condemned to death, 26 hanged one day and "a greate nombre" the next. For other estimates of the executions in London and elsewhere, see David Loades, *Two Tudor Conspiracies* (Cambridge, 1965), pp. 113–27. There was a mass pardon issued on 4 June 1558, containing 245 names. Loades concludes that "the total number who suffered in body or estate was less than five per cent of the number involved." But he also suggests that in London and in Kent the punishments were clearly irrational, and "lacked any constructive value for the stability of the regime. For a few days the government acted as though it intended to pursue a course of terror, but then abandoned this approach in favour of indiscriminate mercy" (pp. 126–27).

3. See Ronald B. McKerrow, *A Dictionary of Printers and Booksellers in England, Scotland, and Ireland . . .* (London, 1910), p. 300.

4. Colm Lennon, *Richard Stanihurst the Dubliner 1547–1618* (Blackrock, County Dublin, 1981), pp. 40–41; Anne Castanien, "Censorship and Historiography in Elizabethan England: The Expurgation of Holinshed's *Chronicles*," unpublished

Ph.D. dissertation, University of California, Davis, 1970, p. 92, n. 11. See *Calendar of State Papers, Domestic,* 1547–1580, p. 689.

5. See *Tudor Royal Proclamations,* ed. Paul L. Hughes and James F. Larkin, 3 vols. (New Haven and London, 1969), 2:312, where it is recorded that on 24 February 1569 the Bishop of London sent to the Privy Council a list of 38 "unlawful books" found in Stow's possession, including recent recusant works by Thomas Dorman, Thomas Heskyns, Robert Pointz, John Rastell, Richard Shacklock, and Thomas Stapleton. For the "great Parcell" of chronicles, see *The Great Chronicle of London,* ed. A. H. Thomas and I. D. Thornley (London, 1938), xvi. The *Great Chronicle* was itself owned and annotated by Stow.

6. See Barrett Beer, "John Stow and Tudor Rebellions, 1549–1569," *Journal of British Studies* 27 (1988), 352–74. For Stow's collections, see J. Gairdner, J. ed., *Three fifteenth-century chronicles.* Camden Society, 3d series. 28 (1880), which contains "Historical Memoranda in the Handwriting of John Stowe," i.e., the demands of Jack Cade's rebellion in 1450. Stow included a version of these demands in his *Chronicle* (1580), along with a document which he called "The complaint of the commons of Kent, and causes of the assembly on the Blackheath" (pp. 654–58) for which there is no fifteenth-century manuscript witness. See British Library Harley MS 545, #17. Both documents, significantly, were inserted by Abraham Fleming into the 1587 edition of the *Chronicles,* with attribution to Stow in the margin. I owe this information to Ellen Caldwell.

7. This tends to undermine the transparency of Stow's claim, in the preface to his *Chronicle* (1580), that the primary function of chronicles is the "discouragement of unnaturall subjects from wicked treasons, pernitious rebellions, and damnable doctrines." My attention was first drawn to Grafton's accusation by David Kastan; but for a full account of the commercial and personal aspects of their quarrel, see C. L. Kingsford, ed., *A Survey of London by John Stow,* 2 vols. (Oxford, 1908), 1:ix–xii. Kingsford also provided a biography of Stow (1:vi–lxvii).

8. See British Museum Harley Ms. 367, fol 12, #10: "when he saythe he hath amended suche things as bifore escaped in the former impression of his abridgment and also added good lessons to trayne subjects to obedience: and to stop the gappes, whiche other hathe openyd, . . . he hathe not folowd one jot of his former abridgement, neyther in order or mater, but all to gethar folowyd the order of my boke, & placid the same morall philosophy to trayne subjects as he hath taken of my boke, as by conference, most playnly may appere. . . . And for my selfe, I say that as I thanke god I have allways abhoryd rebellion, and all the ground thereof, what tytle soever they have pretendyd or may pretend (so the world can testyfy, that towards the laste rebellyon (all thowghe his worke & myne are farre unlyke) I was further chargyd towards the suppression therof than he as was all so my presse, redy to have gone and spent my lyfe agaynst them." Kingsford transcribed several items from Harley 367, including an earlier account by Stow of his dispute with Grafton; he did not, however, transcribe this more interesting self-defence dealing with the charge of political subversiveness.

9. Vernon Snow in his introduction to the 1965 reprint of *Holinshed's Chronicles* (1:ii) asserts, without giving a reference, that Thynne was "a controversial writer who had been in prison for suspected treason several years earlier." However attractive to my thesis, I have been unable to corroborate this statement.

10. Thynne also showed some interest in the history of rebellion. He transcribed from the *Anonimalle Cronicle* in St. Mary's Abbey at York an early account of the Peasants' Revolt of 1381. See B. M. Stowe 1047, Fols. 64 ff.

11. See Elizabeth Story Donno, "Some Aspects of Shakespeare's Holinshed," *Huntington Library Quarterly* 50 (1987), 238; Castanien, p. 254.

12. When Raphael Holinshed dedicated the second volume of the 1577 edition to Sir Henry Sidney, he explained how Campion's manuscript history of Ireland had been incorporated into the project, and that he had no wish "to defraud him of his due deserved praise." This dedication was reprinted in 1587, along with the more fulsome panegyric ("maister Campion, who was so upright in conscience, so deepe in judgement, so ripe in eloquence") included in Stanyhurst's dedication of his *Description of Ireland* to Sir Henry Sidney.

13. This misunderstanding was fostered especially by R. Mark Benbow, "The Providential Theory of Historical Causation in *Holinshed's Chronicles*: 1577 and 1587," *Texas Studies in Literature and Language* 1 (1959), 264–76.

14. Beyond the *Dictionary of National Biography*, biographical information about Fleming appears in Sarah C. Dodson, "Abraham Fleming, Writer and Editor," *University of Texas Studies in English* 34 (1955), 51–66; William E. Miller, "Abraham Fleming: Editor of Shakespeare's Holinshed," *Texas Studies in Literature and Language* 1 (1959), 89–100; and Elizabeth Story Donno, "Abraham Fleming: A Learned Corrector in 1586–87," *Studies in Bibliography* 42 (1989), 200-211.

15. See G. J. R. Parry, *A Protestant Vision: William Harrison and the Reformation of Elizabethan England* (Cambridge, 1987), p. 159. This study, and the doctoral dissertation upon which it was based, "William Harrison (1535–93) and `The Great English Chronology': Puritanism and History in the Reign of Elizabeth," unpublished Ph.D. dissertation, Cambridge University, 1981, contain the fullest account of Harrison's life and thought hitherto, and my debts to it are considerable.

16. See Georges Edelen, "William Harrison (1535–1593)," *Studies in the Renaissance* 9 (1962), 258–59. Edelen "strongly suspected" that Harrison wrote the biographical note himself, "using such phrases as `ut audio' in an attempt to `objectify' and bring it into correspondence with Bale's biographies" (p. 258n). I agree.

17. Parry, "William Harrison," p. 21.

18. Parry, *Protestant Vision*, p. 143.

19. John Ponet, *A Shorte Treatise of Politike Power, D.I.P.B.R.W.* (London, 1556), Sigs. I5v–I6r.

20. For a detailed account of the role played by the Brookes in Wyatt's rebellion, see Loades, *Two Tudor Conspiracies*. Loades, however, probably underestimated the religious motivation of the rebellion. Cf. A. Fletcher, *Tudor Rebellions* (London, 1973), 86–90; and the sixteenth-century *Historie of Wyattes rebellion* by John Proctor (London, 1556), written from a Roman Catholic perspective, which claims that

Wyatt only pretended his quarrel was with the Spanish marriage: "He determined to speake no worde of religion, but to make the colour of hys commotion only to withstand strangers, and to advance libertie" (fol. 3v).

21. Peter Clark, *English Provincial Society from the Reformation to the Revolution: Religion, Politics and Society in Kent 1500–1640* (Hassocks: Harvester Press, 1977), pp. 128.

22. Later, of course, the family fell into disgrace. Two of William's sons were involved in the plots against James (Main and Bye) and Cobham himself incarcerated. Clark calls this the "destruction of Essex's old enemies, Ralegh and Henry, Lord Cobham." Cobham's successor as Lord Warden was Henry Howard, earl of Northampton.

23. Clark, *English Provincial Society*, pp. 137, 174. Clark sees "some support from alienated moderates after Whitgift's onslaught in 1584."

24. This financial detail derives from Parry, "William Harrison," p. 68. This work contains biographical material not incorporated into *A Protestant Vision*, and some of its conclusions have been modified in Parry's later work.

25. See Vernon Snow, *Parliament in Elizabethan England: John Hooker's Order and Usage* (New Haven, 1977), p. 8.

26. For these and the following facts, I am indebted to Snow, *Parliament in Elizabethan England*, pp. 8–22.

27. See also Walter J. Harte, *Gleanings from the Common Place Book of John Hooker . . .* (1485–1590) (Exeter, 1926).

28. Hooker, *The Lyffe of Sir Peter Carewe, late of Mohonese Otrey, in the Countie of Devon, Knyghte, whoe dyed at Rosse, in Ireland, the 27 of November 1575*, ed. J. S. Brewer and W. Bullen (London, 1867; Calendar Manuscripts, 1:lxvii–cxvii).

29. See Snow, *Parliament in Elizabethan England*, p. 126; *Journals of the House of Commons*, 1:84.

Chapter Three: Protocols

1. In the 1577 edition, the first volume contained Harrison's *Description of England*, the early history of Britain up to the Conquest, and the whole of the Scottish and Irish histories, whereas the second volume was devoted to English history after the Conquest. In the 1587 edition, this quantitative disparity was perhaps less obvious. The first volume contained Harrison's *Description* and the pre-Conquest history of Britain. Ireland and Scotland shared the second volume; and the third was devoted to the later history of England.

2. See *Acts of the Privy Council 1586–87*, ed. J. R. Dasent, (London, 1890–1907), p. 312.

3. See *Censorship and Interpretation* (Madison, 1984; repr. 1990).

4. Robert Fabian, *New Chronicles of England and France* (1516 through 1559), ed. Henry Ellis (London, 1811), xxi.

5. Richard Grafton, *Chronicle at Large* (1568), ed. Henry Ellis, 2 vols. (London, 1809), 2:79; Edward Hall, *The Union of the two noble & illustre famelies of Lancastre & Yorke*, ed. Henry Ellis (1548; repr. London 1809; New York, 1965), p. 342.

6. See Grafton, *Chronicle*, 2:527–28.

7. Hooker's dedication of his translation to Sir Walter Ralegh attacks another brance of the Fitzgeralds, the Desmonds, for their "most unnaturall wars . . . against hir sacred majestie," but he lumps all the Geraldines together in his attack (6:103–4); and in translating Giraldus' defence of the family (which Stanyhurst had also inserted into his *Description of Ireland*, 6:47–48), he felt compelled to add a footnote prognosticating the "overthrow of all their houses and families" (6:198).

8. Foxe, *Acts and Monuments*, ed. George Townsend, 8 vols. (London, 1843–49; repr. New York, 1965), 3:353–56, 400–401.

9. One version of this scene appears in Stow's *Summarie of Englyshe Chronicles* (London, 1565). However, the version printed by Holinshed in 1577 is different and matches the text in Stow's *Chronicle*, not published until 1580.

10. Compare also Thynne's subsequent decision to insert a chunk of the Latin text of St. Augustine's account of Bishop Laurence, whom Augustine chose to succèed him as archbishop of Canterbury: "which words I am willinger to write," explained Thynne, "although they be somewhat long, because I will not defraud the author of the true telling of his owne tale, nor posteritie of the spreading by print the part of that booke, which otherwise perhaps might never more come to light" (4:664).

11. See Thynne, 4:783: "But because there maie be some question touching the same, and for that the same Lambard hath not judicialle defined the same; I will leave it as I find it in his owne booke, and Verbatim set downe his words in this sort"; 4:800: "I will Verbatim recite Leland's words"; Fleming or Stow, 4:543: "The submission [of Francis Throckmorton] Verbatim written with his owne hand, followeth."

12. Sir Philip Sidney died on 22 September 1586. The *Chronicles* were evidently in press well before that date, and the proofs were accordingly corrected.

13. Hitherto, however, critiques of the anecdote have emerged from within New Historicist literary scholarship. See Jean Howard, "The New Historicism in Renaissance Studies," *English Literary Renaissance* 16 (1986), pp. 38–39; and Howard Dobin, *Merlin's Disciples: Prophecy, Poetry, and Power in Renaissance England* (Stanford, 1990), pp. 8–16.

14. On the topic of local knowledge and oral transmission, see the important article by D. R. Woolf, "The 'Common Voice': History, Folklore and Oral Tradition in Early Modern England," *Past and Present* 120 (1988), 26–52.

15. Woolf, "The 'Common Voice,'" pp. 34–37.

16. Matthew Parker, *De antiquititate Brittanicae Ecclesiae* (London, 1572), pp. 392–93.

17. C. S. Lewis, *English Literature in the Sixteenth Century* (Oxford, 1954), p. 365. Stanyhurst carried his interest in Virgil into the *Chronicles*, to the extent of citing a rival translation, Thomas Phaer's *The seven first bookes of the Eneidos of Virgill* (1558). He describes the building of Rosse in imitation of Virgil's description of the construction of Carthage (*Aeneid* 2): "Some were tasked to delve, others appointed with mattocks to dig, diverse alloted to the unheaping of rubbish, manie bestowed to the

cariage of stones, sundrie occupied in tempering of morter, the better sort busied in overseeing the workmen, ech one according to his vocation imploied, as though the civitie of Carthage were afresh in building, as it is featlie verified by the golden poet Virgil, and neatlie Englished by master doctor Phaer."

18. Colm Lennon, *Richard Stanihurst the Dubliner 1547–1618* (Blackrock, County Dublin, 1981), p. 115.

19. C. L. Kingsford, *English Historical Literature in the Fifteenth Century* (Oxford, 1913), p. 272. William E. Miller, however, pointed out that the Privy Council had decreed that bishops should introduce the *Anglorum Praelia* into the grammar and free schools of their dioceses. See Miller, "Abraham Fleming: Editor of Shakespeare's Holinshed," *Texas Studies in Literature and Language*, 1 (1959), p. 96, citing *Acts of the Privy Council*, N.S. XIII (1581–82), 389–90. For a summary of Fleming's literary career, see Sarah Dodson, "Abraham Fleming, Writer and Editor," *University of Texas Studies in English* 34 (1955), pp. 51–66.

20. This is taken word for word from Grafton, *Chronicle*, 2:526–27; except that Fleming has added "as saith Grafton," and the marginal pointer, "Policy."

21. See my *Fables of Power* (Durham, N.C., 1990).

22. Thomas Churchyard, *A Discourse of the Queenes Maiesties entertainement in Suffolk and Norfolk* (1579).

23. For a modern edition, see *Entertainments for Elizabeth I*, ed. Jean Wilson (Woodbridge, 1980), pp. 63–85.

24. See Ivan L. Shultze,"The Final Protest against the Elizabeth-Alençon Marriage Proposal," *Modern Language Notes* 58 (1943), 54–57; Conyers Read, *Lord Burghley and Queen Elizabeth* (London, 1960), 258–60; David Bergeron, *English Civic Pageantry 1558–1642* (London, 1971), 44–46; Norman Council, "O Dea Certe: The Allegory of The Fortress of Perfect Beauty," *Huntington Library Quarterly* 39 (1975–76), 329–42.

25. Louis Montrose, "Celebration and Insinuation: Sir Philip Sidney and the Motives of Elizabethan Courtship," *Renaissance Drama* 8 (1977), 3–35; and Catherine Bates, *The Rhetoric of Courtship in Elizabethan Language and Literature* (Cambridge, 1991), pp. 69–75. Bates observes that while some of the participants in the tournament, Sidney, Greville, Perrott, Knollys, Henry Grey, and Edward Denny, were surely part of the antimarriage faction, the same cannot be said of Lord Windsor, who was a Catholic, the earl of Arundel, who had Catholic sympathies, Anthony Cooke, a cousin of Burghley (who supported the match), or Thomas Radcliffe, a relation of the earl of Sussex (who also supported it). "Instead," she concludes," it seems more likely that the show was designed to suppress faction, and to present a picture of Anglo-French concord by subsuming real differences under romantic battles with that "sweet enemy, France" (p. 72).

26. Fleming's inclusion of the Norfolk pageants and the 1581 tournament was noted by Sarah Dodson, "Abraham Fleming, Writer and Editor," *University of Texas Studies in English* 34 (1955), pp. 59–60, but explained it merely as a personal interest.

27. This is how Molyneux described the *Arcadia's* circumstances of composition:

"Not long after his returne from the journeie, and before his further imploiment by hir majestie, at his vacant and spare times of leisure (for he could indure at no time to be idle and void of action) he made his booke which he named Arcadia, a worke (though a meere fansie, toie, and fiction) shewing such excellence of spirit, gallant invention, variete of matter, and orderlie disposition . . . so delightfull to the reader, and pleasant to the hearer, as nothing could be taken out of it to amend it, or added to it that would not impaire it, as few works of like subject hath beene either of some more earnestlie sought choislie kept, nor placed in better place, and amongst better jewels than that was" (4:880). This disingenuous account of Sidney's exile from court matches Molyneux's cosmetic approach to Sidney's 1577 embassy to Germany and the Netherlands, when he exceeded his commission, and attracted too much attention to himself, to Elizabeth's dissatisfaction. According to Molyneux, however, he performed this mission "in such exquisit order, and advised wise course, omitting nothing he should doo, nor supplieng anie thing he should not doo in ceremonie or otherwise, as he exceedinglie therein satisfied hir majestie . . . and won to himselfe great credit and singular commendation" (4:880). For the actual circumstances, see James M. Osborn, *Young Philip Sidney 1572–1577* (New Haven, 1972), pp. 448–500.

Chapter Four: Revision

1. Miller and Power, eds., *Holinshed's Irish Chronicle* (Dublin, 1979), xvii–xviii.

2. Frederick J. Furnivall, *Harrison's Description of England in Shakspere's Youth*, 2 vols. (London, 1887; repr. Vaduz, 1965).

3. I am tempted to forgive Furnivall for his suppression of most of Book I for the sake of his "Temporary Foretalk to *Harrison*, Part III," which begins disarmingly "The Society hasn't money, and I havn't had time, to finish my *Harrison* this year" (p. 1).

4. Georges Edelen, ed., *The Description of England by William Harrison* (Ithaca, 1968).

5. These were: "the catalogue of bishops and deans of London, Harrison's version of the ceremony accompanying ordeal by fire, Canute's forest laws, and the Antonine Itinerary" (viii).

6. By H. Cotton, "Harrison's Chronology," *Notes and Queries* 3 (1851), 105.

7. As Additional M.S. 70984. So recent is this acquisition that at the time of going to press this manuscript was still uncataloged and unavailable for consultation.

8. Parry is presently preparing an edition of the rediscovered Derry manuscript.

9. G. J. R. Parry, *A Protestant Vision: William Harrison and the Reformation of Elizabethan England* (Cambridge, 1987).

10. It is not clear, however, that this does not refer back to another mention of 1579 earlier on the same page (1:361).

11. Cf. *Calendar of State Papers, Domestic*, Eliz. March 11, 1576, CVII, p. 519. "Petition of certain obedient subjects to the House of Lords. Soliciting their order to the Speaker of the House of Commons to read in full the bill for the better cultivation of flax, hemp, and rapeseed."

12. The reference is to Aristotle, *Politics* 2:6. Cf. Louis LeRoy, *Aristotle's Politiques*, trans. I.D. (1598), p. 103: "There doth nothing more debase & weaken the authority of lawes than the too often making of them, without having sufficient care of their observation and maintenance." This work was dedicated to Sir Robert Sidney.

13. In *Shakespeare and the Popular Voice* (Oxford, 1989), pp. 41–48.

14. Sir Thomas More, *Apology* in *Complete Works*, vol. 9, ed. J. B. Trapp (New Haven, 1979), p. 56. See also p. 58–60, 74, 86, 88, 145, 150, 152, 154, 167. For St. German's *A treatise concernynge the division betwene the spirytualitie and temporalitie*, see pp. 177–212. Clearly, St. German's "figure" got under More's skin, which resulted in its having such prominence in the *Apology*. Harrison, who, given his interest in church reform, may well have read both pamphlets, could scarcely have missed it. It is perhaps no coincidence that More's attack on "some say" coincides (pp. 58–60) with his attack on his opponent's pretended "indifference."

15. The Latin quotation sounds like Fleming, and may have been inserted by him; but there is no evidence, such as marginal indicators, that he intervened in Harrison's revisions. The use of the first person, here and elsewhere, makes it clear that Harrison himself has rethought his position.

16. See A. J. Carlson, "The Puritans and the Convocation of 1563," in *Action and Conviction in Early Modern Europe: Essays in Memory of E. H. Harbison*, ed. T. K. Rabb and J. E. Seigel (Princeton, 1969), pp. 133–53. Nowell and a delegation of six others presented the Lords with a series of reform articles on matters of baptismal and communion practice, in which eventually "abrogation of holy days . . . topped the list" (p. 146).

17. Since Archbishop Grindal had been suspended in 1577 and replaced in 1583 by Whitgift, there is no conflict between his intensified critique of the highest ecclesiastical officeholders and his admiration for the Grindalian position on moderate reform.

18. Parry noted the addition (*Protestant Vision*, pp. 181–83) and perceived it as a statement of disobedience to Elizabeth. For the queen's confrontation with Grindal over the prophesyings, see Patrick Collinson, *Archbishop Grindal 1519–1583: The Struggle for a Reformed Church* (Berkeley and Los Angeles, 1979), pp. 233–52. Collinson indicates that both Burghley and Walsingham privately supported Grindal, and cites a letter from the latter to the former that resembles Harrison's amended text: "You see how we proceed still in making war against God . . . God open her Majesty's eyes that she may both see her peril and acknowledge from whence the true remedy is to be sought" (p. 252).

19. Compare Wallace T. MacCaffrey, *Queen Elizabeth and the Making of Policy, 1572–1588* (Princeton, 1981), pp. 80–96, especially p. 89: "The particular catastrophe of Grindal's disgrace came about not through a conscious reaction within the Church against Puritan doctrine and practice but probably as the by-product of local secular politics. . . . We do not know who were the informers or how they reached the queen's ear. . . . In any case it was not a religious reaction which destroyed the exercises but the pressure of royal displeasure, stimulated by private parties for factious ends."

20. Ibid., pp. 110–11.

21. Parry pointed out ("William Harrison (1535–93) and 'The Great English Chronology': Puritanism and History in the Reign of Elizabeth," unpublished dissertation, Cambridge University, 1981, pp. 39–40) that in TCD ms. 165, fol. 22r, Harrison refers to "our Geneva boke (the very best that we have in English)," implying that he used the Geneva Bible rather than the Bishops' Bible.

22. Parry, *Protestant Vision*, pp. 170–71, notes the two selections Furnivall printed from the Derry manuscript of the *Chronology*, which deal with the Elizabethan parliaments of 1589 and 1592–93. In the second of these, dating from two weeks before Harrison's death, there are negative remarks against "precisians." In correspondence, however, he states that the recovered manuscript in its entirety does not alter his view that Harrison remained a committed reformer to the end.

23. Cf. Georges Edelen, "William Harrison (1535–1593)" *Studies in the Renaissance* 9 (1962), p. 256: "On 23 April [1586], Harrison received his last and most important preferment. By letters patent from the queen, who was apparently willing to overlook his attack on prebends in the *Description* as 'but superfluous additaments unto former excesses,' he was made canon of St. George's Chapel at Windsor." Edelen was apparently unaware that this phrase did not appear in the text until January 1587.

24. See John Guy, "The Queen, the Court and the Ecclesiastical Polity," in *The Reign of Elizabeth I: Court and Culture in the Last Decade* (Cambridge, 1993).

25. Christopher Haigh, "Elizabeth's Rule: Image and Reality," in *The Reign of Elizabeth I,*.

Chapter Five: Economics

1. Joyce Appleby, *Economic Thought and Ideology in Seventeenth-Century England* (Princeton, 1978), p. 19.

2. Ibid., pp. 20–21.

3. This was the procedure used by W. G. Hoskins, "Harvest Fluctuations and English Economic History, 1480–1619," *Agricultural History Review* 12 (1964), 28–46. The caveat is entered by Steve Rappaport, *Worlds within Worlds: Structures of Life in Sixteenth-Century London* (Cambridge, 1989), p. 130.

4. See R. B. Outhwaite, *Inflation in Tudor and Early Stuart England* (London, 1969, 2d ed. 1982), pp. 25–60; Peter H. Ramsey, ed., *The Price Revolution in Sixteenth-Century England* (London, 1971), a collection of essays debating this issue; D. M. Palliser, *The Age of Elizabeth* (London, 1983, 1992), pp. 152–86, especially pp. 169–72; and C. G. A. Clay, *Economic Expansion and Social Change: England 1500–1700*, 2 vols. (Cambridge, 1984), pp. 32–37.

5. Rappaport, *Worlds within Worlds*, p. 130.

6. For example, by E. H. Phelps Brown and S. V. Hopkins, *A Perspective of Wages and Prices* (London, 1981).

7. Rappaport, *Worlds within Worlds*, pp. 160–61.

8. Ibid., p. 157.

9. Lawrence Stone, "Social Mobility in England, 1500–1700," *Past and Present* 33

(1966), p. 86; italics added; compare also Clay, *Economic Expansion and Social Change,* 1:97, arguing that in rural England engrossing resulted in "a widening gulf between rich and poor."

10. Paul Slack, "Poverty and Social Regulation in Elizabethan England," in *The Reign of Elizabeth,* ed. Christopher Haigh (Athens, Ga., 1987), p. 227.

11. Ramsey, *Price Revolution,* p. 1.

12. The anonymous *Discourse of the Common Weal* was written in 1549 and first published in revised form in 1581, with a dedication by W. S., possibly William Smith, the nephew of Sir Thomas Smith. Although sometimes attributed to John Hales, it was claimed for Sir Thomas by Mary Dewar, despite the fact that Smith died in 1577. See "The Authorship of the 'Discourse of the Commonweal,'" *Economic History Review,* 2d series, 19 (1966), 388–400. The first version singles out the Henrician currency debasement as the primary cause of the recent price increases; the second adds rack-renting and the importation of American silver. See Ramsey, *The Price Revolution,* p. 5. Typically, it is assumed that the more complicated explanation of the second version could only have been arrived at by reading Jean Bodin's *Response à M. de Malestroit* (1568), ed. H. Hauser (Paris, 1932). See also Outhwaite, *Inflation in Tudor and Early Stuart England,* pp. 23–24.

13. *Tudor Economic Documents,* ed. R. H. Tawney and E. Power, 3 vols. (London, 1924), 3:40.

14. For the commonwealthmen, see Arthur Ferguson, *The Articulate Citizen and the English Renaissance* (Durham, N.C., 1965), pp. 363ff.

15. *Tudor Economic Documents,* 3:315; italics added.

16. He includes among the causes of inflation exchange rates, insufficient exports, the engrossing of lands and enclosures generally, an excessive number of church holidays, which reduce the number of working days, and a mistaken use of "subsidies" or taxes on English products such as cloth, which act as deterrents to industry. And on the last point he returns again to the political motives for economic reform: "And I ensure your grace ther cannot a greatter occasion be geven to make tumulte and insurrection then sodenly to dryve a greate tumulte to gyther oute of ther worke into Idelness *as it maye be evedently sein in many sondry Cronakles yea and of the late here in Englond* in the 16th yere of the reigne of our late sovereigne Lord king Henry the eyght by the dangerus insurrexion in Suffoke and Norfoke which was only by the occasion of the Clotiers ther dyd sodenly (partly perchaunce of a frowardenes) as I feare some will nowe doo, pute a waye there worke men by the reason of a great Subsidie which was then graunted" (3:325; italics added). This last item is apparently in response to a 1548 proposal to exchange the royal right of purveyance for a subsidy on sheep, wool, and cloth.

17. Edward Hall, *The Union of the two noble & illustre famelies of Lancastre & Yorke,* ed. Henry Ellis (1548; repr. London, 1809; New York, 1965), p. 699: "The Duke of Suffolke sat in Suffolke, this season in like commission,and by gentle handlyng, he caused the riche Clothers to assent and graunt to geve the sixt parte, and when thei came home to their houses, they called to them their Spinners, Carders, Fullers, Weavers, & other artificers, whiche were wont to be set a woorke and have their

livynges by cloth makyng, and saied, sirs we be not able to set you a woorke, our goodes be taken from us, wherefore trust to your selves, and not to us, for otherwise it will not be. Then began women to wepe and young folkes to crie, and men that had no woorke began to rage, and assemble theimselfes in compaignies. . . . there rebelled foure thousande men, and put theimselfes in harnes, and rang the belles *Alarme.*"

18. Keith Wrightson, *English Society 1580–1680* (New Brunswick, N.J., 1982), p. 121.

19. On the value of plate as raw bullion, to be coined at need, see Clay, *Economic Expansion and Social Change*, 1:36. Clay alludes to Harrison's discussion.

20. For a defence of primitive accumulation as a Marxist concept applicable, via Etienne Balibar's theoretical restatement of what Marx must have meant by the prehistory of capital, to English Renaissance culture, see Richard Halpern, *The Poetics of Primitive Accumulation: English Renaissance Culture and the Genealogy of Capital* (Ithaca, 1991), pp. 61–75.

21. See Rappaport, *Worlds within Worlds*, p. 149: "Fortunately prices fell briefly after the currency was revalued in 1551 and then stabilised at somewhat lower levels, and consequently real wages began to rise. . . . by the 1560s real wages had returned to the level of the 1530s, the decade preceding the debasements, having recovered *all* of the ground lost during 1542–51. Real wages continued to climb into the late 1560s, reaching an average index of 87 during 1566–70, up by 30 per cent from the depths of 1550–2 and nearly as high as the average for the 1520s."

22. See Norman Jones, *God and the Moneylenders: Usury and Law in Early Modern England* (Oxford, 1989).

23. Clay, *Economic Expansion and Social Change*, 1:96. Nevertheless, this is an invaluable summary, both comprehensive and accessible, of landownership practices during the sixteenth century, including definitions of different legal terms and arrangements.

24. Classical economics accepts the dictum that competition for land ensures that the landlord captures all of the excess profit. In the words of Adam Smith, *The Wealth of Nations*, 2 vols. (London, 1961), 1:161, the rent he collects will be "naturally the highest which the tenant can afford to pay in the actual circumstances of the land." But the secret discovery by the landlord of exactly what his tenant had earned from his agriculture would seem to fall into a category of business ethics not entirely dissimilar from insider trading.

25. Clay, *Economic Expansion and Social Change*, 1:90, cites a sermon by Bishop Hugh Latimer from 1549, which described how his father had rented a farm in Leicestershire at the beginning of the century for three or four pounds a year, by which he was able to keep half a dozen men, "find the king a harness, with himself and his horse," send his son to school, find dowries for his daughters, keep hospitality for his poor neighbours, and give alms to the poor; whereas the tenant of the same farm in 1549 paid sixteen pounds, "and is not able to do anything for his prince, for himself, nor for his children, or give a cup of drink to the poor."

26. Rappaport, *Worlds within Worlds*, pp. 128, 144, citing P. Bowden, "Agricultur-

al Prices, Farm Profits, and Rents," in J. Thirsk, ed., *The Agrarian History of England and Wales* (Cambridge, 1967), 4:607–9.

27. At another point (during Thynne's catalog of archbishops inserted in the 1587 edition) we learn that in the previous year, 1541, Thomas Cranmer had decreed a similar abstemiousness within the church: "For he appointed six dishes of fish and flesh to an archbishop, five to a bishop, to deanes and archdeanes foure, and to inferiour persons three; with foure dishes of fruit, or such like, for an archbishop, three for a bishop, and two for the rest" (4:757). But, added Thynne, "neither Cranmer nor Poole with all their laws (the greater is the pitie) could restreine the inordinat and needles superfluitie of fare in England. For though these orders were for some small time observed; yet within one month after they returned to their accustomed diet and banketing." See also the history of Scotland for the year 1430, when Henry Wardlaw, bishop of St. Andrews, addressed the Scottish parliament on the subject of the "superfluous riot in banketting cheere, and numbers of costlie dishes, as were then taken up and used after the English fashion, both to the great hinderance of mans health, and also to the unprofitable wasting of their goods and substance." Holinshed reported that although there was "order taken" taken for national culinary restraint, "licensing gentlemen onlie, and that on festivall daies, to be served with pies," the legislation quickly became ineffective (5:422).

28. An identical passage occurs in Stow, *Chronicle* (1580), p. 1176. Since the passage appeared in the 1577 edition of the *Chronicles*, it is impossible to determine whose material this was originally.

29. Compare Henry Hastings, third earl of Huntingdon, to Secretary Sir Thomas Smith, President of the Council of the North, 27 November 1573: "All things here are quiet; but the dearth of corn is likely to be very great this year, and yet it is hard to keep some greedy fellows from transporting thereof."

30. See J. D. Gould, *The Great Debasement: Currency and the Economy in Mid-Tudor England* (Oxford, 1970), pp. 8–10.

31. Stow's independent works frequently concern themselves with currency debasement. In his *Survey of London*, Stow wrote more critically of the 1544 debasement that he had witnessed forty years earlier, and which he now saw clearly as having contributed to inflation: "rents of lands and tenements, with prices of victuals, were raised far beyond their former rates, hardly since to be brought down." See Stow, *Survey of London* (1603) in C. L. Kingsford, ed., *A Survey of London. Reprinted from the Text of 1603*, 2 vols. (Oxford, 1971), 1:57; Cited in Rappaport, *Worlds within Worlds*, p. 134.

32. Gould, *The Great Debasement*, p. 27.

33. The effect of the delay was also overlooked by Clay, *Economic Expansion and Social Change*, 1:46, who reported that the Edwardian "calling-down" "had the effect of roughly halving the quantity of money over-night."

34. See *Tudor Royal Proclamations*, ed. Paul L. Hughes and James F. Larkin, 3 vols. (New Haven and London, 1969), 2:8–9, 51–52, 150–58, 160–61, 165–67, 169–70, 179–81, 183–86.

35. See Ramsey, *The Price Revolution*, p. 8. And for a literary and cultural interpretation of currency distrust, see Stephen X. Mead, "'Thou are chang'd': public value

and personal identity in *Troilus and Cressida*," *Journal of Medieval and Renaissance Studies* 22 (1992), pp. 237–59, especially pp. 244–46.

36. Compare S. Herbert Frankel, *Money: Two Philosophies* (Oxford, 1977), p. 31, on the psychological theory of money of Georg Simmel: "to him there was much more at stake here than mere confidence in the money mechanism: that the soundness of the coins of the realm would be maintained as to the prescribed weight and fineness. . . . Something else had to be added. . . . That additional ingredient was nothing other than the faith, belief and trust which the coin symbolizes . . . always, in the last resort, a promise by society as a whole."

37. See *Tudor Royal Proclamations*, 2:183–85, for a draft, dated at Westminster, 13 March 1562) of a proclamation for decrying the new coins. The draft states that *because* of rumors "universally spread and driven into men's minds by sinister means" that the new coins were to be called down, and despite a proclamation of 30 January, 1562, prohibiting such rumors, merchants "have already universally enhanced the prices of all things to be sold for money, according to the rate as though the moneys were already decried," so that now the only solution is to bring the money down in relation to the prices (e.g., the sovereign that was current for 30s. is to be current for 20s.) Although the Crown appears to have thought better of this measure, the text of the draft in the State Papers is interesting for its documentation of the traffic in currency rumors, as also of Elizabeth's emotional commitment to the issue. The draft ends by wishing that "no credit be given to malicious, busy, and curious persons that either of ignorance or malice shall deprave this noble act" for the recovery of fine money and hence "of the ancient fame and wealth of this realm" (2:185).

38. See *Tudor Royal Proclamations*, 2:185–86.

39. *Tudor Royal Proclamations*, 2:179. See also 3:222: draft of a proclamation ca. 1600 "Authorizing Copper Coinage," observes a "great necessity" of halfpence and farthings caused by the suppression of base coins, and the "arrogant disorder used by private persons in making of tokens of lead and tin" to serve as such small money. Rogers Ruding, *Annals of the Coinage of Great Britain and its Dependencies*, 3 vols., 3d ed. (London, 1940), 1:346, notes that some copper was officially coined between 1576 and 1582.

40. *Tudor Royal Proclamations*, 2:170.

41. On "fiat value," see Gould, *The Great Debasement*, pp. 16–18.

42. See E. J. Phelps Brown and S. V. Hopkins,"Seven Centuries of the Prices of Consumables, Compared with Builders' Wage Rates," in *The Price Revolution*, p. 30. This article was first published in *Economica*, No. 92 (November 1956).

43. *Tudor Royal Proclamations*, 2:471–73, 522–24.

44. Slack, "Poverty and Social Regulation," pp. 236–37.

Chapter Six: Government

1. See Nicholas Pronay and John Taylor, *Parliamentary Texts of the Later Middle Ages* (Oxford, 1980), p. 57. Pronay and Taylor were, however, working with too early a

date for the formation of the Society. See Linda Van Norden, "The Elizabethan Society of Antiquaries," Unpublished Ph.D. dissertation, University of Califorina, Los Angeles, 1946; and Van Norden, "Sir Henry Spelman on the Chronology of the Elizabethan College of Antiquaries," *Huntington Library Quarterly* 13 (1949–50), 131–60. See also May McKisack, *Medieval History in the Tudor Age* (Oxford, 1971), pp. 155–69.

2. Richard Helgerson, in *Forms of Nationhood: The Elizabethan Writing of England* (Chicago, 1992), p. 128, stated that "the antiquaries were all loyal to the crown— some, like John Speed, rabidly so. None had any idea of altering the established form of government or even of diminishing the authority of the [monarch]." But Robert Beale, the common law activist in the Elizabethan House of Commons, who challenged Whitgift over the ex officio oath, and William Hakewill, another common lawyer who would side with the Long Parliament, were both members of the Society. Hakewill's edition of the *Modus tenendi* was published in 1641, as was his Jacobean treatise, *The Libertie of the Subject against the pretended Power of Imposition*.

3. J. E. Neale, *Elizabeth I and Her Parliaments*, 2 vols. (London, 1953, 1957); Wallace Notestein, "The Winning of the Initiative by the House of Commons," *Proceedings of the British Academy* 11 (1924–25), pp. 125–75.

4. G. R. Elton, "Parliament in the Sixteenth Century: Functions and Fortunes," *Historical Journal* 22 (1979), 255–56. With Oedipal aplomb, Elton delivered this first as a lecture in the J. E. Neale Memorial Series, at University College, London, on 7 December 1978.

5. These views were subsequently sustained in Elton's magisterial *The Parliament of England 1559–1581* (Cambridge, 1986).

6. In *The Tudor Parliaments: Crown, Lords and Commons, 1485–1603* (London and New York, 1985), M. A. R. Graves provided an overview of revisionism, and claimed that his purpose "is not to preach the revisionist line," but to "synthesise the tested and acceptable elements" in both positions. However, in "Managing Elizabethan Parliaments," in D. M. Dean and N. L. Jones, *The Parliaments of Elizabethan England* (Oxford, 1990), 37–63, his sympathies became clear. In particular, he allowed himself to remark: "Doubtless, Elizabeth would have welcomed Professor Elton's advice, because she understood the realities of Tudor government rather better than Wallace Notestein, Sir John Neale and the rest of their generation did" (p. 46).

7. These include hints that not all of Neale's hypothesis needs to be discarded, particularly in the arena of Parliament's interest in its own historical origins. Jennifer Loach, in *Parliament under the Tudors* (Oxford, 1991), pp. 152–55, noted "an increased interest and pride in the institution of parliament and its history," mentioning John Hooker among the antiquaries, along with Beale, Hakewill, and Whitelocke. She suggested that there had been overconcentration on "management" in the revisionist camp, but concluded that "there is no reason to believe that the increased historical and legal awareness of the Commons was in itself inimical to royal authority," or that boisterousness implied a steady growth of opposition. T. E. Hartley, in *Elizabeth's Parliaments: Queen, Lords and Commons 1559–1601* (Manchester, 1992), while affirming the revisionists' "rejection of the earlier picture of constitu-

tional turmoil driven by a minority of religiously fervent members," in fact broadened the base of opposition from the "Puritan choir" to practically the whole body, united against Catholicism but often frustrated by the queen's own intransigence. "When Elizabeth felt affronted," he concluded, "and even justified herself *constitutionally* against pressure from Parliament, the political allies she thought she could rely on were either nowhere in sight, or were clearly lined up on the other side of the fence" (p. 170). See also the two strong caveats entered by Patrick Collinson, "The Monarchical Republic of Queen Elizabeth I," *Bulletin of the John Rylands University Library* 69 (1987), 394–424; "Puritans, Men of Business and Elizabethan Parliaments," *Parliamentary History* 7 (1988), 188–211.

8. For instance, by the completion of T. E. Hartley's edition of *Proceedings in the Parliaments of Elizabeth I* (Leicester, 1981) or closer investigation of the extraordinary series of "Yelverton" manuscripts associated with Robert Beale, now in the British Library, e.g., Additional MS 48102A (Yelverton CXI), which begins with "The severall opinions of Sundrie Antiquaries touching the Antiquities, power, order, & State, persons, manner and proceedings of the highe courte of Parliament in England," and includes short treatises by Camden, John Doddridge, Joseph Holland, Francis Tate, and Arthur Agard. One of these (anonymous) antiquaries observes: "I have not seene Arthur Hall's booke whereby he disallowes the Commons to have any voyce in Parliament and [for] which he is disabled to be of the same house for ever" (f. 25r.) The present tense suggests a dating close to the publication of Hall's *Letter sent by F.A.* in 1579. These treatises are followed by a description of the "Mirabile" Parliament of 1386 (in Richard II's reign), and William Hakewill's "The Order of passing Bills in the Lower Howse of Parliamente with the Proceedinges thereupon."

9. F. W. Maitland, *Introduction to Memoranda de Parliamentum 1305*; first published in 1893, Rolls Series; reprinted in *Historical Studies of the English Parliament*, ed. E. B. Fryde and Edward Miller, 2 vols. (Cambridge, 1970), 1:91–135. For critique of this view, see Ronald Butt, *A History of Parliament: The Middle Ages* (London, 1989), pp. 82–85. See also R. J. Davies and J. H. Denton, eds. *The English Parliament in the Middle Ages* (Philadelphia, 1981), especially A. L. Brown, "Parliament, c. 1377–1422," pp. 109–40. For an overview of the contest between Maitland's followers and those of different persuasions, see E. Miller, "Introduction," in *Historical Studies of the English Parliament* 1:1–30.

10. Mary Dewar, ed., *De Republica Anglorum* (Cambridge, 1982), Appendix 3, into which she condensed an earlier article, "A question of plagiarism: the `Harrison chapters' in Sir Thomas Smith's *De Republica Anglorum*," *Historical Journal* 22 (1979), 921–29. Dewar set aside the earlier hypothesis of Leonard Alston, ed., *De Republica Anglorum* (Cambridge, 1906), xvii, that Smith or an editor after his death in 1577 read the newly published *Description* in the first edition of the *Chronicles* and wove the new material in at that point. She replaced it with an analysis showing that Smith himself must have done the borrowing, that his fatal illness would have prevented him from making revisions in 1577, but that he could have had access to manuscript parts of Harrison's larger work, the "Chronology," in progress during the 1560s.

11. Likewise, Harrison's editor Georges Edelen, no doubt overinfluenced by Harrison's statement about proceeding "almost word for word," states merely that he borrowed his entire chapter on Parliament "practically verbatim" from Smith, ignoring the semantics of "almost." See Edelen, ed., *The Description of England by William Harrison* (Ithaca, 1968), p. 149, n. 1.

12. Dewar, Introduction to *De Republica Anglorum*, pp. 3–5.

13. Smith, *De Republica Anglorum*, p. 78.

14. Dewar, Introduction to *De Republica Anglorum*, p. 5.

15. See *Dio's Roman History*, ed. and tr. Ernest Cary, 9 vols. (Cambridge, Mass., 1982; Loeb edition), 8:87–88; compare the speech Holinshed translated (1:500) from Tacitus, *Annals*, XIV.35.

16. Polydore Vergil, *Anglica Historia* (Basle, 1570), p. 142.

17. For the apocryphal *leges Edwardi Confessoris* and their appropriation by Coke and Lambarde, see J. G. A. Pocock, *The Ancient Constitution and the Feudal Law* (Cambridge, 1957, 1987), pp. 42-43. For this statement, see p. 43. For an important survey of the use of the Confessor's Laws throughout the seventeenth century, see Janelle Greenberg, "The Confessor's Laws and the Radical Face of the Ancient Constitution," *English Historical Review* 104 (1989), 611–37.

18. Compare Vergil, *Anglica Historia*, p. 154: "His ita constitutis, novissime leges pene omnes a superioribus sanctissimis regibus olim ad bene beataque vivendum latas sustulit, novasque dedit minus aequas, quas posteri non sine suo damno servarunt: perinde quasi nefas esset, eas malas leges irrita facere, quas parvum amicus populi Anglici loco bonarum tulisset. Non possum hoc loco non memorare rem tametsi omnibus notam, admiratione tamen longe dignissimam, atque dictu incredibilem, eiusmodi nanque leges quae ab omnibus intelligi deberent, erant, ut etiam nunc sunt, Normanici linguo scriptae, quam neque Galli, nec Angli recte callebant. Quamobrem videsse iam inde a principio, quotidie partim iniquitate legum, partim inscita eorum, qui illas male interpretabantur, hunc bonis avitis privari, illum iudicio imperitissimorum hominum criminis damnari, morteque mulctari, alium litibus inextricalibus perpetuo irretiri, ac denique divina humanaque misceri, atque ea omnia, ne fidem abroges dictis, publice privateque mortales testari, simulque detestari. Atqui certe quidem Norman pro suo instituto, non potui alias dare leges, quando non alia est natio quae peritius sciat calumniari, praevaricari, atque tergivisari, id est, per fraudem, & cavillationem, ac dissimilationem, frustrationemque litigare, seu vexare litibus."

19. Ibid., p. 179.

20. Cf. *Anglica Historia*, p. 188. In the edition I cite, which contains marginal notes in what may be the hand of Robert Sidney, later earl of Leicester, this passage is marked in the margin, perhaps for removal to a commonplace book: "P.V. The beginning of holding of Parlaments in England."

21. Neale, *Elizabeth I and Her Parliaments*, 1:17.

22. For a balanced account, see Butt, *History of Parliament*, pp. 50–59. In 1215 Magna Carta was nothing but the record of John's reassurance that he would observe customary rights and liberties. Reissued, however, in 1225 as a statement

of law, Magna Carta also came to be regarded as the first English statute, and (by Holinshed's time) was traditionally printed at the beginning of all the collections of statutes. During the seventeenth century it came to be regarded as "a deliberately designed declaration of political liberty," which led to an overreaction that laid stress instead on the crude feudal self-interest of the barons. Between these two distortions, however, lies a compromise, a desirable recognition that Magna Carta did have political significance in its own time as implying that the king was subject to the law; that he could make no law and that subjects owed him no unconditional obedience. These concepts were subsumed in Clause 61 (omitted in 1255) which sanctioned the right of resistance to the king if he abrogated any of the other provisions. See also R. F. Treharne, "Parliament in the Reign of Henry III," in *Historical Studies of the English Parliament,* 1:75–76, where it is pointed out that Henry's own clerks recognized "parliament" as the "occasion when the magnates there assembled imposed upon the king the two most famous and far-reaching restraints upon royal authority known to the century, the Great Charter and the Provisions of Oxford."

23. In contrast, John Bale had represented King John as a Protestant hero in the face of papal oppression, and Shakespeare, while drawing his historical material from Holinshed, notoriously *omitted* Magna Carta from his play on that reign. Edna Zwick Boris, in *Shakespeare's English Kings, the People, and the Law* (London, 1978), p. 124, claimed that Shakespeare omitted the Charter because it was not until the middle of the seventeenth century that it became a strong enough myth for the "forces of liberalism" to rally around it. Clearly, we need another explanation for these divergent emphases.

24. Note also that William Harrison, wishing to "restore one antiquitie to light, which hath hitherto lien as it were raked up in the embers of oblivion," inserted the text of the "great charter" concerning forests derived from Canute into his chapter "Of Parkes and Warrens," stating that it was confirmed by Edward the Confessor and Henry II, and that its abrogation caused "great trouble" under John (1:347).

25. Butt, *History of Parliament,* p. 79.

26. Ibid., p. 78.

27. G. L. Harriss, "The Formation of Parliament 1272–1377," in *The English Parliament in the Middle Ages,* ed. R. G. Davies and J. H. Denton (Philadelphia, 1981), p. 54; versus Butt, *History of Parliament,* p. 78. The contrast is typical of disagreements in this field.

28. Walsingham had represented those who supported the crusade as "the part, whose hearts God had touched," and those who opposed it as an irreligious minority. See Thomas Walsingham, *Historia Anglicana,* ed. Henry Thomas Riley, 2 vols. (London, Rolls Series, 1863–64), 2:84.

29. Henry Knighton, *Chronicon,* ed. Joseph Rawson Lumby, 2 vols. (London, 1895), 2:215–16.

30. Holinshed, however, did not include Knighton's next passage, whereby from another ancient statute (presumably Clause 61 of the original Magna Carta) the Lords Apellant argued that when a king alienates himself from his people, and refuses to rule according to the statutes, he may be deposed. Cf. Knighton, *Chroni-*

con, p. 219. The threat resided in an allusion ("Habent enim ex antiquo statuto et de facto non longe retroactis temporibus experienter") to the recent test of the statute on Edward II. In the margin of Claudius Ms. E.III, the main manuscript containing Knighton's chronicle, it was noted: "Potestas parliamenti in reges."

31. This account of 1386 is largely confirmed by Anthony Tuck, *Richard II and the English Nobility* (New York, 1974), pp. 102–7.

32. See Edward Hall, *The Union of the two noble & illustre famelies of Lancastre & Yorke,* ed. Henry Ellis (1548; repr. London, 1809; New York, 1965), pp. 9–11.

33. See B. Wilkinson, "The Deposition of Richard II and the Accession of Henry IV," in *Historical Studies of the English Parliament*, 1:329–53; versus M. V. Clarke, "Committees of Estates and the Deposition of Edward II," in *Historical Essays in Honour of James Tait* (Manchester, 1933), pp. 27–45. See also Jack B. Gohn, "Richard II: Shakespeare's Legal Brief on the Royal Prerogative and the Succession to the Throne," *Georgetown Law Journal* 70 (1982), 951–52.

34. Hall, *Union*, p. 12: "So that now I can nother amende my mysdedes, nor correcte my offences which suerly I entended to dooe, and especially in my olde age, in the whiche evill thynges be accustomed to be amended and the fautes and offences of youth, to be corrected and reformed. For . . . experience teacheth, that of a rugged colte, commeth a good horse, and of a shreude boye, proveth a good man."

35. *The Great Chronicle of London*, ed. A. H. Thomas and I. D. Thornley (London, 1938), p. 404, pointed out that the *Great Chronicle* and two other London chronicles translated these articles from an official Latin document, the great part of which is to be found in *Rot. Parl.* iii.416–45. Fabian, however, seems to have used an altogether different version, in which the articles appear in the form of letters testimonial, dated 29 September 1399. Since Holinshed used Fabian as a source for the articles, he may not have known of their appearance in *Rotuli Parliamentorum*.

36. Shakespeare's *Richard II* offers a compromise between Hall's psychological account of the resignation and Holinshed's parliamentary one. The deposition scene (notoriously censored from the earliest quartos) is introduced (in the Folio) with an ambiguous stage direction, "Enter *as to the Parliament* Bullingbrook, etc." This may be interpreted as a procession *on its way* to Westminster, or the imaginary opening of a parliamentary session which would require the presence of a problematically empty throne. See Andrew Gurr, ed., *King Richard II* (Cambridge, 1984), p. 137. Shakespeare then invented Richard's appearance in response to Bolingbroke's summons and the famous mirror speech (4:1:275ff.). The articles justifying the deposition are indeed mentioned; but it is Northumberland who attempts, unilaterally, to have Richard himself read the articles aloud, and after three unsuccessful attempts he is turned aside by Bolingbroke's "Urge it no more, my Lord Northumberland." What then, are we to make of Northumberland's reply: "The commons will not then be satisfied?"

37. Henry Ansgar Kelly, *Divine Providence in the England of Shakespeare's Histories* (Cambridge, Mass., 1970), pp. 139–42.

38. John Milton, *Complete Prose Works*, ed. D. M. Wolfe et al., 8 vols. (New Haven, 1953–82), 3:220–21.

39. Milton, *Complete Prose*, 1:446, 454.

40. See J. S. Roskell, *The Commons and their Speakers in English Parliaments, 1376–1523* (Manchester, 1965), pp. 253–54.

41. See Charles Ross, *Edward IV* (Berkeley and Los Angeles, 1974), pp. 341–50.

42. For these events, see John Guy, "Wolsey and the Parliament of 1523," in *Law and Government under the Tudors*, ed. Claire Cross, David Loades, and J. J. Scarisbrick (Cambridge, 1988), pp. 1–18. Guy regarded Hall's *Union* as a legitimate archive, and was particularly interested in Cuthbert Tunstall's opening statement that the Parliament had been called not only for Wolsey's fiscal purposes, but for "commonwealth" matters. Hall had cynically added, however, that "suerlie of these things no word was spoken in the whole parlement, and in effect no good act made, except the grant of a great subsidie were one." Holinshed omitted this comment, apparently intent on delivering a more favorable account of the session.

43. Compare the earl of Surrey's correspondent on May 14: "Sithens the begynnyng of the Parliamente there hath bene the grettiste and soreste hold in the lower House for payemente of [the subsidy] that ever was sene I thinke in any parliamente. . . . There hathe bene suche hold that the Hous was like to have bene dissevered; that is to say the Knights being of the Kings Counsaill, the Kings servaunts, and gentilmen, of the oon partie, whiche in soo long tyme were spoken with and made to sey ye; it may fortune, contrarie to their hert, will, and conscience." See H. Ellis, ed., *Original Letters Illustrative of English History*, 1st series, 3 vols., 2d ed. (London, 1825), 1:220–21.

44. For a guide through the intricacies of the Tudor tax system, see Michael Bush, "Tax Reform and Rebellion in Early Tudor England," *History* 76 (1991), 379–400.

45. Compare Hall, *Union*, p. 696: "All people curssed the Cardinal, and his coadherentes of the Lawes and libertie of Englande. For thei saied, if men should geve their goodes by a Commission, then were it worse then the taxes of Fraunce, and so England should be bond and not free." The intent is the same, but Holinshed's is a specifically parliamentary formulation.

46. Neale, *Elizabeth I and Her Parliaments*, 1:17.

47. Elton, *Parliament of England*, p. 338; italics added.

48. See *Proceedings in the Parliaments of Elizabeth I*, 1:480, 381, 411.

49. Neale, *Elizabeth I and Her Parliaments*, 1:175; cf. *Proceedings*, p. 174.

50. Ibid., 1:189.

51. Ibid., 1:221.

52. See *Proceedings*, p. 237. Wentworth's protest was against Sir Humphrey Gilbert's speech, which he saw as an attempt to intimidate the House, and whom he accused of tale-bearing.

53. Neale, *Elizabeth I and Her Parliaments*, 1:324; for a full text of the speech, see *Proceedings*, pp. 425–34; for Wentworth's examination by the disciplinary committee, see pp. 435–39.

54. Loach, *Parliament under the Tudors*, p. 110.

55. See "Hoker's Journal," ed. J. B. Davidson, in *Transactions of the Devonshire Associ-*

ation for the Advancement of Science, vol. 11 (Plymouth, 1879), 8–9, 479, 480; also reprinted in *Proceedings,* pp. 241–58.

56. "Hoker's *Journal,*" pp. 474–75; italics added. Compare the much briefer version provided by the anonymous diarist of the 1571 parliament, which usually provides so expansive a narrative that Hooker's in comparison seems skeletal. See *Proceedings,* p. 199: "He therefore saied they shoulde doe well to meddle wih noe matters of state but such as should be propounded unto them, and to occupy themselves in other matters concerninge the commenwealth."

57. See Vernon F. Snow, *Parliament in Elizabethan England: John Hooker's Order and Usage* (New Haven, 1977), p. 26.

58. We should note that this search for records took place shortly after the dissolution of the 1572 parliament, whose final weeks featured yet another dispute over privilege (Snagge's speech) and another speech by Yelverton citing precedents, including that of a fifteenth-century speaker who carried tales from the Commons and was punished for it. See Neale, *Elizabeth I and Her Parliaments,* 1:307.

59. For the complex bibliographical details of these two editions, see Snow, *Parliament in Elizabethan England,* pp. 29–38.

60. *Parliamentary Texts,* p. 90.

61. This surely casts doubts on the claim of Pronay and Taylor, *Parliamentary Texts,* p. 25, that the *Modus's* Ricardian phase was without political significance. They saw, however, a "possible reference" to the *Modus* lurking in Knighton's mention of an "ancient statute" invoked by Gloucester and Arundel in 1386 (p. 26).

62. See Snow, *Parliament in Elizabethan England,* p. 89, citing D'Ewes, *A Complete Journal . . . of the House of Lords and House of Commons,* p. 515.

63. See *Order and usage,* in Snow, *Parliament in Elizabethan England,* p. 153.

64. *Order and usage,* pp. 158, 161, 187. Compare "Hoker's *Journal,*" p. 49: "upon this byll one Wentworth toke occasion to speke & toochinge the lyberties & pryveleges of the howse inveighed agaynst [certeyne members of] the howse that had enformed the quene ontrewly of a . . . mocion made in this howse by mr bell . . . to have dysclosed the secrets . . . & to have falsely enformed the Quene."

65. See also his definitions of privilege, *Order and usage,* pp. 179, 186.

66. The allusion, to 2 Chronicles 10: 6–15, is highly rebarbative, however, since the young men who replace the elderly councillors advise King Rehoboam not to respond to the people's appeal for a lessening of their burdens, but rather to threaten them with greater severity. The result is, eventually, the revolt of the Jews at Sechem (1 Kings 12).

Chapter Seven: Religion

1. For Cecil's authorship of *The Execution of Justice,* and the *Declaration* subsequently appended to it, see Robert M. Kingdon, ed., *The Execution of Justice in England* (Ithaca, n.d.), xvii–xviii.

2. William Allen, *A True, Sincere, and Modest Defense of English Catholics,* ed. Robert Kingdon (Ithaca, 1965), p. 70. See also Allen's defence (pp. 64–66) of John Slade

and John Body. Fleming reported that in 1583 "John Slade, sometime a schoole-maister, and John Bodie a maister of art at Oxford [were] both indicted and convicted of high treason" (4:509). Allen points out that these convictions required "two divers sessions . . . (a rare case in our country), the latter sentence being to reform the former (as we may guess in such strange proceedings), which they perceived to be erroneous and insufficient of their own laws." He also drew attention to "R. B.," *The Several Executions of Slade and Body* (London, 1583), and complained that the government suppressed the pamphlet "and punished the author thereof, though he wrote in that point the plain truth as he heard and saw, but *not discreetly enough* nor agreeable to the politic practice they had then in hand, which was to persuade the world that none were put to death for their conscience" (p. 66; italics added).

3. See Anne Castanien, "Censorship and Historiography in Elizabethan England: The Expurgation of Holinshed's *Chronicles*," Unpublished Ph.D. dissertation, University of California, Davis, 1970, pp. 276–78; and C. S. Clegg, "Which Holinshed? Holinshed's *Chronicles* at the Huntington Library," *Huntington Library Quarterly* 55 (1992), p. 566.

4. John Bale, *A brefe Chronycle concerning the examination and death of the Blessed martir of Christ, Sir John Oldecastell the Lord Cobham* (Antwerp, 1544).

5. See Charles L. Kingsford, ed., *Chronicles of London* (Oxford, 1905), pp. 120–21; printed from Cotton m.s. Cleopatra C IV (1441).

6. Thomas Nashe mentions "Henrie the fifth . . . represented on the Stage, leading the French king prisoner, and forcing both him and the Dolphin to sweare fealty" (in *Works*, ed. R. B. McKerrow, Oxford, 1966, 1:213); and the reference in Henslowe's diary refers to a new play of "harey the Vth" in the repertoire of the Admiral's Men in 1595–96, five years too soon for Shakespeare's play. See E. K. Chambers, *The Elizabethan Stage*, 4 vols. (Oxford, 1923), 2:144–45. Shakespeare himself imagined this icon in place in 1450; in *Henry VI, Part 2*, Clifford uses it to persuade Jack Cade's followers to desert him: "Is Cade the son of Henry the Fifth, / That thus you do exclaim you'll go with him? / Will he conduct you through the heart of France, / And make the meanest of you earls and dukes?" (4:8:34–37). And Cade himself remarks its success: "Was ever feather so lightly blown to and fro as this multitude? The name of Henry the Fifth hales them to an hundred mischiefs, and makes them leave me desolate" (4:8:55–58).

7. K. B. McFarlane, "Henry V: A Personal Portrait," in *Lancastrian Kings and Lollard Knights* (Oxford, 1972), p. 133.

8. The statute included a focus on "conventicles and confederations," that is to say, on Lollard groups and meetings, and gave the rights of summary arrest and imprisonment of suspects to the bishops.

9. See Thomas Walsingham, *Historia Anglicana*, ed. Henry Thomas Riley, 2 vols. (London, Rolls Series, 1863–64), 2:282. Walsingham did write that Badby "mugit . . . miserabiliter inter incendia," but when he calls Badby "miser" he means the "wretch" who refused Henry's offer "non dubium quin maligno spiritu induratus."

10. Margaret Aston, *Lollards and Reformers: Images and Literacy in Late Medieval Religion* (London, 1989). But see also, for a very different view, the chapters on Oldcastle's

trial and "The Lollard Rising" in J. H. Wylie, *The Reign of Henry V*, 3 vols. (Cambridge, 1914), 1:236–92.

11. See C. L. Kingsford, *The First English Life of Henry V* (Oxford, 1911), xiii.

12. At the end of his account of the Henry V's reign, Holinshed added to his list of major writers derived from Bale the following interesting note: "Titus Livius de Foro Luuisiis lived also in these daies, an Italian borne: but sith he was both resiant here, and wrote the life of this king, I have thought good to place him among other of our English writers. One there was that translated the same historie into English, adding (as it were by the waie of notes in manie places of that booke) sundrie things for the more large understanding of the historie; a copy whereof I have seene belonging to John Stow citizen of London" (3:136).

13. *First English Life*, pp. 22–23.

14. Ibid., p. 190.

15. Aston, *Lollards and Reformers*, p. 9. This initial scepticism is, however, then qualified. "If the accusations sometimes seem improbable it should be remembered that they also included much circumstantial detail, and when (as in the proceedings against those who had been in contact with Oldcastle in 1417), the jurors were themselves sympathetic, the case is not likely to have been grossly overstated. In general the presentments had at least to be credible enough to make a conviction possible, and some of the more sweeping statements of the Lollards' intentions may have been derived from their own claims." Wylie generally accepts the accounts of the early chroniclers, although he notes (p. 264) that we "have no record of their intentions from their own point of view."

16. Aston, *Lollards and Reformers*, p. 25; italics added. She cites P.R.O King's Bench 27/63, Rex m. 25r., and *Rotuli Parliamentorum*, iv, pp. 107–10. It appears that Aston not only believed in Oldcastle's rebellion but deprecated the contamination of religious reform with political activism. Compare, for instance, her statement on the suppressed rising of 1431: "the foiled plans of 1414 persisting in a debased and still more subversive shape," (p. 31) and later: "Left wing Lollards who helped to give the movement such prominence and discredit may have persisted as long as the heresy itself" (p. 38).

17. On the bias of official records, see also Anne Hudson, *The Premature Reformation: Wycliffite Texts and Lollard History* (Oxford, 1988), p. 59: "If any of the material appears to be impartial, it is probably the more to be distrusted: the records in the episcopal registers, in their formality and verbosity, may resemble a modern law report, but are almost invariably only a 'police memo' of charge and sentence." Hudson's point is to recover Lollard defence testimony, ignored by previous historians, as a historical source. Her work, however, emphasizes Wycliffe's theology and its academic origins (a *trahison des clercs*) in contrast to and indeed in express opposition to Aston's emphasis on the social and political aspects of Lollard history. Hudson points out that Lollardry was not rebellious in theory, that its texts proposed only passive resistance even to tyrannical rulers or resistance only against evil *ecclesiastical* lordship (pp. 366–67). She therefore concludes that "we do not know how Oldcastle justified his rebellion against his king," without questioning

the accounts of that rebellion in the official records whose bias she elsewhere assumes.

18. Aston, *Lollards and Reformers*, p. 7.

19. According to Hudson, *The Premature Reformation*, pp. 367–68, outright pacifism was an extreme position among Lollard opinions, obviously not held by the Lollard knights or by Oldcastle himself; yet her citation of Oldcastle as an exception to later, explicit pacifism assumes as a fact his participation in armed rebellion.

20. These articles are preserved in the *Fasciculi Zizaniorum*, a collection of documents relating to Wycliffe that once belonged to John Bale. See the edition by W. W. Shirley (London, 1858), pp. 360–69. On Bale's possession of the manuscript, and its use by John Foxe, see Aston, *Lollards and Reformers*, pp. 236–37. Netter was the author of Bale's belief that the *Fasciculi Zizaniorum* has been challenged by James Crompton, "Fasciculi Zizaniorum," *Journal of Ecclesiastical History* 12 (1961), 34–45, 155–66. I owe this information to Thomas Freeman.

21. W. T. Waugh, "Sir John Oldcastle," *English Historical Review* 20 (1905), 657–58.

22. Ibid., p. 453.

23. See Hudson, *The Premature Reformation*, pp. 178, 200. Bale explains just how lively was the Lollards' recognition of what was needed to control public opinion. "Whyle the lord Cobham was thus in the tower," he wrote, "he sent out privily unto his frinds. And they at his desire wrote this lytle bill here folowing, causing it to be set up in diverse quarters of London, that the peple shulde not believe the slaundres and lyes that his enemies the bishops servaunts and Priests had made on him abroade" (F2v).

24. Bale, *Brefe Chronycle*, B7v; Walsingham, *Historia Anglicana*, 2:293. The question of whether Bale's account can be trusted cannot be ignored, but neither does my argument depend upon its answering. According to Leslie Fairfield, *John Bale: Mythmaker for the English Reformation* (West Lafayette, Ind., 1976), pp. 128–29, Bale altered the record to make Oldcastle seem more Protestant in doctrine and sympathy, and to counter charges of treason. I owe this reference to John Knott, whose *Discourses of Martyrdom in English Literature, 1563–1694* (Cambridge, 1993), pp. 46–59, contains a section on the Oldcastle legend as retold by Foxe. Waugh himself admits that Bale's account of Oldcastle's examination by Arundel "may furnish something like a true account of what happened" ("Sir John Oldcastle," p. 450).

25. For Netter, see Wylie, *The Reign of Henry V*, 1:238–41. Hudson, *The Premature Reformation*, pp. 50–51. Netter was a Carmelite monk whose six-volume *Doctrinale Fidei Catholicae* constituted a comprehensive attack on Wycliffe's theology and that of his followers. He seems to have been deeply involved in the prosecution of Lollards, participating in the trials of John Badby in 1410, of Oldcastle in 1413, of William Taylor in 1423, and of William White in 1428. He was also a primary influence on Henry from the beginning until, as Wylie put it, the king died in his arms (1:241).

26. *Fasciculi Zizaniorum*, pp. 444–45: "Ulterius dixit idem dominus Johannes alta voce, manibus expansis, alloquendo circumstantes. Isti qui judicant, et volunt

damnare me, seducent vos omnes, et seipsos, et vos ducent ad infernum; idea caveatis ab eis."

27. Waugh, "Sir John Oldcastle," p. 440, regarded it as "apocryphal." For those who credit it, see Aston, *Lollards and Reformers*, p. 21; Wylie, 3:309; Hudson, *The Premature Reformation*, 339–40.

28. See V. H. Galbraith, "Articles Laid before the Parliament of 1371," *English History Review* 34 (1919), 579–82.

29. Aston, *Lollards and Reformers*, p. 42.

30. For an account of the 1584 parliament, and the role played by Robert Beale, the Puritan laywer and son-in-law of Walsingham, see J. E. Neale, *Elizabeth I and Her Parliaments 1584–1601* (New York, 1953, 1957), pp. 62–83.

31. Aston, *Lollards and Reformers*, p. 219.

32. It was among thirty books listed as forbidden in connection with the execution of Richard Bayfield in December 1531. See *Letters and Papers, Foreign and Domestic, of the Reign of Henry VIII*, ed. J. S. Brewer, 22 vols. (London, 1862–1932), 7:69; Aston, *Lollards and Reformers*, pp. 220–21. It appears to have been condemned again in 1542. A single copy survives, as B.M. G12012 (*S.T.C.* 24045).

33. See H. McCusker, *John Bale, Dramatist and Antiquary* (Bryn Mawr, Pa., 1942; repr. Freeport, N.Y., 1971), pp. 16–17.

34. Aston, *Lollards and Reformers*, pp. 235–36. See also William Haller, *The Elect Nation: The Meaning and Relevance of Foxe's Book of Martyrs* (New York, 1963), pp. 58–70.

35. The *Gesta* introduces Oldcastle as an adversary whom God has allowed to rise up against Henry to prove his sanctity "in the furnace of tribulation." It attempts to undermine his military reputation and popularity; (he is "of great popular reputation ["famosus in populo"] but "proud of heart" ["elatus corde"], "strong in body but weak in virtue." It attempts to undo the value of his title: "Slaughtering and pillaging the Welsh secured his promotion to knighthood, and, later still, flattering fortune called him through marriage to be Lord Cobham." It states that after the examination by Archbishop Arundel in which Oldcastle was formally declared a heretic Henry deferred execution in consideration of his knightly rank; and it claims that Oldcastle was able to escape from the Tower after his chains had been removed upon his (broken) promise of recantation. Rhetorically, the clerical author knows unqualified evil when he sees it. Oldcastle is called apostate, tergiversator, a raven of treachery, seditious, a source of venom, an ally of Satan and a second Cain. See *Gesta Henrici Quinti*, trans. Frank Taylor and John Roskell (Oxford, 1975), pp. 3–9.

36. Edward Hall, *The Union of the Two Noble & Illustre Famelies of Lancastre & Yorke*, ed. Henry Ellis (1548; repr. London, 1809; New York, 1965), p. 48.

37. John Foxe, *Acts and Monuments*, ed. George Townsend, 8 vols. (London, 1843–49; repr. New York, 1965), 3:377–78. Foxe was responding to the attack on Bale's Oldcastle by the Catholic polemicist Nicholas Harpsfield, which appeared under the name of Alan Cope, *Dialogi Sex* (Antwerp, 1566).

38. C. L. Kingsford, *English Historical Literature in the Fifteenth Century* (Oxford, 1913), p. 261, claims that there was an earlier edition of Hall's chronicle published

in 1542. He gives no evidence for this assertion, also made in the *Dictionary of National Biography*. There is no trace of this edition in the *Short Title Catalogue*.

39. Foxe, *Acts and Monuments*, 3:378.

40. In this Hall had exceeded Bale in his suspicions. Bale had written more cautiously: "Some wryters have thought this escape to come by the sayd syr Roger Acton and other gentelmen in displeasure of the Priestes, and that to be the chefe occasion of their deathes, which might well be, but Walden doth not so utter it, which Reigned the same selfe time" (F8r). He did, however, cast doubts on the existence of a major insurrection, saying only: "The complaint was made unto the kyng of them that they had made a greate asemble in sainct Gyles . . . As the king was thus infourmed, he erected a banner (saith Walden) with a crosse therupon . . . & with a great nombre of men entred the same felde, *where as he found no such company*" (F7v; italics added). Hall himself states that "a certain unlawfull assemble" occurred, and that Acton, Brown, and Beverly "were brought to the kynges presence, and to hym declared the cause of their commocion and risyng . . . (whiche confession because I have not seen, I leave at large)."

41. Foxe, *Acts and Monuments*, 3:378–79 (italics added).

42. Ibid., 3:402.

43. For an effective, though polemical, defence of Foxe's scholarly methods, see George Townsend's "Life," *Acts and Monuments*, 1:228–34. Hudson, *The Premature Reformation*, p. 40, cites what bibliography exists on Foxe's reliability, and concludes that Foxe "is generally trustworthy to a fairly high degree." See also Patrick Collinson, "Truth and Legend: The Veracity of John Foxe's *Book of Martyrs*," in *Clio's Mirror: Historiography in Britain and the Netherlands*, ed. A. C. Duke and C. A. Tamse (in the series *Britain and the Netherlands*) 8 (Zutphen.1985), 31–54; and G. R. Elton, "Persecution and Toleration in the English Reformation," *Studies in Church History* 21 (1984), 178. In *Forms of Nationhood: The Elizabethan Writing of England* (Chicago and London, 1992), pp. 264–66, Richard Helgerson takes a different approach to Foxe's credibility, via his representation of common people, who answer to their interrogations "with the same articulate and informed conviction, die with the same fortitude as their social betters," precisely what Protestant literacy campaigns had aimed for. Helgerson points out that this was viewed as proof of Foxe's mendacity by the Jesuit Robert Parsons. "But what then do we make of the extraordinary wealth of documentary evidence Foxe presents," asks Helgerson. "Not even Parsons can deny that these men and women died, nor that they died for a faith whose basic tenets and whose source of authority they understood and could express."

44. See Foxe, *Acts and Monuments*, 3:351–59.

45. Waugh, "Sir John Oldcastle," pp. 646–47, admits that the total of those imprisoned, condemned or pardoned was "upwards of a hundred persons." "A 'hundred,' indeed, though better than 'three,' compares badly enough with 'twenty thousand.'" Waugh, "Sir John Oldcastle," pp. 646–47. Wylie, *The Reign of Henry V*, 1:273–76, provides a longer list of those executed and details of hundreds of people pardoned, which can be read either as evidence of Henry's clemency or widespread recognition that most of the arrests, which were carried out on the basis of accusa-

tion, were implausible. But note also the sinister information he records (1:264–65) that although Henry's proclamation declaring that certain Lollards have been brought before him and declared that seditious meetings were to take place is dated 7 January 1414, juries had actually "been empanelled many weeks beforehand." But the equivalent of Foxe's doubts is rather to be found in Waugh's remarkable suggestion that the fact of even the documented prosecutions argues that the rebellion must have taken place. "The execution of so many persons," he wrote, "is in itself an indication that something serious was to be apprehended from their doings. It is impossible to believe, with Foxe, that a man of Henry V's nature would butcher more than forty of his subjects merely for the purpose of discrediting a small section of the nation. Moreover, if the country was the victim of a hoax, the fraud was in truth a most elaborate one. No trouble or expense was spared; large commissions of inquiry were appointed . . . spies were employed and rewarded; numerous proclamations were issued . . . and men were arrested, imprisoned, released on bail, and, for the most part, finally set at liberty and pardoned: and all this to cast discredit on a peaceable sect that was by no means popular and that was becoming less so every day" (p. 646). Note the self-contradictions here especially of that "peaceable."

46. Walsingham, *Historia Anglicana*, 2:297–99.

47. Ibid., 2:326.

48. Ibid., 2:325.

49. Walsingham claimed that Oldcastle told Sir Thomas Erpingham that, if he saw him rise on the third day, he should "procure peace for his sect," and identified the statement as "dementia." See *Historia Anglicana*, 2:328. Bale, who owned a manuscript of Walsingham, wrote in the margin, "Nota de insania Cobam." See Alice Lyle Scoufos, *Shakespeare's Typological Satire* (Athens, Ohio, 1979), p. 109.

50. For a balanced survey of the few facts and multiple hypotheses, see Janet Clare, *"Art Made Tongue-tied by Authority": Elizabethan and Jacobean Dramatic Censorship* (Manchester, 1990), pp. 76–79.

51. See *The First Part of Sir John Oldcastle*, ed. J. R. Macarthur (Chicago, 1907), p. 116.

52. See Mary Grace Adkins, "Sixteenth-century Religious and Political Implications in *Sir John Oldcastle*," *University of Texas Studies in English* 22 (1942), 98–99.

53. See David Bevington, *Tudor Drama and Politics* (Cambridge, Mass., 1968), pp. 256–59; and *The Oldcastle Controversy*, ed. Peter Corbin and Douglas Sedge (Manchester, 1991), p. 16.

54. Compare also Jerome Barlow, *A proper dyalogue betwene a Gentillman and a husbandman* (ca. 1530), ed. Edward Arber, *English Reprints* 28 (1871), pp. 167–68, which directly links the burning of Tyndale's New Testament in 1530 with the censorship of chronicles: "They [the bishops] destroyed cronicles not long a gone / Which for certeyne poyntes unreverently / Soundynge agaynst the kynges auncetrye / As they saye/were brent everychone." Among other heroes of the *Dyalogue* is Sir John Oldcastle, whose destruction is seen as part of the larger pattern (pp. 145–46). The account of the burning of Tyndale's New Testament by Cuthbert Tunstall, bishop of London, appears in the *Chronicles* (3:749).

Chapter Eight: Law

1. David Jardine, *Criminal Trials* (London, 1832), 1:39, 62, *both* regarded this as "the earliest trial reported with sufficient fulness to be adapted for the purpose in view," *and* mysteriously declared that the report is "very imperfect." He did not explain what he regarded as missing. "Unfortunately," he added, "there are no means of rendering it more complete and intelligible; for no other account of the proceedings is to be found, nor are the examinations of the seven witnesses, or of Throckmorton himself, at the State-Paper office."

2. The Throckmorton trial was included in the first series, *A Complete Collection of State Trials*, ed. Thomas Salmon, 4 vols. (London, 1719); it is more accessible in one of the nineteenth-century series, e.g., *A Complete Collection of State Trials*, ed. T. B. Howell, 21 vols. (London, 1816), vol. 1. For an account of the various editions and the agendas they were designed to serve, see Donald Thomas, ed., *State Trials*, 4 vols. (London and Boston, 1972), 1:4–18. My use of the term "whig" here refers broadly to the theory of a progressive advancement in civil and legal rights, rather than party politics. Thomas Salmon's preface in 1719 made it clear that his edition was intended as a contribution to rights theory: "that Learning which shews how life, honour, and innocence are to be defended, when they shall happen to be injuriously attack'd, will not, 'tis presum'd, be thought inferior to that, which instructs us how to defend our less important rights." Yet Salmon himself had a reputation of being an "inveterate enemy" to the Revolution of 1688, and his views were rejected by a subsequent whig editor of *State Trials*, Francis Hargrave. (See Thomas, ed., *State Trials*, 1:8, 20.)

3. David Loades, *Two Tudor Conspiracies* (Cambridge, 1965), p. 17, concluded that they were "indifferent to doctrinal issues" and that their main concern was the queen's Spanish marriage. On the other hand, John Ponet's *A Shorte Treatise of Politike Power*, D.I.P.B.R.W., published from exile in 1556, emphasized the religious motives behind the uprising.

4. Loades, *Two Tudor Conspiracies*, pp. 96–97.

5. Sir Sidney Lee's article on Throckmorton in the *Dictionary of National Biography* is heavily indebted to David Jardine's "Memoir," *Criminal Trials*, 1:40–62. In addition, there exists a peculiar poem about Throckmorton's life, which may have been written by a member of his family. This was first edited by Francis Peck, as *The Legend of Sir Nicholas Throkmorton, Kt. Chief Butler of England & Chamberlain of the Exchecquer; who died of Poison, A.D. 1570, an Historical Poem: By (his Nephew) Sir Thomas Throckmorton of Littleton* . . . (1736). The attribution to Thomas was subsequently disputed by J. G. Nichols, who reedited the poem in 1874 for the Roxburgh Club.

6. See Thomas Andrew Green, *Verdict according to Conscience: Perspectives on the English Criminal Trial Jury 1200–1800* (Chicago, 1985), p. 135.

7. Sir Thomas Smith, *De Republica Anglorum*, ed. Mary Dewar (Cambridge, 1982), p. xx.

8. By residually magic, I mean that the early modern trial demonstrated the staying power of a much older theory of justice, the *judicium dei*, whose belief-system

Throckmorton appropriated even as he uses to perfection the new skills required by the "inquest." For the transfer of judicial decisions from physical to intellectual ordeal, from the hand-to-hand combat of feudal trials to the verbalized (and textualized) combat of the individual against the state, see R. Howard Bloch, *Medieval French Literature and Law* (Berkeley, 1977), pp. 109–40. See also Cynthia Herrup, *The Common Peace: Participation and the Criminal Law in Seventeenth-Century England* (Cambridge, 1987), pp. 2–5, for the continued influence of divine proscription in criminal jurisprudence.

9. Thomas Hobbes, *Leviathan,* ed. C. B. Macpherson (Harmondsworth, Middlesex, 1968), p. 190.

10. Donald Kelley, "Ideas of Resistance before Elizabeth," in *The Historical Renaissance: New Essays on Tudor and Stuart Literature,* ed. Heather Dubrow and Richard Strier (Chicago and London, 1988), p. 51. See also Gerry Bowler, "Marian Protestants and the Idea of Violent Resistance to Tyranny," in *Protestantism and the National Church in Sixteenth Century England,* ed. Peter Lake and Maria Dowling (London, 1987), pp. 124–43.

11. According to Bowler, "Marian Protestants," p. 141 n. 10, *Certayne Questions* was published in Wesel by Josse Lamprecht. The claim that it was "imprinted at London at the . . . requeste of Miles Hogherde" is a rude joke at the expense of Miles Hogarde. Bowler suggests that it must be the "Seditious book of questions in print" which disturbed the Privy Council in the summer of 1555. See *Acts of the Privy Council, 1555,* ed. J. R. Dasent (London, 1890–1907), pp. 153–54.

12. *The Mirror for Magistrates,* ed. Lily B. Campbell (New York, 1960), pp. 73–80.

13. Campbell, *Mirror,* p. 7, insisted that the suppressed edition must have appeared in 1555, which allowed her to argue that, rather than being itself a cause of offence to Mary's government, it merely became a victim of the ban against Hall's *Union,* to which the *Mirror* editors several times refer. This argument has been effectively refuted by Scott Lucas. I am grateful to him for bringing my attention back to Tresilian's tragedy in this context.

14. J. F. Stephen, *History of the Criminal Law in England,* 3 vols. (London, 1883), 1:326–29, contributed a brief description.

15. John Bellamy, *The Tudor Law of Treason* (London, 1979), p. 246.

16. From a literary-historical perspective, we know of nobody who was capable of inventing dialogue like this so early in the sixteenth century. The mature Elizabethan drama is still thirty years in the future, and anyone acquainted with mid-century drama (Bale's *King John* or Norton and Sackville's *Gorboduc*) will immediately see the point. The playwright who did write with this colloquial zest was Shakespeare, who we know found inspiration in Holinshed. Moreover, although Holinshed transcribes the trial in what we now recognize as dramatic form, it is not offered as theater, but as "Dialog."

17. G. Kitson Clark, *The Critical Historian* (New York, 1967), p. 95.

18. See *Fasciculi Zizaniorum,* ed. W. W. Shirley (London, 1858), pp. 435–42. For Netter, see J. H. Wylie, *The Reign of Henry V,* 3 vols. (Cambridge, 1914), 1:238–41, and chapter 7 above.

19. Kitson Clark, *The Critical Historian*, p. 86.
20. Ibid., p. 87.
21. Ibid., p. 94.
22. Duncan Derrett, "Neglected Versions of the Contemporary Account of the Trial of Sir Thomas More," *Bulletin of the Institute of Historical Research*, 33 (1960), p. 204.
23. *The Triall of Lieut. Collonel J. Lilburne . . . Unto which is annexed a necessary Appendix.* Published by Theodorus Verax (Southwark, 1649).
24. Clement Walker is best known as the author of the *History of Independency* (1648–49), which is hostile to the Independents. Although at the beginning of the civil war he joined the parliamentary side, by 1647 he was suspected of being one of the instigators of the London riots, and in 1648 he voted in favor of an agreement with Charles I and was consequently expelled from the House of Commons in Pride's Purge. Like Lilburne himself, Walker was an indefatigable publicist, and from 1643 to 1651 he used the press to promote and defend his opinions.
25. See *State Trials*, 4:1328 (italics added).
26. William Haller and Godfrey Davis, eds. *Leveller Tracts* (Gloucester, Mass., 1964), p. 31; italics added.
27. Other still later examples can be adduced, to explain the relation between unofficial note-taking and unauthorized publication. At the trial of William, Lord Russell in July 1683, Lady Russell was seated beside her husband to handle his papers and take notes for him. Whether or not she was the only notetaker, which seems unlikely, at least six unofficial accounts of his trial and execution were published, notwithstanding an explicit government ban on such pamphlets, including *The Whole Tryal and Defence of William Lord Russel, Who Dyed a Martyr to the Romish Fury, in the Year 1683, with the Learned Arguments of the Council on both sides.* See Lois G. Schwoerer, *Lady Rachel Russell* (Baltimore and London, 1988), pp. 114, 142, 279–80, n. 29. I owe this reference to James Epstein.
28. There is one independent manuscript witness, British Library Stowe 280, once owned by Algernon Capell, earl of Essex. On fols. 75ff. there appears "Tharraignemente of Sir Nycholas Throgmerton in the Gyeldehall at London, the xviith daie of Aprill, anno dni. 1554, expressed in a dialogue for the bettre understanding of every mans parte." The manuscript has many spelling differences, including "Throgmerton" throughout, many changes of word order, different versions of the jurors' names (e.g., Katerwane instead of Cater, fol. 76r.) including two first names that do not appear in the *Chronicles*, and is generally a slightly more expansive text. This would be suggest that the *Chronicles* and the manuscript derive from *separate* originals.
29. *State Trials*, 4:1288.
30. Bellamy, *Tudor Law of Treason*, 82–83.
31. G. R. Elton, *Policy and Police: The Enforcement of the Reformation in the Age of Thomas Cromwell* (Cambridge, 1972), p. 287. See also pp. 263–326, 383–400. It is all the more useful to supplement Bellamy's account of Tudor treason law with that of Sir Geoffrey Elton, because the latter's account of this topic is generally apologetic, and marked by admiration for Thomas Cromwell's regime.

32. Bellamy, *Tudor Law of Treason*, p. 47.

33. The reference is to Sir Roger Cholmley, one of the commissioners, who had been Lord Chief Justice until 1553, when he was dismissed from that post on Mary's accession because he had witnessed the will of Edward VI in favor of Lady Jane Grey.

34. It may, however, be Cholmley's dismissal from the position of Lord Chief Justice that Throckmorton here naughtily alluded to.

35. For "the definitive proceedinges in causes criminall" see Smith, *De Republica Anglorum*, pp. 110–16.

36. Holinshed's account makes no mention of the fact, discovered by Bellamy, that Throckmorton himself challenged *ten* of the jurors. See *Tudor Law of Treason*, p. 140, and his citation of *Public Record Office*, KB 8/29 m.10.

37. Bellamy, *Tudor Law of Treason*, p. 55.

38. See Samuel E. Thorne, ed., *A Discourse upon the Exposicion & Understandinge of Statutes With Sir Thomas Egerton's Additions* (San Marino, 1942), p. 3. Thorne dates the *Discourse* roughly 1557–67; but at one time it looks back to a statute "made in the tyme of Queene Marye" (p. 155), implying, of course, composition after 1559.

39. Throckmorton took this opportunity to cite Scripture and St. Jerome on the subject of false witnesses (4:39). He also used the commonsense argument that, since as Vaughan himself had admitted in court that he was scarcely acquainted with Throckmorton, it was inconceivable that he would "so frankelie discover [his] mind to him in so dangerous a matter" (4:38).

40. Though Thomas Howard, duke of Norfolk, at his own trial for treason in 1571, cited virtually no law in his own defence, he did quote this same sentence: "There is a Maxim in law that penal statutes must be construed strictly, and no penal statute ought to be extended further than the very words." See *State Trials*, 1:1001.

41. That chronicles may be a juridical resource for the citizen is indicated in the exchange between Griffin and Throckmorton on the subject of Jack Cade and "the blacksmith." Cited by Griffin as examples of rebel leaders who pretended they "meant no harme to the king, but [acted] only against his councell," they were countercited by Throckmorton as entirely distinct from himself: "As to Cade and the blacke smith, I am not so well acquainted with their treasons as you be: but *I have read in the chronicle*, they were in the field with a force against the prince, whereby a manifest act did appeere" (4:49).

42. Compare Loades, *Two Tudor Conspiracies*, p. 97. He added that the government only narrowly escaped a second defeat when Croftes was brought to trial on the 28th.

43. Smith, *De Republica Anglorum*, p. 121.

44. See Green, *Verdict According to Conscience*, p. 141, where Throckmorton's case appears in a single footnote; J. S. Cockburn, *History of English Assizes: 1558–1714* (Cambridge, 1972; repr. 1986), where, again, Throckmorton's case appears in a single footnote, p. 123. See also Cockburn, "Twelve Silly Men? The Trial Jury at Assizes, 1560–1670," in *Twelve Good Men and True: The Criminal Trial Jury in England, 1200–1800*, ed. J. S. Cockburn & T. A. Green (Princeton, 1988), pp. 158–81. Green

downplays the claim that packed juries were common: "In general, however, the Crown seems to have relied upon the force of its case and upon the defendant's lack of opportunity to foresee the elements of the Crown's case rather than upon true jury packing" (pp. 132–33); whereas Loades, *Two Tudor Conspiracies*, p. 97, points out that in the trial of Sir James Croftes that followed Throckmorton's the first jury had to be dismissed and replaced with a second, more compliant one. This packed jury duly brought in the required verdict, but Croftes was not executed, and was pardoned in February 1556.

45. See Olivia Smith, *The Politics of Language 1791–1819* (Oxford, 1984), pp. 176–201. I owe this reference too to James Epstein, whose chapter on T. J. Wooler, "Narrating Liberty's Defense: T. J. Wooler," in *Radical Expression: Political Language, Ritual and Symbol in England, 1790–1850* (forthcoming), systematically explores the politics and the mechanics of unofficial accounts of trials in the late eighteenth and early nineteenth centuries.

46. Bellamy, *Tudor Law of Treason*, 143.

47. See *The Legend*, ed. J. G. Nichols (London, 1874), 30.

48. See G. R. Elton, "The Sessional Printing of Statutes, 1484-1547," in *Wealth and Power in Tudor England: Essays Presented to S. T. Bindoff*, ed. E. W. Ives, R. J. Knecht, and J. J. Scarisbrick (London, 1978), pp. 68–86. On the printing and reprinting of William Rastell's *Statutes at large* (1557), see H. S. Bennett, *English Books and Readers 1603–1640* (Cambridge, 1970), pp. 119–21. While the chief readers of these would of course have been lawyers and justices of the peace, the appearance of *several* editions of sessional statutes in years when treason law had been altered suggests a wider national interest.

49. Penry Williams, *The Tudor Regime* (New York, 1979), p. 381. I owe this reference to Jane Strekalovsky.

Chapter Nine: Populism

1. See *Proceedings in Parliament 1610*, ed. Elizabeth Read Foster, 2 vols. (New Haven, 1966), 1:276.

2. See Clifford Geertz, "Thick Description: Toward an Interpretive Theory of Culture," in his *The Interpretation of Cultures* (New York, 1973), pp. 3–30.

3. See Mary Dewar, "A Question of Plagiarism," in her edition of Sir Thomas Smith, *De Republica Anglorum* (Cambridge, 1982), Appendix 3, pp. 157–62.

4. See chapter 2.

5. *Proceedings in Parliament*, 1:276.

6. See chapter 1.

7. See Thomas Walsingham, *Historia Anglicana*, ed. H. T. Riley, 2 vols. (London, Rolls Series, 1863–64), 1:449–50. Walsingham, monk of St. Albans (fl. 1440) is still the chief authority for the reigns of Richard II, Henry IV, and Henry V. Walsingham wrote several chronicles, three of which deal with the Peasants' Revolt. Because Walsingham attacks John of Gaunt in his *Chronicon Angliae*, the monks of St. Alban's suppressed it upon the accession of Henry IV, who was unlikely to have

countenanced these attacks on his father. See E. M. Thompson, ed. *Chronicon Angliae*, 2 vols. (London, Rolls Series, 1874). The *Historia Anglicana* is a condensed version of a longer period of medieval history than that covered by the *Chronicon.*

8. The second version of the story, involving John Leg, derives from the *Chronicon Henrici Knighton*, ed. J. R. Lumby (London, Rolls Series, 1895), vol. 92, 2:130–31:" There was a certain John Leg with three colleagues asked the king to give him a commission to investigate the collectors of this tax in Kent, Norfolk and other parts of the country. They contracted to give the lord king a large sum of money for his assent; and most unfortunately for the king his council agreed. One of these commissioners came to a certain village to investigate the said tax and called together the men and women; he then, horrible to relate, shamelessly lifted the young girls to test whether they had enjoyed intercourse with men. In this way he compelled the friends and parents of these girls to pay the tax for them: many would rather pay for their daughters than see them touched in such a disgraceful way." The translation comes from R. B. Dobson, *Peasants' Revolt of 1381* (London, 1970), p. 135. I have been unable to find a chronicle source for the first version of the story, of which Dobson was apparently unaware. It is interesting that Holinshed preferred the version which stresses the youth of the female victim and leaves her sexual innocence intact.

9. Walsingham, *Historia Anglicana*, 2:32.

10. In 1680 Sir Thomas Browne, an outspoken Royalist during the civil war period, implied that Holinshed was unusually sympathetic to popular protest. In his unpublished antiquarian work, "Repertorium, or Some Account of the Tombs and Monuments in the Cathedrall Church of Norwich," he wrote of Bishop Roger [de Skerning],"in whose time fell out that blooddy contention between the moncks and the citizens begunne at a fayre kept before gate, when the church was sett on fire, which to compose King Henry the third came in person to Norwich. Hollinshed for this confusion layeth much blame upon William de Brunham who was then prior of the convent butt hee who would knowe the names of the citizens who were chief Actors in this tumult, may find them sett downe in the Bull of Pope Gregorie the eleventh." See *Works*, ed. Geoffrey Keynes, 4 vols. (Chicago, 1964), 3:131.

11. For current thinking about this episode of theatrical censorship, see T. H. Howard Hill, ed., *Shakespeare and Sir Thomas More: Essays on the Play and Its Shakespearian Interest* (Cambridge, 1989).

12. Compare Edward Hall, *The Union of the two noble & illustre famelies of Lancastre & Yorke*, ed. Henry Ellis (1548; repr. London 1809; New York, 1965), p. 586, who says that "the poore Englishe artificers could skarce get any lyvynge."

13. John Bellamy, *The Tudor Law of Treason* (London, 1979), pp. 18-19.

14. Bellamy, *Tudor Law of Treason*, p. 20. Bellamy, however, mistakenly attributes this passage to Grafton's *Chronicle at Large*, (London, 1568–69), p. 239, whereas Grafton was obviously taking his information directly from Hall.

15. If one had any doubt of where the *Chronicles* directed the readers' sympathies, they should be dispelled by comparing this account of Ill May Day with that provided by Polydore Vergil, who berated the "ignorant fellows" whose xenophobia

"ruins the commercial activity" of others, and insisted precisely on that which Holinshed denies, that the riot was produced by intention and organized conspiracy: "at the instigation of one John Lincoln, they conspired together against the foreign workmen and merchants. The determined that early on the morning of May Day, when traditionally accustomed to do so, they would pour out into the fields and then return, carrying back leafy branches so that no suspicion of slaughter would be aroused; then they would attack the foreigners, giving some a beating, depriving some of their lives and others of their wealth. But while they murmured threateningly through the streets and public places and boasted that in the near future the wrongs they had endured from the foreigners . . . would be violently avenged, their plans were revealed and exposed." Vergil, who wrote unmistakably from a court perspective, then described the "enormous band of apprentices and watermen" who defied the curfew, and the damage done by "the raving mob." Eventually "an enquiry was held and they established that John Lincoln was the instigator of the wicked plot: he was then staying in the country in order not to seem a member of the conspiracy." Since Vergil's emphasis was, like Grafton and Speed, on the clemency of the authorities, he reports that only Lincoln and four of his associates were executed, along with ten others; but he does admit that some who had fallen in with "that rabble of abandoned men by sudden chance rather than by any set plan . . . shared the punishment." See Polydore Vergil, *Anglica Historia* (Books 24–27), ed. and trans. Denys Hay (London, 1950), pp. 243–44.

16. Compare Hall, *Union*, p. 823.

17. Roger B. Manning, "The Origins of the Doctrine of Sedition," *Albion* 12 (1980), 107.

18. Manning, "Origins," pp. 108-9; see also Lindsay Boynton, "Martial Law and the Petition of Right," *English Historical Review* 89 (1964), 255-84.

19. "I John Hooker the writer herof was present, and *Testis oculatus* of things then doone" (3:939). Compare *The discription of the cittie of Excester, collected and gathered by John Vowel* (London, 1575).

20. Compare Foxe, *Acts and Monuments*, ed. George Townsend, 7:126.

21. See below.

22. Compare Stow, *Chronicle*, pp. 1090–91.

23. Foxe, *Acts and Monuments*, 6:548.

24. The source of the first quotation, inaccurately quoted, is Lucan, *Civil War*, 3:58, "nescit *plebes* jejuna timere." The wider context is important. Caesar, having just driven Pompey out of Italy, turns his attention to the task of "winning the fickle favour of the populace; for he knew that the causes of hatred and mainsprings of popularity are determined by the price of food. Hunger alone makes cities free; and when men in power feed the idle mob, they buy subservience; a starving people is incapable of fear." In *Lucan: The Civil War*, trans. J. D. Duff (Cambridge, Mass., 1928), p. 119.

25. I therefore disagree with Alison Hanham's claim that More's *History* was itself *only* a work of literature, an elaborate joke against historians, a satirical drama, a Shakespearean play in embryo, complete with acts and scenes, and with the Lon-

don citizens brought in as a dramatic chorus, a "much more artificial device" than Mancini's descriptions of men in the street weeping over the fate of the princes in the Tower. "The parallel," wrote Hanham, "with the ubiquitous citizens of Shakespeare's mature histories is obvious." See Hanham, *Richard III and His Early Historians 1483–1535* (Oxford, 1975), pp. 152–90, especially p. 185. This is to read the "source" retroactively in the light of the play it generated.

26. This phenomenon is confirmed by Thomas Nelson, *A Short Discorse Expressing the substaunce of all the late pretended Treasons* (London, 1586), which describes how the people "set their Tables in the streates, with meates of every kinde, where was preparde all signes of joye, that could be had in mind" (Aiiir).

27. See F. J. Levy, *Tudor Historical Thought* (San Marino, 1967), p. 168.

28. See Geertz, "Thick Description," pp. 5, 6, 10, 21.

29. Ibid., p. 23.

Chapter Ten: Women

1. See Louis Montrose, "*A Midsummer Night's Dream* and the Shaping Fantasies of Elizabethan Culture: Gender, Power, Form," in *Rewriting the Renaissance: The Discourses of Sexual Difference in Early Modern Europe*, ed. Margaret Ferguson, Maureen Quilligan, and Nancy Vickers (Chicago, 1986), p. 68.

2. Barbara Kiefer Lewalski, *Writing Women in Jacobean England* (Cambridge, Mass., 1993), p. 3.

3. For "Jane" Shore's correct name, see Alison Hanham, *Richard III and His Early Historians 1483–1535* (Oxford, 1975), p. 179n. She was the daughter of John Lambert, mercer, sheriff of London 1460-61, married to William Shore, and petitioned for annulment on the grounds of his impotence. The discovery was made by Nicolas Barker, *Times Literary Supplement*, 7 July 1972, p. 777.

4. More's defense of Shore goes unmentioned in Constance Jordan, *Renaissance Feminism: Literary Texts and Political Models* (Ithaca, 1990), and Linda Woodbridge's study of defenses and attacks on women, *Women and the English Renaissance* (Brighton, U.K., 1984). Woodbridge remarked that the feminist tendencies of the early humanists, More, Colet, Vives, and others had been "overestimated" (p. 16). Lisa Jardine, *Still Harping on Daughters: Women and Drama in the Age of Shakespeare* (Brighton and Totowa, 1983), mentions More's well-known support of education for women disparagingly, as proof that his real goal was female "docility and obedience." Of his tribute to Catherine of Aragon, she remarked, "This is More's verdict on a lady whose learning he upheld as a paradigm for all English women—she surpassed all notable ancient stereotypes of feminine obedience, loyalty and honour. More's tribute bodes ill for emancipation" (pp. 53–54).

5. It is striking, therefore, to read Alison Hanham's misreading of this portrait. While she found it "charming," she assumes that More had primarily a moral purpose in its introduction, since it "is not apparently very relevant to the history." She therefore calmly states, without textual support, that "More, with his habit of following an abstract statement by a concrete example, sets up Mistress Shore as a

personification of Lechery. . . . The Christian image of the Magdalen was probably
not far below the surface for a contemporary reader, though where More was not
so clumsy as to make any overt reference we would disturb the balance by stress-
ing it." See *Richard III and His Early Historians*, p. 180. Compare Judith P. Jones,
Thomas More (Boston, 1979), p. 57, who perceived More's sympathy for Shore and
that her public humiliation as a lecher is actually exemplary of Richard III's
hypocrisy.

6. *The Mirror for Magistrates*, ed. Lily B. Campbell (Cambridge, 1938; repr. New
York, 1960), pp. 377–78. Note also the exact similarity between More's narrative
and the *Mirror's* version: "My husband then, as one that knew his good, / Refused to
kepe a prynces concubine" (p. 380).

7. See Thomas More, *Complete Works*, vol. 2., ed. Richard S. Sylvester (New
Haven and London, 1963), pp. 56, 230–31. Sylvester comments: "More is obviously amusing himself as he describes the good `mores' of the king's concubine. . . . [He]
evidently thought that [her] ability to read well and write was by no means a normal accomplishment."

8. Hanham, *Richard III and His Early Historians*, p. 179.

9. John Milton, *Complete Prose Works*, ed. D. M. Wolfe et al., 8 vols. (New Haven,
1953–82), vol. 5, part 1, p. 79.

10. John King, *English Reformation Literature* (Princeton, 1982), p. 419. As a sign of
her impact on popular culture, a broadside ballad purporting to be Lady Jane's last
words went through more than one edition in London. See Carole Levin, "Lady
Jane Grey: Protestant Queen and Martyr," in *Silent but for the Word: Tudor Women as Pa-
trons, Translators, and Writers of Religious Works*, ed. Margaret Hannay (Kent, Oh.,
1985), pp. 97–98, 273.

11. The best confirmation of this interpretation is to be found in Shakespeare's
eloquent expansion of Catherine's self-defense, in *Henry VIII*, in act 3, scene 1, and
act 2, scene 4. In the latter, constructed as a trial, Catherine is so bold in her defiance of Cardinal Wolsey that he rebukes her for being out of character: "I do pro-
fess / "You speak not like yourself, who ever yet / Have stood to charity and displayed th'effects / Of disposition gentle and of wisdom / O'ertopping woman's
power." And Cardinal Campeius adds: "The Queen is obstinate, / stubborn to justice, apt to accuse it, and / Disdainful to be tried by't." Her final act of defiance is to
leave the court against Henry's express command that she stay to hear judgment
against her.

12. Keith Thomas, *Religion and the Decline of Magic* (New York, 1971), p. 451.

13. 5 Eliz. c. 16. See *Journals of the House of Commons*, 1:59. This act replaced the
one passed by Henry VIII in 1542 and repealed by Edward VI in 1547.

14. See, for example, Peter Stalleybrass, "*Macbeth* and Witchcraft," in *Focus on
"Macbeth*," ed. John Russell Brown (London, 1982), especially 196–98; Janet Adel-
man, "'Born of Woman': Fantasies of Maternal Power in *Macbeth*," in *Cannibals, Witches, and Divorce: Estranging the Renaissance*, ed. Marjorie Garber (Baltimore and London,
1987), pp. 97–121.

15. See C. L'Estrange Ewen, *Witch Hunting and Witch Trials* (London, 1929), pp.

102–8, who reported that of the 109 persons executed on the Home Circuit only seven were men.

16. Thomas, *Witchcraft and the Decline of Magic*, p. 583. Compare also Alan Macfarlane, *Witchcraft in Tudor and Stuart England* (New York, 1970), pp. 147–207.

17. Thomas, *Religion and the Decline of Magic*, pp. 460–61.

18. Ewen, *Witch Hunting and Witch Trials*, listed this case in an appendix (p. 282) containing trials mentioned in texts for which no indictments could be found in the records.

19. See Thomas, *Religion and the Decline of Magic*, p. 226n, citing Wood, *Athenae Oxonienses*, ed. P. Bliss (Oxford, 1813–20), 1, cols. 188–89.

20. Fleming's contributions to the *Discoverie* are briefly mentioned by William E. Miller, "Abraham Fleming: Editor of Shakespeare's Holinshed," *Texas Studies in Literature and Language* 1 (1959), 93, but without finding any significance in the collaboration.

21. Reginald Scot, *The Discoverie of Witchcraft*, ed. Hugh Ross Williamson (Carbondale, Ill., 1964), pp. 29–30 (italics added).

22. Ibid., p. 36. Cf. Keith Thomas, *Religion and the Decline of Magic*, p. 462: "The most that can be said is that these statutes gave some added publicity to the idea of witchcraft, and that their presence on the statute book helped to sustain the belief, particularly in later years when scepticism was on the increase."

23. See Ewen, *Witch Hunting and Witch Trials*, p. 100.

24. See Miller, "Abraham Fleming," pp. 93–94.

Chapter Eleven: Censorship

1. Stephen Booth, *The Book Called Holinshed's Chronicles* (San Francisco, 1968), p. 72.

2. *Ibid.*, p. 60.

3. In addition to Booth's study, the two most important attempts to describe and analyze the revisions hitherto are Anne Castanien's painstaking thesis, "Censorship and Historiography in Elizabethan England: The Expurgation of Holinshed's *Chronicles*, unpublished Ph.D. dissertation, University of California, Davis, 1970; and Elizabeth Story Donno, "Some Aspects of Shakespeare's Holinshed," *Huntington Library Quarterly* 50 (1987), 229–47. Donno, "Some Aspects of Shakespeare's Holinshed," pp. 242–44, assumed that those relating to the Sidneys were dictated by the queen's hostility to Sir Philip, stemming from his activities in the Low Countries. Castanien, on the contrary, stated that these, "with one possible exception, seem to have been made to make the text more lucid, remove repetitions and to save space rather than because of official disapproval or a desire to lessen the honors paid to the dead" (p. 279). She also assumed that those relating to Leicester's activities were revised in response to the earl's own complaints, and that their objective was to reduce the emphasis on entertainment and to make him seem more efficient and responsible as a military commander (pp. 271–72).

4. Polydore Vergil, *Anglica Historia*, ed. and trans. Denys Hay (London, 1950),

xvi–xvii: "The interval before publication was probably due to the author's anxiety that the political situation should make publication inadvisable. . . . In 1546 a new edition appeared which, like the first, ended at 1509, but which was considerably revised throughout. These revisions were partly designed to improve statements which had become politically undesirable." In regard to the third edition, published in 1555, which adds a new book (27) dealing with Henry VIII's reign up to 1537, Hay continues: "It is reasonable to suppose that in 1523 or 1533, when Vergil planned the first edition, he intended it to have a final book dealing with Henry's reign up to about 1530, i.e., including the rise and fall of Wolsey. In the event, he must have decided that publication would have been dangerous and therefore with- held his draft Book 27 from the printer. In 1546, when he had a new edition print- ed, carefully revised and as politically innocuous as he could make it, Vergil again presumably intended to add the final book, and with this in view carried it down to the birth of Prince Edward. . . . Yet once more the uncertainties of English politics were such that Vergil postponed publication. If it is correct to suppose that Vergil himself carried the text of the 1555 edition with him when he left England for good in 1553, it may be inferred that only the recent accession of Mary provided a con- text in which he felt the last book might safely be made public."

5. Hampton Court, 13, June, 1555, 1 and 2 Philip and Mary. See Paul L. Hugh- es and James F. Larkin, *Tudor Royal Proclamations*, 3 vols. (New Haven and London, 1969), 2:57–60.

6. Robert Fabian, *New Chronicles of England and France* (1516 through 1559), ed. Henry Ellis (London, 1811), xx–xxi.

7. *Acts of the Privy Council, 1586–87*, ed. J. R. Dasent (London, 1890–1907), pp. 311–12.

8. Castanien, "Censorship and Historiography," pp. 9–10; italics added.

9. One of these was Francis Peck, whose *Desiderata Curiososa* (London, 1732–36), vol. 1, Book 6, p. 52, advertised his possession of certain papers once owned by Abraham Fleming, which he promised to publish, along with Fleming's personal ac- count "de Modo Castrandi, Reformandique Chronica." His promise was never ful- filled, and the papers are now assumed lost.

10. Thomas Walsingham, *Historia Anglicana*, ed. Henry Thomas Riley, 2 vols. (London, Rolls Series, 1863–64), 2:317.

11. See Anne Hudson, "Middle English," in *Editing Medieval Texts, English, French, and Latin Written in England*, ed. A. G. Rigg (New York and London, 1977), p. 46: "Provisions extant concerning such dictation in the University of Prague from the 1360s on make it clear that this method of reproducing texts was one so common that official regulation was necessary. . . . Hus completed one of his theological works one evening and assembled eighty scribes the following morning in the Beth- lehem chapel in Prague to copy the text from dictation." She cites, for the regula- tions, *Monumenta historica universitatis Carolo-Ferdinandeae Pragensis* (Prague, 1830–32), 1:13–14, 40–42; and for the story about Hus: John Hus, *Tractatus de ecclesia*, ed. S. Harrison Thomson (Boulder and Cambridge, 1956), xvi, xxix.

12. See Anne Hudson, *The Premature Reformation: Wycliffite Texts and Lollard History*

(Oxford, 1988), pp. 440–41; V. H. H. Green, *Bishop Reginald Pecock* (Cambridge, 1945), pp. 188–204.

13. Green, *Bishop Reginald Pecock*, p. 195. In transcribing Pecock's story from an anonymous fifteenth-century chronicle into his own *Chronicle* (1580) John Stow stated that Pecock "had labored for many yeeres to translate the holy Scripture into Englishe" (p. 682), an assertion that has generated much scholarly speculation, but is now largely discounted.

14. Green, *Bishop Reginald Pecock*, pp. 62–64, points out, however, that Pecock's appeal to the pope after his conviction was interpreted as a challenge to Henry VI's authority and as a threat to the failing Lancastrian dynasty.

15. *The Repressor of Overmuch Blaming the Clergy*, ed. Churchill Babington (London, Rolls Series, vol. 19, 1860), 1:xxxvii.

16. For a detailed account of Pecock's thought and the consequences of his conviction, see E. F. Jacob, "Reynold Pecock, Bishop of Chicester," *Proceedings of the British Academy* 37 (1951), 121–53, especially 137ff.

17. Ibid., p. 139.

18. *Repressor*, 1:xxix; Charles W. Brockwell, Jr., "Answering `the Known Men': Bishop Reginald Pecock and Mr. Richard Hooker," *Church History* 49 (1980), 133–46. As Brockwell points out, both Lollards and Puritans called themselves "the known men." "That term, as a synonym for those known of God or the elect, occurs throughout Foxe's *Acts and Monuments* as a designation of the Protestant martyrs"; and both Pecock and Hooker refer to their opponents as such (p. 134).

19. *Repressor*, 2:331: "But alle the cause, whi yvel cometh fro and bi tho riche possesiouns had in prelacie, is for that vertuose men and weel proved men in leernyng and in lyving ben not chosun and takun into prelacies."

20. Ibid., 1:36–37. However, in the *Book of Faith* he found himself arguing that "it may be that sum oon symple persoone as in fame, or in state, is wiser forto knowe, juge, and declare what is the trewe sense of a certeyn porcioun of Scripture, and what is the treuthe of sum article . . . than is a greet general counceil." See *Book of Faith*, ed. J. L. Morison (Glasgow, 1909), p. 282.

21. Ibid., *Repressor*, 1:xlii.

22. Ibid., 1:30–32. Pecock here produced an extraordinarily circular and complex argument, which on the one hand carries foundationalism to its logical extreme (he constantly uses the term "ground" as a verb that instantiates truth in a particular argument) and on the other illustrates a deconstructionist principle *avant la lettre*; that is to say, by extending the phrase *avant la lettre* to logical absurdity: "Also in caas a greet clerk wolde go into a librarie and over studie there a long proces of feith writun in the Bible, and wolde aftirward reporte and reherce the sentence of the same proces to the peple at Poulis Cros in a sermoun, or wolde write it in a pistle or lettre to hise freendis under entent of reporting the sentence of the said proces, schuld the heerers of thilk reportyng and remembring seie that thilk sentence were foundid and groundid in the seid reporter or in his preching or in his pistle writen? Goddis forbode; for open it is that thei oughten seie and feele rathir that thilk sentence is groundid in the seid book ligging in the librarie. And in case that

this clerk reporting the seid sentence or proces spake or wrote in other wordis thilk sentence than ben the wordis under which thilk sentence is writen in the seid book, thei oughten seid and feele that hise wordis and hise writingis oughten be glosid and be expowned and be brought in to accordaunce with the seid book in the librarie, and the seid book in thilk proces oughht not be expowned and be brought and wrestid into accordaunce with the seid clerkis wordis and writingis; yhe, though Crist and hise Apostlis wolden entende and do the same as this clerk dooth, the peple oughte in noon other wise. . . . And sithen it is so, that all the trouthis of lawe of kind whiche Crist and hise Apostlis taughten and wroten weren bifore her teching and writing, and weren *writen bifore in thilk solempnest inward book or inward writing of resounis doom* passing alle outward bookis in profite to men for to serve God, . . . out of which inward book and writing mowe be taken bi labour and studiyng of clerkis mo conclusiouns and treuthis and governauncis of lawe of kinde and of Goddes moral lawe and service than myghten be writen in so manie bokis whiche schulden fille the greet chirche of Seint Poul in London" (italics added).

23. *The Union of the two noble & illustre famelies of Lancastre & Yorke*, ed. Henry Ellis (1548; repr. London 1809; New York, 1965), p. 237.

24. Cf. *Repressor*, 1:xxv–xxvi: "He carried his notions on the papal supremacy almost as far as an ultramontane could desire, and was blamed even by men like [Thomas] Gascoigne, [abbot of St. Albans] for giving more than its due to the pope's temporal authority."

25. Ibid., 1:xlviii–xlix.

26. Several of these survive in manuscript, and two in print. See Babington, ed., *Repressor*, 1:lxi–lxxxiii. "Of Christian Religion" was at one time in the collection of Sir Thomas Phillips of Middlehill. The *Donet* and its *Follower* are extant in manuscript (as Bodleian Ms. n. 916 and British Museum Bibl. Reg. 17 D. ix, respectively). According to the *Dictonary of National Biography* the former was intended "to be of little quantity, that well-nigh each poor person may by some means get cost to have it as his own." The *Booke of Faith*, extant in manuscript in Trinity College, Cambridge (B. 14, 45), was first published by Henry Wharton (London, 1688).

27. Babington, ed., *Repressor*, 1:lxv–lxvi. Peter Munz, *The Place of Hooker in the History of Thought* (London, 1952), pp. 41–42, 45, raised the possibility that Richard Hooker might have consulted Stow's copy of the *Repressor* when working on his *Laws*.

28. *The Mirror for Magistrates*, ed. Lily B. Campbell (Cambridge, 1938; repr. New York, 1960), p. 350.

29. Ibid., p. 354.

30. Ibid., p. 359; italics added.

31. See Campbell, *Mirror for Magistrates*, p. 47: In the editorial framing of the tale, John Higgins, one of the contributors, remarks, "I was willed my maisters . . . by Maister Holinshed, to bring Sir Nicholas Burdet unto you."

32. *The Great Chronicle of London*, ed. A. H. Thomas and I. D. Thornley (London, 1938), p. 236: "a sedicious Ryme [was] fastenyd upon the Crosse In Chepe & other placys of the Cyte . . . ffor the devysers of this Ryme much serch was made and

sundry accusyd to Theyr Chargys, But ffynally two Gentylmen namyd Turburvyle & Colingbourn were ffor that & othyr thyngys layd to theyr charge, arestid & cast In prison, ffor whom shortly afftyr . . . was holden at the Guyldhalle an Oyer determyner where the said ii Gentylmen were aregnyd, and that oone off theym callid Colyngbourn convyct of that Cryme & other, ffor the which. . .he was drawyin unto the Towyr hyll and there ffull Cruelly put to deth. . . . This man was gretly monyd of the people for his goodly personage and ffavour of vysage." The *Great Chronicle,* i.e., Guildhall Library Mss. 3313, is a history of England from Richard I through 1512, from a London citizen's perspective. It is now attributed to Robert Fabian. Between 1563 and 1570 it came into the possession of John Stow, who copied from it word for word this account of Collingbourne's trial and execution for the 1601 edition of his *Annales* (p. 780). It appears that Stow may have lent it to John Foxe (xiv–xv). Neither Hall's nor Holinshed's accounts, which omit Turberville, derive from it, although Holinshed might have been led by its hints of "othyr thyngys layd to theyr charge," as well as by the specification of a commission of oyer and terminer at the Guildhall, the traditional locale of treason trials, to inquire further.

33. See *The Chronicle of Queen Jane, and of Two Years of Queen Mary,* ed. J. G. Nichols (London, 1850), pp. 78–79: "But after the king was passed, the bushoppe of Winchester, noting the book in Henry the eightes hande, shortely afterwards called the paynter before him, and with ville wourdes calling him traytour, askte why and who bad him describe king Henry with a boke in his hande . . . thretenyng him therfore to go the Flete. And the paynter made answer, that he thought he had don well, and that no man bad him do the contrary, `for (sayth he) yf I had knowen the same had ben agaynst your lordeship's pleasure, I wold not so have made him.' `Nay, (sayde the bushoppe,) yt is agaynst the quenes catholicke proceedings,' &c. And so he paynted him shortly after, in the sted of the booke of *Verbum Dei,* to have in his handes a newe payre of gloves." This entire passage was crossed out in the manuscript. Nichols also notes that this version, with the "ominous fact of the biblé being painted out, and replaced by a pair of gloves," is corroborated by yet another version in Harleian m.s. 419, f. 131.

34. Hall, *Union,* pp. 762–63.

35. Hall, *Union,* pp. 762–63.

36. See Foxe, *Acts and Monuments,* ed. George Townsend, 8 vols. (London, 1843–49; repr. New York, 1965), 5:565.

37. See *Letters and Papers, Foreign and Domestic, of the Reign of Henry VIII,* ed. J. S. Brewer, 22 vols. (London, 1862–1932), 4: no. 2607.

38. D. M. Loades, "The Press under the Early Tudors: A Study in Censorship and Sedition," *Transactions of the Cambridge Bibliographical Society* 4 (1964–65), 29–50. See also his parallel essay, "Illicit Presses and Clandestine in England, 1520–1590," in *Too Mighty to be Free: Censorship and the Press in Britain and the Netherlands,* ed. A. C. Duke and C. A. Tamse (Zutphen, 1987), 9–27.

39. Loades, "Press under the Early Tudors," p. 32.

40. Ibid., pp. 33–34.

41. *Acts of the Privy Council,* 2:312.

42. Loades, "Press under the Early Tudors," p. 35.

43. Ibid., p. 42.

44. It is worth noting here that Richard Grafton, the printer of Hall's chronicle, had already been imprisoned briefly in 1541 for printing a protest by Melanchthon against Henry's notorious Six Articles; and he now, for his support of Lady Jane Grey, lost his position of king's printer to John Cawood. See Loades, "Press under the Early Tudors," pp. 34, 45.

45. See *Tudor Royal Proclamations*, 1:xx.

46. Edward Arber, *A Transcript of the Registers of the Company of Stationers of London, 1554–1640*, 2 vols. (London, 1875), 2:784.

47. Ibid., 2:799.

48. Loades, "Press under the Early Tudors," p. 45.

49. Arber, *Transcript*, 2:803.

50. S. L. Goldberg, "A Note on John Wolfe, Elizabethan Printer," *Historical Studies, Australia & New Zealand* 7 (1955), 55–56. See also H. R. Hoppe, "John Wolfe, Printer and Publisher, 1579–1601," *The Library*, 4th series, 14 (1933); Joseph Loewenstein, "For a History of Literary Property: John Wolfe's Reformation," *English Literary Renaissance* 18 (1988), 389–412; and C. C. Huffman, *Elizabethan Impressions: John Wolfe and His Press* (New York, 1986).

51. Goldberg, p. 56. See also Loewenstein, p. 405, who concludes from the appointment of Wolfe as beadle of the Stationers' Company in 1587 that he had turned his coat. "No longer identifying his interests with those of the least powerful, we find him instead *policing* the company, securing the rights of capital, rights that he had now arrogated to himself."

52. From a literary perspective, the most tantalizing aspect of Wolfe's career is as printer of the second edition of Spenser's *Shepheardes Calender* in 1586, the year of the Babington Plot; to be followed by his printing, in 1590, of the first installment of Spenser's *Faerie Queene*.

53. Loades, "Press under the Early Tudors," p. 50.

54. See F. S. Siebert, *Freedom of the Press in England 1476–1776* (Urbana, 1952), p. 54. For the text of the *Injunctions*, see *Documents Illustrative of English Church History*, ed. Henry Gee and W. J. Harvey (London, 1910), pp. 417–42.

55. Holinshed noted, however, that in April 1559 a royal proclamation was issued, "inhibiting, that from thenceforth no plaies nor interludes should be exercised, till Alhallowes tide next insuing" (4:134).

56. See *Tudor Royal Proclamations*, 2:375. The *Admonition* was printed at a secret press in June 1572, and went through three editions before the end of August. In August 1573 Bishop Sandys reported to Burghley that he had ferreted out a Puritan printing press in the country. The printer Lacy and his confederates had been arrested while working on another edition of Cartwright's *Reply*. See Patrick McGrath, *Papists and Puritans under Elizabeth I* (London, 1967), pp. 133, 144.

57. *Tudor Royal Proclamations*, 2:376–79.

58. Ibid., 2:400–401.

59. Ibid., 2:449.

60. William Camden, *Annals* (London, 1625–29), Book 3, pp. 15–16.

61. *Tudor Royal Proclamations*, 2:506. Hughes and Larkin report that a list of such books seized this same year included: twenty copies of *A Treatise of Treasons* (Antwerp, 1572), STC 7601; 367 copies of Richard Bristowe's *Motives* (Antwerp, 1574), STC 3799; nine copies of Possevino's *Treatise of the Holy Sacrifice of the Altar*, trans. Thomas Butler (Louvain, 1570), a copy of Bede's *History*, trans. Thomas Stapleton (Antwerp, 1565); and twenty-eight copies of Thomas More's *Dialogue of Comfort* (Antwerp, 1573), STC 18,083.

62. For an argument that the Babington Plot was from the start encouraged and to some extent actually set in motion by Walsingham, Burghley and other members of the Council, with the set purpose of incriminating Mary, Queen of Scots, see Alan Gordon Smith, *The Babington Plot* (London, 1936). Smith argues that the Council employed agents, especially Gilbert, to draw in Ballard, Gifford, and Babington. Smith contended that Walsingham deliberately prevented Babington from withdrawing himself from the conspiracy, which itself "proved to be so harmless—never at any time more than the silly talk of boys—that it was only by the wilful distortion and suppression of evidence that it was possible to make any case in court" (pp. 245–46.)

63. "The horrible conspiracie of Babington and other his fellow traitors discovered by A.F." (4:898).

64. Fleming, however, connects Babington with "Throgmorton the traitor," that is, Sir Francis Throckmorton, whose trial in 1584 he had also recorded in detail.

65. Arnold Stein, *The House of Death* (Baltimore, 1987), pp. 76–83.

66. See my *Fables of Power* (Durham, N.C., 1991), pp. 70–72, 91–95, and for an earlier version of this argument, pp. 54–59.

67. Castanien, "Censorship and Historiography," pp. 296–97.

68. Ibid., p. 12.

69. There were three editions of Thynne's *Chaucer* involved; a first, canceled edition, which must have preceded Wolsey's impeachment in 1529; the first extant edition of 1532, and the second of 1542, in which it was the "Plowman's Tale" that barely escaped suppression.

70. Francis Thynne, *Animadversions upon the Annotacions and Corrections . . . of Chaucers workes* (1598), ed. G. H. Kingsley (London, 1865), rev. ed. F. J. Furnivall (London, 1875; repr. London, New York and Toronto, 1965), pp. 7–10.

71. The prevalence of bishops in this narrative is in no way accidental. It must be remembered that the 1587 *Chronicles* were completed in the atmosphere of a still further increased control over the press, the direct result of John Whitgift's accession to the archbishopric. The Star Chamber decree of June 1584 was superseded by the far more rigorous decree of June 1586, drafted by Whitgift himself. Any infringement of the regulations was punishable by destruction of the presses and other materials, and six months' imprisonment, offenders to be brought before Whitgift's court of High Commission. This decree is usually interpreted primarily as an attempt to reinforce the monopoly over the printing trade by the Stationers' Company; but its political implications, in heralding the reign of Whitgift over English culture, must have been equally evident.

Chapter Twelve: Readers

1. D. R. Woolf, "Genre into Artifact: The Decline of the English Chronicle in the Sixteenth Century," *Sixteenth Century Journal* 19 (1988): 322–23.

2. Thomas Nashe, *Works*, ed. R. B. McKerrow, 5 vols. (London, 1904), 1:194.

3. Virginia F. Stern, *Gabriel Harvey: His Life, Marginalia and Library* (Oxford, 1979), 152.

4. Woolf, "Genre into Artifact," pp. 331–32.

5. Thomas Nashe, *Works*, ed. R. B. McKerrow, 5 vols. (Oxford, 1966), 3:37. For the passage about the flea, and the chain fashioned for it by Mark Scaliot, blacksmith of London, see *Chronicles*, 4:406. It carries Abraham Fleming's personal certificate: "a thing almost incredible, but that my selfe (amongs manie others) have seene it, and therfore must affirme it to be true."

6. Note by R. B. McKerrow in Nashe, *Works*, 5:167.

7. Nashe, *Works*, 1:317–18; see *Chronicles*, 4:510–11, which in fact provides a far more sympathetic account of Harvey's pamphlet than Nashe would have it, mentioning the fear of "a marvellous fearfull and horrible alteration of empire, kingdoms, segniories and estates, . . . desperat treasons and commotions."

8. For Harvey's career, see V. F. Stern, *Gabriel Harvey: His Life, Marginalia and Library* (Oxford, 1979).

9. See *Elizabethan Critical Essays*, ed. G. Gregory Smith, 2 vols. (Oxford, 1904), 1:100. Evidently this refers to William Harrison's *Description* and shows that Spenser did *not* know Holinshed personally.

10. Ibid., 2:253.

11. Samuel Daniel, *Complete Works*, ed. A. B. Grosart, 5 vols. (London, 1896; repr. New York, 1963), 4:82.

12. Jardine and Grafton, "'Studied for Action': How Gabriel Harvey Read His Livy," *Past and Present* 129 (1990), 30–78.

13. For Essex's copy of the *Chronicles*, see chapter 1. For Daniel's problems over his tragedy *Philotas*, see Joan Rees, *Samuel Daniel: A Critical and Biographical Study* (Liverpool, 1964), pp. 98–101; G. A. Wilkes, "Daniel's *Philotas* and the Essex Case," *Modern Language Quarterly* 23 (1962), 233–42.

14. David Underdown, *Fire from Heaven: Life in an English Town in the Seventeenth Century* (New Haven and London, 1992), p. 53.

15. Ibid., p. 56.

16. The most interesting of these is entitled "A Libell found at the Court, and presented to the King by the Bp of London, Dr Laude. 8 March 1628," Cambridge University Library MS. Dd.xi.73, f. 102v. While the direction of its satire is unclear, the reasons for Whiteway's interest in it are not. See, for example, the following:

> Good brother Barnes, Elder at Amsterdam,
> Shut up at home the wild Arminian Ram,
> If here he comes these men will cut his throte,
> Blest Buchanan sings them a bitter note.

He teacheth how to put downe power of Kings,
And shows us how to clip the Eagles Wings.
[. . .]
Against the Papists we have got the day,
Blind Bishops onely stand now in our Way,
And we will have a tricke to tame their pride,
Tonnage and Pondage it shalbe denide.

17. Underdown, *Fire from Heaven*, pp. 189, 190.

18. Whiteway, commonplace book, f. 180r.

19. See Helgerson, *Forms of Nationhood: The Elizabethan Writing of England* (Chicago, 1992), p. 89.

20. Helgerson, *Forms of Nationhood*, p. 91; citing *Calendar of State Papers Domestic, 1621–1631*, p. 490. See also Kevin Sharpe, *The Personal Rule of Charles I* (New Haven, 1992), pp. 656–57.

21. Helgerson, *Forms of Nationhood*, p. 320, n. 62.

22. See W. O. Hassall, ed., *A Catalogue of the Library of Sir Edward Coke* (London, 1950), nos. 509, 510, 511.

23. Coke, *Institutes*, Fourth Part (London, 1645), p. 34: "In Anno 16 H.8. to furnish the King for his going in his royal person into France, a new device for getting of mony was set on foot, which made the headlesse and heedlesse multitude to rise in rebellion. Hollensh Chron. 891." The reference is to *Chronicles*, 3:891. On the next page Coke added: "In 4 H.7 another like new found Subsidy was granted, which raised rebellion in the North. Hollensh. Chron. 769." The reference is to the account of demands for a tenth in 1489, and the murder of the earl of Northumberland by rebels incited by John a Chamber, who blamed him as "chiefe author of the tax." See *Chronicles*, 3:769.

24. John Milton, *Complete Prose Works*, ed. D. M. Wolfe et al., 8 vols. (New Haven, 1953–82), 1:426.

25. In *Eikonoklastes*, in connection with Charles's claim in *Eikon Basilike* that he only left Westminster for shame at the public disturbances in London, Milton had found a useful parallel in the events of 1388: "Our forefathers were of that courage and severity of zeale to Justice, and thir native Liberty, against the proud contempt and misrule of hir Kings, that when Richard the Second departed but from a Committie of Lords, who sat preparing matter for the Parlament not yet assembl'd, to the removal of his evil Counselors, they . . . comming up to London with a huge Army, requir'd the King then withdrawn for feare, but no furder off then the Tower, to come to Westminster. Which he refusing, they told him flatly, that unless he came, they would choose another" (*Prose Works*, 3:407).

26. See the anonymous pamphlet, *A True Description, or Rather a Parallel betweene . . . Wolsey and . . . Laud* (1641). See also the Smectymnuan pamphlet, *A Postscript* (1641), now attributed to Milton, which contains thirty-two references to the 1587 *Chronicles*, including the following: "After this, though the Bishops ceased to bee Papists; for they preached against the Popes Supremacie, to please the King, yet they

ceased not to oppugne the Gospel, causing Tindals translation to be burnt, yet they agreed to the suppressing of Monasteries, leaving their revenewes to the King, to make way for the six bloodie Articles, which proceedings with all crueltie of inquisition are set downe Holinsh. pag. 946."

27. A. H. Smith, ed., The Writings of B. Franklin (New York, 1906), 9:103–5. Cited in Caroline Robbins, "The Strenuous Whig, Thomas Hollis of Lincoln's Inn," William and Mary Quarterly 7 (1950): 408. Robbins also cites from J. Nichols, Illustrations of Literary History (London, 1831), 6:157, the accusation of the Reverand Baptist-Noel Turner that Hollis "might be said even to have laid the first train of combustibles for the American explosion."

28. Brand Hollis was also well acquainted with "Throgmorton's long trial, as a conspirator with Wyat." See Memoirs, 2:560.

♨ Index